THE RIDDLE OF THE PACIFIC

THE RIDDLE OF THE PACIFIC

BY
J. MACMILLAN BROWN

ADVENTURES UNLIMITED PRESS

THE RIDDLE OF THE PACIFIC
©1924 John Macmillan Brown

First published by
T. Fisher Unwin Ltd.
Adelphi Terrace, London

This edition
© 1996 Adventures Unlimited Press

ISBN 0-932813-29-1

This edition published by
Adventures Unlimited Press
303 Main Street
Kempton, Illinois 60619 USA

Distributed in New Zealand & Australia by
Adventures Unlimited NZ
221 Symonds Street
P.O. Box 8199
Auckland,
New Zealand

PREFACE

THIS book was written on Easter Island and is the result of five months' residence there and many years' personal observation and study of the islands of the Pacific, their peoples, customs and language. The visit had to be postponed from year to year because of the difficulty of getting to the island ; and it was only the kindness of the Government and the Admiralty of Chili and of Captain Wiegand of the *General Baquedano* that made it possible. It was due to the generosity of the lessees of the island, Messrs. Williamson, Balfour & Co. of Valparaiso, and the help of their manager, Mr. Percy Edmunds, and his assistant, Mr. Clarke, that the visit was as efficient as it was under trying conditions.

The author's notebooks are full of minute observations on the various burial platforms and the statues ; but he has used them only to a limited extent and that only in the first few chapters, nor has he made any attempt to give a full description of the monuments of the island, as he considered that Mrs. Routledge's book " The Mystery of Easter Island," the result of long and careful work, and to a much smaller extent, the Smithsonian article of Paymaster Thomson of the *Mohican*, somewhat marred by the inaccuracies that necessarily attach to too rapid a survey, have rendered that superfluous.

Professor J. Macmillan Brown

CONTENTS

THE SCULPTORS' FRONT SHOP WINDOW ON RANO RARAKU

LIST OF ILLUSTRATIONS

FULL PAGE

IN THE TEXT

IN FRONT OF IMAGE-SLOPE

How still the tyranny of ocean sleeps,
With infant innocence its face agleam ;
O'er all the ghostly secrets that she keeps
She lies adream, adream.

And on the stony features of each god
There broods the same far mystic smile,
As if they knew the world was at their nod,
Alone on their lone isle.

Who made their mates of stone to fall they know,
What tyrant broke their golden thread of fate ;
They turn their backs upon their ruthless foe,
Their looks all scorn and hate.

As kings they conquered and as kings they ruled,
As vikings dared the tempests of her rages,
And dying, in the stones their serfs had tooled
They'd live for countless ages.

A flash of anger and their empire sank
Deep down in the unfathomable deep ;
One draught of all their hopes and dreams she drank,
And then she went to sleep.

And where hath vanished all their pomp and glory ?
Who now can tell their deeds or even their name ?
Ask these mute gods, who know the tragic story,
What is eternal fame.

And, as the stars wink out upon the blue,
The Titans turn their questioning eyes to heaven ;
The starry answer is a question too ;
"Ah ! whither are we driven ?

" We die, the same old story to rehearse ;
For being is an everlasting quest ;
Change, ever change, in every universe ;
There is no rest, no rest.

" Yon farthest world that on the horizon looms,
What are its deathless fames but dying breath ?
Each cosmos is an isle of nameless tombs,
Its life oblivious death."

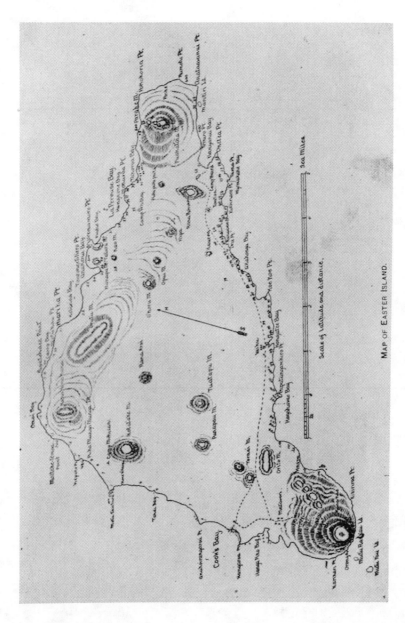

MAP OF EASTER ISLAND.

THE CHILIAN GOVERNMENT SURVEY MAP MARKED BY PAYMASTER THOMSON WITH THE RING OF BURIAL PLATFORMS ALONG THE COASTS
AND THE BEGINNING OF A RING FARTHER INLAND

THE RIDDLE OF THE PACIFIC

CHAPTER I

THE ISLAND OF MAGNIFICENT SEPULTURE—EASTER ISLAND

(1) If Westminster Abbey were left isolated on the only insular relic of submerged Europe, the anthropologist of the far future would have the same task in reconstructing its past as he has to-day in Easter Island. (2) And the masonry that has gone into the Abbey is but a fraction of all that has been achieved on this speck of dust on the unbroken vastitude of the Southern Pacific. (3) and (4) No concentration of mortuary memorials has ever surpassed this in the sense of the infinite it stirs or in the innocuousness of the ghosts or diseases of the buried dust ; (5) None in greatness of conception, even though it is but the crowning effort of Polynesian architecture to immortalize the divine chiefs. (6) Nor was the conception fully realized when some cataclysm put an end to the attempt. (7) There were to be statued avenues breaking the monotony of zones of burial platforms. (8) Along these would move the funeral trains of dead heroes and the festal throngs to celebrate their memory. (9) But all was stopped as suddenly as when a world is shattered.

(1) **IF BRITAIN SANK ALL BUT WESTMINSTER.** If the civilization of Europe should again vanish through change of land-surface and climate, and but a fragment of the South of England stand out solitary in a waste of waters, and that fragment the island of Westminster with its Abbey, we should have an Easter Island of the Atlantic, or rather of the East-to-West sea, which Suess, the Austrian geologist, calls T e t h y s, half-girdling the globe. And if the memory of the British Empire and of all the other empires it struggled with had worn to a shadow, a mere shred of tradition, the observer from the Eastern world looking at the ruin with its statues, and across the fissure of ten thousand years to the nucleus of fact fading to a minute cloud on the horizon, would have a task as speculative and as difficult to piece together the shadows out of the past into something like reality as the visitor to Easter Island has to-day. Here as I sit, surrounded with the enormous squared and tooled stones, that turn the edge of the toughest modern steel, away over its precipitous coasts across the endless levels of the Pacific that far out seem to justify the name, whilst the thunder of the surf for ever in my ears gives them the lie, I feel, like all my predecessors, as baffled and desolate in thought as that far-off Oriental visitor to the statued and isolated relic

of our far-spreading empire and our western civilization would be. Nor would he find much aid in the solution of his problem if he came across a few hundred survivors wandering about inept and purposeless, except for the quest of food, like the dwellers in the native village of Hangaroa close by.

(2) **AN INFINITY OF ORGANIZED LABOUR.** Nor must it be presumed that Easter Island is dwarfed by. the comparison. One has only to ride round the bold coasts and see the great burial platforms stretch in an almost unbroken line round the three dozen miles of its circumference to realize that it is not this mortuary speck in the greatest of oceans that is over-shadowed by the imaginary parallel. Every mile or even half-mile, especially along the south coast and the east coast, you stumble across one of those great memorials of the forgotten great; and in some of the sheltered nooks, like A n a k e n a Bay or La Perouse Bay, from half a dozen to a dozen are crowded together in a space no larger than Westminster Abbey and its precincts. Some of them are inchoate, almost shapeless, heaps of the myriads of millions of stones that cover the surface of the island; but these are a small minority. Into some of the largest must have gone the labour of tens of thousands of men for many years. It is not merely the piecing together of the large and small stones into platforms, some of which are four to five hundred feet long; that would, indeed, take vast masses of organized labour. It is the individual labour expended; there are in many of the platforms scores of immense stones ranging in weight from two to twenty tons, all shaped and tooled, each one of which must have taken a workman with his stone implements, aided by sand and water, years to cut and groove; they are most of them of a vesicular basalt that European masons would find it hard to work even with tools toughened by admixture of the rare metals. There must be tens of thousands of tons of these adamantine and titanic stones all worked into shape on the coasts of the island. And there must be hundreds of thousands of tons of such cyclopean blocks chipped into the requisite form, though untooled. A building like Westminster Abbey would not need a tenth part of the labour in tooling and handling and erecting that these hundreds of platforms took. No one can realize the amount of human muscle and the concentration of it that would be needed to fit out this islet as a place of sepulture till he has slowly ridden round all the coasts, and that is a task of days.

TOMBS OF THE TUITONGAS AS REPRESENTED IN "THE MISSIONARY VOYAGE OF THE DUFF," 1799

(3) **EASTER ISLAND DOES NOT SUFFER BY THE COMPARISON.**
Nor does the comparison throw Easter Island into shadow,
even when we look at it from the point of view of art. Our
great ecclesiastical buildings, our cathedrals and abbeys, are
magnificent in their design and impressive in their effect on
the human mind. But the use of them as memorial halls
of the great is an afterthought suggested by their use as
places of sepulture for those who lavished gifts upon them.
And in some we feel as if the shrines and statues were excres-
cences, they are so clotted together, without thought of their
relationship to the general design. The *campo-santos* of Latin
Europe and Spanish America with their marble corridors and
statued vaults have doubtless developed out of this idea of
concentration of memorial sepulture. But as we wander round
gazing at the winged angels and other marble forms we soon
feel that this concentration of the dead is not without its
danger to the living : lead and marble have no more power
to imprison bacteria than to imprison Röntgen rays ; and
bacteria are far more efficient enemies of the human race
than the old ghosts.

(4) Here the bacteria of the memorialled dead are innocuous.
The cathedral roof is the firmament ; the aisles are the great
precipices that fret the Pacific into an endless dirge ; and the
trade wind tempers the fierceness of the summer sun and
carries the healing salt spray over the whole island. It is
difficult to imagine a sleeping-place for the dead so sanitary
for both body and soul of the living as this islet a thousand
miles from every speck of land and open to all the skyey
influences, tropic or antarctic.

(5) **THE CLIMAX OF A POLYNESIAN IDEA.** It is as difficult
to imagine a more artistic or impressive memorial place
for the great dead. No architect of the historical civilizations has ever reached a conception so magnificent for
immortalizing the past. The Polynesian mind had been slowly
finding its way to it in working out cyclopean monuments
for the dead. Back in Micronesia it had made a beginning in
Tinian in the avenue of stone pillars bearing aloft their mortuary
semicircles of stone. In Tongatabu (Holy Tonga) the truncated
pyramids of huge coral blocks near the old native capital,
Mua, marking the tombs of the Tuitongas, or priestly kings,
show the idea still developing in the most westerly of the
Polynesian groups. In the south of Upolu of the Samoan

group Mr. Edgar N. Heycock has just found numerous truncated and stepped pyramids of stone ranging from ten to
thirty feet in height, twenty to sixty feet in width and ninety
to two hundred feet in length ; and from these there are traces
of paved ways down to the sea. Farther east and not far
from the Equator Malden Island, as small a speck as this and
the haunt of no living thing but sea-birds through all time,
is covered with truncated pyramids of coral blocks capped
with dolmens and approached by paved ways from the sea ;
and though there is no sign of burial or dead, these temples
and altars must have been connected with ceremonials intended
to immortalize chiefs that had passed. These reveal tentative
efforts towards such a conception of a concentrated mausoleum
as has been carried out on this islet and show a clear line of
development towards it; but they are dwarfed by its embodi-
ment on Easter Island. Here for more than thirty miles you
can ride and never come to the end of these titanic attempts
to immortalize the great dead.

(6) **DUPLICATION OF THE PLATFORMS HAD BEGUN WHEN
THE END CAME.** And when the catastrophe came that slit the
thread of these attempts as suddenly as if by "the abhorred
shears" of "the blind Fury" there were still greater
plans in contemplation. On the south coast especially
the platforms close to the precipices were getting duplicated
by platforms almost similar a half a mile to a mile inland.
On the south-west, round the northern bases of Rano Kao,
we find two a mile inland ; and away up the west coast about
two miles inland from the great platform of Tepeu there lie
on a broad plain the ruins of Ahu Ativi, which must have been
as extensive a platform ; it was three hundred feet long ; the
seven great images that stood upon it have fallen like all the
others ; but unlike the others they have faced the sea and not
looked inland ; nor have they had like the others red tufa
caps ; there is not a trace of red tufa to be found in the *débris*
that the wreckers of the platform have left scattered about ;
and the flat tops of their heads bear petroglyphs that are
evidently as old as the statues and that were not meant to
be covered.

(7) **STATUES FALLEN BY THE WAY.** The plan of the
architect was clearly far from completion when the work
suddenly stopped ; the whole thirty thousand acres of this
solitary islet were to be included in the resting-place of those

A *langi*, OR TOMB OF THE TUITONGAS NEAR MUA, THE ANCIENT CAPITAL OF TONGATABU,
WHEN PARTIALLY CLEARED OF ITS FOREST GROWTH

THE APPROACH TO THE WORKSHOP OF THE SCULPTORS ON RANO RARAKU WITH
AVENUE OF FALLEN STATUES ON THE WAT

that had vanished. Line by line from the precipitous coast would stretch the circles of burial platforms. But there are indications perhaps of another part of his plan that would break the monotony of those circles. Looking westwards from the workshop of the sculptors on the south-west side of Rano Raraku one can see that the fallen images group themselves on either side of the ancient way that leads to the conical hill of Maunga Toatoa, two miles off. And again, riding north to Anakena one seemed to see some arrangement in the statues that had fallen by the wayside. It looked as if from Rano Raraku there rayed out roads that were ultimately meant to be avenues of statues. Of course, there are many statues lying, usually face down, all over the island that cannot be taken as indicating such an avenue, especially away to the north-west of the island ; there are two or three huge statues a mile or two from platforms and credited by tradition with being on the way to platforms ; one of them said to be for the great *Ahu* of Waimataa has rain-grooves down its back, though it is quite level ; but it may have stood for some years in the front shop-window of the sculptors on the south-west slope of Rano Raraku, where so many still stand ; and statues cut along the strike of the strata tend to weather in this way, whilst others that have been cut across it tend to have grooves and ridges askew. We must assume that at least some of these statues fallen in solitary places were abandoned at the general abandonment of all such work on the island.

(8) **STATUED AVENUES ONLY BEGUN WHEN DESTINY BROKE THE THREAD.** But there is clear room for conjecture that the plan of the architect included statued avenues by which the funeral train of some great chief was to pass from the landing-place to his final rest. By these, too, would pass the gay throng that with song and dance marched to some platform to celebrate the memory of a great warrior by long feast. The architect that planned on the landward side of most *ahus* great paved dancing-grounds, great round holes filled with stones for the erection of huge figures of wickerwork and bark-cloth, and numerous permanent stone foundations for the erection of guest-houses, would not neglect the spectacular approach or fail to provide it with long lines of images.

(9) With or without the statued avenues the conception of Easter Island as a memorial islet holding out its great

burial platforms everlastingly over the ocean is both magnificent and original. It was slowly developed in the mind of the megalithic Polynesian; but it reaches its climax and realization here. That it was abandoned long before completion and still more that the idea of approaches to the platforms with long vistas of statues on either side of them was abandoned almost at its inception, shows how great must have been the cataclysm that broke off the history of Easter Island as a mausoleum of the heroic dead and left it hanging in air, an undying mystery.

THE REMAINS OF ONE OF THE PYRAMIDAL ERECTIONS ON MALDEN ISLAND

THE PYRAMIDAL STRUCTURES OF MALDEN ISLAND AS THEY WERE IN 1825 BEFORE THE GUANO
BEGAN TO BE WORKED. (*From "Byron's Voyage."*)

CHAPTER II

THE BURIAL PLATFORMS

(1) The unbroken ring of a h u s *round the coast over precipice as well as bay negatives the idea that they were placed near the habitations of men. (2) But close to some of the greatest are great foundation-stones where immense houses stood. (3) They are far too cyclopean and tooled with too titanic work to have borne only the flimsy structures that the voyagers saw them bear. (4) The conception of a ring of coastal* a h u s *was as great as that of an islet dedicated to the memory of the dead. (5) But the statues have their backs to the ocean and cast their frown of mystery on the festal crowd that celebrate the memory of the dead. (6) Why should these Titans have been perched where nothing could save them from downfall when their brethren in the sculptor's shop, stuck solidly in the earth, still defy the storms? (7) Busts with flat uncarved backs as they are, they were evidently meant to stand in the earth* r e l i e v o s *against the high sea-wall of the* a h u s, *their potent frown threatening the billows. (8) But this was the final idea towards which the architects and the sculptors had slowly found their way. (9) Nature gave them their models in the countless volcanic dykes, and laughs at her own jest, as she thinks how all these* a h u s *and statues that were to make the dead immortal are oblivion itself and live only as the mystery of the anthropologist.*

(1) **THE ISLAND RINGED WITH MEMORIAL PLATFORMS.** One of the most striking features of the mausoleum design is that there is an almost unbroken line of burial platforms right round the islet. They are all but a few on the coast and most of the inland exceptions are duplicates of the coastal. A feasible explanation of this might be that the population was wholly coastal ; the legends sometimes refer to inland dwellers ; but they are solitary hermits or beings of the supernatural type usually styled after the introduction of Christianity *tatanis*. Most of the cultivations are in soakages at the mouth of hollows ; and round some of these, especially where there is a spring on the beach between high and low tide, there is generally the chief agglomeration of platforms, sometimes as many as half a dozen. But this will not explain the often magnificent specimens of them on almost inaccessible bluffs and precipices ; the *Mohican* party in 1886 describe an *ahu* Ahurikiriki " on the face of a perpendicular cliff nearly a thousand feet high and midway between the sea and the top," with sixteen small images on it and with no road to it from above or from below or from either side ; it was a long way from any village or possibility of a settlement and now lies in fragments far below. And away on the north-west coast some of the finest platforms have striking sites close to the edge of precipices that dominate the ocean, and far from

7

any spot that could have supported a community of men. Nor will the hypothesis of the habitable sites dictating the sites of burials explain the continuity of the line of *ahus* along the sea-coast irrespective of feasibility of approach or sustenance of the builders.

(2) **THE MYSTERY OF THE FOUNDATION-STONES.** One exception must be made to this generalization as to the distance of the platforms from the dwelling-places of men. On the landward side of some of the finest of them are the foundations of many houses that have manifestly had close connection with them. The foundation-stones are of the hardest basalt and are tooled to perfection; most of those round M a t a v e r i, where I write, are ten feet by two-and-a-half by two and must weigh not less than four tons, some of them nearer ten; they are some of them rounded on one side and others grooved, whilst most of them have beautifully rounded holes two inches in diameter drilled into them; there was on this site a great guest-house called H a r e m o a i, or house of the statue, in which all the great men of the island lived when they came to the annual feasts, and there was down below on a bluff above the sea a platform long vanished into the stone dykes that one manager of the stock built all over the island. Most of these finely shaped stones of adamant have been otherwise utilized, some in the old days in lining earth ovens or shelters under the fallen statues or in edging the rude heaps of gathered stones that cover newer graves, some in the new days of sheep and cattle and horses in the dykes that vainly attempt to paddock the animals. In some places they still remain embedded in the earth, revealing the shape that the ancient houses took, a shape that none of the old voyaging visitors to the island failed to compare to an upturned canoe, a narrow ellipse tapering to blunt ends. The most complete specimens are to be found inland from A h u T e p e u and coastwards from the far inland A h u A t i v i on the west coast, and inland from A h u H a n g a h a h a v e on the south coast. And for these T u u k o i h u, the contemporary and fellow-adventurer of H o t u M a t u a, is said to have been responsible; it was in his south coast residence, called H a r e K o k a, or the house of the cockroach, that he made the first wooden images; and it was in his west coast residence that, by means of cords controlled from inside, he made them move like marionettes round the roof of the house. It is this

A SOUTH COAST BURIAL PLATFORM

A WEST COAST BURIAL PLATFORM (TEPEU

ONE OF THE HUGE TOOLED FOUNDATION STONES
USED IN THE FOUNDATIONS OF THE MANAGER'S
HOUSE AT MATAVERI, WHICH WAS BLOWN OVER
IN 1921

last that was one of the largest; it measures close on three hundred feet long. These two pioneers of Easter Island seem to have indulged in houses; for H o t u M a t u a built a new one every year on the hill M a u n g a K o U a in Anakena Bay; and he built a house at intervals along the old road from Rano Raraku to Rano Kao, where he died, beginning from the platform called H a r e o A r a , or house of the road, the special burial-place of kings, where he and his sons were buried.

(3) These immense foundation-stones, tooled with a care that meant years of work on each piece of adamant, were evidently intended by their original architects to bear the framework of great structures. What the voyagers and Brother Eyraud, the first adventurous missionary in 1864, saw them bear was a flimsy haystack-like roof of poles and thatch with an entrance two feet wide and two feet high that compelled crawling in or out on the stomach. It could be put together in a few days, if not in a few hours when plenty of hands were available. That these immense foundation-stones of adamant, tooled with years and years of work, were meant to carry nothing more than this is the very irony of architecture. In the Easter Island that we know from tales of Roggewein, its discoverer, and Cook, and La Perouse, and from tradition, they did carry nothing but these flimsy structures that sheltered the guests who gathered to the great feasts from all parts of the island; and every new feast the low-rounded roof was re-erected, to be the sport and wreckage of winter's storms, whilst the bearing stones were to last a thousand years. But the first use of them was to house the builders of the platforms and the kings and chiefs who came to bury or commemorate some dead warrior.

(4) **THE RING OF** *AHUS* **ONE OF THE GREATEST OF ARCHITECTURAL IDEAS.** The site of the *ahus* was not dictated by the site of residences but dictated it. Those adamantine foundation-stones were tooled and set by the builders of a platform, not merely to carry the houses that were to shelter them during the years they were working at it, but to carry the palaces that were to house the princes and chiefs who came to honour the dead in the after generations. And that these came in great numbers and stayed long is evident in the great round house twelve feet in diameter that covers the earth-oven, the supplier of food to the temporary

occupants of the houses. There is not much in the hypothesis, therefore, that it was the residential nature of parts of the coast that made the line of burial platforms coastal. In fact, we may take the continuity of the coastal line of *ahus* as a deliberate architectural plan. And the conception is as great as that of a sacred burial islet devoted solely to the honour of the heroes who have passed. It is most probably the child of the same brain that bred the other, and was intended to impress a maritime aristocracy, vikings that swept the often stormy spaces of the Pacific without fear. As they sailed round the islet to find the shelter of H a n g a r o a on the west, or of A n a k e n a or L a P e r o u s e on the east, they could, as an ancestor-worshipping people, feel drawn to the dead in the burial vaults that crowned every surge-defying precipice they passed. And Moerenhout, the observant and thoughtful visitor to Easter Island a hundred years ago, thinks that the giant statues standing on these platforms were, like those he saw on R a i v a v a i guarding the isthmus that led to the open billow-swept taro-ground of the people, intended to be *tikis* or boundary-gods warning the ocean not to repeat its trespass on the land.

(5) **WHY WERE THE STATUES PLACED LIKE NINEPINS TO BE BOWLED OVER?** But the statues had their backs to the ocean, except on the inland *ahu* on the west. They had all a look of menace on their faces, emphasized by the pout of the thin lips and the strength of the great chin. If they threatened anything it was the land and not the sea, the crowds of festal singers and dancers and not the thunder of the billows that insolently ate their way into the everlasting cliffs their pedestals. It is true that the site chosen in every case was meant to command the sea and that the sea-wall of every platform is solidly built and imposing, and in many beautifully tooled and fitted. But the little square-built burial-vaults are on the landward side, and so are the paved dancing-grounds and the guest-houses and the great spaces for the crowds of feasters. Then there was the A r a M a h i v a or road of the strangers, that was to go all round the island inland from the *ahus* and to carry all the victims (*ika*) that were to be slain on the altars ; and there were the beginnings of those statued avenues that were to lead the festal crowd to every platform.

(6) And yet there is something to be said for Moerenhout's

THE PLATFORM OF TONGARIKI, WITH THE PEDESTAL STONE OF A STATUE STILL STANDING

THE FALLEN STATUES OF TONGARIKI, WITH TWO RED HATS IN FRONT

idea. The statues do not seem to have had their natural and permanent place where they stood on the highest part of the *ahus ;* their height, especially with their huge red hats on and the two-to-three foot thick pedestal stones on which they were perched made it quite certain that they would fall sooner or later, as they have all done, by either natural or human means. Why sculptors should carve these titanic figures and architects should have them conveyed safely to their platforms only to set them up as gigantic ninepins for the tempests of the air or the human mind to bowl over is perhaps one of the deepest mysteries of Easter Island ; they were meant to be everlasting memorials of the great dead, and they were placed where nothing but a miracle could save them for more than a brief period from destruction. The sculptors on Rano Raraku gave a practical illustration of what ought to have been done and what was ultimately meant to be done to these titans if they were to be permanent. They stuck them in upright on the sides of the crater within or on the south-west slope without. And there they stand to this day, in spite of the storms and rains and landslides of two centuries, one of the most striking sights in the world.

(7) **MEANT TO BE IN RELIEF.** At least the sculptors knew what alone would save their works from destruction. And two features of the images show that they knew ; they made them without legs or feet and the thighs were inchoate. It was only from the abdomen upwards they meant them to be seen ; and it is across this well-nurtured rondure that the hands from the wrists, with the long thin fingers, are bent at right angles to the stout arms. The lowest two or three feet might be buried in the earth without spoiling the effect of the statue. The other feature is the flat back of all the images ; only in one or two cases has anything been carved on that side, and generally it looks as if this had been a later performance. The back was not intended to be seen ; all the carving is on the front ; and the sea-wall of every platform seems to have been made for such a back. Set up in the earth against this as a figure in relief a statue would have stood the ravages of time and the assaults of war as long as those on Rano Raraku have done. And the resolution and menace on their faces would have dared the violence of the billows that gnawed into the adamant cliffs.

(8) **DEVELOPMENT OF THE** *AHUS.* But not all *ahus* were

built thus; in fact, more than half of them are without
statues and were never meant for statues. Some are but
slightly arranged heaps (the original meaning of *ahu*) of
untooled stones. There is, in fact, a fairly clear evolution in
the burial platform. The first stage is a loose heap of stones
collected from the surrounding country, such as those the
Easter Islanders continued to bury their dead in up till recent
times. The second is a heap shaped into a long rectangle;
one form of this is concave on top and is supposed to represent
a *boat* (*ahu poepoe*), though the boat model must be post-
European; another rises gradually from the two ends to a
point in the centre, and though steep on the seaward side
slopes up on the landward. But the stones were apt to get
adrift and leave the burial vault uncovered. The only remedy
was to confine the rubble within the lines of great blocks of
stones; thus the platform arose. At first the blocks, though
huge, were shaped to fit each other, but untooled; and the
long slope of rubble covered the vaults and the low landward
retaining wall. It was this low wall of more easily manipulated
blocks that came to be tooled first as well as shaped, and it
rose ultimately with its fine lines clear of all the rubble. The
next stage was the tooling and shaping of the blocks that went
to make the great seaward wall; and then the huge pedestal
stones could be laid with safety on the top of the great platform
made solid by its confining walls. On these the images, which
were at first of medium size, began to be erected. And as the
ideas of the architects expanded, so did the platforms, so as
to have long wings with seaface set farther back than the
solid centre, at first only of roughly shaped blocks and without
statues, but later finely tooled and bearing statues of their
own. Then followed modifications that distinguish *ahu* from
ahu; one has subsidiary platforms in front on the edge of the
precipice; another has them at right angles to the central;
another has taken advantage of a volcanic dyke to continue
the platform at an angle or in a circle. The final stage was
the shaping of every block of the two containing walls so that
they would fit exactly into each other. One of the best examples
of this is *V i n a p u* on the south coast at the root of Rano
Kao; though perhaps even finer was the *ahu* of H a n g a r o a,
the destruction of which the first missionaries began by taking
the blocks as well as the untooled stones to build their house;
the fragment that remains, like the platform of V i n a p u,

PICTURE OF STATUES AND NATIVES FROM " THE VOYAGE OF LA PEROUSE." THE NARROW HEADS AND HUGE HATS ARE WELL SHOWN. BUT NO PLATFORM IS IN THIS SHAPE; NOR HAS THE MOUTH OF ANY STATUE THE ENDS AS DRAWN DOWN

where it was not shattered by the scientific vandalism of the Americans in 1886, is equal to the best to be seen in the Inca work and pre-Inca masonry of Peru.

(9) **NATURE SHOWED THE WAY.** And yet every stage is to be seen as one rides over the island in the work of Nature. The outcrop of volcanic dykes weathers at times into heaps of small loose angular stones like the first stage of the *ahu*, again into the boat-shape, or into the pyramidal shape. Away up the west coast towards the north point I asked my guide to take me to what Paymaster Thomson calls in his Smithsonian article A h u K i n o k i n o ; I noticed a flickering smile on his face ; and when we came to it I found it to be a weathered dyke shaped like a pyramidal *ahu ;* it was Nature copying man. My guide's father accompanied the *Mohican* party round the *ahus ;* and this was one of the little jokes the natives perpetrated on the scientists ; *Kino-kino* means " very bad," " gone to ruin." And to show that Nature enjoyed the jest and seemed conscious of man's attempt to imitate her, I found every stage of the *ahu,* even the most advanced like the C u z c o cyclopean work imitated by the weathered volcanic dyke ; it weathers often into geometrical crystals that look as if tooled and shaped and set together by the hand of man. It became quite manifest to me as I rode where that architectural genius who thought out the plan of the sacred isle of sepulture borrowed the ideas of his burial platforms.

CHAPTER III

THE WORKSHOP OF THE SCULPTORS

(1) The Colosseum of the stone-Titans looks another Olympus come down from the heavens and frozen stiff at the sight of pigmy man and his works. (2) The greatest romance of all is the suddenness with which the titanesque sculpture ceased as if a bolt from the hand of Jove had laid low the makers of the Titans. (3) The back of the head of these giants was flat; and so were the nostrils, whilst the fingers were made long and slender because these enter into the Polynesian ideal of beauty. (4) The face has such an imperious expression that they seem stone Alexanders the Great with typical Greek features. (5) And each statue has its own individual expression on its face, though cut by blunt adzes out of puddingstone. (6) The sculptors gave a lesson to the architects in placing their images in their front shop-window, firmly set up in the earth. (7) The greatest mystery about the images is not their making but their transport without mishap. (8) The miracle was probably achieved by keeled sledges for the images, and great hawsers hauled by tens of thousands of slaves.

(1) **AN AMPHITHEATRE OF THE GODS.** One of the most picturesque rides in Easter Island is that along the south coast from the great platform of Akahanga eastwards. In front, at the extreme south-eastern point, stretches the elevated plateau of Poike, the ancient dwelling-place of all wizards and witches and *tatanis*, and off its bold cliffs the spearhead of Marotiri rising from the ocean, once, not so long ago, a part of those cliffs and like them the favourite resort of supernatural beings. The sea foams and spouts along the coast in futile rage against the black volcanic basis of the island, only its flying spray or at times a darting tongue reaching the softer precipices over which the burial platforms preside, their memorial giants fallen athwart them. Miles off inland at last there comes into view one of the strangest sights that one can see on the face of the earth, the slope of a cone that looks volcanic peopled with stone giants gazing out into infinity. And as we round the cone of Maunga Toatoa, every few hundred yards a titan lies biting the dust, as if driven from the mountain by the victorious Olympians. And they look down in stony arrogance along the vista of their fallen foes, and as we get nearer, smaller though most of them are than those that bow before them, their ruthless majesty becomes more and more pronounced. At the foot of the mountain, as we gaze up, the first impression is deepened; there is a look of pitiless scorn on those stony faces. Nor does

14

PART OF THE PLATFORM OF VINAPU WITH WELL-TOOLED STONES

A PLATFORM THAT RESEMBLES A LAVA-DYKE

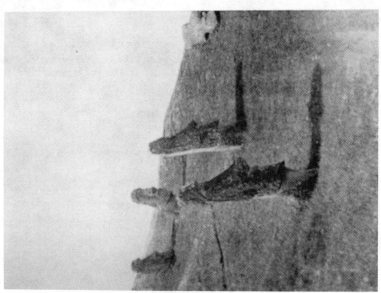

FOUR STATUES SET UP BY THE SCULPTORS AT THE
FOOT OF THEIR WORKSHOP, AND ONE FALLEN

the impressiveness of the scene wear off as we settle down in the lee of Orohie, an even greater titan, while the guide pitches our tent just above the bird-man's *ahu*, one of the most insignificant on the island. Hours and hours passed as I sat and gazed up at this gallery of the stone-gods, and every minute I seemed to discover some new giant asleep in his niche, contemplating his canopy of rock or the sky above. Tier above tier they lay far up the hill, most of them still part of the rock out of which they were carved, one here and there needing only a few blows of the chisel to detach it, another lying on its keel as if ready to be launched, a third seeming to need but a touch to send it headlong down the slope. On every level were empty benches whence images had been cut and removed. Below one was a headless trunk, the head left far below, a fate that it is difficult to imagine how most of the statues did not suffer in their descent, so steep were the slopes, so ridged with the docks of their launched brethren. That hill-face surely presented as many problems in engineering as in sculpture. I never wearied of looking up at that ancient workshop as the sun westered. Every minute the light changed and brought out new shadows or blotted them out ; it was as if a master hand was manipulating the limelight he threw upon this theatre of the gods.

(2) **EVIDENCES OF DIRECTIVE SKILL AND CATASTROPHIC ENDING.** Nor did a day or two of climbing from bench to bench and level to level attenuate the first impression ; it rather deepened it, especially as I saw sign after sign of the sudden cessation of all the operations in the workshop, as if a tremendous blast of poison gas had asphyxiated all the workmen and left them to sleep the everlasting sleep of the stony giants they were shaping ; but they have mouldered away whilst a sleep of two centuries has left the beings they created almost unchanged. Tools lie as they were thrown away the day the workshop fell silent. Images lie in all stages of creation, from measuring and roughing out to preparation for launching. One immense statue, seventy feet long, and broad in proportion, intended, it is said, to adorn an *ahu* away along the south coast, called Tahiri, almost an annexe of Vinapu, has only had its face and body outlined ; it is one of the few statues that have been cut out vertically instead of horizontally, doubtless to ensure a safe descent ; for far up the hill above it the trunkless head of an image has warned the

sculptors against the dangers in front of the statues when finished. Everything speaks of the catastrophic suddenness of the last strike ; and that was a universal strike ; for every feature of the workshop reveals the marks of careful organization and foresight. There must have been brains and strong will directing the sculptors, as there were directing the emplacement and building of the platforms. Directive skill is not so apparent in the first workshop inside the crater ; the images have been cut more at random up and down the slope. On the outside the whole strata have been mapped out so as to get as many statues out of them as they were capable of ; though the map must have been frequently changed as the ideas of the clients enlarged and rivalry amongst them arose as to who would have the largest images. For the chief development apparent is in size and not in fineness of sculpture. There is a tradition that the statues set up on the mounds of sculptors' *débris* round the lower levels of the slope were left severely alone by the later clients because they were not large enough to suit their fancy.

(3) **THE POLYNESIAN MOTHER'S HAND DICTATED THE FEATURES OF THE GIANTS.** There is, however, an advance, or at least a change in the direction of slicing off the back of the head so as to make the top very narrow, so narrow indeed that it could not have borne the immense red hats. This is an exaggeration of the ideal that dictated the flat back for the head from the first. To this day the Easter Island mothers or midwives massage the plastic skull of the babies into the fashionable Polynesian shape, flat back, domed top and sloping forehead ; I was fairly certain before I came to the island that it could not form the exception to the Polynesian custom, and inquiry brought out a clear confirmation, though there are cases of unmassaged heads, doubtless because of the breaking of the thread of Polynesian customs through the influence of the new religion ; whilst some that have been massaged in infancy still show a prominent occipital bulge and a head that looks rather long than round ; for the massaging hands of some mothers would be less severe upon the heads of their babies. The nearest approach to uniformity would be secured in Samoa, where the head of the infant was set between stones, and in Manihiki, where a board was used to slope the brow. Had a cradle-mould been used as in Borneo, or a mat-bandage as in the little islands Tomman and Hambi

A TYPICAL PLATFORM OVERLOOKING THE OCEAN ON THE SOUTH COAST.
IT WAS BUILT IN TWO SECTIONS

ONE OF THE STATUES STILL UNDETACHED FROM ITS NICHE IN THE
ROCK. ABOVE AND BELOW IT ARE EMPTY ROCK-BENCHES FROM
WHICH THE STATUES HAVE BEEN REMOVED

on the south coast of Malekula, the Polynesian skull would
have been much more uniformly round, or rather armenoid.
And the fashion of a domed head with the topknot on the top
of that would explain the height of the red stone-hat with its
rounded protuberance, though it is possible the shape may
have some relationship to the curious little straw hats the
Easter Islanders make for themselves, and the colour may be
due to the monopoly by Polynesian chiefs of the red tail-
feathers of the tropic-bird for their diadems. Another peculiar
feature of all the images may be explained by this practice of
massaging parts of the infant's anatomy ; it is the extra-
ordinarily long and slender fingers ; here as in other parts of
Polynesia the fingers of the baby are lengthened out by massage
to their full capacity. In Easter Island, at least, its legs and
especially its ankles were also massaged in order to give the
adult agility in speeding over the stone-covered surface. There
is another feature of the statues that is due to the custom of
infantile massage ; it is the breadth of the nostrils ; flattened-
out nostrils are an important element in the Polynesian ideal
of beauty, often grotesquely incongruous with the aquiline
or Grecian bridge ; Cook's officers saw an Areoi drama of an
accouchement, and the six-foot baby, as soon as he was born,
had his nostrils violently rubbed down by his six-foot nurses.

(4) **A RACE OF ALEXANDERS SEEKING OTHER WORLDS TO
CONQUER.** But there is more than acquiescence with ancient
Polynesian custom in the shaping of the noses of the
statues. They are given an openness and an upturn of the
nostril that add to the imperious expression every face bears.
This makes the noses of many " tip-tilted," and in the case
of one tall image set up at the bottom of the slope, makes
its nose look as if it were experiencing an offensive smell ;
it is called Piropiro, which means in the language " Bad smell."
But as a rule the raised nostrils are in full harmony with the
short upper lip, the thin, closed, pouting lips, and the large
commanding chin. Taken as a whole they express haughty
scorn and imperious will ; it is the expression of victorious
warriors and empire-makers ; and when added to the upturned
gaze it seems to indicate a series of Alexanders looking for
other worlds to conquer. Though the arrogant and resolute
look is given to the faces of all the statues, it is never the
same on two faces ; every one looks as if it had been intended
to be an individual portrait ; one has the domineering look

toned down almost to meekness, if not pity ; another has it
raised almost into the diabolic ; in one we are struck more by
the contemplative eye, in another by the strength of the chin ;
and in most of the skulls that I saw exposed in the burial
vaults of the *ahus* the strength of the jaw and chin was as
pronounced as in the statues. My guide insisted that every
platform bore the name of the first warrior buried in it ; I
pointed out that some of the names would bear local interpretation ; Paukura, for example, meant " the end of the red,"
and it was erected exactly where a stratum of red tufa that
crowned the cliffs of the coast stopped ; and another called
" Hare o Ara," or " the house of the road," was on the road
that, he had just told me, Hotu Matua had punctuated with
residences. But he stuck to his point with an obstinacy that
characterizes most Easter Islanders as well as their flies. And,
though I still think with him that every statue was meant to
represent an individual, I have to confess that the statues were
peppered over the platforms, even the largest, like Tongariki,
without regard to the place of the burial vaults below. Of one
thing I am certain that, even if the images are not portrait
statues, they represent the imperious leaders of a race that if
they failed to conquer or build an empire had all the will and
talents to do so. And if the fine oval faces, the large eyes,
the short upper lip and the thin, often Apollo's bow lips, are
any guide to race, they indicate a caucasoid race ; and these
are features that one meets in every group of Polynesian
islands.

(5) **THE STATUES SEEMED TO SOME VOYAGERS MOULDED
OUT OF CLAY.** That the sculptors were able to give so much
character and individuality to the separate faces shows no
mean skill in their art when we consider the material
in which they had to work and the clumsy tools they had to
work with. Some of it is friable as unmoistened putty, and
on some of the *ahus*, where the images have been shattered,
the pieces have gone almost to mullock and will ultimately
disappear. In fact, it looks not volcanic stone but sedimentary.
The rim of the crater of Rano Raraku against the skyline
shows the corrugations of the strata set on end. The material
is puddingstone, or conglomerate ; the original dust has been
perhaps laid in shallow water and sprayed with angular
fragments of shattered rock, some volcanic, others that look
like altered slate or fire-hardened clay, and others that may

THE BUTT OF THE SEVENTY-FOOT LONG STATUE INTENDED FOR TAHIRI PLATFORM ONLY HALF FINISHED
AND STILL ATTACHED TO THE ROCK ; IT IS ONE OF THE FEW CUT UP AND DOWN THE SLOPE OF THE
HILL INSTEAD OF HORIZONTALLY

A STATUE SHOWING THE GREAT CHIN, SHORT UPPER LIP, POUTING
THIN LIPS FLAT BACK AND NARROW HEAD

be granite. The strata have been hardened by pressure and
then forced from the horizontal to the vertical position by the
volcanic thrust of the lava below. But it is the angular
fragments so liberally sprinkled through it that bind the
material together. The sculptors saw this and attempted only
once to make a statue from the sheer cliff of pure compressed
clayey mud that flanks Rano Raraku on its south-east side.
Where the rock-raisins in the pudding were few, the statue
soon went to pieces ; where they were too many or too large
the carving of the statue had to be abandoned.

(6) **HOW WERE THOSE FIFTY-TON TITANS OF PLASTER-OF-
PARIS HAULED WITHOUT MISHAP ?** Why they chose such
soft and friable material to represent and immortalize their
great dead is a question difficult to answer. It may have
been the clumsiness and bluntness of their tools ; and yet
they were able to shape and chisel the adamantine basalt
of the foundation-stones, to cut the *vulva* on the less hard
boundary-stones and to carve out a still softer volcanic
stone into statues like Hoa-haka-nanaia. The architects of the
platforms built one of these carved from the harder volcanic
stone into an *ahu* called Maitaki-te-Moa, away up the west
coast, and, perhaps to express their disapproval of such small
images, turned its back to the front of the sea-wall. In any
case, there seems to have been a disagreement between the
sculptors and the architects of the platforms ; for the images
set up at the foot of the workshop are placed without order or
system ; one is placed right in front of another so as to block
the view of it ; one is set in a reclining position, another leaning
forward ; some look north-west, others south-east, and that
side by side ; the one feature common to the position of all is
that their backs are to the hill, a feature that even the most
infantile of artists would see to in placing the products of his
art ; he would never turn the face to the wall. It is perfectly
manifest that though they are all dug in they intended to
serve no purpose but exhibition in the front shop-window, so
as to be removed by clients to avenues or platforms.

(7) And here we strike upon one of the deepest mysteries of
this islet. How were they able to haul those brittle statues,
weighing up to fifty or sixty tons (the seventy-foot long image
intended for Ahu Tahiri would have been more than that, and
there is one as large going to pieces far inland), over the most
uneven of surfaces, all littered with angular stones, as far as

twelve or fifteen miles without an accident such as they not
infrequently had in lowering them from their benches on the
hillside ?   Imagine statues of material that seems no harder
than the mixture of putty and pebbles well compressed being
dragged over even our macadamized roads ; how much of
them would be left before they reached their destination ?
And here across the stoniest, most uneven, islet in the world,
dozens of them were hauled without a mishap, without even
a scratch.   There is a tradition that the sailors who brought
the statue of Rano Raraku material from the Ahu Moihava
to the beach of Hangaroa, less than two miles over a cleared
road, rubbed off one of the features of its face, probably the
nose, and when they got it on board of the *Topaz*, reconstructed
the missing protuberance from materials they had at hand.
The remaining statue on the *ahu* is certainly of the usual
friable stuff.   The tradition that pebbles from the beach were
generally used to facilitate the transport only deepens the
mystery.

(8) If one were allowed to make a conjecture as to how the
miracle was accomplished, there are a custom and a tradition
that would suggest the means.   Down almost every hill-side
and always down the steeply sloping there are grooves or
rûns that seem to be very old ; and to this day they are used
for tobogganing ; the sledge, called *pei*, consists of one stem
or more of a banana tree.   A slight adaptation of this in the
shape of a cradle or canoe on two keels, provided large enough
stems were procurable, would ensure the transport of these
giants over the roughest ground in safety.   And for hawsers
to haul such weights, we have the tradition of an aerial
gravitation tramway from the top of Rano Raraku down to
the great platform of *Tongariki*, nearly a mile off on the coast,
and one from the same height to the foot of Maunga Toatoa,
close on two miles distant.   On the ridge of the image-mountain
there are large circular holes drilled deep in the rock ; into
these, the tradition tells, were wedged high circular beams,
and from the top of those beams huge ropes were stretched,
and down these men and cargo passed by their own weight ;
for lubrication yams, strangely enough, were used, though it
is not so strange when we know the poverty of the land.
Whence the great beams and enough material for the hawsers
could come is the problem in a piece of land that shows no
sign of ever having had any forest on it.   But once these were

TWO STATUE-HEADS FROM THE FRONT SHOP-WINDOW OF THE
SCULPTORS, SHOWING THE STRONG CHARACTERISATION

THE PROFILE OF ONE OF THE STATUES, SHOWING THE POWERFUL NOSE, MOUTH AND CHIN
THAT INDICATE A RACE OF CONQUERORS

forthcoming, it was only a question of the concentration of human muscle on the enormous weights. There must have been thousands, if not tens of thousands, of adult manhood under the discipline of slaves, to achieve the transport of such weights as the statues and the stones of the platforms.

CHAPTER IV

THE ISLAND

(1) No great outburst of art is without a natural cause. (2) Easter Island is the Robinson Crusoe of the lands of the world; (3) Out of the track of all voyaging and commerce, and incapable of oceanic navigation; (4) Infertile; (5) Leaky; (6) Bearing only a narrow range of vegetation that flourishes with difficulty; (7) Without humus or worms, a land on which pigs cannot live wild, having nothing to grub; a land on which land-birds have never been able to live. (8) Nor did the sea make up for the deficiency, the sea-birds think, and give it largely the go-by. (9) Whence could the luxury come that is implied in the monuments?

(1) **GREAT ART HAS EVER GREAT CAUSE.** Is there anything in the position or character of Easter Island to explain this marvellous outburst of the memorial arts? As a rule where we have had any striking exhibition of artistic talent in history or prehistory we are able to explain it. The civilization of ancient Egypt with its lavish development of the memorial arts finds its explanation in the Nile and the rich soil that it bears down from the mountains of Central Africa and yearly strews on its banks and delta. The arts and culture of Mesopotamia are explicable on similar grounds; the Euphrates and the Tigris were the kindly teachers and nurses of agriculture in early times, and made Babylon and Nineveh and Assyria not only possible but probable. Cyprus and Crete and the Ægean stood right in the current of eastern- and western-moving commerce, and ancient Greek art and literature were the consequence. Carthage and Rome, with their more westerly position and their command of lands that shot out into the Mediterranean, were the natural heirs of the arts of empire-builders. Then, as the Atlantic became the maritime centre of the world, Spain and Portugal, and after them Holland, took up the tale of human development on its occidental course. It was a preparation for the British Empire, the first maritime and world-wide empire in history; and the art and literature of the Elizabethan and Victorian eras have their natural genesis in the position of Britain as commanding the commercial and maritime interests of Europe and pioneering its industrial and imperial interests. And the position of the United States between the two great oceans will explain all

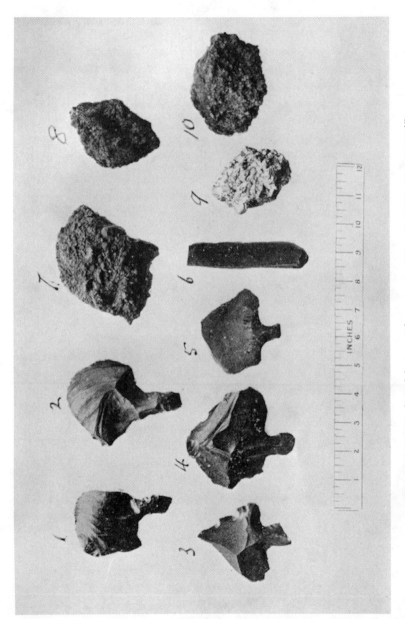

OBSIDIAN SPEARHEADS (*mataa*) (1, 2, 3, 4, 5).   ONE RASP OF FILE OF OBSIDIAN (6).
THREE FRAGMENTS OF THE STATUES (7, 9, 10).   ONE FRAGMENT OF RED HAT (8).

that she may do in invention and thought and art. The great art that China developed in her isolation thousands of years ago were due to the silt of her great rivers and her protection by the mountains on the west and the south and by the sea on the east. Whilst the architectural and other arts of the empires of Peru and Central America have close relationship to their particular agriculture and their naturally protected unity of position.

(2) **A RAT-CURRENCY THE ISLAND'S COMMERCIAL BASIS.** The position of Easter Island is the very antithesis of that which explains all the artistic outbursts that the world has known. It is more than a thousand miles from the nearest land, the uninhabited Ducie Island ; it is more than two thousand miles from the nearest of the ancient empires of the new world ; it is eight or nine thousand miles from the nearest of the empires of the old world. It is far out of the routes of both commerce and empire. Even from the Polynesian groups that attained to monarchic unity it is separated by the twelve hundred miles of the undeveloped and undevelopable low islands of the Paumotus. It is more side-tracked from all possible commercial routes than St. Helena ; and even if it were in the line of commerce, its congeners in Polynesia have never got farther than the beginnings of barter ; the far less cultured peoples of Melanesia and New Guinea had advanced much further towards commerce ; they had developed a currency of strings of shells and feathers. Polynesia had come no nearer to the idea of money than the old mats of Samoa. In fact, the only Polynesian island that ever developed the conception of a medium of trade was Easter Island ; and its currency was rats ; if a man wanted anything another man had he went out during the night to the haunts of rats, and by stoning them as they returned to their holes from their nocturnal raids, he was able to amass as much of the coin of the realm as would purchase the coveted object ; the only problem was the higgling of the market.

(3) **ELEMENTARY TRANSPORT AND VAST OCEANS TO CROSS.** But the greatest of rat-millionaires would never have been able to buy one of those gigantic images or command the immense labour-gang or the architectural talent that would produce one of these great burial platforms. Easter Island was as little likely to amass wealth by commerce as Tristan da Acunha ; it is so far from everywhere in the world. And the

biggest canoe it could produce was not more than eighteen feet long and two broad and incapable of carrying sail. The planks of which it was sewn together were never more than four feet long and never more than twelve inches broad ; it was caulked with dry grass and bailing was the never-ceasing necessity of sailing. No voyager ever saw more than two or three canoes on the islet. They never ventured more than a mile or two from land ; for the only thing they had to rely on against a breeze was a paddle no more effective for propulsion in water than a hockey stick ; it was a three-foot branch with an expansion at the business end not unlike a closed clasp-knife ; Paymaster Thomson in giving a picture of it was evidently so impressed with its inefficiency as a paddle that he calls it a scull for steering. What commerce could arise over the thousands of miles between the island and all communities that needed more than the bare necessities of life with means of transport like this is another of the mysteries of Easter Island. And how without commerce the wealth could be amassed that would make such great memorial arts as sculpture and architecture possible, if not essential, is a still greater one.

(4) **THE BARRENEST OF ISLETS.** But the wealth that gives leisure and demands luxury is sometimes amassed as in ancient Egypt and Mesopotamia and in China by tilling of the soil. And this might have been the foundation of the wonderful development of the memorial arts in Easter Island. Seeing that it has only thirty thousand acres, every acre must have been cultivated intensively and have had exceptional fertility to produce such a result. And it is the most infertile island I have been on in the Pacific. The least productive of the low coral islands can grow the coco-nut and the pandanus to perfection ; both trees lived a death-in-life on this island, once they were imported from Tahiti, although it is evident from the name for the tree (niu) being old in the language, and from one of the most valued ornaments in ceremonials and dances, the *t a h o n g a*, being a wooden imitation of a coco-nut, that that universal provider of the South Seas once grew and bore fruit in the island. The banana, too, has grown in many varieties and in considerable profusion since Hotu Matua introduced it ; and it undoubtedly exhausts the soil and needs considerable richness in it. It is generally grown now like the taro in stony hollows, where the unweathered volcanic dyke

MAITAKI TE MOA BURIAL PLATFORM WITH A BASALT STATUE
BUILT IN BACK TO THE FRONT

THE SCULPTORS' FRONT SHOP WINDOW, SHOWING ITS LACK OF ORDER.   THE STATUES ALL FACE
DIFFERENT WAYS.   THE LARGEST HAS EVIDENTLY NEVER BEEN SET UP

below prevents the moisture leaking away too rapidly to the sea and the weathered fragments above prevent it evaporating too rapidly in the heat of the sun.

(5) **NO FRESH WATER EXCEPT IN THE CRATERS.** The greatest defect of the island is its porous character. It has a rainfall of more than forty inches in the year, and the showers fall in about 250 days out of the 365. All these summer months I have spent here few days have passed without a shower falling some time in the twenty-four hours ; and the summer is not the wet season. Yet the whole island looks yellow and parched. A half an hour after a downpour the ground is as dry as before it. Even the rocks seem all of them to be porous ; they are certainly all vesicular as if they had been laid in water, the steam bubbles of which prevented complete solidity. The result is that, though there are out-crops of lava dykes every hundred yards on the more level parts, there are no springs except at sea-level. The old voyagers reported that the natives drank salt water systemat-ically ; and one early manager of the stock on the island built a stone wall along the coast to prevent the animals continuing to go down to the beach to drink. The only springs ooze up below the line of high tide, and, though they are most of them brackish, they are not too much so for natives and stock to drink the water of at low tide. The natives never made salt like the Hawaiians, and never took salt water as a seasoning like the other Polynesians. The reason doubtless is that the water they drink and the air they breathe have enough salt in them ; the spray from either coast is ever saturating the atmosphere. The great reservoirs of fresh water are in the craters ; they are called *r a n o* from a Pacific Ocean word meaning water or lake ; for they have each a permanent lake in them, though covered with a thick felting of soil and reeds. A procession of native horsemen and horsewomen passes up the slope of Rano Kao here every Saturday with bundles of clothes to wash. And the reason for the permanence of this reservoir of rain-water is that there is a plug of lava in the throat of the crater less permeable than most of the lavas of the levels. And this partial impermeability must belong to a hard black basalt that forms the sea-leve foundation of the island and resists so sturdily the assaults o the surge at least on the south coast.

(6) **VEGETATION STILL HAS A HARD STRUGGLE.** It is this

porosity, added to the unbroken violence of the winds, that makes all the trees planted on the island lead so hard a life; the only chance for them is huddling together; you can see the eucalyptus trees raise bare poles above a moderate height and their vitality is at best poor. The trees that seem to persist most are the melia azadarach, the fig and the cupressus macrocarpa. For any tree to thrive in Easter Island it must be exceptionally deep rooting so as to get down to the reservoir of water below, and exceptionally tough in the grain to resist the onslaught of the winter winds. The natives always used to build high stone walls (*manavai*) round their mahute, which gave them their bark-cloth and their hauhau, from which they got their cord fibre; else the moisture round their roots would have evaporated in the sun and the winds would have torn them to rags. They still do the same for their bananas; though that may be partly for protection from the stock which have eaten out all the native trees, like the toromiro (the sophora tetraptera of New Zealand) and the naunau, the bastard sandalwood, which grew fairly well on the heights of Poike; the latter has vanished, and the former is to be found only at the bottom of unapproachable precipices six hundred feet from the rim of Rano Kao, down by its lake. The sugar cane was one of the Polynesian food-plants that was brought to Easter Island and was cultivated with care; but it did not thrive, and has ceased to have any place on the *menu* of the natives, much to the detriment of their teeth. The ti, or dracaena, was another plant that was carried by the Polynesians in all their migrations and still lives here, though only in the bottom of Rano Kao; its leaves were burned to furnish the powder which, moistened with sap, formed the tattooing and painting mixtures; whilst its main use was that of its highly saccharine root as a confection; but the introduction of lump-sugar has displaced it. Their staple food consisted of the Polynesian tubers; but none of them grew to perfection except the sweet potato (kumara); for it could do well without the constant moisture that the taro and the yam required. And to this day the sweet potato is always a synonym of food.

(7) **NOTHING FOR BIRDS TO CATCH OR PIGS TO GRUB.** What the island most lacks is humus, the accumulation of the vegetable growth of thousands of years; it is geologi-

AN EASTER ISLAND CANOE ; FROM " LA PEROUSE'S VOYAGE." THE PADDLE HERE DIFFERS FROM
THOSE ACQUIRED BY PAYMASTER THOMSON

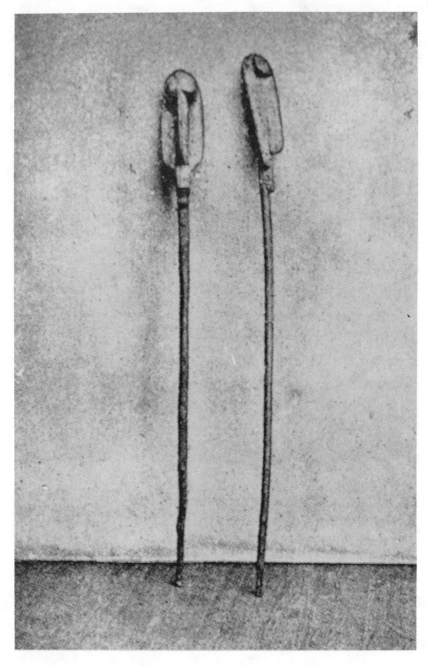

CANOE PADDLES.   NOW UNPROCURABLE
From Paymaster Thomson's " Smithsonian " article.

cally speaking quite a young island, and all the indigenous
vegetation on it, even the two native grasses, the low bunch-
grass (*m a u k u*) and the tall cyperis (*u k o k o k o*) is
attributed to the horticultural energy of that great pioneer
of the island, Hotu Matua. That there never has been a
forest on it is patent to anyone who rides over the country.
The leaves of generations of trees have never gone to the
making of mould ; it is only in the hollows that one sees any
of the black soil that is the basis of fertility ; the rest looks
still the crude *débris* of weathered rocks ; though the stock
that wander everywhere and the introduced grasses that form
their feed have made some difference in the last half century
and in time will make it fairly fertile. But there are no
earth-worms to be seen, those essential digesters and trans-
formers of the raw earth and its vegetable matter. And this
may be the reason, too, that there are no land-birds ; twice
have they been introduced and they have vanished. None
but sea-birds are to be seen or heard, and these only by the
precipitous coasts. The small indigenous fly, which has the
arrogant aggressiveness of a monopolist, and the introduced
house-fly count the island and the faces of all its human
residents as their own. The mosquito, that ubiquitous all-
adaptive enemy of the human race, took up its camp here
fifty years ago, and has thriven in spite of the paucity of human
flesh to sink for blood in ; and it has tabooed the night as its
own, the only section of the twenty-four hours that the flies
had left free, though the flea dares the taboo. It is a pleasure
to see that sworn foe of the mosquito spawn, the dragonfly,
thrive well, and that indefatigable hunter of the fly, the
indigenous jumping spider (the h o n u n a n a i a) so skil-
fully leap on its prey. And I hope that the two cockroaches,
the small indigenous one and the big new-comer, and the
sizzling cricket, which has in five years covered the land,
have added fly-and-mosquito pie to their menu. The rat is
everywhere, but not the small indigenous rat that used to
form so tasty a change from human flesh in the olden days ;
that has died out and the bigger new-comer seems to defy the
hunting skill of the wild cats, the posterity of the first pair
that ventured off a ship. The rabbit was introduced, evidently
at first from Tahiti ; for it was originally called *r a p i n i*
from the French *lapin;* afterwards English speakers must
have reintroduced it, for it was later called *r a p i t i;* but

the natives have again eaten it out. The pig is not so omni-
present as he is in most other Polynesian islands; for he has
nothing to grub for, neither wild tubers nor burrowing insects
or worms; he only turns over the stones for the little lizards
or the introduced wood-lice, crickets and ground-beetles. And
a country in which pigs cannot thrive out in the open is a
poor country indeed.

(8) **THE SEA NOT MUCH MORE FERTILE THAN THE LAND.**
But if the land was infertile, perhaps the sea supplied the
deficiency. The natives were expert fishermen; but they
had to be, if they were to have any sea food. The fish are
by no means plentiful round this islet. For it has no reef with
its calm water and its *débris* to welcome fish; it must have
come up or sunk by successive jumps, leaving no long period
for the zoophyte to build its coral wall. But still worse it
stands on the southern angle of the triangular A l b a t r o s s
plateau from which Agassiz, on his dredging expedition,
brought up no living thing, vegetable or animal, in his dredges;
nor does one often encounter p l a n k t o n , the natural
sustenance of fishlife, when sailing through these seas. Even
the seaweed is far from plentiful round the coast; and yet
many of the shallow-water fish taste of it. Some of the small
fish are good; but in the olden days the best of them were
reserved by taboo for the king's table. The bigger fish of the
deeper sea, like the tunny (k a h i), are coarse. The sea-
birds long ago came to the same conclusion; for they are
never seen in the vast numbers one sees along the Pacific
coast of South America, or round the less inhabited islands
of the great ocean. It was crustaceans and cuttlefish and
shellfish that the Easter Islanders had mainly to depend on
as sea-trove. They were expert divers; one sees their naked
bodies disappear for minutes at a time and reappear, crayfish
or cuttlefish in hand. The women used to go out at night
with four little baskets, hanging around their middle from
the belt, into each of which they gathered a different kind of
crustacean, or cuttlefish, or little fish. The shell-heaps near
the bays and by the sites of old villages show how large a
part shell-fish took in their diet. Stinging though the trailers
of the nautilus were, and dangerous for the naked feet the
spines of the sea-urchin, they were greedily eaten, and the
latter reserved for the women. The Easter Islanders were
almost as omnivorous as the Australian blacks.

ACROSS THE LAKE OF RANO KAO, WITH THE RIM OF THE CRATER LOWERED BY THE
OCEAN AND THE WINDS

THE CRATER LAKE OF RANO KAO FELTED OVER WITH REEDS (*From Agassiz*)

(9) **RAIN-MAKING A NECESSITY.** It is doubtful if their food-supply was in any way more extensive or varied than that of the people who made the shell-heaps on so many of the coasts of the old-world. And when a drought came, as it does sometimes even yet, on this island, it is difficult to see how the old inhabitants were to live except on each other—a necessarily vanishing quantity. And so the kings monopolized the profession of rain-bringing, one of the commonest bases of power among primitive peoples all over the world. The king, when rain had ceased to fall for months, sent up one of his skilled men, or *maoris*, to a stone altar on a lonely mountain with a white stone in a little basket; there he prayed and prayed and nursed the stone; no one was permitted to approach him nor was he allowed to descend till he had got the first drops and planted the stone, and having got them he perambulated the whole island, drawing the much-needed shower with him. Where any luxury could come in amidst a life like this it is somewhat difficult to see.

CHAPTER V

THE PEOPLE

(1) Harsh conditions, if not too harsh, often breed a great people ; but they develop will rather than imagination or artistic talent. (2) But who in this hard-bitten islet could afford to pay for withdrawing talent or energy from the life-and-death struggle for food ? (3) A people without organization filled the islet, every man a law unto himself. (4) There were quasi-confederations and a king, but they were mere mockeries unable to prevent the ever-lasting wars. (5) A feast or a famine was their normal state ; and wars were welcome as suppliers of meat. (6) The only organization they had was the feast and the feast had as sequel famine or war, which had as sequel another feast. (7) Any government they seemed to have was of the opera-bouffe variety. (8) Imitativeness and theft were their chief talents ; they had no initiative. (9) They cannot and never could stick at any work to a finish ; nor is or was their physique fitted for continuous or hard work. (10) If no other explanations of the monuments of Easter Island is forthcoming, we must accept the native resort to the supernatural.

(1) **HARD CONDITIONS OFTEN BREED GREAT TALENTS AND IDEAS.** We have seen that neither the position nor the fertility of Easter Island can account for its extraordinary outburst of memorial art. Yet difficulties to be met with often develop exceptional talent, and a hard environment has often bred a people of fine courage and capacity. Mountaineers are proverbially great patriots and warriors and often supply some of the best talent of the adjacent lowland nations. Norway, with its long winter, deep fiords, and barren mountains, was the home of the Vikings who threatened most of the coasts of Europe and conquered or founded kingdoms. Scotland, with its small area of cultivated land and its bleak hills, has, perhaps, supplied more talent to the British Empire than any other portion of Britain of equal size. The mountains of Persia and of India have sent forth successive conquerors and administrators of the prosperous lowlands. Japan, small and mountainous though she is, has produced an edition of Chinese art all her own and threatens to disturb the peace of the world. And if we turn to the new world, it was the Aztecs from the islands and mountains of the north that re-edited the art of the Mayas, and looked, when Cortez arrived, as if they would extend their empire over all central America. And in Peru, before the Incas came, there were kingdoms down on the barren and rainless coast that made astonishing advances in

30

LOOKING TOWARDS THE SCULPTORS' QUARRY OUTSIDE RANO RARAKU.
IT SHOWS THE RICHER TYPE OF LAND WITH PLAINS OF LONG GRASS AND
LOW SCRUB AT THE FOOT OF THE HILL

A PLATFORM ON THE SOUTH COAST, WITH RANO KAO IN THE DISTANCE.
A TYPE OF COUNTRY INLAND FROM THE COAST

the arts of gold-and-silver work, of pottery, and of weaving. Whilst one of the factors that led to the rise and dominance of the Incas was the difficulty their people had in raising food on those cultivation-terraces that are still seen on the slopes of the Andes up to seventeen thousand feet. Undoubtedly an environment that puts a man or a nation on its mettle develops where it is not so harsh as to stunt or crush. But the talent that this evolves is rather of the aggressive and enterprising, oftenest of the warlike and empire-building, type than of that which produces works of art or great ideas in art. For the harshness of the conditions tends to strengthen the will at the expense of the imagination and the emotional side of the nature.

(2) **PERHAPS EASTER ISLAND FORCED TALENT TO THE FRONT.** It is worth while investigating whether the character of the Easter Islanders as developed by their untoward environment has had anything to do with this surpassing fertilization of the glyptic and architectural imagination. We have seen that Nature had furnished models for the *a h u s* in the outcrops of lava dykes and their varied types of weathering. So we can imagine the ancestors of the men of Hangaroa of to-day who chip pieces of wood or stone into the form of little images to sell to visitors or to the sailors of passing or shipwrecked ships, sitting in the crater or on the slopes of R a n o R a r a k u , and finding as they chipped with their axes or chisels that it cut as easily as the softest of wood, set themselves to carve the outlines of a human face. But the stimulus now is ever present, the chance of getting money or European clothes in return. Who were the clients on this hard-bitten islet that could afford to draw the bulk of the talent and muscle of the population away from the life-and-death struggle for food ? Who were the patrons that could afford to copy nature and bury their dead in such huge and magnificently architected platforms ? Who could pay for such finely-cut and fitted cyclopean masonry, as only the great prehistoric empires of Greece and Crete, or that of Egypt, or that of the Incas at the zenith of their power have indulged in ?

(3) **NO JUSTICE BUT BY FEIGNING MADNESS AND GOING TO WAR.** But let us suppose that they had the wealth that would be capable of such a rare luxury, were the people capable of achieving its great results ? There would be

needed not only talent but organization and directive power. Is there any sign of these in the history of the people as it is given in their own traditions ? It echoes with increasing strife. There was practically no law ; every man had to be a law unto himself. If a man or woman was murdered the nearest relative became responsible for finding out the murderer and getting him disposed of ; he laid the corpse upon the neighbouring burial platform, turning it over every day and taking a *timoika*, or broad pear-shaped paddle, in each hand as chief mourner and avenger (t i m o) of the victim (i k a), he danced and sang and waved them about and banged them together so as to affect the u r e of the slayer. Or he went mad, or feigned madness, and painted himself black, and taking a living rat between his teeth danced over the island ; when he met people he groaned and shouted " heheva " (" I'm mad "), and the answer came, " heheva " ; for they all knew what the performance meant and those who pitied him and had the secret pointed out the assassin to him. Instead of carrying out the task of vengeance on the spot, he threw the rat away and went home and washed the paint off his body and appeared again in his own skin and his right mind. He took a hearty meal and, shouting for joy, called all the men of his clan together to a great feast he had prepared ; and, though all knew, he told them the name and clan of the murderer. They prepared for war, as did also the enemy. No clansman dared refuse such a call. And when they met they fought till the slayer was slain, and then it ended with a sociable banquet on the bodies of those that had fallen. But that did not prevent reprisals ; the vendetta was endless and closely interwoven with the appetite for human flesh. The H e h e v a , or assumption of madness, seems often to have been welcomed as an opportunity for additions to the larder.

(4) **WARS NEVER CEASED IN THE ISLET.** Now there were about a dozen clans (some have reported ten and others fifteen) marked off rather by localization than by common blood or ancestry. It is true that the clans round the north coast, east and west, often ranged themselves with the royal clan, the *M i r u*, under the name *K o t u u* and that those along the south coast from Poike to Hangaroa ranged themselves with the *T u p a h o t u* on *R a n o R a r a k u*, under the name *H o t u i t i*. They were mere quasi-confederations that

LOOKING ACROSS HANGAROA BAY (IN WHICH COOK ANCHORED)
TOWARDS RANO KAO. IT GIVES AN IDEA OF THE LOWER COAST-
LINE, ON WHICH THE PLATFORMS ARE INDISTINGUISHABLE
FROM THE LAVA DYKES RUNNING OUT INTO THE SEA

BELOW THE PLATFORM OF TONGARIKI.   A TYPICAL COASTAL SCENE

might occasionally be rearranged ; for example, *T u p a h o t u* joined with *M i r u* in rescuing the last-effective king, N g a a r a , from his captors, the N g a u r e . It is easy to see that with this perpetual friction and all this combustible material there were but few years without a conflagration on the islet. There was a king, the head of the royal clan of the M i r u , who was supposed to be divine, sacred, and inviolable. But he had not even the shadow of power ; he was a comic-opera king : else these wars would have been reduced to a minimum ; and justice would have been meted out for murder without resort to the Heheva and the embattlement of clans.

(5) **STATUES TUMBLED INTO RUIN ;** *A H U S* **PRESERVED.** One of the legitimate and recognized methods of warfare was to tumble the statues from the burial platforms in the enemy's locality—a by no means difficult task, considering how unstable they were with their narrow bases and their top-heavy hats. In many cases they have all fallen one way and look like a series of gigantic violoncello cases, as they lie. Half of them were broken by their fall into two or three pieces, and the hats were quoited away sometimes a distance of hundreds of yards. But the avengers do not seem to have mutilated them in any other way, though one fixed on the hill-side, called H a i v e , said to belong to the T u p a h o t u , shows chisel marks around the neck, and their enemies, the Miru, are said to have attempted to behead it. If any damage was done in the wars to the *ahus* it was but small compared with what the *Mohican* party did to some of the finest of them in their enthusiasm to dig out the secret of the mystery. The probable reason for the saving of the platforms was the *p a i n a ,* or great feast, sometimes lasting for a month, that took place periodically at one or other of them. To this all the people of the island gathered, each trying to outrival his neighbour in the amount of provisions he brought to it. Sometimes the *u m u ,* or earth-oven for cooking the food, stretched the whole length of an *a h u ,* from two to three hundred feet long. And if there is one thing that has always been able to quell all other passions, whether warlike or amorous, in the Easter Island breast, it is the chance of a feast, especially if prolonged for weeks, even though it should mean practical starvation for months after. If ever there was a people to whose life the proverbial phrase " Either a feast or a famine " could be applied literally, it was the Easter Islanders.

It reveals the straits they were often in for food. Starvation was the normal state, feasting the abnormal ; and hence feasting became a passion that must be gratified at all costs. And this explains the slenderness of build and figure that observers have from the earliest visits noticed in the islanders, a striking exception to the tendency of the Polynesian in all ages and to the ideal of his aristocracy ; to grow stout was the mark of the noble.

(6) **THE PASSION FOR FEASTING ALONE QUELLED WAR.** Perhaps it may be argued that these feasts show evidence of organizing capacity. And there was always a host who gave the *p a i n a* in honour of a dead father or mother ; he erected a huge figure of wickerwork and bark-cloth, and climbing up inside it with baskets full of food threw it out of the open mouth to be scrambled for by the crowd of feasters below. And he called in a *maori,* or skilled entertainer and artist, to organize the music and dancing and to keep all the young folks in a state of hilarious enjoyment. And it must be confessed that for the purpose of feasting and ceremonials they had some talent in organizing—the talent of an *entrepreneur.* They had the master-passion of the people—the love of eating—to work with them and stimulate order. The moment the feast was over they returned to their Donnybrook Fairs.

(7) **SHODDY KINGS THE ONLY SHADOW OF DIRECTIVE POWER.** For there was no governmental organization on the island for the purposes either of peace or of war. It was true there was a king, the descendant in the right line from Hotu Matua ; but he was only a religious figurehead to superintend the reading of the ancient tablets, and tattooing, to select the *maoris,* or men of letters and arts, and to impress upon the superstitious minds of the natives the physical evils of infringing taboos. He was a pasteboard king, not much more honoured or observed than that other mock-monarch, the bird-man, whose servant had been successful in getting the first egg of the sooty tern for the year. If these two institutions, the caricature of monarchy, have any significance, it is that this people was absolutely incapable of self-government or discipline. By some accident, perhaps the act of Hotu Matua, as tradition says, they were spaced out along the coast in so-called clans. But not one of them, except the royal clan, the M i r u , had a chief. None of them had

THE *timoika*, OR BATON OF VENGEANCE. SUCH RARITIES ARE
NOW UNSEEN ON THE ISLAND
From Paymaster Thomson's " Smithsonian" article.

THE BURIAL PLATFORM OF HANGAHAHAVE ON THE SOUTH COAST. THE STATUES HAVE
FALLEN, SOME GONE TO PIECES, AND THE RED TUFA HATS FLUNG FAR

either by election or natural selection a leader in war; even the king was supposed to stand aside and take no part in wars; and hence his person was considered inviolable by both sides in a fight. Their wars were nothing but local shindies or riots arising from the lack of all apparatus for securing justice or keeping the peace, and ending in an amicable banquet on the bodies of those that had been knocked on the head. If there is one thing more apparent than another in the history of these, at most two or three thousand people, it is that they were as incapable of organization either from within or from without as an Irish free fight.

(8) **THE APE OF PEOPLES.** The only things they showed themselves capable of as a whole were a free feast and the adoption of some custom or costume brought in from abroad. They were perhaps the most imitative of all primitive peoples, certainly the most imitative of all Polynesian peoples. It was in the eighteenth century that foreigners began to appear on the island; they were all men and none of them had holes in the lobes of their ears; the Easter Island men soon abandoned the ancient custom of piercing the ear, whilst the women continued it up till close on our own day; there were no women in the ships that came or in the camps of the stock-breeders who tried to utilize the island in the latter half of the last century. They are the one Polynesian people who have given up completely the old welcome by the pressing of noses together for the European custom of shaking hands; and this was at the behest of Father Roussel, one of the first missionaries in the sixties of last century; doubtless he saw the evil of a custom that was called *h o n g i*, when the duplication of the word, *hongihongi*, had an obscene meaning. They accepted the new religion at one gulp; they were as easily and suddenly converted as those wild German tribes that Charlemagne made Christian by jostling them through a stream for baptism. The transference was as easy as their change of dress; it is long since the old bark-cloth girdle and mantle were entirely abandoned for European jackets and shirts and trousers; and most of the trade with visiting ships is for European articles of clothing. The making of native cloth from the inner bark of the *m a h u t e* is forgotten; the low tree is found now only at the bottom of the crater of Rano Kao; my guide is collecting pieces of the bark thence, and his mother, who was a staid matron when the Peruvian

raid occurred in 1863, perhaps the only one in the island who
knows the art, is going to manufacture them for me into cloth.
It was this love of adopting the customs of aliens that made
them snatch the hats from the heads of the sailors of the old
voyagers and filch the handkerchiefs from the pockets of those
who were making them presents. And since I have studied
their natural imitativeness here I am not so disinclined to
accept the suggestion sometimes made that the tattooing of
the women from waist to knee was an imitation of the bathing
drawers they had seen on swimmers, and the other that their
curious little straw hats and the huge red tufa hats of the
statues had their original model in the hat of some visiting
or shipwrecked sailor.

(9) **A "FECKLESS," "GO-SLOW" RACE.** It is difficult to
imagine a people like this originating anything, let alone
producing great ideas in sculpture and architecture, or being
capable of having in their ranks one of the greatest
originators in architecture. But suppose we granted them
organizing powers and directive talent on the one hand and
originative ideas and geniuses on the other, had they the
physique and industry to carry out these great works that
would need generations, if not centuries, of continuous and
well-directed toil ? You have only to ask people who have
employed them in Tahiti or Mangareva or here to have this
possibility ruled out. As they are now, one can see they have
no such muscular physique as is to be found in all the other
islands of Polynesia ; they have not the brawny shoulders
and chest or stout legs that are the distinctive mark of the
Polynesian as contrasted with the Melanesian and other
negroids ; they have not the tall stature that makes the
Polynesian on the average the tallest race in the world, although
they are moderately tall and although Behrens, the Luxem-
bourger sergeant-major of Roggewein's marines, says, in that
French pamphlet of his which so enthralled and misled Europe,
that his soldiers could walk between the legs of the islanders
without bending. And one does not need to ask employers
if they are industrious and persevering in their work ; the
answer is a smile of amusement at the question ; for they are
to be seen everywhere doing naturally what the " go-slow "
policy of European union leaders cultivates with *malice
prepense ;* they are work-shy, and give it a holiday every few
minutes ; they look afraid that it might suffer by too close

EASTER ISLAND STATUES AND HATS AS THEY APPEARED TO COOK'S ARTIST, HODGES. NO STATUE EVEN NOW
WHEN LONG FALLEN HAS THE FEATURES SO OBLITERATED

Compare with La Perouse's picture, Chapter II, page 13.

application. They have taken to riding " as to the manner born," and gallop wildly over the stone-littered country as if there was not a stone anywhere to stumble over or a hoof to split. It is the one work they have taken to with undiluted enthusiasm. And yet, when there is added to it a purpose such as shepherding, they have to get down every mile or two to have a smoke or a chat. All this desultoriness is to be seen in other Polynesian islands; for the Polynesians are immemorial socialists; every man is expected to share his meal or his goods with any other who wants it; it worked all right so long as there was a tyrant with the taboo in his hand like a whiplash to compel work; when the missionaries came and dissolved the power of taboo, the chief was whipless, and work fell into decay through the lack of its natural stimulus, necessity, where every one trusted to his neighbour to help him out with what sustains life. In Easter Island it is no new phenomenon; for they had no chiefs. And the first voyagers and observers are as decided as to the " fecklessness " of the natives as the employers and the most recent visitors. And they are equally decided as to their poor musculature and inefficient physique.

(10) **NOTHING BUT THE SUPERNATURAL CAN EXPLAIN THE MYSTERY.** Is it any wonder that the building of these many and great platforms and the tooling and transport of these immense stones and statues have been taken as a miracle and constitute the mystery of Easter Island? Even the natives attribute the moving of the statues to supernatural powers and the dropping of so many of them by the way to the caprice of some old woman, a cook, at being cheated of her due rations or some other childish cause. So the *A y m a r a*, when the Incas asked them who built the great cyclopean city of T i a h u a n a c o at the south end of Lake Titicaca, answered " Giants in the night." The primitive mind has to give some simple reason for what it cannot understand.

CHAPTER VI

THE CENTRE OF THE WORLD

(1) The only alternative to the supernatural is the catastrophic ; but there is no sign of recent vulcanism on the island. (2) There is a traditional beginner of all flora and fauna ;—Hotgu Matua. (3) He had been driven from his archipelago to the north-west—Marae Renga and Marae Toiho—by its submergence. (4) Arriving at Anakena with his two canoes and three hundred followers, he planted the cuttings and suckers and seeds that he had brought. (5) Davis and Wafer in The Bachelor's Delight saw an archipelago east of Easter Island stretching away over the horizon in 1686. (6) Roggewein in 1722 and Gonzalez in 1771 searched for Davis Land and failed to find it. (7) An archipelago to the east of Easter Island and in the same latitude had gone down. (8) A great land with " the mouths of very large rivers " and peopled with well-clad white inhabitants, had gone down farther south, if we are to believe the report of Juan Fernandez in 1506. (9) " Te pito te henua," the only native name of the island meaning " the navel of the world," indicates that there had been archipelagoes all round. (10) Sala-y-Gomez is probably the remains of the eastern mountainous archipelago ; thence the great god of Easter Island, M a k e m a k e, brought the sea-birds and the fishes ; and various legends show a consciousness of islands near. (11) In this we have probably the solution of the mystery of Easter Island.

(1) **CATASTROPHIC EXPLANATIONS.** To avoid the supernatural the modern imagination, saturated as it is with science, naturally resorts to the catastrophic. The *Mohican* party in 1886, the first to visit the island with scientific purpose, seeing so many of the giant statues " fallen by the way " far from any burial platform, and so many images on R a n o R a r a k u roughed out, half-cut, or even ready for launching, with the workmen's tools lying where they had thrown them, came to the conclusion that this meant the sudden hand of Nature. Agassiz, on his dredging expedition early this century, spent some weeks on the island and endorsed the decision. But there is no sign of any great volcanic outburst or any movement of the rock strata in such recent times. And even if there had been such an upheaval, it might explain the entire abandonment of the island, but not the sudden and complete cessation of the two great arts of the little community ; why the artists should not return to their work after the shake was over and all fear of its repetition had faded away is a problem as difficult to solve as the fundamental mystery. And most solutions of this last assume the submergence of the larger part of the island, a part so large as to admit of luxuries and especially the exceptional luxury of these two memorial arts. But there is no sign around the coast of great sections of the land going down. There is no reef and little coral to indicate

A MARQUESAN, A SPECIMEN OF POLYNESIAN MUSCULARITY AND
PHYSIQUE, AS CONTRASTED WITH THOSE OF EASTER ISLANDERS. HE
WAS SUPPOSED TO BE IN PRISON MAKING THATCH. THE TATTOOING
ALL OVER HIS LEGS DID NOT COME OUT IN THE PHOTOGRAPH

THE CAPTAIN OF THE SCHOONER "FALCON." A PURE ABORIGINAL OF
THE ISLAND OF CHILOE IN THE SOUTH OF CHILI, STANDING IN FRONT
OF A GROUP OF EASTER ISLANDERS, SOME OF WHOM WEAR THE
PECULIAR EASTER ISLAND HAT

slow subsidence or elevation, though in latitudes farther south
these are to be found. And oceanic depths occur not far from
the coasts, whilst the island lies on an angle of the Albatross
plateau rising out of the depths. The only change that has
been going on in so recent times is the erosion of the south
coast by the seas from the south-west and south and south-east
in winter. The knife-edge ridge that separates the steep
crater of R a n o K a o from the ocean shows how rapidly
the south-west billows are engineering a crater harbour for
Easter Island, to be ready, perhaps, when the stock and
conservation of the rainfall have made it fit for cultivation.

(2) **CULTIVATION BEGAN WITH HOTU MATUA.** There is a
tradition that indicates a more natural solution of the mystery
than these. H o t u M a t u a is proclaimed by all the stories
that have come out of the past as the pioneer of all food-
production on the island and all horticulture and forestry ;
he brought the various useful and cultivated plants, all of
which were carried by the Polynesians wherever they migrated. The tubers were introduced by him in very many
varieties, although they were only propagated by cuttings.
The banana and the sugar-cane and the dracaena (*ti*), propagated only by suckers, he brought to gratify the sweet-tooth
of the inhabitants. It was due to him that the *m a h u t e*
and the *h a u h a u*, the cloth and cordage plants, and the
bastard sandalwood (*n a u n a u*) and *t o r o m i r o*, which
supplied timber for their implements, weapons, houses, and
canoes, grew on the island. It was his forethought that gave
them the *pia*, or arrowroot plant, which has now died out
before the grosser-tubered but less delicately flavoured arrowroot of South America, the *m a n i o c*. In fact, there is
nothing that ever grew on the island but its introduction is
credited by tradition to him. He was the beginning of all that
lives about this volcanic speck except men, sea-birds and fishes.

(3) **THE SUBMERGENCE OF HIS HOME DROVE H O T U TO
EASTER ISLAND.** The birds and fishes belong to the realm
of another great name in Easter Island history, M a k e m a k e.
And man preceded the great immigrant, if we are to trust
tradition. He had been deprived of his royal honours and
driven out of his native archipelago, M a r a e R e n g a and
M a r a e T o i h o. Where he went at first the story does
not tell ; but the ultimate destination was to be a little
island like Easter Island, which was indicated in a dream.

And shortly after he set out in his canoes the king of
Marae Renga, called Haumaka, had a similar
dream (*moe mata*) descriptive of the islet which Hotu Matua
was to make for and of the bay where he should land. When
he awoke he sent off six men, Ira, Kuukuu, Ringaringa,
Parenga, Moomona, and Ure, in a canoe named Orao-
rangaru ("Saved from the billows") to spy out the land
for the great pioneer. They came to Motunui, the bird-
island off Rano Kao, on the south-west point of the island
(in the legends all voyagers arrive at this south-west island);
they found their way up into the crater and planted the
yam-cuttings they had brought with them by its lake. Then
they explored the south coast and rounding the south-east
angle went up the eastern coast. When they came to the
little white shell beach among the black rocks of La Perouse
Bay, they thought that this was the landing-place their king
had dreamt of. But to make sure they went north to Ovahe
Bay, and, rejecting that as the promised land, they returned
to Anakena Bay, and were quite satisfied that its shell-
sand beach was the dreamt-of port for the great immigrant.
Then they lost one of their number, Kuukuu, who was fatally
injured by the flipper of a turtle that he had found on the
beach. The remaining five left him in a cave to die and
hurried back to Mataveri at the foot of Rano Kao,
so that they might be ready to tell Hotu Matua when he
arrived the results of their inspection ; and here they found
that the gap in their ranks had been filled up by a man called
Ratavake, who, it seems, immediately made off to
Motunui, where he promptly fell asleep. Ira went up
to the crater-lake and found all the yams he had planted
smothered with grass ; he followed Ratavake to the bird-island,
where he joined him in his slumbers. As they slept, Hotu
Matua arrived and tied up his two canoes to the islet. And
on the morning, when Ira found the immigrants had arrived,
he told them "The land is worthless ; grass smothers all you
plant." Hotu answered that he would do his best with the
plants he had brought, and when the other four, who had been
making wreaths for his royal head at Hangaroa, came up in
their canoe and, upbraiding Ira for his rash report, for all that,
declared that they were on their way back to their own good
country, Marae Renga. Hotu at once told them it was useless
going back ; for " the sea has come up and drowned all the

TE PITO KURA, A ROUND TOOLED STONE IN LA PEROUSE BAY
"THE NAVEL OF THE ISLAND"

THE GAP THAT THE OCEAN HAS BROKEN IN THE RIM OF THE
CRATER OF RANO KAO

people on Marae Renga." They would have their way and
went off westwards, leaving their new-found comrade, Ratavake, with the three hundred in the two canoes. Hotu Matua
preferred a barren little islet above the ocean to an archipelago, however rich, below it.

(4) **PLANTING FOR POSTERITY.** The two great canoes separated to meet at Anakena ; that commanded by the leader
himself went eastwards to round the south-east point ; the
other commanded by his lieutenant and brother-in-law,
T u u k o i h u , explored the west coast and rounded the
north angle. When they arrived in the sheltered little
cove with its white beach, the leader's wife and his sister,
A v a r i p u a , the wife of his second in command, were
promptly and simultaneously delivered of boys, the one to
be called Tumaheke and the other Avaripua. But before
the naming ceremony there was a more important function.
The leader bade his second make an *a t a* , or sacred place ;
the navel-strings were cut and a *p u r e* performed. Then
the three hundred longears and shortears, after their four
months' voyage, trooped on shore. Koteke, who was the
guardian of the plants and seeds, though he was in disgrace
for having forgotten the sandalwood (*naunau*), for which
another had to be sent back to Marae Renga before it was
submerged, doubtless saw to their planting. My guide remembers seeing, when a boy, sandalwood trees and toromiro trees
eighteen inches in diameter at Anakena ; they were probably
the trees that Koteke brought overseas in the canoes and
planted. For trees on this island are slow of growth.

(5) **A LOW SANDY ISLAND AND A LONG HIGH ARCHI-
PELAGO.** In this tradition we have clearly expressed the
consciousness of archipelagoes to the west of Easter Island
having gone down, and the submersion being the cause of
ocean-voyaging immigrants settling on its infertile soil. It
is worth while asking if a similar submergence had not occurred
to the east. In Wafer's " Description of the Isthmus of Darien.
London, 1688 " there is a passage that has been much quoted
and much discussed ; it is worth quoting again : " we came
to latitude 27° 20′ south when about two hours before day we
fell in with a low sandy island and heard a great roaring noise
like that of sea beating upon the shore ahead of the ship " ;—
" So we plyed off till day and then stood in again with the
land, which proved to be a small flat island without the guard

of any rocks " ; ... " To the westward about twelve leagues by
judgment we saw a range of high land which we took to be
islands ; for there were several partitions in the prospect.
This land seemed to reach about fourteen or fifteen leagues
in a range, and there came thence great flocks of fowls."
The captain would not consent to their desire to make this
land and go ashore. " The small island bears from Copaipo
almost due East five hundred leagues and from the Gallapagos
under the line six hundred leagues." Wafer was the lieutenant
on *The Bachelor's Delight*, returning from raids about Panama,
and commanded by the buccaneer, John Davis, a Dutchman,
though the ship was English in ownership and crew. And
they had just been pitchforked up by the sea to their great
alarm in latitude 12° 30′ S., and afterwards found that the
cause was the great earthquake of Callao of 1687 ; they kept
steering south and by east half east for fifteen degrees of
latitude. Dampier in his two volumes of voyages, " London
1699 " said : " Captain Davis told me lately that . . . about
five hundred leagues from Copaype on the coast of Chili in
latitude 27° S. he saw a small sandy island just by him ; and
that they saw to the westward of it a long tract of pretty high
land tending away to the north-west out of sight."

(6) **DAVIS LAND SOUGHT FOR IN VAIN ; VANISHED.** Roggewein, the Dutch admiral, thirty-five years after sailed along
the latitude in search of Davis Land and thought he had
found it when he saw the great number of birds "amongst
which were many teal." But he could not find it ; so he stood
west twelve degrees from longitude 251°, and continually saw
several sea and land birds which accompanied his ships till on
April 6th, Easter Day, he came across an island which he
named from the day, Easter Island. He claims that this was
not what Davis had seen, but was a new discovery. Gonzalez,
a Spanish navigator, in 1771, ignorant of or ignoring the
Dutchman's discovery, sailed again in search of " David's
land," and not finding it, found Easter Island, which he
proclaimed Spanish territory. Beechey, visiting the island
in 1825, argues that Davis had found Easter Island, because
currents would carry him far to the east ; and he rejects the
conjecture of La Perouse that Davis in stating the distance
from the American coast had by mistake added on a cipher
to fifty leagues, and that what he had discovered was the islands
of St. Felix and St. Ambrose, sixteen hundred miles east of

Easter Island. And some have gone as far in the other direction and ignoring Wafer's latitude have identified Davis Land with Mangareva, away to the north-west.

(7) This is the midsummer madness of criticism and theory. Once you begin to whittle away the facts and figures of a piece of evidence that has had no motive for distortion and no reason for inaccuracy there is no absurdity to which imagination will not carry the theorist. Beechey's argument is the only sound one, based as it is on a sailor's practical knowledge of the great and variable currents in this region of the Pacific. And yet no one who has visited Easter Island but must deny its identity with either of the lands that Davis saw, either the low, flat, sandy island or the long, partitioned range of land stretching away to the north-west over the horizon. If we have any respect for a sailor's evidence on a sailor's question, we must accept the existence of both lands in 1687 and their non-existence in 1722 when Roggewein sailed along the latitude in search of them. In other words, land of considerable extent, probably archipelagic, has gone down in the south-east Pacific away to the east of Easter Island.

(8) **THE DISCOVERY BY JUAN FERNANDEZ IN 1576.** And there is evidence, though of a less definite kind, long before, of land having vanished in this region. Juan Fernandez was a great Spanish pilot in the southern Pacific in the latter part of the sixteenth century. His name is known from the island to which he gave it in 1572. But four years later he wished to avoid the current and wind from the south that make a voyage from Callao to Valparaiso for a sailing ship difficult all the year round and shot away to the south-west into the Pacific, and after a month's sailing came across what he thought to be the coast of the great Southern Continent that so many voyagers in the sixteenth, seventeenth, and eighteenth centuries set out to find ; he saw " the mouths of very large rivers, from whence and from what the natives intimated and because they were people so white and so well-clad and in everything so different from those of Chili and all Peru " that he had no doubt this was part of the so much talked-of continent. His ship was small and he resolved when he got to Chili to return " properly fitted " and to keep it a secret till the fitting time came. But he died without having fulfilled his purpose. Dalrymple in his " Southsea Voyages," published some years before Cook set out to find

this southern continent, tells the story as he found it in Arias's Memorial. And, though the obsession of a great continent yet to be discovered doubtless biassed the judgment of the Spanish pilot, and discounts his report, we cannot entirely reject his evidence that considerable tracts of land in the south-east Pacific have gone down. In 1909 the ship *Guinevere* reported a reef in about 95° longitude east and 35° latitude south, which may be the remains of this submerged land.

(9) **THE NAVEL OF LANDS KNOWN BY EASTER ISLANDERS.** We are not without warrant then in assuming that this scrap of land in a waste of waters was not always so. The only name that the natives have ever given to their island as a whole confirms the assumption; it is T e p i t o t e h e n u a. In other Polynesian dialects *p i t o* means "end" as well as "navel." But in that of Easter Island it means only "navel." There is a sphere of stone near the great *ahu* in La Perouse Bay that is called T e P i t o K u r a; it is about thirty inches in diameter and carefully tooled, and is considered the navel of the island. And much ingenuity has been expended in getting a meaning for the name of the island from this word; one is to take another sense of "henua" and explain "the navel and the uterus" from the volcanic cones; but the proper meaning of this "*henua*" is "placenta"; the oldest name for a covering or mantle was "*nua*." As applied to a land, it is the other sense of "*henua*" that must be taken—"land" or "world." The true meaning of the name is "The navel" (or centre) of "the world" (or the lands known to the inhabitants). And, according to the tradition, it was Hotu Matua, the great pioneer, who named it so as he landed in Anakena Bay. And he was just finishing a voyage that occupied one hundred and twenty days, and he had been in lands where it was so hot that in summer the sun shrivelled up vegetation by its heat; this was probably the Marquesas; for he brought in both of his great canoes, men with long ears, and it was the Marquesans alone of the Polynesians who cut the hole in the lobes of the ears so large as to make them like those of the Easter Islanders reach their shoulders. That there were Marquesans in the island before is certain from their predominance at all times of the history of the island and from the fact that all the statues have long ears, the only one pointed out as short-eared having ears only a little less long than the others. He also visited New

PAVED ROAD OF THE MARAE OF TANGAROA IN RARATONGA

SALA-Y-GOMEZ, FROM THE SOUTH
From the "Albatross" Expedition of Alexander Agassiz.

Zealand ; for the timber tree that he brought, the toromiro, is the yellow-flowering *kowhai* of that land ; his " short ears " that arrived in his canoes probably also came thence, if we are to trust the number of customs that are peculiar to Easter Islanders and Maoris amongst the Polynesians and the number of words peculiar to their dialects.

(10) **A RING OF ARCHIPELAGOES AROUND IT.** It is by no means improbable that Sala-y-Gomez, a rocky islet just above water nearly three hundred miles to the east of Easter Island, is the remains of Davis Land ; for there are numerous reefs round about it and the water in its vicinity is shallow compared with the depths in that region of the Pacific. The natives of our island have a name for it, Motu Matiro Hiva, and they bring their great god M a k e m a k e thence ; he was the prince of it, and from it he brought all the sea-birds and all the nets, taking care of them after he brought them, preventing the people eating all the eggs lest the birds should die out and seeing that only men, and those skilled men, should use the nets. And this eastern archipelago was balanced by the western from which Hotu Matua came ; that *M a r a e R e n g a* and *M a r a e T o i h o* were towards the west is plain from the closing scene of his life. When he had become old and wished to die he went to the volcano on the southwestern point, R a n o K a o , and looking out westward he called to the spirits that hovered round his old submerged home to bid the cocks crow, and when the cocks crew he gave up the ghost. And from several of the legendary stories of the supernatural still told by the older people on the island we can see that they were conscious of other islands and archipelagoes lying round their home at some distance ; a beautiful maiden is carried away by a turtle to a far-off island whose king, a master of enchantment, marries her ; two enchanters, the masters of all beautiful dyes, hear of an old woman in Easter Island, a famous maker of mats and *ketes*, being hard up for a fast, yellow dye and fly from their distant isle to teach her the secret ; and T a n g a r o a , king of a far-off archipelago, hearing of the straits the people of this little island were in for food, swims across the ocean to relieve them and is cooked alive for his pains, yet comes out of the oven untouched by the fire and escapes east, his giant brother with league-long strides following after to find what has become of him.

(11) Thus, tradition, legend and the observation of modern

European sailors combine to indicate Easter Island as the centre of an archipelagic world that surrounded it at various distances. One of these to the west was distinguished as being a land of temples, probably cyclopean, like the *maraes* of R a r o t o n g a and the M a r q u e s a s. Another, that to the east, as seen by Davis and his crew, stretched from the south-east away to the north-west beyond the horizon, probably right across the tropic ; and it was marked by lofty mountains, which probably with the rains from the tropics bore great forests and sheltered in their valleys rich gardens and cultivations. In this, perhaps, we have a solution of the mystery of Easter Island.

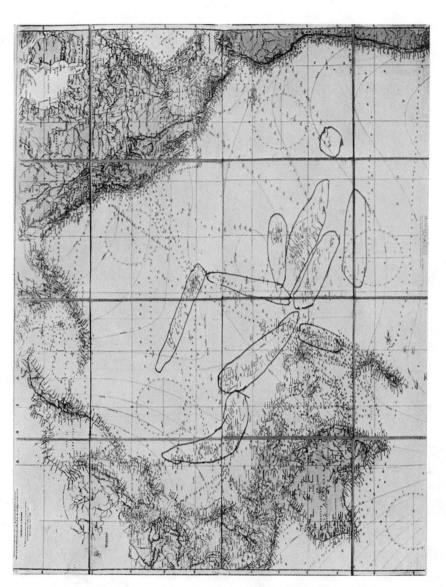

THE PACIFIC OCEAN, WITH PROBABLE ARCHIPELAGIC LAND BRIDGES DOWN TO HUMAN TIMES, STILL SLOWLY SUBSIDING.
THE RING INDICATES THE ARCHIPELAGOES ROUND EASTER ISLAND

From Perrier's "La Terre avant l'histoire."

CHAPTER VII

SUBSIDENCE DOMINANT IN POLYNESIA AND MICRONESIA

(1) *A Pacific continent is assumed by many geologists; by the end of the Secondary Period it was foundering.* (2) *At any rate we have to assume land connection between the Hawaiian archipelago and those of the south-west to explain the identity of most of their flora and fauna; and the foundering of Pacific lands went on through all time and still goes on.* (3) *It is a question not of continents but of archipelagoes such as still stretch across the ocean; and the rise of the Andes and the South American coast still going on must have had compensatory subsidence in the neighbouring ocean.* (4) *No such stretch of landless sea exists anywhere else on the earth.* (5) *The stuff from which the images are carved is a stratified volcanic conglomerate laid either in a shallow sea by rivers that descended from lofty mountains, or by neighbouring volcanoes; and the arc of coral islets from the Ladrones to Easter Island is a line of buoys over a great range of mountains submerged.* (6) *With spurts of elevation the subsidence has gone on through all human times; and Ocean Island with its earth-oven volcanic stones deep in the phosphate show that Polynesians lived on it before one subsidence at least.* (7) *The cyclopean Venice on Ponape was the capital of a great archipelagic empire that has vanished.* (8) *The existence of a syllabic script to the west argues a second empire gone down, and a taboo tribute to an obscure chief in Yap argues a third.* (9) *Away east the Polynesians exhibit a unique racial and cultural unity though spread over a greater area than any empire ever occupied.* (10) *Quarantined for thousands of years they must have lived under an organized government that had primogeniture and monarchy.* (11) *Their fatherland in the east central Pacific went down slowly and sent off migration after migration.* (12) *Their language is marked by primeval simplicity, and, along with that, in the larger areas, a vocabulary of great scope.* (13) *A sound-law stricter than Grimm's governs the relationships of the consonants in the far-scattered dialects.* (14) *Tuanaki to the south of the Cook group went down with all its inhabitants in the late thirties of the last century; was this the case with the archipelagoes round Easter Island?*

(1) **A HYPOTHETICAL PACIFIC OCEAN CONTINENT.** Most geologists who study the whole surface and crust of the earth assume a hypothetical Pacific continent from the latter part of the Primary period to the end of the Secondary, ringed round by an ocean that communicates to the north with the ancient Arctic Ocean and on its east and west with the narrow and shallow M e s o g e a n Sea, the T e t h y s o f S u e s s . At the end of the Primary period this ocean flows over what is now the region of the A n d e s and the Rocky mountains on the east and over the long sinuous strip on the west in which New Zealand and Melanesia, Papuasia, and eastern Indonesia, the Philippines and Japan now rise above the sea. By the end of the Secondary period the Pacific continent is in process of foundering; and the west coast of America, with its great range of mountains, is in process of elevation, whilst the islands to the west are preparing to appear. And Poly-

47

nesian cosmology is not without consciousness of such great areas of land; for example, in the T a h i t i a n R u the god of the winds broke up the f e n u a n u i, or single continent, into the existing islands.

(2) **SLOW SUBSIDENCE THROUGH MILLIONS OF YEARS.** Whether we assume a continental area in the central region of the Pacific or not there must have been enormously more land than there is now, if not some land connection between the Hawaiian Archipelago and the south-west of Polynesia; for the American scientists, working from the former find a close affinity between its flora and fauna and those of the latter, whilst there is no evidence of connection with the American continent. In the flora, for example, the only great genera of the south-west that are absent in the north-east are the aroids, ficoids, and pines. The affinity of the land-shells is even more convincing. But the north and south connection was the first to disappear, leaving traces in scattered coral islands like Washington, Fanning, Christmas, Malden, Manihiki. The trend of the ancient high land was from north-west to south-east. And as the archipelagoes from New Zealand through Melanesia, Papuasia, Indonesia, the Philippines and Japan rose, Micronesia and southern Polynesia sank; and from the M a r i a n n e s down to M a n g a r e v a and Easter Island there are more coral islets than in any other region of the world. And it is growing more and more clear from the reports on the boring on F u n a f u t i in the Ellice group, bringing out the shallow water formation of every part of the core, that Darwin's and Dana's theory of the formation of atolls and reefs is in accordance with facts. In the Pacific Ocean at least, wherever there is a coral island there has been subsidence, even if followed by elevation. And it is to be granted that along with subsidence in the coral arcs of the Pacific there is sporadic elevation. For the volcanic activity that raised the high land primevally becomes not suddenly but slowly quiescent. In some coral groups there are volcanic islands as in the Tongan, Samoan, Society, and Marquesan groups; and raised coral islands, like Niue and Rimatara are not infrequent. In fact, there is clear evidence of alternate subsidences and elevations; the phosphate islands, M a k a t e a in the north-west of the P a u m o t u s, and Ocean Island and N a u r u in the west of the G i l - b e r t s, have gone down to leach out the nitrates of their

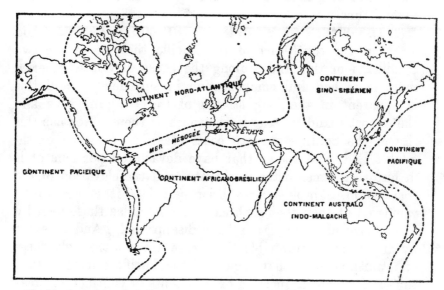

The Earth at the end of the Primary Period; the Andes and the Rocky Mountains under the sea; the Pacific continent still persisting.

(From Perrier's "La Terre avant l'Histoire.")

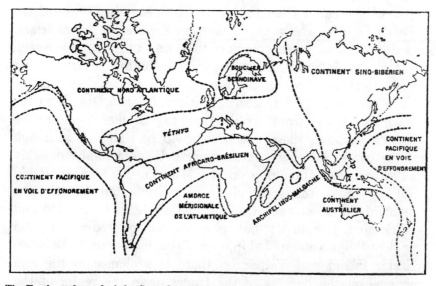

The Earth at the end of the Secondary Period; the Andes and Rocky Mountains emerging; the Pacific continent foundering.

(From Perrier's "La Terre avant l'Histoire.")

blanket of bird manure and come up to have a new blanket
several times.

(3) **THE WASTE OF WATERS OF THE SOUTH PACIFIC.** And
away in the south-east of the Pacific the rise of the two
cordilleras of the Andes along the coast of South America
must have had full compensation in subsidence; and this
is apparent in the long stretch of the P a u m o t u s and
the almost islandless seas to the south of them. Nor has this
rise of the South American coast ceased; the great earthquakes and tidal waves that have devastated portions of it
in historical times make it patent; and the elevation of the
coast is measurable within brief periods. It is not to be
wondered at then that such extensive lands as those seen by
Juan Fernandez and Davis have disappeared. And it is not
by any means improbable that these are not the only cases
of evanishment in that region of the Pacific during human
times. It is not a question of continents or continental areas
over the south Pacific but of archipelagoes such as are still
strewn in definite arcs or lines across the great ocean.

(4) The worst of it is that it is difficult to find proof where
so little has been left, especially outside the tropics, above the
surface of the ocean. There is no such landless area on the
face of the earth than this same south-eastern region of the
Pacific Ocean. The voyage from New Zealand to Easter Island
is drearier and more eventless than any other in the world.
I have made many long voyages, including several round
Cape Horn or through the Straits of Magellan, but none of
them can compare for desolate outlook to that I made in the
B a q u e d a n o from Wellington to Easter Island; we
sighted no land, there was no land to be sighted; although
if the course had been farther north the sea might possibly
have been seen breaking on the M a r i a T h e r e s a Reef;
nothing broke the great circle of solitude but the sinuous
flight of the albatross. One cyclone drove us on in rain and
murk for a few days; but as a rule we loitered on in calm
or slept " like a painted ship upon a painted ocean." Between
Easter Island and Valparaiso there is a chance of life and
change, on the borders of the trades or in the realm of the
southerlies.

(5) **INDICATIONS OF LOFTY MOUNTAINS IN THE SOUTH
PACIFIC.** If Easter Island can throw no light on what this
blank region has been in the past, there is nothing to

INSIDE THE CRATER OF RANO RARAKU, WITH STRATIFICATION SHOWING ON THE SKYLINE

THE SCULPTORS' QUARRY ON THE OUTSIDE SLOPE OF RANO RARAKU

go upon but the chance reports from Juan Fernandez and Davis and the traditions of this solitary speck. But in the great statues and the strata from which they have been cut there is an indication of a different condition of land in so landless a region. So little like lava is the stuff out of which they have been carved that some of the old voyagers took them for composite. Though filled with angular fragments of various kinds of rocks, any piece of them when broken off tends to crumble away if not handled with care. The rocks out of which they came look like a sedimentary conglomerate, though probably a volcanic breccia laid in water. In fact, there is no sign of lava or volcanic rock in the crater of R a n o R a r a k u or on its slopes till just above the plains that surround it ; there volcanic dykes weather into their constituent crystals as over the whole of the island ; down the northern slope of R a n o K a o there is a similar absence of volcanic outcrops, although this volcano has had lava flows on its south and south-western rim. Against the skyline the south-west rim of R a n o R a r a k u shows clear stratification ; the strata have been tilted into the vertical. They have been laid in a shallow inland sea with its bottom rising through the ages ; the volcanic dust showered into it from high mountains has been allowed to settle without disturbance. There is no sign of shells or shell-dust in the conglomerate. In some of the distant islands there are indications that they are but fragments of loftier islands ; in T u b u a i and R u r u t u the lava-flows that cap their heights slope at a considerable angle from the rims or slopes of craters that must have risen to many thousands of feet, but have vanished ages ago. As we recede north-westwards from the deep that fringes the South American coast we have less and less of the wide landless expanse of waters that is so characteristic of the south-east Pacific. The surface of the ocean is stippled with islands, chiefly coral. And, if the subsidence theory of these far-sprent coral islets is accepted, we may take them as buoying the highest peaks of a great mountain range that once ran across the hypothetical Pacific continent in an arc from the L a d r o n e s to Easter Island.

(6) **ISLANDS GONE DOWN IN HUMAN TIMES.** That this range has not gone down suddenly we may take for granted if we believe in the slow processes of Nature taken as a whole. Through the Tertiary period and the Pleistocene and right

up to our own day the process must have been going on, in one part slow, in another rapid, with occasional compensatory elevations and volcanic spurts. Not infrequently the same point would reverse the process several times; examples are the phosphate islands, M a k a t e a, O c e a n I s l a n d, and N a u r u. And in the case of Ocean Island at least, Polynesians perched on the island before one of its submersions; for deep down in the phosphatic rock there were found fire-marked volcanic stones such as are used in the earth-oven; and such stones are not to be found nearer than K u s a i e, six hundred miles away.

(7) **A VANISHED EMPIRE HAD PONAPE AS CENTRE.** Four hundred miles to the north-west of this last, on the southeast reef of P o n a p e, there is a great cyclopean ruin that implies a vast subsidence of archipelagic land in the near or distant vicinity; there are eleven square miles of huge public buildings erected on square or rectangular islets artificially raised out of the water by a breastwork of great basalt crystals fencing in masses of coral *débris*. The walls of some of them, twelve feet thick, still rise thirty feet above the level of the surrounding water-streets; and to judge by the masses of cyclopean stones tumbled into their courtyards they must have been twice as high in their original condition. And these were only the temples and assembly halls of the great capital. The houses and huts of the nobles and commoners and slaves must have vanished centuries ago. The rafting over the reef at high tide and the hauling up of these immense blocks, most of them from five to twenty-five tons weight, to such a height as sixty feet must have meant tens of thousands of organized labour; and it had to be housed and clothed and fed. Yet within a radius of fifteen hundred miles from this as a centre there are not more than fifty thousand people to-day. It is one of the miracles of the Pacific unless we assume a subsidence of twenty times as much land as now exists.

(8) **ISLAND EMPIRES VANISHED FARTHER WEST.** And a thousand miles to the west of it there is a little coral island called O l e a i with six hundred inhabitants that is at least a hundred miles from every one of the half score islets that lie round about it. There I found, in 1913, script of some sixty characters, a syllabary quite unlike any other in the world.[1] It was in use by the young chief of the island and was

---

[1] See Chapter X, p. 84, for a picture of this script.

THE OUTER WALL OF THE GREAT DOUBLE-WALLED EDIFICE OF NANTAUACH IN THE EXTENSIVE
RUINS OF METALANIM, AN ANCIENT VENICE ON THE REEF ON THE SOUTH-EAST COAST OF
PONAPE IN THE CAROLINES. THE AUTHOR IS SEATED AT THE ENTRANCE OF A SUBTERRANEAN
PASSAGE

THE COMMUNITY HOUSE OF GATSEPAR ON THE EAST COAST OF YAP

known to only five on it, though it was also in use in
F a r a u l e p, an islet about a hundred miles to the north-
east. If this has any significance, it is that an archipelagic
empire of considerable extent needed means of communication
that would enable the central authority to keep in touch with
its subordinates. Some maker or unifier of the island-empire
needed a more explicit method of conveying his commands
to his lieutenants than the knotted cords which are used freely
over most of the Caroline Islands. And when a monarch's
needs are known they elicit invention as surely as the needs
of a democratic people, though never so widely or so usefully.
And nothing but the necessities of communication in an
island-empire could have kept alive this script once it was
put into form. And another five hundred miles farther west
there is an indication of a third organized archipelago that
has gone down. On the east coast of the island of Y a p
there is a village called G a t s e p a r, and its chief, though
of no significance or power in his own island, has canoes come
over hundreds of miles of sea to pay him annual tribute ;
when the tributers are asked why they do so to so powerless
a chief, they say that if they did not keep paying the tribute,
he would shake their islands with his earthquakes and the
sea with his tempests.

The meaning seems to be that his ancestors built an island-
empire to the east of Y a p, and when some intermediate
islets had gone down the others continued still to look to the
ruler in the west as the holder of all power natural and
supernatural.

(9) **THE UNIQUE UNITY OF POLYNESIA.** All this is in
M i c r o n e s i a away to the north-west. Is there any
evidence of similar submersion of organized archipelagoes or
large islands farther east ? Polynesia covers a greater space
than most of the larger empires of the world have covered ;
and is occupied by a people more of a piece in physique,
culture, and language than the people of any one of the great
empires. This people exhibits a combination of highly
advanced and highly primitive culture which is unique in
history or prehistory. They are far beyond any of the island
peoples to the west of them in canoe-building and house-
building and in the arts of navigation and war, although their
implements and weapons are as primitive, if not more primitive ;
in social and political organization there is nothing to approach

E

them till we get near to the continent of Asia. And yet they
have never made pottery, an art that is common from Fiji
to the Malay Archipelago, or fought with a bow or shield, or
invented a spindle or loom, or applied their cord-drill to
relieve them of the great and concentrated effort in ploughing
fire out of a piece of soft wood. It is one of the marvels of
migration that they should spread over so vast a space of
sparsely islanded ocean and at often thousands of miles apart
and yet be easily recognized as one people by their physique
and culture.

(10) It is easy to see that if they have come into contact
with other races and cultures it has been only in a superficial
way and for a brief period ; and that they have been quarantined long enough to have their character and mould so deeply
imprinted on them that they are indelible and easily distin-
guishable from those of all other races. And so alike is the
development of their social constitution and customs and
political tendencies that we will not be far wrong in concluding
that they were united for a long period, probably thousands
of years, under one regime and in an archipelago or island
isolated from the rest of the world. They have relics of
matrilineality, but have overlaid them with the patrilineal
so far that they have preferred primogeniture to every other
social form. They have laid great stress on ancestry in both
social life and religion and have kept their genealogies, sometimes for thousands of years. Wherever they have got scope
in the larger groups their feudalistic monarchy has developed
into military empire, with sections of society rigidly distinguished.

(11) We can scarcely avoid the conclusion that they have
lived unitedly under such a government and in such a social
system for a long period ; and that the slow submergence of
their fatherland has driven them off migration after migration
to seek other lands to dwell upon, each marked by some new
habit into which they were driven by the gradual narrowing
of their cultivable area, such as abortion and female infanticide
and the cannibalism that marks off four groups from all the
others. All the indications point to an empire in the east
Central Pacific having gone down.

(12) **THE POLYNESIAN LANGUAGE MAKES PRIMEVAL UNITY
AXIOMATIC.** If we turn to the language we find the same
conclusion as clearly indicated. Every group has its own

version of the common language; and that common language has the same combination of primeval simplicity and advanced elaboration as the culture. It has the narrowest range of sounds and the simplest phonological laws of all the languages of the world. It has only five vowels, without diphthongs, and seven to nine consonants; and it must end every syllable and word in a vowel. And yet the vocabularies of some of the larger groups, like Hawaiian and Maori, are as extensive as those of two-thirds of the languages of Europe; they have above twenty-thousand words and without having many abstract words they have distinctions as nice as those of many highly cultivated languages; whilst the ideas of cosmology and poetry deserve and need great breadth and nicety of language.

(13) But there is a characteristic of these dialects that makes a long residence in a common fatherland and under a common and highly efficient system of government an axiom. Like all dialects, they have taken each its own phonological way: but unlike the dialects of most other languages, each has modified the common sounds in the strictest relation to the changes of the others. If we know the law that governs these modifications we can tell the form that a common word will take in each of them. Where Maori uses *k*, Samoan and Hawaiian and Tahitian omit it. Where Tongan and Samoan and Hawaiian use *l*, all the rest use *r* except Marquesan, which as a rule omits it. Where Maori uses *ng*, Tahitian abandons it and Hawaiian uses *n*. It is the same all through the gamut of Polynesian sounds; a strict law rules all the modifications in the dialects. How this could have come about with the thousands of miles of sea now separating the peoples that speak the dialects it is impossible to imagine. The changes could not have come about in strict relation to one another unless the speakers had frequent peaceful intercourse; and that must have been in an island or archipelago under one government, and that an efficient one. In other words, an empire must have gone down in mid-Pacific.

(14) **DID THE EASTER ISLAND ARCHIPELAGOES GO DOWN AN IMPERIAL UNITY?** We have seen that Easter Island was the navel of a surrounding archipelagic world. Is there anything in its traditions or in the customs or peculiarities of its people that would lead us to think that this world was united under an empire, and would the existence

of such an empire help to explain anything that has hitherto been inexplicable ? We have full warrant for thinking that large areas of land have gone down in the south-east Pacific opposite that South American coast which has been on the rise for millions of years and is still on the rise. We have definite reports of land having gone down in recent centuries in the neighbourhood of Easter Island ; was that land peopled and did all the people go down with the archipelagoes ? We have an instance analogous in the submergence of T u a n a k i to the south of the Cook group in the thirties of last century. Two M a n g a i a n s had been on a whaler and landed on it, and reported to the missionaries that its people had much the same customs and language as their own island and that the chief, having heard of the social revolution the new religion had produced in the Cook group, was anxious to have a missionary for his people. The missionary schooner was sent out under the guidance of these two native sailors ; but it never found the island, and no one has seen it since, although up till recently there was at least one native living in Rarotonga who had lived in it and one who had visited it. Had the two Mangaians not landed on it and reported it to the missionaries, would anyone ever have known of the submergence of it and its people ? There might have been a vague rumour, easily disbelieved and easily discounted ; and that would have been all the record.

CHAPTER VIII

HOTU MATUA

(1) *After reporting to his emperor on the great archipelago to the east, the great pioneer visited the Marquesas and New Zealand for long-eared and short-eared warriors to replace him in his satrapy to the west.* (2) *Even in Easter Island he had enemies to subdue ; else he would never have got his Maori warriors to entrench a hill at his landing-place in Anakena Bay or taught the boys of his followers to fight.* (3) *He had to subdue tens of thousands of slaves unshackled by the submergence of the empire and their masters ; he introduced all the food plants ; they had depended on the archipelagoes for their food and were now a starving mob.* (4) *This will explain the after-history of the island—anarchy tempered by feasts.* (5) *There was nothing before the foodless mob but cannibalism ; it would reduce the numbers to be fed as well as fill their stomachs ; and the free fight that the disappearance of all organization meant furnished forth the banquet.* (6) *The Marquesans, the Longears, and the Maoris, the Shortears, who formed the bulk of the population, were inveterate cannibals.* (7) *As a change from human flesh they ate up the pig and the dog that Hotu Matua brought and their broods, and to this inappeasable hunger all later introductions have fallen victims.* (8) *Hunger has left its brand on all their history, even the coco-nut vanishing before it.* (9) *And it was all the worse that female infanticide and polygamy made women, the surest raisers of food, scarce.*

(1) **HOTU MATUA'S FOUR MONTHS' VOYAGE TO THE MARQUESAS AND NEW ZEALAND.** There is no mention of Hotu Matua's having any connection with M o t u M a t i r o H i v a, the archipelago away to the east. And yet in the earlier version of his story recorded by Paymaster Thomson and probably collected from some of the older survivors of the Peruvian raid, he is said to have come from the direction of the rising sun. To reconcile the two versions we must assume either that he was ruler of the whole circle of archipelagoes or that he was subordinate ruler of the western, and had been to the greater land to the east in order to report on the rebellion in his own particular section of the empire. The latter is the more probable ; and after consultation with his chief, he set out on his travels around the Pacific in order to find some other land to settle on like so many Polynesians before him, or perhaps to gather warriors from other groups to reinstate him in his satrapy. One cue for conjecture as to the course he took is the tradition that he had Longears in both his canoes when he landed in A n a k e n a Bay. That indicates the Marquesas ; for amongst the Polynesians it is only the people of that archipelago besides the Easter Islanders

57

that make the holes in their ear lobes so wide as to lengthen them almost to the shoulder. And we know that as late as the eighteenth century great expeditions set out from it and that later some P a u m o t a n s were recognized as having names and physique recalling Marquesans. The temple with its carved stone statues that the mutineers of the *Bounty* found on the upper levels of Pitcairn Island was probably due to a Marquesan immigration ; for along with the coco-nut palms and breadfruit trees that were discovered planted in regular rows in convenient places, there was the banian, and that tree generally gives shade to the great stone temples of the Marquesas. The Mangarevan-French Dictionary identifies with Pitcairn the E i r a n g i to which tradition makes T o a t u t e a lead a Mangarevan emigration. But Mangareva never had the banian, nor was a stone image ever made there or any large cyclopean temple such as are carved and built in the Marquesas. To push so far south as the Paumotus and so far south-east as Pitcairn Island probably implies that Marquesan migrations took this direction and ended in crossing the tropic and reaching the archipelagoes around Easter Island. That he had to go south-west in order to get east in a latitude more than twenty degrees to the south is confirmed by the course that whalers in a later age had to take when having got to the west they wished to go east. The south-east trades would carry his canoes with ease up to the Marquesas ; it would suit their great sails to cross them to the south-west ; for Polynesian canoes never sailed so well as with a beam wind. When he got to Rarotonga it would be his natural course to follow on the track of expeditions to New Zealand. Once there he could have his canoes refitted from the ancient forests and reprovisioned for his voyage before the westerlies to the south. And it would be natural for such bold navigators and warriors as the Maoris to join him in the venture. Doubtless they had been preceded by other emigrants to the eastern archipelagoes. And when there, the Shortears, with their physique and will and courage, trained in a cool temperate-zone climate and in a country that demanded and encouraged war, as is seen from the great number of trench-fortified positions of strength in it, would be certain to gain the upper hand.

(2) **HE HAD ENEMIES TO GUARD AGAINST.** And the leader had evidently much need of their warlike prowess, even

though the western islands in which he expected by their aid to be reinstated in power had gone down; he could expect no aid from the east. All the builders of the burial platforms and carvers and transporters of the statues had lost the strong hand that had kept them organized and busy. Had the leader found the little mausoleum-island as empty of men as the tradition makes him find it empty of vegetation, he would have had no need to take the warlike measures he adopted. The earthwork fortifications on the conical hill closest to the sea on the south-east side of A n a k e n a Bay were not dug by him if there was no enemy to oppose his landing; the hill is called M a u n g a H a u E p e, the Hill of the Long-ears; and yet the whole character of the defence identified it as a work of Maoris from New Zealand; it is a *p a*. For no other Polynesian people developed the art of entrenchment as the Maoris did. In most of the other groups the strong places and places of refuge are defended by stone walls; and this is the case in the Marquesas. Although stone-fortifications were found in New Zealand, the majority consist of earthwork entrenchments and palisades; and it is generally their situation that makes them secure. So it is here in A n a k e n a Bay; there is no position on Easter Island that could be made so easily impregnable as the top of this steep hill, if only water was procurable; and, for the three hundred landing in this little bay, that would be looked after as a first necessity on an island that has springs only on the beach between low and high tide. There are two other hills as high in the bay, P u h a r o a and M a u n g a K o u a. But in Easter Island there were no bows and arrows and no slings; the only missile was the spear and the beach-stone thrown by the hand, and the tops of these hills are too far from the fortified hill-top to allow of such missiles having effect. Tradition indicates one other measure of the leader that means nothing if it does not signify an enemy to be met who could not be put down in one battle or one series of operations. He is said to have trained the youths to fight in line; he set even the youngest, row against row, armed with *h e k e k e o h e*, a tall reed-like cane of some strength and suppleness; as they grew older he gave them the stalks of sugar-cane to try their strength and skill with; and when they reached the thews and sinews of manhood he substituted spears made of *t o r o m i r o* for these fragile weapons. One thing is mani-

fest from these two measures, that he either had to defend
himself or feared that he might have to defend himself.

(3) **ARMIES OF TOILERS ; ALL FOOD IMPORTED.** Who
were the people that might be his enemies ? The archipelagoes that had gone down doubtless held the empire that
had been using this barren land as a mausoleum for its
rulers and warriors. There is little probability that any but
a wealthy and highly organized power could have carried out
so great an architectural conception in such a manner as is
apparent on this islet. In other words, some warrior must
have unified the archipelagic ring round it and developed its
wealth so far that it could employ its talent in arts that imply
peace though applied to the glorification of war. Nothing
but great wealth in the hands of a powerful ruler could afford
to draft off from the essentials of an empire, the raising of
food, and the warlike pursuits on which its security depended
to employment on such luxurious arts as architecture and
sculpture. Who but an absolute monarch and his nobles
with unlimited resources could entertain such an idea of
posthumous self-immortalizing as is largely realized in this
islet of magnificent sepulture ?

For this realization there was needed not only talented
architects and sculptors but great armies of workmen who
could tool the huge blocks and raise them into position and
haul the enormous weights of the statues over the rough
surface of the islet. There were, if we are to judge by the
amount of work done and assume that it was done in a
moderately brief period, far larger numbers on this infertile
piece of land than it could ever have supported, even if they
had been all employed in nothing else than raising their own
food. If we are to estimate the time during which the work
went on by the condition of the statues, it cannot have been
longer than a few generations ; and in that case the labour
needed to do all the stone-work of the burial-platforms and
the foundations of the houses must have mounted into the
tens of thousands. And the food to support this huge population occupied solely in the subsidiary work of these luxurious
arts must have come from the archipelagoes around. Doubtless it was the policy of the masters to make the labourers
wholly dependent on them for their sustenance ; if they had
raised their own food they might have at some time plucked
up courage to assert their independence, especially when they

knew their rulers were at such a distance over the sea. Something like this is needed to explain why tradition attributes to Hotu Matua the first introduction of all the food plants and clothing and timber plants ; according to this he found it a *tabula rasa* for his horticultural and forestry pioneering. He did only what all other Polynesian leaders of migrations did ; they carried the plants and animals (with some significant omissions in his case) that would stock the new islands they settled on. Most other migrations have trusted for the supply of their wants to the natural products of the lands they were transferring to ; even in modern times they rarely think of introducing the plants and animals they have been accustomed to until they are settled. Polynesian migratoriness was always marked by deliberateness and preparation. Doubtless they found much in their new islands that could be utilized for sustenance. But the striking thing about the tradition of this Polynesian arrival is that Hotu Matua is credited with the introduction of every useful plant into Easter Island.

(4) **ALL BONDS RELAXED ; WAR TEMPERED BY FEASTS.** This will help us to understand the suddenness with which all work on the platforms and statues was stopped. The effect of the cessation of the supplies of food on the large population of an island that produced nothing would be far more alarming than an earthquake or a volcanic explosion ; it would threaten the life of all. No wonder the statues were abandoned *en route* and the tools thrown away promiscuously. Without sustenance it was only a matter of a few weeks when their energy would ooze away and work would be impossible. And even if this had not been the case, all organization would founder whenever it was realized that the source of the power that directed it had vanished. It is easy to imagine what would occur if ten thousand slaves suddenly felt themselves master of their organizers and foremen. The long discipline, once it was relaxed, would make the indiscipline and riot all the more pronounced ; every man would be master. And this relaxation of all bonds and general scrimmage continued through the history of Easter Island thereafter, modified by some mimicry of organization and some taboo. I have never heard or read of any human community so continually torn by feuds and wars. Barataria, under Sancho Panza, would have been a model society compared to

it. Every man's hand was against his neighbour unless his
whole neighbourhood joined in the mêlée. I have heard one
of my most intelligent Easter Islander friends insist that when
a man in the old days was assassinated, his nearest relative
and sponsor, his *t i m o*, had not only the right but the duty
to run amuck in the island in order to get justice. This is
the apotheosis of anarchy and would soon have ended in
leaving the island in its primeval solitude. But happily it
was tempered with feasting; feuds and wars were laid aside
during a *p a i n a* so that everybody should have a good
satiation of hunger. Nothing is so conspicuous in the history
of this islet as the prolonged feasting unless it be the prolonged
bellicosity to which it gave a yearly holiday.

(5) **CANNIBALISM A NECESSITY.** Of course, the main question when the source of supplies went to the bottom of
the sea was how they were to live, how to get enough to keep
life in, an important question yet as through all the history
of the island. With tens of thousands of mouths to fill what
was to be done ? The roots of ferns, and reeds, and those of
the wild beach convolvulus, to be found on every island in
the south Pacific would not go far ; moreover, the last caused
swellings of the head and face and even death. The fish were
scarce and difficult to catch ; the crustaceans, the most
plentiful sea-food on the coast, had to be dived for. The rat-
currency was limited and not over-filling. The sea-birds had
to be caught, and their eggs and young could be more easily
taken ; but that would mean the early exhaustion of the
supply. There was no solution of the difficulty but banqueting
on themselves ; there was an over-supply of both banqueters
and banquetees. There is a story of the origin of cannibalism
that places it later in the history of the island, as a result of
the war between the Longears and the Shortears, when the
refugees of the defeated, driven into caves and on to the islet
of M a r o t i r i, had, through lack of food, to resort to
human flesh. There is nothing ceremonial about Easter
Island cannibalism ; nor has it anything mystic in it like
that of the warriors who think they absorb the courage of
the enemy they kill by eating his heart or his left eye, or that
of those tribes who think they will get the service of the spirit
of the eaten when they go to the world of spirits. The Easter
Islander had no belief in a world beyond; nor did he choose
for his banquet the organs that were supposed to concentrate

courage ; his titbits were the palms of the hands and the buttocks. He ate the people he had killed because his larder was empty ; his hunger for flesh was not stayed by rats and fish. The doctor of the *O'Higgins,* the Chilian warship which visited the island in 1871, declares in his report to the commander that he could see a striking difference between the old men and the young in physical activity and muscular force, and attributes this to the diet of human flesh the former had fed on and the fight they had had to put up in order to get it.

(6) **MARQUESANS AND MAORIS TAUGHT THE CUSTOM.** If culture and language are to guide us in finding affinities, the Marquesans furnished a considerable contingent to the circle of archipelagoes that were submerged ; it is more than likely that they were the source of the Longears, who figure so largely in the history of the island ; for they alone of the Polynesians, except the Easter Islanders, extended the lobes of the ears by piercing and by increasingly large insertions. That the men of the island gave up the custom more than a century ago may have been due to the defeat of the Longears that tradition reports ; but the arrival of whalers about this time stimulated the abandonment of the custom. It is equally clear that they must have been in the ascendant when the sculptors gave all the images long ears. But when the archipelagoes plunged they must have been the toilers in the central island ; for they were, till their defeat later on, the stronger and the more numerous element in the population. And the Marquesans were the most inveterate cannibals in Polynesia ; it is even said that the practice of eating human flesh continues, though in secret, to the present day. But cannibals, too, were the Shortears who, to judge from culture and language, represent the contingent from New Zealand and had been in the ascendant before the catastrophe if we accept the tradition that Hotu Matua was one of them and led them. The Maoris amongst the Polynesians rank next to the Marquesans as eaters of human flesh, though they do not seem to have taken to it from famine. It is little wonder then that this islet adopted the diet when its population was thrown on its own resources.

(7) **THE PIG AND THE DOG THRICE INTRODUCED AND THRICE EATEN OUT.** The straits to which all of them were driven, even the new arrivals under responsible leaders, nothing

so clearly shows as the fate of some of Hotu Matua's introductions. The language reveals that the Easter Islanders knew the pig and the dog far back in their history; when they got on board Roggewein's ships and saw the pig they called it *p u a k a*, the Polynesian name for it, and they kept the Polynesian word for dog (*k u r i*) till the first cat came off some European ship (tradition says an American whaler from the coast of Peru), and then the four rapid-moving legs and the comparatively low stature of the newcomer appropriated the old name of the lost dog. Both pig and dog must have vanished with the submerged archipelagoes. But, according to tradition, H o t u M a t u a brought specimens of similar animals; the piglike animal, described as having short front legs and high fat buttocks, brought a new name with it, "p e p e k u"; so the dog brought another new name "p a i h e n g a," which is the Easter Island word for the animal to this day. But both of them were eaten before they could propagate their kind. The same fate overtook a third pig that was landed on the island by La Perouse; it and its mate were taken away up to the plateau of P o i k e; a huge hole was dug for the pair and they were fed upon the best of the land, bananas and taro and sweet potatoes; the sow littered, but the litter was generally distributed to other parts of the island; and they were all, as well as the boar and sow, sacrificed to the hunger of the islanders. But they left a new name for pig in the language ("*o r u*" evidently imitative of the grunt) and that is the name the pig is now known by on the island. The tradition seems to have passed through about half a dozen generations and to point to two of the animals that La Perouse left as a legacy of his visit.

(8) **EVEN THE COCO-NUT EATEN OUT.** This inordinate passion for eating everything eatable that lands on the island is not confined to ancient times or to flesh. Famine leaves its brand on the whole history and it evidently took Hotu Matua all his capacity as a leader to prevent his seeds and his plants going the same road as his "p e p e k u" and his "p a i h e n g a ." The nearest analogy one can find is the story of the great Australian effort to realize the socialistic ideal in "New Australia" and "Cosme" in Paraguay; the tons of seed-wheat that were taken to sow were all eaten and the hundreds of milch cows went into the

pot without a pound of butter having been made. There are considerable gaps in the Easter Island list of plants that all Polynesian migrations carried with them, and one cannot be too sure that the absences are not due to this voracity. Hotu is said to have brought the coco-nut, and the coco-nut will undoubtedly grow and bear in Easter Island; there are two or three of the palms still growing and bearing that the Tahitian firm planted some fifty years ago. And in a former generation, there were two on the south coast, one on Poike and one near *Maunga Toatoa*; they were cut down in the wars between the Miru and the Tupahotu. Whether these were raised and planted by *Hotu Matua* is very doubtful; for the coco-nut does not live hundreds of years. There are to be found in the shallow crater of R a n o A r o i, towards the north of the island, many small brown nuts about an inch in diameter that look like miniature coco-nuts and are said by the natives to be coco-nuts. They pierce them with a pointed stick through the centre and spin them as tops; and they call them not *n i u*, the Polynesian name for a coco-nut, but *m a k o i*, the Easter Island word for a top. That this means an abundance of coco-nut palms in former days often dropping their immature nuts is not very probable. The nuts may be the fruit of a different palm. They are also found close to the sea at the foot of high cliffs.

(9) **WOMEN ALWAYS SCARCE.** Starvation has undoubtedly left its mark on the people of Easter Island and their history. And Hotu Matua's troubles in his attempt to stock it with plants and animals show that it began centuries ago. He had probably to face a worse form of it than any leader since. For his rich archipelago to the west had vanished and his failure to get food for the famishing population from any other direction indicates that the other archipelagoes had also gone. How long he stood siege on M a u n g a H a u E p e it is impossible to say. He was able at last to get out and plant the seeds, or suckers, or cuttings that remained uneaten. But men in peace as well as in war would be more needed than women, though Easter Island women took their share, not only in the cultivation of tubers and in nocturnal fishing, but in war, going forward to encourage their men in the fight, if not themselves taking part in it. And the universal Polynesian custom of female infanticide, probably a legacy from a sinking and narrowing fatherland, was emphasized here

by the frequent lack of food. Some of the voyagers, like Cook, observed a singular disproportion between the numbers of men and women. And it is more than likely that this was even more the case when the island was full of toilers at the *a h u s* and the images ; the masters on the archipelagoes would not favour households among the subjects on the central island, and when it was left to itself there would be few women upon it. Nor would the canoes of Hotu Matua contribute a large contingent to its female population. This scarcity of women, increased by the custom of polygamy, may be the reason why such stress is laid upon sexuality in its customs and legends. And this stress is apparent in all the reports of the voyagers. Some of them thought from the way the men traded off the women promiscuously when ships arrived that there was community of women. But this can be easily disproved. Marriage existed as throughout Polynesia ; but it was only a loose bond, easily made and easily broken ; for unlike all the other incidents of Polynesian life, like naming and haircutting, it had no sanction from religion or connection with it. It was polygamy that seemed to be identical with promiscuity, leaving in the hands of some men a superfluity at their disposal. *H o t u   M a t u a* brought only one wife, as far as we know, though many ancestors, in his canoe ; and so did his lieutenant, *T u u k o i h u*. Had he begun to interfere with the immemorial right of polygamy, he would have but made little headway with his reforms.

APPENDIX

REPORT OF PROFESSOR SPEIGHT, PROFESSOR OF GEOLOGY AND CURATOR OF MUSEUM, CANTERBURY UNIVERSITY COLLEGE, ON THE STUFF OF THE STATUES

Judging from the samples submitted to me, the material of the images appears to be a basic volcanic agglomerate, consisting of fine-grained matter in which are angular fragments ranging in size through lapilli up to pieces $2\frac{1}{2}$ inches in diameter. The colour is yellowish in the hand specimen. Under the microscope the smaller rock fragments appear to be composed chiefly of glass, yellowish in colour like palagonite, and containing numerous broken pieces and shreds of basic felspar. I noticed no calcite in the slides nor in the hand specimens, which might give by its presence some indication that the deposit from which the specimens were obtained was laid down on a sea bottom. I looked for this specially, since the marked stratification of the agglomerate as seen on the island, according to Professor Macmillan Brown, strongly suggests that such were the conditions of deposit, and this evidence might be considered conclusive were there not numerous instances of the occurrence of well-marked stratification in fragmental volcanic material resulting from the sifting action of wind. This possibility must be considered in such a connection.

The larger fragments of the agglomerate show a range in character from an andesite to a basalt. The specimens at my disposal did not indicate a strongly basic character for the rock, and they should be classed as augite andesites. No olivine was observed in the slides.

The hats of the images are composed of very scoriaceous basic rock, strongly coloured by oxide of iron, and are very glassy in texture, as disclosed by the microscope.

One of the hammers kindly presented to the Museum by Professor Macmillan Brown, from which no slides were made, is probably an andesite similar to the other fragments ; no olivine could be detected with a hand lens, which might suggest that it be called a basalt.

The spear heads are of volcanic glass, but whether acidic or basic I was unable to determine definitely, as I did not feel justified in breaking one in order to obtain a section. The specific gravity, 2·45, points to their being more acidic than the material of the agglomerate, allowing for the fact that a glass is likely to have a lower density than the corresponding crystalline rock.

CHAPTER IX

THE DIVINE KING

(1) *Whence the timbers for the big canoes?* (2) *Easter Island had never any trees more than eighteen inches in diameter.* (3) *The timbers so greatly needed for all the cyclopean work on the island must have come from the archipelagoes, which would need huge craft to convey slaves and supplies and funeral trains.* (4) *With only three hundred followers the great pioneer had to act on the defensive against the tens of thousands of enfranchised slaves.* (5) *His only offensive was to play upon the superstition of the Longears.* (6) *He had to use the taboo of the Polynesian a r i k i and conquer the soul of the mob, instead of attempting to subdue their bodies.* (7) *For this he reconstructed society on the Polynesian king and a r i k i system; but only he and his descendants were to be kings, and only his followers and their descendants were to be a r i k i; he would be strictly neutral in all the wars of the clans that he had divided all the slaves into.* (8) *He placed the system on a religious footing, calling his own tribe M i r u, a name of supernatural power amongst Polynesians.* (9) *M i r u was the name of the learned priest of a blond aboriginal tribe in the fatherland.* (10) *By adopting this name for his clan he meant to indicate that they were in touch with the occult.* (11) *But in order to prevent the rise of unofficial dealers in the occult, the natural result of a monopolistic official religion, he established an order of learned priests to be the repository of all the arts and learning and called them indigenes (m a o r i s).* (12) *They were to exercise especially the art of making indelible picture galleries of the skin—tattooing.* (13) *But to secure perfection of the art he and his successors held an annual review of all the tattooed.* (14) *To this the people had to bring their tribute, including the foods that were taboo to all but the king.* (15) *There was a painful disease believed to follow the breach of any taboo, and by this he managed to make the sacred clan endogamous and pure; whilst the royal head, even when dead, was the most efficient of fertilizers.* (16) *These do-nothing kings were to continue long in the land by having no part in action and by resigning, when he eldest son set up house, so as to avoid senility.*

(1) **WHERE DID THE TIMBER COME FROM?** H o t u M a t u a and his band arrived in two large canoes, each evidently capable of carrying one hundred and fifty people under all circumstances, calm or storm. Tradition does not say whether they were like most of the Polynesian large canoes for oceanic travel, double with a platform between and bearing a house that would shelter all but the fighters and seamen. If anything, it seems to indicate that they were single canoes like the warcraft of the north island of New Zealand. For my guide, the depository of so much of the legendary lore of the island through his aged mother and his father, who died only three or four years ago, declared that Hotu's was a mile long and promised to show me the proof when we reached the landing-place of the great pioneer. When at A n a k e n a B a y he pointed out to me the stern on the flank of the fortified hill; it was a weathered outcrop of a lava dyke. I did not ask to be shown the prow after that, and he did not volunteer to point it out.

(2) The canoes were certainly not of stone. But where they could have got the timber in Easter Island to build such large craft is one of the mysteries. In Paymaster Thomson's version of the defeat of the Longears and the origin of cannibalism a double canoe is mentioned : " A chief, named P o y a , had just finished a large double canoe at Hangaroa, which he called T u a p o i . This was dragged across the island and launched at A n a h a v a . ' ' No tree larger than eighteen inches in diameter is reported by voyager or native or tradition. And there are no traces of roots or stumps round Hangaroa or on the slopes of R a n o K a o that would bear trunks capable of supporting timbers for such a canoe. No visitor ever saw more than two or three canoes on the island with timbers above four feet long. And it is well known that no canoe large enough to carry sail was ever made or used on the island ; there is no native word for sail in the language, though the vocabularies give compounds that are supposed to express " jib " and even " royal "; they are of post-European Tahitian manufacture.

(3) **TRANSPORT FROM THE ARCHIPELAGOES MEANT FLEETS OF LARGE CRAFT.** We may take it for granted that all the oceanic canoes that tradition attributes to Easter Island came from elsewhere. The archipelagoes that surrounded it, especially such an archipelago as Davis and Wafer saw on the horizon fading into the distance towards the northwest, were certain, if they were ancient lands, to carry great forests. And it was these that supplied Easter Island with the thick beams and ropes needed for levering and hauling the statues and manipulating the huge shaped or tooled stones for the platforms and house foundations and with the long thick timbers needed for building oceanic canoes. And the traffic over those long sea distances between would require huge craft, such as Hotu Matua travelled in, to bring the supplies of food for the *ahu*-workers on the islet or new supplies of labour superintendence, if not finer double canoes for the dead warrior and the train that was to convey him to his burial platform. There are paved ways or slides down to the sea close to several of the great platforms, as, for example, at the northern end of the finest in L a P e r o u s e B a y , called H a n g a k o u r e , behind which lie the pieces of the last great statue to be overthrown (P a r o). My guide thought it was for the people to come down for water ; but the shoeless

feet of the natives would be hampered instead of helped by such a pavement ; it is so broad and the stones so carefully fitted and at the foot of it the high tide is so deep, that there would be no difficulty in hauling up even a double canoe. And on the white sand of A n a k e n a B a y the beaching of many of the largest of canoes would be managed with ease. Or if rafts were used, as in M a n g a r e v a , for transporting the great beams on the island, their unloading would be accomplished without difficulty.

(4) **THE TASK BEFORE HOTU MATUA.** Assuming that the island was full of toilers at the great works of art, subjects of the powers in the archipelagoes, and dependent on them for organization and sustenance, we can imagine what a chaos it would be when the source of authority and of food had gone down ; we can imagine what a task lay in front of *Hotu Matua*, the only representative of the vanished government. What could he do with his three hundred against the thousands who felt that their chains were broken, and that if organized and led they could do what they liked with the island and the officials of their old masters ? His dilemma is manifest in the entrenched fort on the top of M a u n g a H a u E p e. He felt that he could act only on the defensive. And he prepared for future emergencies by training and drilling even the youngest of his followers.

(5) He had forgotten how defenceless was an unorganized mob that had risen against all organization. And he remembered what a power the aristocracy had over the commoners through their religious imagination. He knew the reverence they had for the sacred persons of the king and the *a r i k i* . And he set himself deliberately to assume the character and to direct the old veneration of royalty towards himself. It is by no means unlikely that the names of the two islands from which he was expelled, including as they do the Polynesian word for a temple (M a r a e R e n g a and M a r a e T o i h o) mark them as sanctuaries of the archipelagoes ; and their governor had probably something of the position and character of a priest-king like the T u i t o n g a s of the Tongan group. It would be perfectly natural, then, for him to take up the rôle of sacred royalty and to concentrate on himself all the worship that had been bent towards the distant centre of the empire now vanished. He represented that imperial government ; he was its only remaining official ;

and for years, if not for generations, the Longears had been accustomed to look upon it as divine, and had been helping to perpetuate the glory of its noble families by raising these great memorials in whose vaults the bones of the greatest of them were to be interred. They had looked upon the faces of those gigantic statues with awe ; for on them they saw the defiant resolve and majesty of conquerors. Surely the courage and might that were so plainly marked upon the countenance of these memorial images would not be awanting in the last of the imperial line.

(6) **THERE WAS NOTHING FOR IT BUT CONQUEST OF THE SOUL.** There was no other rôle for him to play; for he had no army to enforce his commands. If he hesitated, he was lost. So he set himself deliberately like all Polynesian *a r i k i* to cultivate the religious sense of the people, and to focus it on his own person and that of his followers and children. The people were Longears ; but he had Longears also new-comers in his canoes. The two would doubtless fraternize, and he would use those of his own band as missionaries amongst the others to saturate their minds with the new ideas of re-ligion based on the old and developed out of them. The new ideas were a fuller use of the old Polynesian taboo, and an application of it to secure the influence of him and his descen-dants as well as of his clan over the minds of the whole com-munity. The chains he forged for their new subjection were far more powerful than the old, which had their power and sanction only in the distant M o t u M a t i r a H i v a ; they were spiritual and bound the mind through its illusions.

(7) **HE LOCALISED THE PEOPLE AS CLANS WITH ONE SACRED CLAN, THE M I R U.** But he had to substitute some new social organization for the old. This he managed by spreading the people along the coast where they would be likely to make his new plants grow, and where they might secure at least brackish water from the low-tide springs. He divided them up into tribes or clans according to their locality, giving them charge of the burial platforms in their neighbourhood. His own following also he moulded into a clan, and gave them command of A n a k e n a B a y and its vicinity, where all the best landing-places for canoes were situated. He made every member of this clan sacred, so that their smallness of numbers might not be overborne by larger clans. They and they alone were *a r i k i ,* the Polynesian

word for aristocracy. And they were the only clan that had a chief or king, himself and after him his descendants. He was the *ariki mau*, or constant representative, of all that was noble in the island or had been noble in the archipelagoes around ; and his descendants were so also by right of primogeniture. The others were *ariki paka*, or the cream of noble blood, *paka* being an intensive in the language. That the other clans might not feel themselves slighted he distributed his sons amongst them, as soon as he had enough sons to distribute. Each was to have some connection with his sacred blood by taking its name from one of his sons and counting him as the founder of the clan. But there was to be no nucleus of rivalry with his headship in any chief who should be hereditary or elective or war-selected. He and his successors were to take no side in any quarrel or war ; nor were they to enter into any fight, so that their persons should be inviolable, like that of a war-herald in other nations. The more the others quarrelled and fought the less chance would there be of any rebellion against the central power, provided that kept neutral, and based its influence only upon religion and taboo.

(8) **THE RELIGIOUS SIGNIFICANCE OF THE NAME** *MIRU*. That he meant religion to be the basis of all his power and paramount in all social and political affairs is apparent in the name he adopted for the clan he formed his followers into—*Miru*. This is a name of great potency in many Polynesian groups, and is generally applied to the power that presides over the land of the common dead, *Po* or *Hawaiki*, although it is a Tahitian name for heaven, Ellis says ; in *Hawaii* it is a god ; in New Zealand and the Cook group it is a goddess. In Hawaii he led a rebellion of the spirits against the new and powerful gods ; and T a n e , the Jupiter of the new Olympus, tumbled him with his crew into outer darkness. In New Zealand, though *Miru* is a goddess, there are indications that she was the deity of an earlier race subdued or driven into the wilds. It was from her realm, Maori mythology acknowledges, that the Maoris learned their art of carving, their songs, dances and games, including cat's cradle or string-figures, as well as witchcraft and anti-witchcraft and all love charms. Mr. James Cowan recently described in the Journal of the Polynesian Society (June, 1921) the P a t u p a i a r e h e, one of the aboriginal tribes of New Zealand, from information gathered amongst

the K a u m a t u a s, or old sages of various tribes in both
the north and the south island, and especially those of the
N g a t i - M a n i a p o t o , whose ancestors were deeply influenced by this "mysterious forest-dwelling race spoken of
as an *i v i a t u a*, a race of supernatural beings." This word
i v i a t u a appears also in Easter Island as the name of a self-
appointed profession of wizards and sorceresses, which sprang
up outside the *M i r u* clan and gained boundless influence
over the minds of the people by their successful manipulation
of the *a t u a s*, or gods, and *a k u a k u s*, or filmy shadows
of the dead ; since the conversion they are *d i a b o l o s*, or
t a t a n i s; but before they threatened the religious omnipotence of the King and his *M i r u* clan.

(9) Mr. Cowan tells a story of this blond race that comes
from the Polynesian fatherland H a w a i k i, "dating back
untold centuries." A P a t u p a i a r e h e man called M i r u,
the chief and priest of his tribe, fell in love with H i n e r -
a n g i , the puhi or virgin daughter of " a man of this world,"
and marrying her had two sons by her ; but getting homesick
he returned to his tribe, taking with him some companions,
including his father-in-law and sister-in-law. As the *t o h u n -
g a* of his tribe he taught them in H u i - t e - r a n g i o r a
all the incantations and charms of his race, and various games,
including " the working of the wooden marionettes that were
caused to imitate h a k a and other dances," another striking
hint of Easter Island ; for T u u k o i h u, the lieutenant of
Hotu Matua made the little wooden images that he was the
first to carve dance round the roof of his great house on the
west coast of the island. The father-in-law of M i r u in return
bestowed on him the hand of his second daughter, and " returned to this world " and built a H u i - t e - r a n g i o r a
there and taught in it all the sacred wisdom and charms he
had learned. "That is how the people of this world came
to possess the knowledge of these." And the N g a t i - M a n -
i o p o t o continue to honour this name for a house of learning
and council, H u i - t e - r a n g i o r a .

(10) It is by no means a rash conclusion to draw from
these indications that M i r u was an honoured name in the
Polynesian fatherland amongst a lighter-coloured race, who,
though probably of higher culture, was driven into the wilds
by the bolder sea-rovers that came later and ruled in Polynesia. Whether H o t u M a t u a chose the name for his clan

as representing the older race and culture that taught the new-comers witchcraft and charms, dancing and carving and other arts, or as the name of the ruler of the land of spirits, it is difficult to say. H e n r i M a g e r, in his ''M o n d e P o l y n e s i e n,'' gives one hint that seems to suggest the latter: he says that H o t u M a t u a reigned twenty-five years ''at M'A v a i - t u''; whence he gets this name he does not say; but *A v a i* is the Polynesian fatherland, and in the Marquesas and other groups the land of spirits. It looks as if the choice of the name M i r u was dictated by his desire to give a religious atmosphere to his clan, and to make men think of them as above common humanity and in touch with the mysterious and occult.

(11) **THE MAORIS A PRIESTLY ORDER OF SAGES AND ARTISTS.** It is probable that he anticipated the rise amongst the other clans of men and women claiming knowledge of the occult; perhaps they had already arisen; for there are few branches of the Polynesian race that have not had practitioners of *makutu* or black magic; they seem to spring up at a certain stage of the development of a primitive religion as a complement and foil to the priesthood, professing to get into touch with the gods and the spirits of the dead by means apart from traditional ceremonial. H o t u M a t u a knew how inevitably this phase of human superstition takes command of the simpler mind, and he established an order of wise men learned in the arts and wise in all the traditions of the supernatural and, to avoid any suggestion of foreign derivation of their skill and wisdom, called them *m a o r i s ,* or indigenous sages. Nor did he choose them from his own clan alone; that would have stirred the jealousy and suspicion of the others and left them unaffected by the new order. He selected them from every clan and trained them in all the traditional arts and learning of which his own clan was the repository. He brought them together once a year to A n a - k e n a B a y , where he tested their knowledge of the various arts that they had been taught, reciting and singing and dancing and the method of healing.

(12) **TATTOOING BOTH ART AND RELIGION.** But one of the most important was tattooing, which made men and women beautiful for ever; the decoration of the human face and figure was now considered more important than the carving of images in the likeness of men; and the permanence

of the picture gallery on the skin was secured by this art.
It was an honour and glory to be tattooed from head to foot;
and the M i r u generally gave the example of this. My guide
remembers the magnificent tattooing over the whole face
and body of the last of the *ariki paka*, old M a t i, who
died at the end of the eighties of last century. His mother is
tattooed only from waist to knee and with the little netlike
circles on the brow. But he remembers as a boy in the sixties,
when nothing but the *hami mama*, or perineal bandage,
was still worn, seeing three old women set out every morning
to their work; and their skin from brow to toe was a picture
gallery in blue. From the Marquesans or the Maoris or both
this elaborate tattooing must have been acquired, especially
the tattooing on the face; and a spiral over the lower ribs
on each side seems to indicate the latter as the models and
teachers; the spiral was of little importance in Marquesan
tattooing.

(13) Such an important art as this in the life of the people
the king could not leave to the individual taste or fumbling
of the *maori* of each clan. For it was a business of years
to complete the task of beautifying the skin of any man or
woman, and the symmetry and design of the whole might be
spoiled by some unskilful detail any year. So he called all the
people together every year to inspect their tattooing. At the
foot of the hill on which stood his houses there is a little circular
cistern lined with tooled basalt; here he bored the lobes of
the ears of every man and woman and then examined their
tattooing; those that were well tattooed he sent over to
A h u R u n g a; those who were not were sent to the opposite
side. Thus were careless or unskilful professors of the art
rebuked; for the clan of every one was known and the name
of the *maori*. And to the same review the people brought
their tribute, each a stick of fowls' feathers in alternate black
and white bands and a tuber of *pua* on the end, the source
of their red dye. The mythology of the natives of New Zealand
attributes their tattooing to a visit of one M a t a o r a to the
underworld. And there is in this annual review of the work
of tattooing by the Miru priest-king the suggestion of an
underworld or religious significance.

(14) **TABOO THE CHIEF INSTRUMENT OF POLYNESIAN
POWER.** These sticks of feathers were of importance; for
they were to form the *huhu*, or royal banner, that

would mark off for the year the house of the king from all other houses. But it was not merely decorative material that they brought. As important were the foods that were delivered to the royal household; they were not given as compulsory tribute to a master, but as something that was reserved for a divine personage. Certain fish, for example, were tabooed for the king; if anyone else ate them they were harassed with various diseases. Father Gaspar, who established a mission at V a i h u on the south coast, and had a score or more of young Easter Islanders in training in his house, found one of them convulsed with agony one day; examined as to what was the matter, he said: " Oh, Father, I have eaten K a h i, '' a fish supposed to be sacred to the king. M a h a k i, a fish of fine flavour, is probably meant; for *K a h i* is a very large and coarse fish, and it is delicate eating that is generally reserved for an aristocracy. The belief, so long inculcated in the people, that the breach of a taboo would bring some painful disease, was sure to bring it in primitive natures; belief was the chief weapon in the hands of the Polynesian chiefs and sorcerers, as it is the most efficient medicine in the pharmacopœia of a modern physician. It was this in the hands of the Miru king that secured any supremacy he had.

(15) **THE SACRED HEAD AND ITS USES.** In order to retain the monopoly of this sacredness in the hands of his successors and their clan he made endogamy compulsory. But no decree or command of his was efficient without some taboo. He made all the other clans believe that if any member of them married or had intercourse with any one of the M i r u clan, he or she would at once have *t u t a e h i h i*, a painful disease of the intestines; and to this day the belief exists in full strength. That was the negative side of the priest-king's use of the supernatural. There was also a positive side. All the people believed that the head of the king had the most marvellous fertilizing power. If it came near any crop it would double or treble the growth. If it approached one of the *a n a m o a* it enormously increased the laying power of the hens. Even when dead there was a struggle to get hold of the skull and mark it with a hieroglyph, probably a highly conventionalized version of the *K o m a r i* or *vulva;* for this was considered highly efficient against trespassers when carved on the boundary-stones and was always

Hine, DAUGHTER OF THE LAST KING *Riroroko*, WHO DIED IN VALPARAISO
IN THE LAST YEARS OF LAST CENTURY

held to be a sign and a stimulus of fertility. When the last king in working order, N g a a r a , died, just before the Peruvian raid, in Hangaroa, and his bones were placed along with his tablets and other insignia of his position and art in the burial platform of T a h a i , the skull was promptly stolen. And all the Easter Island skulls that have those marks on them in the museums of the world may be taken for royal. For the king's head was sacred; he who touches it even to do the necessary hair-cleaning or cutting (and the only comb in old Easter Island was the fingers) had his hands taboo and dared not use them to carry food to his mouth. M a u r a t a , the last acknowledged king, when he was raided by the Peruvians left a boy who was afterwards brought up by the missionaries and called G r e g o r i o . When he was twelve he fell ill of a fever and it was essential that he should have his hair cut; but he was descended from the divine king and had been brought up in the belief that his head was sacred; he refused to let anyone touch it and he died. Of course, this sacredness of the head of the chief or king belongs to all branches of the Polynesian race; but it was never thought of as utilitarian even when dead by any branch but that of Easter Island.

(16) **HOW TO PREVENT SENILITY IN THE DIVINE KING.** There is "a divinity doth hedge a king"; but here is a line of kings (some give a list of fifty-seven, others thirty) who were not merely hedged with divinity but were divinity itself. They were r o i s f a i n e a n t s ; but that did not matter, they were gods; and gods are the more omnipotent the less that their omnipotence is tested in action. The founder of this dynasty hedged them in so that they should never have to act; they only reviewed the results of the actions of others. But what if they fell into senility and decay? Would not their divinity be a laughing-stock instead of a thing of awe? As a rule, when there is such an inert divine king in a community, provision is made that he vanish before senility or decay sets in. The founder of this Easter Island monarchy thought he had guarded against all such contingencies in enacting that when the eldest son of a king married and set up house for himself the father should resign and retire into private life. He probably made this provision when he was in the prime of life and his sons were still children. For, when he grew old, tradition tells, he quarrelled with his eldest son

and with his own wife, doubtless because they insisted that this enactment should be carried out. What he did secure for this divine line of kings, who were no kings, was that the line should be long in the land. Had no Peruvian slave-raiders been about in the Pacific and no Europeans reached Easter Island it might have lasted many centuries; there was nothing to bring it to an end but a repetition of its founders' refusal to carry out his own enactment and resign in favour of an eldest son.

CHAPTER X

THE SCRIPT

(1) *His most potent instrument for the subjugation of the people's soul was the tablets.* (2) *There was no need for script or any mnemonic system of long-distance communication on an islet that at its longest could be walked over in a day.* (3) *In the Polynesian fatherland the knotted cord system of mnemonics was evidently developed as far as the Easter Island script, both for recording and sending long-distance communications.* (4) *This often bars the way to the invention and adoption of script ; and its use as a talisman leads to the rosary so common in advanced religions.* (5) *Tattooing had led to the development of script ; the k o m a r i, or conventionalized pudenda muliebria, was liberally tattooed and liberally used in the script, which was ever connected with sexuality.* (6) *But the composite figure of the great god Makemake, representing fish, flesh and fowl, is by far the most frequent of the characters. He is the omnipotent and was probably the deified conqueror and founder of the empire.* (7) *Bishop Jaussen's attempt to get the meaning of the tablets ended in his saying : " We must give it up—there is nothing in it."* (8) *Another attempt in Papeete led to three different translations of the same tablet by one* maori *on three consecutive Sundays.* (9) *Eyraud was the first to report their existence, and he thought that " the characters are relics of a primitive writing, and that they are now preserved without enquiring the sense of them."* (10) *The American visitors in 1886 got Ure Vaeiko, an old man who was supposed to know the script, so far tipsy that he translated the tablets fluently though they were interchanged and shifted ; and another old man, Kaitae, is asserted to have given the same translation.* (11) *Ure Vaeiko was the cook of Ngaara, the last effective king, and doubtless heard his master recite them often ; all the old people agree that he did not know the script, though he might have been able to recite some of the hymns and songs ; and Kaitae's portrait in Thomson's pamphlet was recognized by nobody and his name was unknown. The Easter Island language translations are full of Tahitian words.* (12) *The attempt of C. de Harlez, of Louvain, in 1895, still leaves much to imagination.* (13) *The sixty-seven tablets brought by Hotu Matua had already passed from secular use into religious turbidity, and were only things to be listened to* (rongorongo), *not things to be read. The lining of them was probably imitation of some European book or document, and the boustrophedon was due perhaps to scarcity of material.* (14) *He made these talismans to put the souls of the people into the hollow of his hand ; but Eyraud declares they were little esteemed by the people.* (15) *Yet a few relics of them survived,* (16) *chiefly through the sexual and procreative tinge in them.*

(1) There was one introduction of H o t u M a t u a ' s that served him well in his endeavours to get the mind of the people into the hollow of his hand. It was the r o n g o - r o n g o, or collection of hymns and songs, genealogies, and traditions which he brought with him from M a r a e R e n g a, away to the west, or from their primeval source M o t u M a t i r o H i v a, away to the east. That they came originally from the eastern archipelago is to be inferred from the fact that the traditional form of the god M a k e - m a k e appears more than any other character in the script, and that this god had his origin and home in this ; it is he, according to the legends, who brought the sea-birds and the nets thence to Easter Island.

(2) AN ISLET THAT COULD BE WALKED OVER IN A FEW HOURS HAD NO NEED OF LONG-DISTANCE COMMUNICATION. It is clear to anyone who has visited the islet that the script could not have had any necessity for its invention or persistence there. The primary purpose of any recording method is not to preserve the memory of the past but to communicate information or commands or advice to some part of a political unity too distant from the centre to permit of frequent personal visits. As a rule it arises, or is invented, when the peoples of a large territory or archipelago have been unified either by conquest or federation. It could never have appeared in the history of man as long as he lived in isolated units without commercial intercourse or war. As far as we know, its appearance in the old world was due to the growth of monarchic institutions in Egypt and in Mesopotamia. And in the new world it originated in the pre-Aztec empires of Central America, whilst in Peru the knotted-string record became a necessity when the little, yet highly cultured, empires of the coast and of the Andes were united under the Incas. It is easy to cross from any coast of Easter Island to any other coast in a day on foot; and, even if the people had not always been at sixes and sevens, as the tradition represents them, but completely unified, the king would have had no necessity for any fixed mnemonic system ; he could have taken his message himself, or, if he had sent a messenger, the few hours occupied in the transit would not have shaken out of his mind any detail of a verbal message. There could have been no real necessity on this minute surface of the globe and amongst a people constantly torn by feuds for any means of long-distance communication. There might have been need for placing on record numbers, as for example, of fish taboo to the king caught, or of strings of feathers contributed at his reviews, or of the sweet potatoes or bananas or fowls brought in to the feasts. But fidelity in accounts was secured by religious means ; Hotu Matua and his successors had all the people inoculated with the belief that if they broke the taboo or failed in their duty to the divine king they would be afflicted with painful diseases ; and the diseases sure enough resulted from the depth of the belief. If any accounts had to be kept, the knotted-cords so common amongst the Polynesians and Micronesians would have been sufficient for the purpose, as amongst the Incas. But Easter Island tradition reports no

Lines of the Santiago tablet enlarged to show the great variety of forms the Makemake character takes and the large place it fills in the script. Out of one hundred and ten characters here there are sixty-eight which are forms of Makemake; most of the others are sea creatures or features separated from the Makemake character. (It should be noted that the first four lines are all from left to right and boustrophedon.)

use of this method at any time ; it is not in existence amongst the natives of to-day ; nor do the oldest know anything about it ; whilst no voyager or visitor has ever reported its use. Of islands that have indications of past imperial organization it is the one exception in Polynesia and Micronesia ; it may be taken, when found in an island, as a mark of former organization spread over a wide area.

(3) **RECORD AND COMMUNICATION BY KNOTTED CORDS.**
It was evidently employed in the Polynesian fatherland—

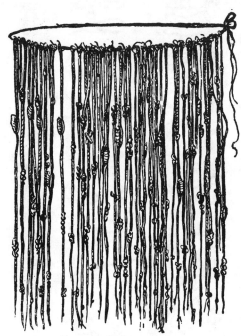

Peruvian Quipu or knotted cord, mnemonic system.

Hawaiki—at least as a numeration record. For when the Hawaiian islands were unified under Kamehameha the old method came into full use as the organization of tribute from the outlying islands and districts ; had the whole people not been familiar with it from old monarchical times the new monarch would have adopted from his European advisers the European method of checking the accounts of the taxpayers and tax-gatherers. But it is the Maoris of New Zealand that show in their language the antiquity of the method in Polynesia ; it has the compound words *t a u p o n a- p o n a* and *a h o p o n a p o n a* for the *quipu* or knotted cord record ; and, as Mr. Elsdon Best points out in an article in "The New Zealand Journal of Science" for April, 1921, *p o n a* in Maori means not merely "a knot," its original sense perhaps besides that of "knuckle," but a message or command, as *h a k a t a p o n a* in Easter Island means to beg for what one has not got and another has. That undoubtedly implies that the knotted cord was used in the ancient Polynesian empires for the communication of the wishes of the government. Mr. Best, in his interesting article, quotes a story from ancient Maori tradition that seems to point to a very advanced use of methods for conveying ideas and information. W h a t o n g a, a pioneer of migration to New Zealand, long before the six canoes, when voyaging from Hawaiki, had to rest in R a n g i a t e a (probably Raiatea in the Society group) for a time on account of stress of weather; his grandmother at home, wanting to know what had become of him, sent off a tame P i p i w h a r a u r o a, or bird of Long Voyage, with a message in knotted cords tied round its neck asking where he had got to; he sent the reply by the same messenger, and on his way home intercepted it with another message asking if he was returning. This bird, the Shining Cuckoo, arrives in the north of New Zealand early in November and leaves for its homeward flight in March; Cook came across what seems to be a specimen of it in M a n u a o, in the Cook group; and evidently the Society group lies also in its line of flight. We have here a development of the *quipu* that goes far in the direction of the Easter Island script, the conveyance of ideas by means of conventional combinations of forms agreed upon. That the *quipu* was used in the Society group centuries before Pomare moulded it into an empire points back to the Polynesian fatherland as its source. For just after this unification M o e r e n h o u t reports quite a different kind of mnemonic method in describing that highly licentious brotherhood, the A r e o i, the keepers of the mysteries of Oro: " Their liturgy consisted of long prayers, eternal catalogues of their divinities, and endless legends and traditions, all in obscure and metaphorical language demanding a prodigious memory "; " And when the ceremonies spun out they had as guides bundles of little sticks of different sizes and thicknesses that they drew from their parcel and placed beside them to help out a prolonged prayer. They must not make a slip." And this was the method of T u p a i a, the Tahitian high priest who accompanied Cook, when he wished to record the islands and countries that he visited.

(4) I am inclined to think that these mnemonic methods of recording, or recalling, or transmitting ideas often bar the way to script, as the early elaboration of the ideographs in the history of China barred the way to the development of an alphabet or even a syllabary. It is, perhaps, the explanation of so cultured a people as the Incas never having advanced to writing when the Mayas in Central America without it did. And yet we have an instance to the contrary in China, which

had the knotted-cord method of numeration in early times, leading later to the *a b a c u s*, and which probably transmitted it to Micronesia. And in the Caroline Islands the existence of the *q u i p u* down to our own day did not prevent the invention and persistence of a syllabic script

Characters Used in Oleai
Written by the Chief Egilimar.

na	tsehra	rä	P N Runge		
goo	mmä	lüh			
dâa	tschä	sthah	EYE		
bä	moâ	tŏo	BROUN		
tschroa	ro	wä	HGNE		
nôo	ma	schä	EGILIMAR		
pui	boa	kŭ			
ru	tä	soâ	The mark ^ indicates accent.		
ma	pä	baq			
bö	vôa	ku			
mä	schrü	schrö			
ngä	pu	gkœ			
boa	lö	rü			
warr	tüt	nga			
râa	va	môo			
uh	lä	gä			
dôo	moi	du			

Collected by the Author in Oleai, in the West of the Carolines, Herr Runge assisting.
(See article in "Man," Aug. 1914.)

such as I found in U l e a i in 1913. Nor did the use of the knotted cords prevent it degenerating into the instrument of sorcery. At the south end of Y a p I saw a long queue of natives line up to consult a hunchback wizard, called F a t u m a k, on the welfare of their relatives who were working in the P e l e w s, four hundred miles off; he made them tie knots in a green leaf from the frond of a coco-nut, as they wound it round their fingers, and according to the combination of knot and knuckle he gave his answer. Such a use of knots on cords for the purpose of divination probably explains their use as a talisman and the widespread use of the rosary throughout the religions of the world.

(5) **TATTOOING AND PETROGLYPHS ON THE ROAD TO WRITING.** The script of Easter Island had gone far before it reached the religious stage. It had not the knotted-cord or bundle-of-sticks system to compete with in the archipelago to the east, else Easter Islanders would have retained some relic of one or other in their religion or in their sorcery. It doubtless began in religious symbolism connected with the food supply, or the sexual relations. The *komari* carved on so many stones, cut on so many ceremonial pieces of wood, tattooed on so much of the skin of men and women, and inscribed on the fertilizing skull of the king, shows the way the characters originated; and it is said to occur again and again on some of the tablets. It is more than likely that tattooing had much to do with popularizing and conventionalizing such representations into characters that ultimately bore a wider significance. In New Zealand the face-tattooing of the Maori chief would tell his tribe his ancestry and the war deeds of himself and his forefathers; and when the foremost chiefs came to sign the treaty of Waitangi with the British, they each used part of their tattoo as signature, and these signatures seem to be of the same order as those that Gonzalez, the voyager from the American coast, got in 1771 the representative Easter Islanders to attach to the document assigning the island to Spain. Undoubtedly tattooing, like petroglyphs, was one start on the road to writing. And in the Easter Island region it must be taken into consideration in explaining the development of the script. For not only was the *Komari* carved on the back of the statue Hoahaka-nanaia when a young woman was taken up to Orongo to pass her examination before the *maori* or professor of tattooing; but it and other significant sexual conventions were tattooed on her back; whilst on the cheek of the virgin was tattooed another conventional form of it in the shape of a V with double lines, what is called the *puhi*, which in Maori means virgin, whilst in Easter Island the word is *neru*. On the backs of the men's

G

hands the *k o m a r i* was also tattooed. There is little
doubt about it that sexualism was greatly emphasized amongst
the people of Easter Island, as also perhaps amongst those
of the archipelagoes around, to judge from the characters
in the script. It was probably the emphasis on sexuality in
them that made the basis of the Easter Island belief in the
virtue of the tablets as aids to conception.

(6) **THE FIGURE OF MAKEMAKE IN THE TABLETS.** But
there are other religious cues of the characters than this.
Most of the characters are repeated to monotony in the
tablets. But that which is by far the most frequently repeated

A few of the Signatures of Maori Chiefs to the Treaty of Waitangi ceding
New Zealand to Britain in 1840.

is the composite figure that is supposed to represent the great
god M a k e m a k e ; it is made up of bird, mammal (sometimes human) and fish, and appears in many varieties of form,
sometimes with fish in hand or in both hands, sometimes with
spear or curved weapon in one hand, often in duplicate or
triplicate hand in hand, oftenest seated or standing with the
forked tail of the fish developed into straddling human legs.
At times the fish or the weapons are separated from the hands
of the figure and often in duplicate or triplicate. A composite
of bird and human or of animal and human is not infrequent
in the carvings of the natives of New Zealand, in the totem
poles of the north-west coast of North America, and in some
of the ornamentation of the most ancient art of China. But
none are so conventionalized and repeated as this figure of

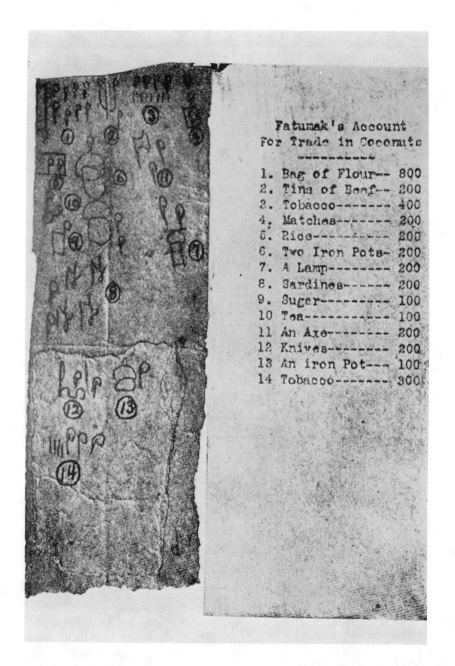

Fatumak's Account
For Trade in Coconuts

1. Bag of Flour--- 800
2. Tins of Beef--- 200
3. Tobacco-------- 400
4. Matches-------- 200
5. Rice----------- 200
6. Two Iron Pots- 200
7. A Lamp--------- 200
8. Sardines------- 200
9. Sugar---------- 100
10 Tea------------ 100
11 An Axe--------- 200
12 Knives--------- 200
13 An Iron Pot--- 100
14 Tobacco-------- 300

FROM FURNESS'S "ISLAND OF STONE MONEY"; IN ORDER TO SHOW HOW CRUDE A SCRIPT COULD BE
INVENTED BY ONE OF THE KEENEST MINDED NATIVES OF THE CAROLINES, A STRONG CONTRAST TO
THE SYLLABARY KNOWN TO THE CHIEFS OF OLEAI

the Easter Island script. M a k e m a k e is evidently the god of fish, and flesh, and fowl, in short, of all food but vegetable. But he is more ; he is the representative of power ; he is seated on his throne ; he has the symbols of royal authority in his hands ; his head touches the heavens and he wields the lightning and thunder. He may possibly have been the conqueror or unifier of the empire that could realize the idea of Easter Island as a great mausoleum. And H o t u M a t u a as the surviving representative of that empire made the most of its god.

(7) **ATTEMPTS TO GET TRANSLATIONS OF THE TABLETS ; JAUSSEN'S.** Various attempts have been made to get a translation of the tablets out of natives who professed to

The Signatures of the Easter Island Chiefs
obtained by Gonzalez in 1771.

know. One of the first to get tablets was Bishop Tepano J a u s s e n of Tahiti; he heard of them through his missionaries, E y r a u d and R o u s s e l, and heard, too, that they were getting used as firewood; so he bade them send him four of them. And, as there were some two hundred Easter Islanders working on Brander and Salmon's sugar plantations, not far from P a p e e t e, he made inquiries as to which of them had any knowledge of the script, and found that one, M e t o r o, was reputed to be one of the *maoris*, or artists and learned men, who were accustomed to copy the tablets and recite them at the great feasts. He got him to come to him and explain the tablets and the characters. But the translation of the tablets was evidently unsatisfactory; for the Bishop gives none of it in the paper he wrote for the Paris Académie. He gives only the meanings of some of the characters explained by Metoro. But when these meanings are applied to the translation of the tablets no sense can be got out of them. It is little wonder that the Bishop in his introduction says, "We must give it up; there is nothing in it."

(8) **CROFT'S ATTEMPT.** An American, a Mr. Croft, resident at Papeete, writes in 1874 to the president of the Californian Academy of Sciences about photographs of the Bishop's tablets that he is sending and tells how he was "cruelly disappointed in his interpreter" of them; the Easter Islander who was recommended as capable of interpreting them came one Sunday and translated one; he wrote down the translation, but mislaid it, and the next time he got him to start again on the same tablet; it struck him that it was different and that there was some deception; so he asked him to come again. Meantime he had found the missing manuscript and saw that he was right in thinking the interpretations very different. The third time the interpreter came he gave a third translation which differed from both the others. He dismissed him with the remark that it was impossible the same characters should have three different meanings on three different Sundays; and he warned the Bishop to be on his guard against such discrepancies in the so-called translations of the tablets. Mr. Croft is one of those who report the destruction of many of the tablets at the behest of the missionaries. Some natives told him that " the missionaries persuaded many of their people to consume by fire all the blocks in their possession, stating to them that they were but heathen records and that the possession of them would have a tendency to attach them to their heathenism and prevent their thorough conversion to the new religion and the consequent saving of their souls." These were " employed by Mr. Brander, a merchant and planter here." Those who " are living with the Bishop deny this statement altogether."

(9) The first missionary, Brother Eugenio Eyraud, in his letter to the superior of his order in Valparaiso in 1864 says of them: " In all the c h o z a s (huts) are found tablets of wood or sticks covered with hieroglyphs; these are figures of animals unknown in the island, which the aborigines form with sharp stones. Each figure has its name; but the little esteem they show for these tablets make me think that the characters are relics of a primitive writing and that they are now preserved without enquiring the sense of them." He was the first to report on their existence and probably one of

PHOTOGRAPH OF THE SCRIPT ON THE TABLET IN THE MUSEUM OF SANTIAGO, CHILI

the first to write of them to Bishop J a u s s e n . And, when he observed them, the natives were still uninfluenced by European opinion of them. One of the strangest things is that though at least La P e r o u s e and G o n z a l e z saw a festival, at which these tablets usually came into prominence, .they report only the appearance of a wicker or bark-cloth figure, one of the features of their feasts.

(10) **HOW FAR THE TRANSLATIONS GOT BY THE** *MOHICAN* **PARTY ARE TO BE TRUSTED.** The next to make an effort to get at the meaning of some of the tablets was the "M o h i c a n" party in December, 1886. When at Tahiti they took photographs of the Bishop's tablets, and by the help of Mr. Salmon they purchased the only two that were to be heard of as remaining in the island, one a piece of driftwood and the other of the native *t o r o m i r o* wood. They got hold of an old man, U r e V a e i k o , who was supposed to know the script ; he refused to translate lest touching heathen things he should "ruin his chances for salvation "; to escape from all temptation he took to the hills ; but one night of storm and rain they found he had taken shelter in his home. By cautious management they got him so far tipsy that he became garrulous and the photograph of one after another of the Bishop's tablets was placed before him. Mr. Salmon, who was with them, wrote down the translation. "U r e V a e i k o 's fluent interpretation of the tablet was not interrupted, though it became evident that he was not actually reading the characters. It was noticed that the shifting of position did not accord with the number of symbols on the lines, and afterwards, when the photograph of another tablet was substituted, the same story was continued without change being discovered." Nor could he "give the signification of hieroglyphs copied indiscriminately from tablets already marked. He explained at great length that the actual value and significance of the symbols had been forgotten, but the tablets were recognized by unmistakable features "; "just as a person might recognize a book in a foreign language and be perfectly sure of the contents without being able to actually read it." "An old man, K a i t a e , who claims relationship to the last king, M a u r a t a , afterwards recognized several of the tablets from the photographs and related the same story exactly as that given previously by U r e V a e i k o ."

(11) I made inquiries of the old people about these two interpreters of the tablets. U r e V a e i k o was known as a servant of N g a a r a the king who died just before the Peruvian raid. But he was declared to be ignorant of the script; he was the king's cook, and often heard the tablets being recited by him, so that with a retentive memory he was able to recognize some and repeat the hymn or song intended to be brought to memory by it. The other, K a i t a e , no one knew by name, and when the portrait of him in Paymaster Thomson's pamphlet was presented to them, no one recognized him ; it was agreed that he was not an Easter Islander at all. My guide, J u a n T e p a n o , had been working with me over the whole vocabulary of the Easter Island dialect for weeks, and we started on the hymns and songs in that dialect given in the pamphlet as the transliteration of the tablets. It was soon very evident that a considerable number of the words were Tahitian and that the English translation was anything but literal or even accurate. In spite of all this, it is by no means improbable that the genealogies and hymns and songs given were really what the tablets stood for ; for at the annual feast the people were taught to recognize each tablet as they recited or heard recited what it contained, and in 1886 the old language had been mutilated and filled with words from Tahiti and Mangareva.

(12) A third attempt was made in 1895 by a Mons. C. de Harlez, of Louvain ; a Brother Tauvel, of the Congregation of Picpus, had brought him a tablet and a long manuscript written by Bishop Jaussen, containing explanations of the signs and long texts in the language of Easter Island, and asked him to try to find out the meaning of the figures and of the texts. He gives the results of his attempts in a small monograph published by J. B. I s t a s , Brussels, evidently basing his attempts on the work of the Bishop ; the translation still needs much imagination to see how the figures represent it ; and the sequence or connection of ideas is by no means apparent. He acknowledges that the *lacunæ* are many and that some characters defied all his efforts ; for, he explains, the characters represent only in a general way a word of an explanatory phrase, sometimes two, very rarely three. So he attempted only the first four lines of one tablet and the first line of each of two others ; it cannot be said that he has made anything very intelligible out of them, though some of his phrases have

Four lines of the Santiago tablet enlarged to show the great variety of forms the Makemake character takes and the large place it fills in the script. Out of one hundred and ten characters here there are sixty-eight which are forms of Makemake; most of the others are sea creatures of features separated from the Makemake character. (It should be noted that the first four lines are all from left to right and boustrophedon.)

evidently some connection with some of the figures they are supposed to translate.

(13) **THE STAGE THE SCRIPT HAD REACHED WHEN BROUGHT BY HOTU MATUA.** It is beyond the power of even imagination to get sequent, reasonable ideas out of what were never meant to give expression to them. Some of the characters clearly bear their source and immediate significance upon them whilst others are as clearly conventionalized with a meaning that the original users had agreed upon like the knots on the *quipu*. But none of them are intended to convey what we would express by a sentence or series of sentences ; there is only the suggestion of it, and, as many of the characters have only a conventional meaning known only to those who have agreed upon it or who are informed of it, transmission without the prayer or hymn or allegory or genealogy the tablet was put together to represent would end in mystery or fog. Before H o t u M a t u a brought his sixty-seven tablets from his homeland, they had already fallen into the befogged stage, and their meaning had to be handed down as carefully as the tablets ; they were already called *r o n g o r o n g o*, things to be listened to or recited, not things to be seen or read. The original sense of the characters may have been known to the great pioneer ; but it is doubtful whether he attached any importance to them as means of human communication. The script had largely arisen or persisted out of religious necessities, as is evident in the constant repetition of the M a k e m a k e figure and his constituent elements, perhaps the religion that grew up round the apotheosized founder of the empire, and probably based upon his efforts to find a means of communication with its distant parts, was apparent in the conventionalized and symbolic characters. Where the priests picked up the idea of setting the characters in lines as in a European book or letter it is impossible to say. Considering the imitative tendency that has clung to Easter Islanders to the last, I might conjecture that it was mimicry of some Spanish book or document that had fallen into their hands in the sixteenth, or early years of the seventeenth, century, perhaps from the ships of Q u i r o s , who came across the island of L o s Q u a t r o C o r o n a d o s on February 4th, 1606, a fortnight after having set out from Callao on his expedition to the Solomons. The boustrophedon or consecutive line-reversal method of the tablets is against this, though that is not always

PHOTOGRAPH OF THE SCRIPT ON THE TABLET IN THE MUSEUM OF SANTIAGO, CHILI

adopted, and the later scarcity of materials to engrave on, apparent in the necessity of writing on both sides, may have led to it.

(14) Certain it is that Hotu Matua had already, when he arrived at Anakena Bay, in his hands the most efficient instrument for the religious subjugation of the people of Easter Island. He at once set himself to apply it. He put the tablets into the hands of the *maoris* whom he had chosen and appointed from each clan and made them commit to memory the traditions, and hymns, and genealogies connected with each; they were the mysterious *abracadabra* with which these artist and sages would be able to enthrall the Easter Island mind and bind it to the feet of himself and his descendants, the only representative of the great empire that had produced them. He had brought them on the paper, that is, bark-cloth, on which they had been probably painted in Motu Matiro Hiva. But that was scarce and coarse in Easter Island. So he soon substituted the inner bark of the banana stem. But this, too, had its disadvantages; for, though the fibres were not interlaced and crossed like those of the *mahute*, but linear, the paint would run and be easily blurred or washed off. With the new obsidian which he found in such plenty in Easter Island he taught them to etch the script in lines on boards cut from the great beams that had come from the archipelagoes or even from the planks of his great canoes once they began, from disuse, to go to pieces. Every year he called all the *maoris* of the island together with their new-cut copies of the old tablets, to inspect them and to hear them recite the traditions and genealogies and prayers they were supposed to represent. This was the great annual feast of the tablets kept up till the Peruvian raid had carried off most, if not all, who were directly and professionally acquainted with them. He made them introduce the *rongorongo* into all the feasts and ceremonies and even into the crises of domestic and individual life. In short, he made the tablets the sacred book of their religion interwoven into all their sacredest feelings and used as a never-failing talisman or amulet to save them out of dilemmas or diseases. It was a bold attempt, and was worked up by himself and his descendants by means of constantly repeated festivals such as had occurred when a prince or noble from the archipelagoes was brought to be buried or the memory of some great man was celebrated. But it failed. It never gave him or his

descendants a tittle of the influence he meant it to give them. And when the professional etchers and reciters of the tablets were carried away to Peru we have the authority of Brother Eyraud, who spent nine months in the island just after, that they were little esteemed by the people. It was the official religion artificially created and artificially kept up.

(15) **ORIGIN, PURPOSE AND SURVIVALS OF THE SCRIPT.** That new tablets were never made by either Hotu Matua or any of his successors or by any of his *maoris* or priest-artists makes it probable that only the meaning of each of the sixty-seven tablets brought to the island and not the significance of the characters was known to anyone who survived the submergence of the archipelagoes. It is true that some of the characters, including that drawn from the figure of the great god, M a k e m a k e , were used as signatures by representatives of the islanders, when G o n z a l e z , in 1771, got them to sign a transfer of possession of the island to Spain, though most of these, especially those like the beaks of birds, may have been from their own tattoos like the signatures of the Maori chiefs to the treaty of W a i t a n g i , acknowledging the suzerainty of Britain. And it is a tradition that after any one of their unending fights the warriors of a clan came to the m a o r i and made him record the number of men each had slain. All this shows that there was some use of conventionalized characters in the life of the actual Easter Islanders up till recent times ; and certain figures are petroglyphed on the rocks and boulders of O r o n g o , chiefly that of M a k e m a k e , whilst that from the *vulva* was cut on boundary stones and on the skull of the dead king, and was tattooed on the skin of both men and women. But these are isolated survivals of the script ; had the significance of all the characters survived, the names and genealogies of the kings would have been engraved in the script on the burial platforms in which they were buried. Not even on the statues of the warriors of the empire or on the platforms built to cover their bones was any record of their names or deeds cut ; and this seems to imply that the script was a priestly secret, not to be used for any but religious purposes or by anyone but the priests themselves in their ceremonies. Even in its inception each character was probably nothing more than an aid to memory, giving the cue to some sentence or idea or even lengthy prayer or hymn or incantation that so brief a form

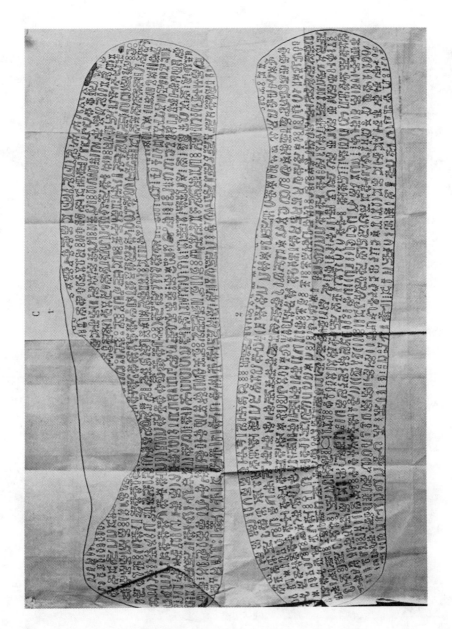

PHOTOGRAPH OF THE SCRIPT ON THE TABLET IN THE MUSEUM OF SANTIAGO, CHILI

PORTRAIT OF A MARQUESAN CHIEF OF THE ISLAND OF TAHUATA. THE TATTOOING ON THE
FACE SUGGESTS SCRIPT; IT IS NOT UNLIKE SHORTHAND

From Hodge's Illustrations of " Cook's Voyages."

could never express. This is probably the explanation of the perpetual repetition of the character that is taken from the figure of M a k e m a k e ; the whole religion centred round the supreme god ; and his form became a sacred and mystic symbol that stirred religious emotions rather than ideas or trains of ideas ; the script is pathographic rather than ideographic.

(16) **THE TABLETS AS STIMULI OF FERTILITY.** The prominence given to the conventionalized *v u l v a* amongst the characters was probably the source of the fertilizing power that, the natives believed, belonged to the tablets ; it is repeated over and over again, and probably stood for a hundred different forms of emotions connected with procreation and fecundity ; this was doubtless the reason why it was tattooed on the young virgin to certify that she was marriageable and on the hands of men to indicate that they were producers, and carved on the rocks and on the boundary stones. It was probably the reason why the tablets, like the king's skull, were cherished as stimulators of fertility, and why so many of them, according to Brother Eyraud, were to be found in every hut ; perhaps the main reason why their recitation was an essential part of every feast, which, usually followed as it was by a period of starvation in every household, naturally brought into the mind of the feasters a longing for increase in the productivity of land and sea. An island that was so far from prolific of the various kinds of food never allowed the idea of reproduction to be long out of the minds of its inhabitants ; and had they had a paradise it would have been one that teemed with all that is edible. Even the prolonged ceremonies at O r o n g o , though primarily established to preserve the sea-birds and the deep sea fish from the improvident voracity of the participants, had as a constant undercurrent and motive the increase of fecundity ; the symbol of it is repeatedly carved on the face of the rocks. Had the tablets not had the procreative passion placed in the forefront of them and not been closely interwoven in all their feastings the great pioneer of the island would have failed to make them an instrument of religion and supremacy, or even to make them survive. Of the sixty-seven that he brought with him to the island, probably taken on his voyage for religious purposes, and probably but a small percentage of those that existed on the archipelagoes, there are only a few extant, two in the

Smithsonian Museum, one in the British Museum and one brought to the Santiago Museum by the Chilian warship *O'Higgins* in 1871 ; one in the San Francisco Academy of Science perished in the great earthquake, and those that Bishop Jaussen had are now in the priory of Braine-le-Comte, to the south of Waterloo in Belgium.   Why the natives failed to reproduce those that remained unburnt after they discovered the value that visitors attached to them is one of the many mysteries of the island.

PHOTOGRAPH OF THE SCRIPT ON THE TABLET IN THE MUSEUM OF SANTIAGO, CHILI

PETROGLYPHS IN RAIATEA, SOCIETY ISLANDS

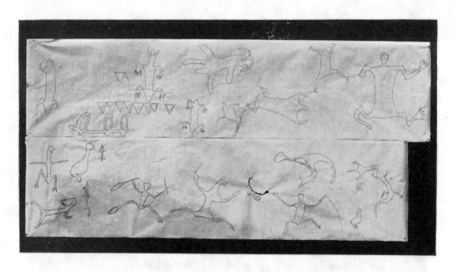

ROCK PAINTINGS FROM SOUTH CANTERBURY (NEW ZEALAND). BOTH THESE HAVE A TOTEMIC ORIGIN AND ARE ON THE WAY TO SCRIPT

From Otago Museum.

CHAPTER XI

THE FISH-AND-BIRD CULT AND TABOO

(1) The great pioneer recognized improvident voracity as the master-passion of the Easter Islanders. (2) They ate out his pig and dog before they could establish themselves, and, if human flesh was the only variation on tubers and fish, they might eat the human species out like " Kilkenny cats " ; the sea-birds and fish were the only bar to that consummation, and if their voracity had free scope it would eat these out, and they would be left to starve. (3) Makemake brought the sea-birds from the remains of the great archipelago to the east ; but he saw they grew fewer and fewer on Easter Island ; the people devoured the eggs. So he placed them on Motunui, which was guarded by a belt of ocean filled with devouring monsters. (4) He was the god of Hotu Matua, who, to prevent the extirpation of deep sea fish, taught the people that they were poisonous till the first egg of the new season's sooty tern had been got, and to preserve the birds he gave them a ceremonial, (5) and bolstered it up with festivals for months, and a competition for another pasteboard kingship, the office of the bird-man of the year. Not till the young were hatched were the eggs to be eaten. (6) So popular did the manufactured amusement become that the sorcerers had to take a hand and predict the winner. (7) It all centred in the great god of the Miru clan, Makemake, a composite god of fish, flesh and fowl. (8) The frigate-bird, the pirate of the air naturally gives him his head. (9) His fish tail probably comes from the shark the pirate of the sea. (10) Whence the mammal body with the long arms ? (11) The Orongo version differs somewhat from the version in the script. (12) It has far longer flippers than a seal ; it is called by the natives n i u h i, *unlike the shark or whale or saurian. Some Easter Islanders encountered it recently near Motunui. (13) A sceptical question about Jonah brought instances of the monster's depredations from authentic and even recent history. (14) Ngaara, the king, tried to stop its depredations in the middle of last century by killing his ten-year old boy. (15) This monster, whether real or fabulous, went to the making of Makemake, and is represented amongst the carvings of Orongo.*

(1) To make a system, religious, political, or social, take root it must appeal to one or more of the master-passions of human nature. In an island that is not fitted to produce more than a bare subsistence the master-passion is that for food ; it is even greater than the sexual, which when Europeans arrived was inordinately developed in Polynesia. The great pioneer and law-giver of Easter Island recognized the secret of possible success and laid himself out to interweave his religion and politics with the overwhelming desire the people of the half-starved islet had for food, once the great source of its supply had subsided. He had brought the seeds or cuttings or suckers of all the usual Polynesian vegetable foods. He had brought the animals, too, that supplied the Polynesian with flesh food, the porcine (*p e p e k u*) and the canine (*p a i h e n g a*) ; but they were eaten up, like after importations of them and like the rabbit in these latter days, by the improvident voracity of the people, before they could establish themselves in the island. The rat was a nocturnal and secretive animal, and escaped destruction better than the rabbit afterwards

did by hiding in the earth, only to be overcome by strangers from the new ships, the European rat and the cat.

(2) **THE SEA-BIRD SUPPLY WAS THREATENED BY THE HUNGER OF THE PEOPLE.** But the rat was insufficient for the animal food of all the people, and it might lead to their annihilation to trust to human flesh too much. In the archipelagoes it is likely that the people, made up largely as they were of immigrants from New Zealand and the Marquesas, were cannibals; but there was the flesh of the pig and the dog to prevent too great a run on that of man. What could he get to supplement the rat and keep the demand for human flesh within the danger point? There were only the sea and the air to search for it; and the sea was not too lavish of supplies, and there were no land-birds to fall back upon. The only thing he could rely on was the sea-birds. What could he do to conserve the supply so that it should not fail them when a drought came and they were on the verge of starvation? He must do everything in his power to check that ravenous appetite, the product of long hunger, and prevent it suicidally swallowing the only chance of its permanent satiation as it did with the *pepeku* and the *paihenga* he had brought them. There was not the smallest likelihood of his curing it of its improvidence, that had been so long and so deeply rooted during the period after the cessation of all supplies from the archipelagoes. It was perfectly clear that they would not stop till the sea-birds followed the pig and the dog into their devouring maw. When the archipelagoes sank, their sea-birds flocked in vast clouds to Easter Island; it looked as if the supply was inexhaustible. Who would have been rash enough to anticipate that all these myriads could disappear? But all the people were gathered round the coasts; for it was there the burial-platforms had been getting erected, and it was there the people were likely to remain near the springs of water on the beach and near the shell-fish and the seaweed, and the patches suited for taro and yam and banana. The cliffs were sure to be the nesting-places of the new-comers, and the nests would be within reach of a people so expert in scaling precipitous rocks as he had to deal with. The favourite haunt of the birds was P o i k e , its high plateau and beetling cliffs, and next to it M a r o t i r i , the rocky islet near it. It turned out as was to be expected. The people took the eggs and fed upon them.

PETROGLYPHS FROM HAWAII, PROBABLY DIRECTIONS FOR TRAVELLERS. AS THEY ARE ON AN ANCIENT HIGHWAY.—*Photograph by Rev. Dr. Baker, of Kona.*

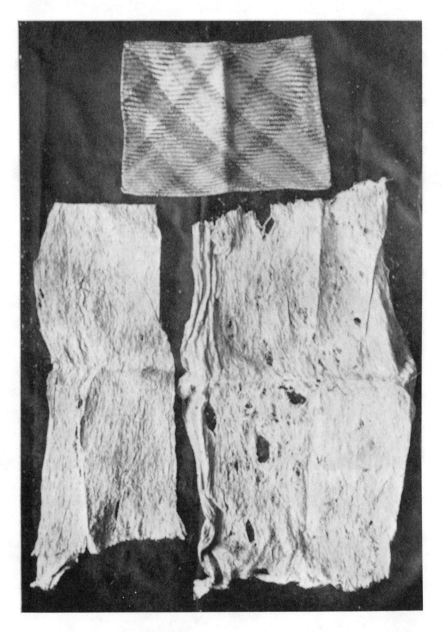

(TOP) A *kete*, OR BASKET WOVEN OF RUSHES FROM RANO KAO ; THE *pora*, OR RAFT, WAS SIMILARLY WOVEN. (BELOW) TWO PIECES OF BARK-CLOTH (*Mahute*) ; THESE WERE GENERALLY POORLY MADE COMPARED WITH THE *tapa* FROM OTHER POLYNESIAN ISLANDS

The result was that the generations of sea-birds died out on the south-east point of the island. And before this the boobies (kena) that gave A n a k e n a its name by their numbers had deserted all the cliffs of the north and west coasts. And now they and their fellows found no nesting-place but the south coast ; only one kind of tern still clung to the unscalable clay cliffs on the south-east side of R a n o R a r a k u ; it was the beautiful little pure-white tern, the k i a - k i a , which now adds the only sign of life to the ancient workshop of the sculptors ; its eggs are too small to be worth the trouble of scaling cliffs to find. And at last even the south coast began to lose its winged life ; the eggs were too tempting a morsel for voracious appetites to be let alone. The last resort was M o t u n u i , and its lesser fellows guarded by a stretch of ocean that was troubled by both south-east winds and north-west winds, and guarded still more by the unscalable precipices that their billows have cut on the seaward side of R a n o K a o .

(3) **MAKEMAKE TAKES A HAND.** This is the meaning of a legend of M a k e m a k e and the sea-birds. He was doubtless buried in the great platform of *Tongariki ;* for the story tells that a famous sorceress, H i t u , had been set to watch his skull in front of the *a h u ;* but she saw it carried away by a wave and swam after it for many days till she arrived at the bird-haunted rocks of M o t u M a t i r o H i v a . There she saw it change into a magnificent prince by the usual fairy-tale process. He had been the king of the realm that is called from a little fish that leaps in the shallow waters of a shore (m a t i r o). His old viceroy, *H a u a* , and his mate, *H o a* , and his own widow, *K e n a t e a* (the white booby), and all their retinue came to meet him, and they welcomed *H i t u*, too, after her long swim of nearly three hundred miles. Now M a k e m a k e had deputed these to watch over sea-birds that nested there ; and he bade them collect a large number of the birds for him, and with them he returned to T o n g a r i k i and let them loose to nest in the cliffs of P o i k e . He watched over them himself and began to see that they grew fewer and fewer in numbers. He guessed that the people had been stealing and eating the eggs. So he gathered them again and tried them on various cliffs of the south coast. But all was of no avail ; the eggs disappeared and the birds would soon have vanished altogether from the

island. So he gathered all that remained and let them fly on M o t u n u i and its sister-islets ; for he noticed that this was the only place in all P i t o t e H e n u a which was protected by the sea and its monsters and the wildest cliffs from the voracity of the islanders.

(4) **TABOO AND CEREMONIAL TO PRESERVE THE FISH AND THE BIRDS.** M a k e m a k e was the god of H o t u M a t u a and his sacred clan, the *M i r u*. And it may be taken for granted that the pioneer of the island saw how one of the main sources of the animal food of its inhabitants was about to be extirpated by their improvident rapacity. He guessed that even those on M o t u n u i would disappear if no measures were taken to protect their eggs from the greed of the natives. So, too, he saw that the deep sea fish, their mainstay from the sea, as the shallow water fish were small and not too plentiful, would vanish as quickly, if they were not protected during their spawning season. To teach them the suicidal effect of their improvidence was useless ; he had tried it before and failed to preserve the animals he had introduced or the birds that his god, *M a k e m a k e*, had introduced. There was nothing for it but to play upon their superstitions and make them afraid or give them a strong social and religious interest in guarding the sure victims of their rapacity. For the deep sea fish he made them believe that they were poisonous, and would kill them if eaten before a fixed date, and that was the time in September when the sooty tern arrived from the warmer north to lay its eggs and hatch its young.

(5) That was the proper date for both birds and fish. But the eggs must not be touched till most of the young were hatched. He thought that to enlist the vanity of the clans amongst whom he had spaced out the coasts would be more effective than to rouse their fears by a taboo. He manufactured an elaborate ceremonial to be accompanied by feasts and dancing and singing extending over many months, so as to prolong the period of inaction as far as the birds were concerned well into the spring. And in order to concentrate their inaction on a purpose and touch their vanity, he invented an imitation king, whose royalty should depend on, and mainly consist of, securing the first egg laid by the sooty terns on their arrival from the north. If he had made it an election of this avian president of an imaginary republic, the clans would

PETROGLYPHS FROM ANEITEUM, THE SOUTHERNMOST OF THE NEW HEBRIDES; MOST OF THEM TOTEMIC
Photograph by Rev. Dr. Gunn.

have been constantly at each other's throats ; even as it was
it was difficult to keep the disappointed clans and the successful
clans from war ; for he made it a competition between the
H o t u i t i alliance and the K o t u u alliance.   They were
rigidly partitioned off in the half subterranean village they
built of slatelike *laminœ* at O r o n g o on the south-western
edge of the crater of R a n o K a o , opposite the bird islands,
and also on *M o t u n u i*, where the watchers awaited the
coming of the first sooty terns.   It kept the thoughts of the
islanders engaged for months, and so secured an interval of
comparative peace.   Almost half the year the whole of the
clans were occupied in this innocent enthusiasm as to who
was to be the new bird-man.   It was an empty honour ; but
it served its purpose.   It kept them all from meddling with
the eggs till the young were hatched ; and then it was only
the unsuccessful federation that indulged in them ; they were
probably all addled ; that was the reason, doubtless, that
they were left severely alone by the victors in the competition.
Not till these latter swam with the first young birds to the
mainland and marched round the island was it lawful for the
defeated to gather and eat the eggs ; they were under taboo
before that, and to break it would have meant death ; the
contents were poison.

(6) **THE SORCERERS WERE BOUND TO SHARE IN SO
POPULAR AN INSTITUTION.**   The competition and ceremonial
had an atmosphere of religion thrown round them.   The
m a o r i s of the various clans were sent up to O r o n g o to
recite the *r o n g o r o n g o* and superintend the singing and
dancing ; it was they probably who carved the sacred symbols
so frequently repeated on the rocks up there ; for they were
the artists as well as the priests and learned men ; they corre-
sponded to the *t o h u n g a s* of other Polynesian groups ; but
over and above this they represented the tradition of the
sculptors on *R a n o R a r a k u ;* hence it was that they had
the image, *H o a h a k a n a n a i a* up at Orongo, in order to
have the sacred symbols carved on its back, the *p u h i*, the
k o m a r i, the *a o*, and the *M a k e m a k e ;* though of
volcanic stone, it was too soft to stand the winter storms in
the open ; all the new carvings would have been obliterated ;
it was therefore placed inside one of the houses.   So important did this competition become and so large a place did
it take in the life of the community that it could not be left

H

as a monopoly to the official priests or *m a o r i s*. Those self-constituted dealers in the occult, the *i v i a t u a s*, had to have a hand in it. They were like the " bookmen " in the modern racing world ; they " spotted " the winner, and had a vision of the member of it that was to succeed and the name he was to assume after his success, the name by which the year was to be known, just as amongst racing men of to-day a year is known by the name of the winner of the Derby. Here they did not show the astuteness that had given them a grip on the superstitious mind of the native ; when so many were predicting the winner only one could be right ; they tried to stave off the discredit of a false prophecy by making it cover

several generations ; if the man named did not succeed it was his son or his grandson that was to be the birdman—a *ruse* that failed to satisfy some. Why these blundering predictions did not discredit not only the *i v i a t u a s* but the *a k u a k u s* who gave them the name of the winner in dream, it is difficult for the modern educated mind to understand. But the belief was too deeply seated to be dislodged by such failures ; in fact, it is not yet dislodged by nearly sixty years of a more advanced religion. The belief in *a k u a k u s* and sorcery is as strong

The usual form that Make-make takes in the Script.

as ever ; it is only that there are no open practitioners that the latter seems under the horizon.

(7) **A COMPOSITE DEITY.** But the connection of religion with this competition that took such a firm hold on the minds of the islanders was not merely external and ceremonial. It revolved round a deity who is sometimes assumed to be supreme, and the creator of all things. His name is M a k e m a k e ; and it is so difficult to find any derivation or cognate for the word even in other Polynesian dialects, that it is almost safe to assume that he was an apotheosized hero of old, probably the founder of the empire, of which Easter Island was " the navel." He was really the special deity of the sacred clan of *H o t u M a t u a*, the *M i r u*. His importance in the bird-and-fish cult brings out clearly how much the great pioneer had to do with its foundation. The figure of M a k e m a k e quite overshadows all the other carvings on the rocks of Orongo ;

STONE HOUSES AT ORONGO FROM WHICH THE " MOHICAN " EXPEDITION TOOK PICTURED SLABS

STONE HOUSES AT ORONGO.   MOST OF THESE HOUSES ARE NOW IN RUINS
Photograph taken on the "Albatross" Expedition of Alexander Agassiz in 1904–5.

it is ten times more numerous than any other figure. It is, of course, very varied in form, sometimes showing more of the bird, sometimes more of the mammal, sometimes bringing the fishtail into greatest prominence by changing the divisions of it into something like human legs. Often it departs completely from the merely animal and becomes almost human. There is generally the suggestion of the human in some part of it or in the attitude.

(8) **THE FRIGATE-BIRD.** What the different elements in it mean it is worth while investigating. The bird head is often most pronounced, and, though sometimes having a straight beak, it has the beak fairly often bent sharply at the point, and swelling into protuberance on the throat below as in the pouched birds. There is little doubt that this is meant for the frigate-bird ; there is no other sea-bird had the combination. The pouch is that of a fishing-bird that travels long distances from its nest, and can accommodate many fish to feed its young. But the beak is not that of a fishing-bird capable of diving rapidly and seizing its prey. It is an instrument of offence, used for getting from other birds what they have caught. Its habit is to haunt where fishing-birds are numerous, and, chasing any one that has evidently been successful in its catch, bully it into vomiting all it has got. As a rule it prefers to go in pairs, sometimes three or four together, so that all the fish that are ejected may be secured in falling before they reach the sea. Its favourite victim is the booby, called the *k e n a* in this island, a large fat bird that can stow away many fish before it returns to its nestlings. Failing this easy prey it will hustle a tropic-bird (t a v a k e) or a sooty tern (m a n u t a r a) into abandoning its fish. It is a regular visitor of Easter Island, haunting especially *M o t u n u i* and *P o i k e* . But it never nests in the island. The nearest land is S a l a - y - G o m e z , almost three hundred miles distant. And it is from that direction I have generally seen them come, somewhat north of east, a huge dark shadow high in the air, making for the south coast ; I have seen six together before a shower. Though S a l a - y - G o m e z is a mere collection of rocks without trees, but bearing low bushes, it must be there it nests ; it is not likely it will fly more than a thousand miles, with its load of fish. The natives regard this pirate of the air with great awe, if not veneration ; it is so powerful in its predatory work that few of the peoples of the

Pacific, with their admiration of the overpowering, but almost worship it. It must have haunted S a l a - y - G o m e z in great numbers when it was the long archipelago that Davis and Wafer saw stretching away towards the tropics ; for then there would be plenty of trees for it to nest in and myriads of diving birds to pirate. It must have been the most common thing in the world for the people of *M o t u M a t i r o H i v a*, when it was above the waters, to see the great bird of prey following its piratical practices, and the most natural thing to count it with its powerful flight and its capacity for plunder almost as a god. Whether they called it *m a k o h e*, like the Easter Islanders of to-day, or *m o k o h e*, like the Mangare-vans or Marquesans, we cannot say ; but they looked up to it with the same awe that the builders of T i a h u a n a c o , the great ruin south of Lake T i t i c a c a , felt towards the condor when they carved him crowned as a king all over their immense monolithic gateway. To the Oceanic peoples the frigate-bird is exactly what the condor is to the people of the high Andes. And yet in the low islands, in the Ellice group and the Paumotus I have seen him domesticated and used as the carrier of messages to other islands. Here the natives can tame the tropic-bird and the m a n u t a r a , but not the *m a k o h e*, probably because, though he is sometimes caught for his feathers, he never nests in Easter Island, so that he is never caught young. That he should go into the composition of M a k e m a k e in M o t u M a t i r o H i v a is exactly what we should expect. Even if he had been manu-factured in Easter Island, this great plunderer of the air was almost certain to have gone to the making of their god of the bird-and-fish cult, especially as he came from a far-off island and remained untameable.

(9) **THE SHARK AND MAKEMAKE.** It is not unlikely that the fish-tail given to Makemake comes from the greater pirate of the sea, the shark. He is looked upon with awe and often with worship in many of the Polynesian groups. In Hawaii victims were often offered to him, as the monarch of the sea and the most formidable marine enemy of man ; yet sometimes a shark was accepted as the friend of a family ; for into it had passed the spirit of some close relative ; and then it was an *a u m a k u a* , the senior and patron of the family. In other groups, especially the south-western, the octopus took its place as the marine source of fear and was sometimes

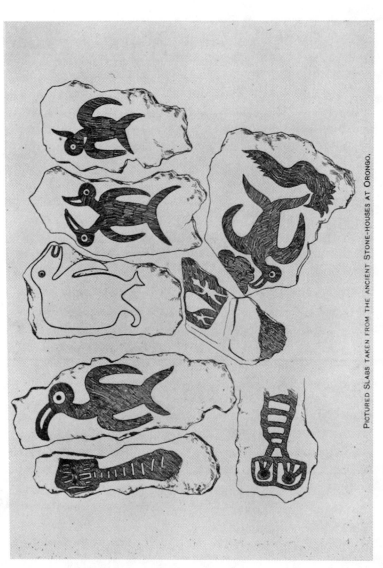

PICTURED SLABS TAKEN FROM THE ANCIENT STONE-HOUSES AT ORONGO.

MAKEMAKE AS REPRESENTED PICTORIALLY AT ORONGO. ONE FORM IS DOUBLE-HEADED, LIKE THE WOODEN IMAGE OF CHAPTER XIV., PAGE 132. TWO HAVE BEEN HIGHLY CONVENTIONALISED. ONE HAS TWO HUMAN FIGURES WITH A PEAR-SHAPED FIGURE BETWEEN. ON ONE SLAB OF A MAKEMAKE IS A SEA ANIMAL WORM-SHAPED. THESE PICTURED SLABS WERE TAKEN BY THE "MOHICAN" PARTY IN 1888 AND ARE NOW IN THE NATIONAL MUSEUM, WASHINGTON.

From Paymaster Thomson's "Smithsonian" article.

accepted as divine. In Easter Island, the natives tell me, the shark is not one of the terrors of the sea ; though it is regarded with awe as the powerful marauder. It is round islands that swarm with fish he is most in evidence, like the *makohe* in the air. The naturalist of the *Blonde*, which discovered M a l d e n I s l a n d in 1825, on its return voyage from H a w a i i , was amazed at the enormous number of fish and sea-birds, and especially frigate-birds, and at the numbers and ferocity of the sharks ; they bit at the oars as the boat pulled to land. So must the shark have been round M o t u M a t i r o H i v a , when its waters swarmed with fish, as the air swarmed with sea-birds and especially frigate-birds. It is not then very far-fetched to think that the fish-tail of Makemake, its great god, should be a shark's.

(10) **MAKEMAKE OF THE SCRIPT AND OF ORONGO IS THE SAME, YET DIFFERENT.** There remains the body to explain. It is clearly that of a mammal with a reminiscence of the human and a tendency to become the human. The prevailing type is not unlike the body of a seal ; and the seal is not infrequently seen on the coasts of Easter Island and is called by the natives *pakia*. But the flippers are longer and more armlike than those of the seals ; they are easily developed in the characters of the script into something meant to simulate a human arm, and in the carvings of Orongo they often become the human arm, whilst the legs which the forked fish-tail has already become in the script tend at times to develop at Orongo into heavy after-limbs, more like those of an animal than human. There is a distinct change in the form of Makemake from the script to the Orongo carvings ; in the former there is more made of the flippers as long arms, some- times with, oftenest without, hands ; they occasionally simulate the hooked beak of the frigate-bird, whilst the hooked beak of the head simulates long flippers, especially when the head is duplicated, or the long ears of the head extended at right angles ; so do the legs generally retain more of the appearance of their original, the forked tail, though occasionally they are represented seated astraddle, or with a male organ in the middle highly developed. Yet the two are fundamentally akin ; it is only the prominence of the fish as the object to be held and offered in the script and the prominence of the egg to be held up in the Orongo carving that leads to the greater differentiation.

(11) **A MONSTER OF THE PRIME.** The body is evidently a modification of the same animal, an animal that has flippers or arms much longer than those of the seal. There is an animal with long arms that is said by the natives to haunt the waters of Easter Island and to indulge in fish and sometimes in man. It is the *n i u h i*, the only sea animal that inspires the Easter Islander with terror. It is not a shark; the Easter Island shark (*mongo*) does not seem to be a man-killer. It is not a whale (*taoraha*); for besides the large mouth that is one of its prominent features it has a large throat capable of swallowing a man and sharp teeth capable of lacerating him. The long upper jaw, projecting beyond the lower, might suggest a saurian of some kind; but it has not the hard scaly back or the short legs of the saurian. When mention of it cropped up I was extremely sceptical, as I had seen no notice of it by any of the visitors to the island, the description of it would tally with nothing I had read or heard of in the natural history of the water, and the natives who reported it were inclined to attribute its vicious, man-eating character to an *a k u a k u*. So I cross-questioned and investigated with a pertinacity that seemed to the reporters to be uncalled-for. I mentioned it to the Europeans who have resided for some time on the island; none of them had heard of it; but they started off questioning their native employees. The result seems to confirm the description of my first informant except in unessential details.

(12) The animal is about thirty feet long and is also very broad even in the head. Its arms are at least four feet long, stretching from the shoulders or below the head; when swimming these are stretched behind the neck; but when in action they are thrust forward towards the prey, which it enfolds with them and draws towards its capacious mouth; the natives call them *r a p e*, whilst its claws or hands they call *k a r a*. It generally swims in pairs and it has a pilot-fish which the natives call *m a m a   n i u h i*, and think, points the prey. My informant had encountered one when out fishing in a boat near Motunui with friends. He had hooked a large *k a h i*, or tunny, and as he drew it in he saw the monster following it with arms outstretched; by the time it reached the surface and was near the boat, it had swallowed the fish and still pushed on. They struck it vigorously on the head with the oars and at last it dived. Again, on the island itself,

ANOTHER VIEW OF THE BIRD-ISLANDS TAKEN FROM THE SEA WITH
THE SMALLER IN THE FOREGROUND

THE BIRD-ISLANDS, THE LARGER MOTUNUI WHERE THE WATCHERS
WAITED FOR THE RETURN OF THE SOOTY TERN. VIEW FROM ORONGO

he and some others saw a *niuhi* approaching; the sun
was behind them and threw their shadows on the water; it
snapped at the shadows and disappeared.

(13) **RIVALS OF JONAH.** Nor are the traditions of the
island without mention of its depredations. When *T u u k -
o i h u*, the co-voyager of H o t u   M a t u a , was about to
celebrate a great feast at his house behind A h u   T e p e u ,
one follower contributed more bananas and sweet potatoes
and sugar-cane than all the rest put together, and, in order
to complete his contribution he went into the sea to get fish.
In diving, a *niuhi* caught him as he was emerging; the
pioneer's attention was called to the incident, and he shouted
out to the monster, "Let my follower alone; he is the most
generous contributor to my feast"; struck with remorse,
the *niuhi*, after having swallowed its victim, disgorged
him. I asked the teller of this tale if he had ever heard of
a prophet called *J o n a h;* his eyes as well as his tongue
confessed ignorance of the name. But he could evidently
detect scepticism in my tone; for he proceeded to give me
later instances of the feats of the *niuhi*. About the
middle of last century a very fat native (a fat native has always
been a striking exception) called M a t a n g a u was fishing
up the west coast near A h u   O h a u , when a *niuhi*
caught and swallowed him; but he had the presence of mind
to pull about its intestines and the agony made the monster
reject him. He was covered with wounds and sores; but,
by careful treatment, he recovered and lived till just before
the Peruvian raid. My sceptical reiteration of the name
J o n a h elicited still more recent instances of the rapacity
of this unheard-of monster. One, N o e , who died only
the other day, was fishing for crabs at A p i n a , not far from
the village, when two *niuhi* tried to get him; he escaped
and got home all trembling and he was a month in bed before
he recovered from the experience. This is minus the Jonah
feature. So was the other that he told of, one *U r i h e h e u;*
he was seated on a stone on the beach of *H a n g a h i o*, a bay
just below M a t a v e r i , when a *niuhi* swam right up and
caught him by the feet and pulled him into the water; but a
second *niuhi* thought he ought to have a share of the prey
and swam in front of the captor in such a way that the victim
escaped, though with his thighs and buttocks all bitten. The
beach was full of people, who helped to pull him out of the water.

(14) A PRIMITIVE CURE FOR THE RAVENING MONSTER.
It seems as if the *n i u h i* grew especially aggressive during
the reign of *N g a a r a* in the middle of last century. It
became quite a common occurrence for men to lose their
lives. Women too were killed ; for example, two went out
opposite the platform of M a h a t u a on the east side to
catch crabs ; they saw one of the monsters swimming towards
them and climbed up on a rock that rose out of the sea. But he
swam round and round till the tide was high enough for him to
seize them by the legs, and both disappeared down his maw. So

frequent did similar incidents become
that at last the king had to take action.
He put his ten year old boy and heir,
R o k o r o k o h e t a u, to sleep and
carried him off to a cave in the centre
of the island ; leaving him there for
a time he visited the A h u O h a u
on the west coast. The people asked
him what had become of the boy. He
answered nothing, but went off to the
cave and cut the throat of the sleeper.
Thereafter the operations of the *n i u h i*
ceased for a time. It shows a singular
lack of common-sense that he could
not invent a less drastic remedy for
the aggressions of the beast than this,
especially as it gave warning by its
stench that it was near ; it stank at
long distance. Perhaps the king was
too sensitive of smell to act P e r s e u s to his Easter Island
A n d r o m e d a s.

An unidentified animal on
one of the painted stones taken
by the *Mohican* party from
one of the Orongo houses. It is
manifestly an attempt to represent the *n i u h i,* whether that
sea mammal is fabulous or real.

(15) THIS MONSTER WENT TO THE MAKING OF MAKEMAKE.
Whatever truth is to be attached to these stories, the natives
believe that a ravening sea-mammal, fabulous or real, is
about in these waters. The natives have caught and killed
young *n i u h i* and can describe its dark blue skin, and
have promised to keep the skeleton of the next they take.
And it is this that has contributed the body with the long
flippers or arms to Makemake. There is a large sea-animal
of similar name in the M a r q u e s a s; but whether it
is the same it is impossible to say. And in Hawaiian *niuhi*
is " a shark of the larger kind." That it was a frequenter

of the waters round M o t u M a t i r o H i v a is to be
expected, and probably in larger numbers than round Easter
Island and its ill-stocked waters. It was doubtless more
feared than any other animal by a water-frequenting race.
And it was most natural that it should be taken as the symbol
of divine power. My reporter here was quite convinced that
its malignity was due to *a k u a k u s;* in fact, he said that
the hero of the last story, *U r i h e h e u* was a *T u p a h o t u*
and it was two M i r u *tatanis,* living above on the volcanic
R a n o K a o, called R a e r a e h u and M a t a m a t a p e a,
who entered into the *n i u h i* and stimulated the attack;
they would never have injured a M i r u. The supernatural
element in this monster was probably more pronounced in
the archipelago more frequented by it. The result is that it
contributes the body and the long arms to the great god
M a k e m a k e. And amongst the carvings on the rocks
of Orongo and the painted slabs taken by the *Mohican* party
from the Orongo houses there is one with fat pig-like body,
mammal head and mouth, long flippers and abortive legs,
that evidently gives the native idea of a *n i u h i*. Hotu
Matua could not have chosen anything more efficient against
the improvidence that was threatening to reduce the deep-sea
food to a minimum than the deity that embodied this great
man-and-fish-eating sea-monster.

CHAPTER XII

(1) The only rival to Makemake was Mahiva or Raraiahopa or Ra, the god of the Tupa-hotu or Longears, who lived in and around the workshop of the sculptors. (2) The defeat of the Longears made Makemake supreme and fulfilled the projects of Hotu Matua ; all the children at every crisis of their lives were entangled in his religion. (3) He probably found the disposal of the navelstring, the bond of the generations, already fixed to be on the top of the pipi hereko, *or solid towers, that have been one of the mysteries of the island. (4) Easter Island agrees with the smaller Polynesian islands in having no secrecy or taboo about preg-nancy or birth. (5) Hotu Matua most entangled their religious faculty by appealing to their appetite for food. (6) All the clans but the Miru were the common people ; only the Miru were* a r i k i; *but the feasts he established were for all. (7) They wore their most fantastic outfit and brought all their food to the feasts ; and they ate to repletion, even if they should starve for weeks. (8) They honoured the dead by letting the living gorge, and all for Make-make. (9) He is the supreme creator, but his making of man out of clay differs seriously from the story in Genesis. (10) He sent the rain when famine threatened. (11) The later legends make him dispense good to those who worshipped him and evil to those who were profane. (12) This is strange, as they believed in no life after death.*

(1) **A RIVAL TO MAKEMAKE WAS RARAIAHOPA.**
Hotu Matua made every endeavour to entangle the religious or superstitious feelings of all the clans in the meshes of his own religion. Every clan had its own god ; but so much were most of them overshadowed by that of the Miru that it is difficult to get the names ; the only one that seems to have escaped oblivion is that of the Tupahotu, the head of the Hotuiti or eastern alliance. When they went to Orongo it was to worship the god of their own clan. One name by which he was known was Hiva or Mahiva, which means the stranger or foreigner. Whether that implies that he was brought in from some other island or that the clan itself was looked upon as immigrants from abroad it is impos-sible to say. Their territory covered the workshop of the sculptors, and Poike, where most of the sculptors had lived ; and Poike was also the home of the Longears, supposed to have been overwhelmed by the Shortears whom Hotu Matua and his descendants represented and led. The sculptors were certainly long-eared, if their employers from the archipelagoes were not so also ; for all the statues (one is doubtful) are long-eared. And the descendants of the Tupahotu seem to keep up their immemorial hostility to those of the *Miru* even though they are all now inter-

married. The attempt to preserve the sacred clan pure by
the taboo of threatened disease is probably the explanation
of this enmity; for the intolerance of special holiness and
the monopoly of sacredness produce intolerance. Whether
it was the defeat of the Longears or the first visits of foreign
ships that was the cause, long-ears were discredited, amongst
the men at least, long before the missionaries arrived. Even
those who lived about R a n o R a r a k u and P o i k e ,
the realm of Longears, seem to have dropped not only the
fashion, but all claim of descent from them. But it is a significant thing in most of the legends and traditional stories,
wherever a wizard is introduced, his home is generally in the
district of the T u p a h o t u . This indicates that some
difference in race or in capacity was recognized in this clan,
by the M i r u at least, if not by the other clans too. The
other name of its god was R a r a i a h o p a , the only name
in Easter Island that seems to suggest any kinship with the
great gods of the other branches of the Polynesian race ; it
looks like an expansion of *R a*, the sun, belonging like
R a n g i and P a p a to the primeval mythology of some
of the groups.

(2) **ORONGO SECURED TO MAKEMAKE ALL THE ENTRANTS
INTO LIFE.** Such tumbling of the gods and the priests
of a defeated race into shadow is not an uncommon
occurrence in the history of primitive religion. It was what
the pioneer of the island and his successors played for in the
game of life. Had the Shortears been annihilated in the ditch
that was prepared for them, M a h i v a or R a r a i a h o p a
would have taken the place of M a k e m a k e in the
ceremonials of Orongo and in the traditions. But once the
Longears were defeated the M i r u had it all their own way
and the religious measures of H o t u M a t u a attained
their aim in making the god he had brought from the archipelagoes supreme amongst all the other clans but T u p a -
h o t u . He made the *maoris* go up to Orongo with the
r o n g o r o n g o to recite or sing and by means of one of the
harder-stone statues to connect the new ritual with the old
arts. And this led to the birdman of the year dancing along
the south coast and playing the hermit under taboo just
below the workshop and front shop-window of the sculptors.
He got all the young men and maidens linked up with the
worship of M a k e m a k e by having them go up to Orongo

and get into the hands of the *maoris,* who began the tattooing of both. The maiden had been secluded before ; but now as child of the bird-ceremonial (p o k i m a n u) she had the circles or spirals tattooed on her buttocks ; whilst the boy, like her, donned the perineal bandage (*h a m i m a m a*) for the first time. Later on, when the two had reached puberty after their long period of seclusion, they were examined by the *maori* to see if they were fit for marriage or for entry into the great-house the *m a o r i s* had for training them to sing and dance at the festivals ; and if the maiden was virgin the *p u h i* was tattooed upon her cheeks, whilst the canoe was tattooed on the cheeks of the youth. This was their " coming out " and then it was that matrimonial choices were made. And when the wife knew she was to have child, she went up to O r o n g o, and the *m a o r i*, stripped to the waist and with the new *t a u r a r e n g a*, or yellow and red cord round it, he painted a similar set of coloured lines round her abdomen. And a record of these rituals was often cut on the statue H o a - h a k a - n a n a i a, which was also painted with red and yellow stripes and hence called T a u r a r e n g a, *t a u r a* meaning not only cord but " make red " and *r e n g a* meaning yellow.

(3) **THE MEANING OF THE STONE TOWERS, SOLID AND HOLLOW.** Thus did H o t u M a t u a interweave the new ritual of the bird-and-fish taboo at Orongo with most of the great happenings in the life of the people he wished to hold in leash. There was one, however, perhaps the most important, that he did not connect with Orongo. It was the first ceremonial in the life of the infant, the cutting and disposal of the navel-string ; that was what bound it to its ancestry, and in an ancestor-worshipping people like the Polynesians it was of as great importance as the final disposal of the bones. In the H a w a i i a n group the navel-string of the child is taken secretly by the parent and plugged into a hole he has made in the face of a precipitous rock, and no one but himself knows the hiding-place. On Easter Island there was not the same secrecy ; but safety was the first consideration ; the navel-string was placed in a gourd and hung or set on the top of one of those solid towers that have formed another of the mysteries of Easter Island. There are two types of circular and high stone erections ; one has an entrance and room below, evidently for the accommodation of a watcher when

FROM DOMENY DE RIENZI'S "OCEANIE"; DESCRIBED AS "ORDINARY HOUSE AND SUBTERRANEAN HOUSE"; BUT THE TOWER WAS PART OF A TURTLE WATCH-HOUSE, USUALLY WITH A LOWER HOUSE ATTACHED; IF SOLID, IT WOULD HAVE BEEN A NAVEL-STRING TOWER. THE SUBTERRANEAN HOUSES ARE REFERRED TO BY FORSTER

he needed shelter; this is the *ana-* or *hare-honu*, the turtle cave or house, intended primarily to be by the shelly beach on Anakena Bay or that on La Perouse, to watch for the rare visit of the turtle when it came to place its eggs in the sand, but later built in other places to observe the approach of the shoals of small fish like the *nua* or the *ature*, that was so necessary as bait for the bigger deep-sea fish. The other type of tower, found not only by the sea but inland, is called *pipi hereko*, and was built solid, and high for the sole purpose of keeping the navel-strings out of the reach of meddling fingers. It shows a certain lack of ingenuity on the part of Easter Islanders when there are so many unscalable and solitary precipices all round the island, and so many caves all over it. It looks as if this institution was in existence before Hotu Matua landed, for in the history of the six fuglemen from M a r a e R e n g a who were sent to spy out the land, it is told that the five who remained after K u u was fatally injured by the flipper of a turtle, each erected a *pipi hereko* in Anakena Bay.

(4) **BIRTH CUSTOMS.** In Easter Island there was not likely to be secrecy in the cutting and disposal of the navel-string. For to this day it is the custom for the neighbours and friends to crowd into the house in which the event is to occur; and not only the husband, but the visitors, assist in the operation. This is a contrast to the custom in most of the larger groups of Polynesia and Micronesia. There the expectant mother is taboo, and a special hut is assigned to her. In Tahiti the parents alone were admitted to this; but if any others had to enter, as, for example, the women who brought food to the mother, they had to doff their clothes before they crossed the threshold. This taboo on the parents was not removed till they went to the *marae*, or temple, and made offerings and prayers, a sheet of bark-cloth being laid for the mother to walk on, not to save her feet, but to save the temple from the pollution that it would suffer from contact with a woman's foot. It may have been different in the smaller groups or islands, as it was also in Tonga, where the whole of a neighbourhood was present at an *accouchement;* for in *Manihiki* the mother went into the street or road to be delivered *coram populo*. Hotu Matua must have known of the Polynesian taboo on the woman about to be delivered of a child; but failed to apply it for purposes of

government in his new realm. Perhaps he thought that by making the pregnant woman go up to *O r o n g o* and get the *t a u r a r e n g a* painted round her waist by the *maori* he would secure a sufficient hall-mark of his religion of Makemake and sufficient sign of proprietorship in the life of the child to come. One universal Polynesian custom this did not secure the abolition of was the shortening of the life of the child either in the womb or immediately on being born and on being discovered to be female. Abortion and infanticide, especially female infanticide, are not unknown even now when the population is reduced to less than three hundred. Doubtless it was the same reason actuated the great pioneer in letting the custom persist as it originated in the fatherland, H a w a i k i—the threat of famine.

(5) **GREAT CANNIBAL FEASTS AT MATAVERI.** What afforded him the finest opportunity for laying the seal of the old empire on the people he had to rule and keep in order was the result of this disproportion between the mouths to be filled and what was to fill them. He saw that the long periods of famine had ended in making the desire of food the ruling motive and eating the greatest of all pleasures. He set himself to cultivate the passion and give it satisfaction in connection with the new rituals and the old celebrations of the empire. The burial platforms were erected to keep the memory of the imperial dead alive ; and at the interment of the bones of any prince or noble in one of them or at any commemoration of a dead hero there had been elaborate ceremonials and feasts ; and for this there was a space reserved on the landward side of the greater *a h u s*, with a paved dancing-place in front of the burial vaults and permanent foundations for the erections that were to house the visitors and feed them. Everything was ready to his hand. There were, at the foot of R a n o K a o, on one rim of which the new ritual was to be celebrated, two or three of the finest platforms and the huge foundation-stones of a great house at M a t a v e r i. He rebuilt the H a r e m o a i, or house of the statue, every year (there have been several well-carved stone statues dug up quite close to it) ; and to it he called together all the leaders of the clans for feasting and entertainment in preparation for the new ritual on the rim of R a n o K a o just above them. And the *pièce de résistance* at the feasts here was human flesh ; whence it came tradition does

not say ; but not far off, just below the village of H a n g a -
r o a , there are the extensive ruins of a platform at which
the connoisseurs in the flesh of men used to meet ; it is called
A h u   P e k e   t e   U a ; whether it means " Follow the
wave " (the sea is quite close) or " Seek the veins " it is
difficult to say ; most Polynesian names may be translated
several ways and are unsafe to draw conclusions from ; but
if *u a* had meant " buttocks " as it is given in some vocabularies of the dialect and were not in that sense a Tahitian
introduction it would have been easy to find an appropriate
meaning for the dining-place of cannibal *gourmets ;* for the
choice pieces in such a banquet were the buttocks and the
heel and palms. Of course, at the H a r e m o a i there was
more than eating at the annual assemblies ; for just below
was the great house of the *m a o r i s* who came up often and
recited and sang the *r o n g o r o n g o* or sacred tablets ;
they brought their trained choruses, who danced as well as
sang. There was no lack of entertainment to engage the
minds of the great men of the clans in the interests of Hotu
Matua and his religion.

(6) **FESTIVALS ALL THE YEAR ROUND.** But he did not
confine his attention to the outstanding men of the clans.
One of the singular things about Easter Island, distinguishing
it from all the rest of Polynesia, is that there was no common
people, as there were no *a r i k i* except in the sacred clan,
the M i r u , which was all *a r i k i.* In Tahiti, for example, there were three distinct classes, the highest the
a r i i, or nobles, below this the *r a a t i r a,* or farmers,
and lowest the *m a n a h u n e,* or common people. In
Easter Island there were no intermediates between the members
of the sacred clan or *a r i k i* and the members of the other
clans ; *k i o,* or slaves, are mentioned ; but this meant only
that a clan defeated in war had to do certain work for the
victorious clan, not that the *k i o* were a permanent class
or caste. The great pioneer had to think of all the other
clans as the common people with whom the influence of
himself and his successors had to be secured, if there was to
be any religious or social order on the island. He must enlist
their ruling passion in the interests of his clan and his religion.
He must not allow the great body of the people to think
that they were neglected when he was arranging feasts and
entertainments. He established the great spring festival of

the *P a i n a*, at which all the people of the island gathered
and feasted, and enjoyed themselves for many days; it passed
in order from tribe to tribe and was always celebrated at
one of the great burial platforms. As a rule someone was
supposed to give it, calling in a *maori* to preside and conduct
it; but all those who came were expected to bring as much
as they could; some brought their whole crop of food, as
even now, and starved thereafter for months. And yet the
chief host had a great figure erected of wickerwork and bark-
cloth with frigate-bird wings or feathers to adorn its head of
human hair, and into this he climbed with *k e t e s* of food,
and through its great mouth he distributed the food amongst
the crowd below; and a division or apportionment is called
in the dialect *p a i n g a*, whence perhaps the name of the
festival. Then the feasting began; and when all was over,
though the figure was supposed to stand for the father or
mother of the man who acted as host, he put ropes round its
neck and catching the ends of these the assembled people
pulled it over with acclamation. It is safe to assume that
the *p a i n a* occurred oftener at some of the great *a h u s*
than once in ten years (ten was probably the number of the
clans); for there is on the landward side of them, close to
the paved court, a paved round hole over which the huge
figure was erected.

(7) Father Eyraud, who remained on the island nine months
in 1864, speaks of the *p a i n a* as a summer festival, whilst
he calls the spring festival m a t a v e r i, "a kind of
c h a m p s d e M a r s" that "lasts two months"; but it
is "knit up with the p a i n a." "On occasion of these
feasts there is an ostentation of luxury; each brings his best.
Then are seen the most extravagant costumes. They paint
themselves with great care, getting a skilled hand to fix the
colour and trace the lines on the face. The women put on
their ear-rings, enormous wheels of bark." "They must
have some kind of hat," "a gourd, a half of a water melon,
a sea-bird whose body they have opened." "Happy those
who can add pieces of iron and other sounding objects";
T o r o m e t i, his patron and would-be proprietor, stirred
boundless applause "by wearing a little bell that the missionary
had brought for ecclesiastical purposes." In the autumn and
winter, seasons of the rains, the feasts take another aspect.
To the *painas* succeed the "*a r e a n t i*"; but, whatever

these may be, no Easter Islander knows the word or its meaning ; and the combination of two consonants, n and t, makes the form an impossibility in Polynesian. These autumn and winter festivals had "no succulent banquets of potatoes!"; the people merely ranged themselves " in two rows and began singing " about any subject that was the topic of the day, such as the smallpox that was sending hundreds into the grave. The time of rains always ruins the sweet potatoes, and there is little or no food to feast upon in these two seasons. It shows the amazing vitality of their love of " fun and feasting " that half of them had been rounded up and carried off to Peru the year before, and in the very year of these repeated festivals they were dying " like flies " with the disease that the few survivors of the raid had brought back with them. But there is this to be said, that, through all their history up to the present day, they never lost an opportunity of a death, even when only reported, to have a feast. This is Polynesian.

(8) There was one festival that repeated itself, if not monthly, at least frequently throughout the year. This was the *k o r o*. There was here a host who gave it in honour of some dead relative and a temporary representation of the departed was erected. A *m a o r i* was called in to conduct it with the young men and women whom he had trained in his *h a r e n u i* to sing and dance. They sang behind the statue and danced in front of it. Though this was said to be in honour of some one dead, he was seldom mentioned, and, as at funeral feasts, the prayers and the offers of food were to M a k e m a k e. The regular formula in both was "*K a t o mo te atua ma Makemake*"; "Take this for the gods with Makemake." They were all religious festivals in their origination, though the religious element practically disappeared in the shadow of the feasting. And they were evidently, even the funeral feasts, arranged, if not founded, by the founder of the M i r u clan; for it was their god Makemake who was honoured. If any religion remained in the almost continuous feasting, it was that which centred round Makemake.

(9) **MAKEMAKE MAKES MAN FROM CLAY.** In fact, Hotu Matua almost succeeded in elevating the god he had brought from Motu Matiro Hiva into a supreme being, overshadowing and ultimately annihilating all other gods, so potent was his appeal through the feasts to the ruling passion of

I

the people. It is more than likely that Christianity has tinged the legends with regard to Makemake. For he is sometimes represented as the maker of all things, even the maker of man, in spite of the composite bestial form that he retains in the ritual of O r o n g o. Yet in the story of his making of man there are many touches that are evidently not taken from Genesis. When he came down from the heavens to H a n g a n u i on the south-east coast of the island he made a hole in a rock, he urinated into it and with the liquid made clay and moulded it without turning it into the man he wished to make ; he moistened it again with the same liquid and moulded it without producing the form he desired ; but by repeating the process a third time and kneading the clay more thoroughly there came out a most beautiful human form, a man. There is no mention of the making of a mate for him, a deficiency that appears in some of the Polynesian stories of the making of man out of clay. And this creation of man from clay by a people that never made earthenware is one of the anomalies of Polynesian cosmology. The only feasible explanation is that the neolithic and megalithic migrations into Polynesia knew of the art of pottery, but as mere men could not persuade the women of the household, constituted as it had been in palæolithic times, to take up this woman's art. Behrens, the writer of the French pamphlet on the Dutch discovery of Easter Island, set afloat the fiction that the people of the island had pottery ; and it was only in 1839 that the log of his admiral, Roggewein, was published, in which it is said that it was inconceivable how the natives cooked their food, having no earthenware. But it was far too late to overtake the lie ; it appears in most anthropological books about the Pacific Ocean. There is clay on the island and the natives sometimes make use of it for teetotums (*m a k o i*) ; but these are only sun-dried and they never made vessels of it.

(10) **MAKEMAKE THE RAINGIVER.** They also believed that Makemake could send rain when there was a drought and their plantations threatened to die. To stave off the menace of famine, they went to the *a r i k i m a u* of the sacred clan whose god was Makemake and asked him to appeal for help. And he sent up one of his *a r i k i p a k a s* to one of the rough cylindrical stone altars on the heights ; and the *M i r u* put a *K a r a k a m a* or white stone and a leaf

of *miritonu* (seaweed) in a *kete* and covered his body
with the leaves of the sandalwood (*naunau*), and he went
up a hill, generally Tuatapu on Punapau (the hat quarry) ;
and he walked round and round, turning his face to the sky
and uttering the prayer to Makemake " E to uka matavai
roa ahiro e Katopa mai " ; (in great fear we pray thee to let
thy tears fall in long swirls of rain upon this place). And
tradition says he kept on thus till the rain came. He planted
the white stone that the earth now blessed should make the
plants to grow, and all over the island he went taking the
bounteous shower with him.

(11) **EVOLUTION OF MAKEMAKE.** It is even said by tradition that Makemake distinguished between the good (i.e. the
religious) and the bad (i.e. the irreligious) in his favours.
One story runs of an Easter Islander called *Pekuan-
gooohu* who refused to sacrifice to the god ; and the god,
lifting him up, took him to his own ancient kingdom, Motu
Matiro Hiva, where he set him the task of looking after the
fish that were left aground by the tide. But another Easter
Islander, a holy man, in his devotion followed the god to his
old realm, and, arriving there, found only *Peku* the profane ; he taught the blasphemer to pray and offer sacrifice,
and, in reply, the god taught *Peku* to make houses and
implements and other useful things, and sent them both back
to Easter Island rejoicing and pious. There is no mention
of *Peku's* being taught to make nets, the special ancient
province of Makemake, or to protect the sea-birds who were
under his care. He was evidently at first the god of a people
who depended largely on fishing and sea-birds, and it was he
who brought the nets and the sea-birds to Easter Island from
his old realm. It was as such a primeval deity that he became
the centre and pivot of the Orongo ritual and taboo. He
had a long way to travel before he became the supreme deity
and the dispenser of good and evil that the later legends
make him.

(12) **NO WORLD OF SPIRITS.** This later development is
very astonishing when we know that the Easter Islanders did
not believe in a world of spirits beyond the grave. When a
man died, his *akuaku* had nowhere to go to even for
annihilation ; it hung about the house a malignant ghost
ready to pounce upon any of its living occupants and do them
harm. I narrowly questioned on this an Easter Islander who

is a devoted son ; he speaks of his dead father not infrequently with a quiver on his lip ; and his still living, though aged, mother he constantly quotes with admiration and affection. After he had repeated again and again his doctrine of the malignity of the *a k u a k u* to the friends who lived I pressed home on him the question whether, when his mother died, who evidently returned all the affection he had for her, her *a k u a k u* would haunt his house and his footsteps to do him injury, to kill him if it could ; the answer came unhesitatingly in the affirmative. It was only from T a h i t i , when those returned who had been working there on the sugar-plantations, that the Polynesian idea of P o , or Hades, came into their thoughts ; it seemed to them no more natural or harmless than the leprosy they also brought back with them. There still remains in their inner nature the feeling that there is no more life beyond the grave than there is in the bones and skulls that they haul so heedlessly from the burial vaults of the platforms. And what there is is not a thing to be desired.

CHAPTER XIII

RELIGION AND SORCERY

(1) Why does Easter Island form the one exception to the Polynesian belief in a world of spirits ? (2) It seems to prove that when the archipelagoes went down there were none but slaves on the island ; for the Polynesians hold that slaves have no souls. (3) There is only a filmy something after death, a fluttering malignant ghost that has but a short career. (4) The sorcerers taught this doctrine and held that the only cure for sickness was to catch and burn the ghost that caused it. (5) The surest cure was to burn down the house of the sick man. (6) The belief in the character and functions of ghosts is full of contradictions. (7) Only the sorcerer had full command of the ghosts, and through the ghosts of the gods. (8) These sorcerers appear in every Polynesian island, or group, as the natural antithesis to the official monopoly of the supernatural by the priests. (9) In Easter Island the i v i a t u a s, or intermediaries between the clan and the gods, belonged to the clans other than the Miru. (10) Now that there are none, the ghosts and the diseases they cause accumulate in spite of the sign of the cross and holy water and medicine. (11) The m a o r i too had medical, especially surgical, duties. (12) But Hotu Matua defeated his own object by spreading the duties too thick upon his m a o r i s. (13) And they willingly abandoned their medical duties to their unofficial rivals, the sorcerers. (14) The maoris had enough to do as troubadours, artists, teachers and priests ; the a h u s were their temples and the feasts their worship. (15) The great pioneer saw that the stomach was the religious faculty, and let the whole Polynesian mythology and cosmology lapse except perhaps the worship of ancestry if we take " m o a i " (the images) to mean " sacred to ancestors."

(1) NO WORLD OF SPIRITS IN EASTER ISLAND. THE SPIRIT DIES. All Polynesians believe in the after life of at least one section of their society. That is as a rule the *a r i k i* or nobles, probably the last conquering immigrants into the fatherland, H a w a i k i. The other classes may have had souls ; but they went to P o, the land of darkness, the underworld, or to H a w a i k i submerged ; they dived into the sea to get to it. The aristocracy went in Tonga and Samoa to B u l o t u, the delightful land of the gods, in Tahiti to *R o h u t u N o a n o a*, as delightful a place in the sky, where every wish was readily gratified. How is it that the Easter Islanders make an exception to this universal belief in another world, a world of spirits beyond the grave ? All who are familiar with the old life before the Peruvian raid and the coming of the missionaries have no hesitation in declaring that there was no such thing as belief in another world ; there was neither a heaven for the aristocrats nor a realm of slow annihilation for the spirits of common people ; there was no life at all after death but that of a poor fluttering malignant ghost, ephemeral and noxious as a stinging, poisonous insect of the night.

121

(2) There must be some natural cause of this striking exception to the spiritual attitude of the Polynesians. Perhaps we may find it in the Polynesian belief that slaves had no souls to live or die after death. If the archipelagoes around Te Pito te Henua had the platforms on it erected to bury their noble dead in and the statues cut to represent them, then the toilers on the island who hauled the huge blocks and the statues must have been subject to their imperial masters as the result of defeat and conquest, and must have been compelled to do whatever their masters required, in other words, were slaves. And as slaves they were certain to have it well ground into them that they had no souls and would vanish when they died.

(3) **BELIEF IN AKUAKUS.** But there must have been something else at the shaping of the belief. For there is a self-contradictory element in it; there is something remains after death that is neither soul nor body, but is immaterial and malignant and evanescent. My chief informant on this point, though an Easter Islander of some education and haracter and of considerable experience of European customs, and modes of thought, had a deep-seated belief in the existence and malignity of those *akuakus*. He told me of a specimen incident in his life as a policeman. He was on his beat one moonlight night, not far from midnight, when he saw the filmy form of a woman in front of him; as he moved she moved, and when he stopped, she stopped. At last he made the sign of the cross on his forehead and breast and she vanished. There were men *tatanis* about too; he made " chot " (church) and put his hands together and they squatted. They were very white; and, as he moved, they moved. He finally looked up to the sky and appealed to " my mamma above, Maria." He was close to his house by this time; he passed in and they did not follow. Next morning he found that one woman had died in the night and two men.

(4) **THE IVIATUAS BURNED THE AKUAKU.** The source of this belief was, we may be sure, the *iviatuas*, or sorcerers, who had grown into great influence outside of Hotu Matua's religious system. They were the real medical men of the community and were called in whenever sickness appeared in any household. The source of all sickness, they laid it down as a general principle, was some *akuaku*, or ghost, who was haunting the house in order to kill its victims.

They were of both sexes and were, the natives now say, all wizards and witches. When one was called in he at once got to business; he left an assistant outside of the house whilst he went in and hung a net over the entrance. It may be said here that the houses had no doors in our sense of the word; the *harepaenga*, or house with stone foundations, closed the low square hole with a net hung from a rod or twig (h a k a r a v a); the poorer houses had three bundles (p a p a e) of dry grass (*mauku*) to do the same duty. It was, therefore, no out-of-the-way proceeding for the *iviatua* to hang up a net over the entrance. But its use was out-of-the-way; it was intended to catch the *akuaku* that was causing all the trouble in the house, a use analogous to the use of the net in Easter Island warfare for catching an enemy who had taken refuge in a house or a cave. The sorcerer fumbled about in the house, especially about the sick man, till he was certain he had secured the ghost in the net; then he called to his assistant outside to light a fire, and he crumpled up the net with the ghost in it, and, going out, threw it all into the fire; thus was the malignant spirit disposed of, and the sick person was supposed to get better; if it were not any deep-seated disease or fatal illness, doubtless faith would go far to secure recovery. If there was no recovery, then it was evident that another *akuaku* had been at work as well as that which had been burned.

(5) **THE MOST SUCCESSFUL BURNED THE HOUSE IN WHICH THE AKUAKU WAS CAUGHT.** Of course, some *iviatuas* had great reputations for their success in catching *akuakus*, whilst others, like one called *Rengaroiroi*, had to go out of business because, it was believed, they never caught any. There was one famous *iviatua* called *Ngavovo*, who lived at La Perouse Bay, the realm of the Miru, though he was a T u p a h o t u whose region was P o i k e and R a n o R a r a k u. He was so skilful that he did not need a net to catch the malignant ghost with. When he was called in he made an earth-oven on one side of the invalid's mat and, telling the people outside to hide and be silent, he promptly caught the *akuaku* and got him into the *umu*. He bade his assistants come and carry the sick man outside, and then he set the house on fire, in order to make quite sure that he had finally disposed of the mischievous ghost. The man got well. This prescription

is not unlike Hoti's of Charles Lamb's essay for making
"cracklings"; his house was burned down when a litter of
pigs happened to be in it; and, tasting the delicious morsel
after the conflagration, he burned down a house every time
he wanted cracklings. But there is more sense in N g a -
v o v o ' s prescription than in Hoti's. For the Easter
Island house is a dark cave into which nothing but bacteria
and insects penetrate ; a good breath of air and some curative
sunlight were sure to be effective. No wonder this sorcerer
gained such a reputation ; for he not only cured the patient
but burnt out the real *a k u a k u s*, the bacteria and the
lice, their hosts that carried the malignity to other houses,
when a death occurred. This practitioner in ghosts was so
efficient that, though a T u p a h o t u , he had not only
M a h i v a , the god of his clan, acting in his service, but
Makemake, the god of the *Miru*, and his assistant, *Haua*. It
is not impossible that the keener *i v i a t u a s* may have had
some inkling of the real cause of sickness ; for after burning
the *a k u a k u* that was the supernatural cause of it, they
often put the bark stripped from banana stems and long
flag-like leaves (r i k u) into the *u m u* and gave the patient
a steam bath and liberally used massage, the favourite remedy
of all Polynesians for most diseases.

(6) **CONTRADICTORY BELIEFS AS TO AKUAKUS.** The
i v i a t u a s , however, not only burned the *a k u a k u s*,
but used them as the medium of their predictions. When
they wished to know the future, as, for example, how a
threatened war would turn out or who was to be the winner
in the first-egg competition, they went into a trance and an
a k u a k u appeared to them in a dream and told them all
they wanted to know. This utilitarian employment of the
most malignant of beings seems irreconcilable with their
malignance and their ephemeral existence. And the informants
who laid such stress on these two characteristics of the shadows
of the dead also volunteered the statement that the only reward
the host of one of the feasts looked for was to be commended
in a dream (*m o e m a t a*) by the ghost of the father or mother
in whose honour he had organized it ; it was useless pointing
out that was not malignity. In fact, it is useless attempting
to reconcile with reason beliefs, in the origination and
making of which reason had no part.

(7) **THE SORCERERS, THE GHOSTS, AND THE GODS.** The

sorcerers seem to have had great influence not merely over
the shadows of the dead, but over the gods with whose mind
these seemed to be in touch. They could command not merely
the gods of their own clan, but those of another clan, and
even the supreme god, Makemake, and ancient gods who had
disappeared under the horizon of Easter Island life. There
were two very ancient and powerful gods called Rapahango
and Kotare, the latter sometimes identified with Makemake.
One informant told how these two had been so endowed with
vitality in recent times that they troubled an ancient relative ;
they took half the food out of her *u m u* and went off laughing to eat it. She had to call in a famous *i v i a t u a* called
K o p u h i   A n g a t a k i ; even then they continued to
speak to her and to laugh. But *K o p u h i* spoke to them
and put them to sleep. The result was that they did not
trouble her more. As a rule it was through the *a k u a k u s*
that the gods spoke or acted ; and they were at the command
of the *i v i a t u a*, acting independently only when they were
on malignity intent, making a relative sick, or interfering
with the success of a fishing expedition, or entering into a
n i u h i to stir it to aggression on men and women. The
mere man or woman who had no reputation as a sorcerer
could neither catch this shadow of the dead nor make it act
with effect on an enemy. He might become a *t a n g a t a
t a k u* and threaten the life of one whom he hated by
prayers and incantations ; but this threat was futile unless
he called in the professional practitioner to his aid. The
latter could threaten with certainty of the threat taking
effect ; for he had consulted the *a k u a k u* and knew.

(8). **THE SORCERY OF POLYNESIA.** These powerful dealers
in the supernatural belong to almost all branches of the
Polynesian race ; it is uncertain whether they originated
in the fatherland as an excrescence on the official priesthood
or sprang up in the various colonies of migrants from the same
elements in human nature. In Easter Island it looks as if
the latter were the case ; for the gods and the religion round
which sorcery clambered were new, having no relationship.
to the fundamental Polynesian Olympus. In Tahiti these
unofficial sorcerers became so influential that even the priests
of the great gods, who conducted the worship of the temples
(*m a r a e s*), and occasionally the chief himself, entered their
ranks and assumed the rôle of inspired representatives of

the gods. They could pass without fear from camp to camp
in war like the priest-king of Easter Island. They were the
arbiters of war, as they could say which side the gods would
favour. Hence they were wooed and caressed by women of
the noblest birth; and when inspired they assumed an
imperious air as if they were the wielders of human destiny.
The priests commanded the most humble obeisance from even
the greatest; but they never elicited the flattery and signs
of fear that these sorcerers did. In New Zealand the
t o h u n g a - m a k u t u professed the same power over the
destinies and lives of men. But they were never men of high
rank or influence; and they turned their powers against
each other; and there even arose a section of them who
practised a kind of anti-sorcery; they used charms and
incantations for the protection of those who were threatened
by sorcerers. These were more like the sorcerers of Easter
Island who were called in to heal people and guard them from
the malignity of the ever-present ghosts. There are, in fact,
in the sorcery of each Polynesian group features that distinguish it from that of the others. But everywhere it has the
appearance of being rather the rival and parasite of the official
cult than its origin or outgrowth.

(9) **THE DERIVATION OF "IVIATUA."** In Easter Island at
least it is not under the wing of the sacred clan. And yet
the name *i v i a t u a* seems to imply that the profession had
some connection with the *a t u a* or older type of gods;
a t u a is the regular Polynesian word for a god and is of
uncertain derivation; it may be the original of *m a t u a*,
the common word in all the Polynesian dialects for a fore-
father or first ancestor, and the same as Maori *w h a t u a*,
ancestor; there are many words in Polynesian that appear
with *m* as the first letter and without it, so that *m* seems to
be a primeval prefix; or it may be connected with the root
t u, strong or powerful. Probably both have influenced
the meaning of the word. It was the usual word in old Easter
Island as in all the Polynesian groups for "a god," but, as
in many, a new religion has tended to give it the sense of
"*devil*," like *a k u a k u*. What *i v i* means is disputable;
the only native sense of it is "*bone*"; and the bone, or permanent framework, or backbone of the gods does not seem to
throw much light on the appropriateness of the word; whilst
the not infrequent Polynesian sense of "*i v i*" as ancestry,

clan, tribe, though given in some vocabularies of the dialect, seems to have been introduced by the missionaries from Mangareva. But there are many compound words in the language that can be derived only by resort to cognate dialects. Whatever be its meaning or derivation, and however much the element " atua " may indicate a connection with the old Polynesian religion, it seems plain that the profession arose in other clans than the Miru, probably as an offset to the assumption by that clan of the monopoly of religion and relationship to the supernatural.

(10) **AKUAKUS STILL ACCUMULATING IN THE ISLAND.** My informant left no doubt as to their belief that, when a man or woman died, the *a k u a k u* still proceeded to cause sickness and ultimately death in the household or some related or neighbouring household. They acknowledged that there were now no *i v i a t u a s* to catch this shadow of the dead and burn it, in fact, had been none since the missionaries came. I asked them what substitute there was for those old shadow-catchers ; they said there was the sign of the cross and holy water, and the appeal to " Maria," and, as a last resort, medicine. But, when pressed, they acknowledged that these only frightened and checked the *akuakus* and did not destroy them. I suggested that the island must have in this half century or more got over-populated with these malignant immaterialities. They could not dispute the suggestion and rather seemed to think it proven by the fact that they had never been free from sickness since the profession had ceased to exist and that disease in the village was on the increase instead of the decrease.

(11) **MEDICAL DUTIES OF THE MAORIS.** Whatever their attitude to the Miru may have been, the *i v i a t u a s* seem to have had no quarrel with the *m a o r i s*. This may have been due to the fact that these latter were not confined to the sacred clan. Hotu Matua showed his wisdom in selecting the official conservators of the great and imperial past and official performers of the rites and ceremonials of the religion from all the clans and not from the Miru, his own clan, alone. He probably thought that this would prevent the rise of rivals to his priesthood. Whether they arose in his day or not till his power had passed into the weaker hands of his descendants, is not clear from the traditions. But rise the unofficial profession did, and to such influence that it

threatened that of the *m a o r i s*. It is not unlikely that
he staved off the evil day by giving the *m a o r i s* as one
of their duties the care of the health of the people. The
profession that superintended the feasts and amusements of
the people was the natural protector of their bodies from the
assaults of disease or wounds. And we hear of their being
called in as physicians or surgeons. One aged resident in the
village remembers the case of a man who had been seriously
wounded in a fight ; he had been pierced by several spears,
yet lived to be carried to his home. A *maori* was called in
and opening the abdomen took out a large *m a t a a*, or
spearhead ; he sewed up the aperture again and went off.
But the man still suffered great pain. Another *maori* was
called in and he opened the intestines and found a small
m a t a a. He sewed the wounds up and gave the patient a
banana to eat. This carried off all the *débris* of the spearheads
and the operations ; and the man recovered rapidly.

(12) **THE "POOH BAS" OF EASTER ISLAND.** But it was
plain that the great pioneer had overloaded the profession.
They had to etch copies of the old ritual and genealogies and
traditions on new boards and show these every year to the
king at a great review. They had to keep reciting these so
that at the annual festival they should be letter-perfect.
When a war or battle occurred the warriors came to them and
told them of all the men they had killed, and they had to put
the number of all the victims (i k a) in permanent record,
so that they should go down to posterity, when they were
recited at the festivals. They had to carry the tablets and
the sacred clubs (*a o* and *u a*) into the battle with the
warriors. They were the professional troubadours of the
island. Thus they had to do what was assigned to a profession
in Tahiti, the *h a r e p o*, as their whole duty ; these
" runners in the night " had to remember every word of the
traditions ; and had to keep reciting in the night at the temples
in order to have perfect remembrance of them. The *maoris*
had to arrange and conduct all the festivals of the island ; and
tradition as well as present practice seems to make these almost
continuous throughout the year. They managed and conducted all the singing and dancing. And thus one section of
their duties covered all that a special freemasonry guild had
to perform in the Society Islands ; that singular brotherhood,
the *A r e o i*, went from island to island reciting and singing

the stories of the gods and heroes, or representing them in dramatic form ; they were a religious body and their religion was overshadowed by their feasting and entertainment. The *m a o r i s* were also the teachers of the community ; they picked out the young men who were to be their understudies and taught them how to etch the tablets as well as giving them verbally all that the tablets contained or suggested. They had also great houses (h a r e n u i) or colleges where they kept and taught those pure young men and women, who had shown themselves competent, the songs and dances for the festivals. It was they who did all the tattooing, a work of long and patient artistic skill, generally assigned in the larger groups to a special profession ; for where the whole body was covered with a permanent picture-gallery, as in the Marquesas, New Zealand, and Easter Island, the process in the case of each individual must have been extended over many years and the skill of the artist must have been exact as well as fine. When there were thousands on the island and all had to have the work of many years printed on their skin, the wonder is that any set of men could get through all. They were really the successors of the old sculptors and architects in all artistic work and had doubtless much to do with the conservation of the larger *a h u s* and the planning of any that may have been erected in times succeeding the great breach in the development and tradition. They were doubtless grieved to see the havoc of the later internecine wars ; but with their hands so full they were helpless in trying to prevent it.

(13) **MEDICINE HAD TO PASS INTO THE HANDS OF THE IVIATUAS**. When there was added to their duties that of medical superintendence and even surgical operations, we may be certain that something was neglected ; especially as the new bird-and-fish ritual of Orongo was placed under their care. The duties of these last two departments of their work would have been enough for two professions. It was not likely that they would give up what was to enshrine the ancient religion of Motu Matiro Hiva in the new ritual that was to economize the sea-birds and the deep-sea fish, and to occupy the minds of the people for a large part of the year with the competition for the honour of being bird-man and giving the name to the year. It was of the utmost importance that the deity of the empire, Makemake, should be ruler of the mind of the

island, and that the learned men of all the clans should be occupied in the duties of his new ritual. It was inevitable therefore
that the medical work should pass into the hands of another
profession without any protest on the part of the *m a o r i s.*
And the *i v i a t u a s* had probably already become a feature
of the community from the necessity of prediction, a necessity
that arises in primitive as well as advanced societies. They
were ready to take up the duties and naturally found an easy
solution of their new difficulties and a general principle for
all cases in the supernatural; the *a k u a k u* was a surer
card to play in every disease, and to catch it was the universal
prescription and panacea. They had found the blessed word
that every community, or section of a community, every
generation and profession must have to eke out its knowledge
when that knowledge fails. They had no acknowledged or
official position ; none the less did they take possession of
that "no-man's land" of the human mind which is so fertile
in faiths and superstitions.

(14) **RELIGION AND THE STOMACH IN EASTER ISLAND.**
And what was left for the *m a o r i s,* the real priests of
the community, though sacredness was monopolized by one
clan ? There was the whole sphere of history (they were
the story-tellers of the community), of art, of education,
and, most of all, of religion. And in what did the religion
consist, if we put aside the new Orongo cult ? In all the other
Polynesian groups, especially the larger, there were always
sacred places where the great gods were worshipped ; where
were the sacred places of the Easter Islanders ? Roggewein's
party seemed to see worship going on before the great statues
and fire on altars in front of the platforms. No voyagers
after that have been able to confirm this observation. It is
generally agreed that the statues were not gods and the
a h u s not temples or sacred places where worship went on.
The first missionary, Eyraud, says, " Religion seems to occupy
the most insignificant place in their lives. I have never been
able to notice any act truly religious." The little wooden
figures he saw in every hovel ought to have been idols, he
thinks ; but he has never seen the natives render any kind of
honour to them. Nor did he see any religious rites in relation to
death. Of course, he did not go to Orongo. He failed to realize
that the feasts he saw, the " *Mataveri,*" the *paina,* and the others
that followed in an almost continuous series were religious.

(15) It is these feasts that constituted their worship ; even to this day they are far more concerned as to what they shall eat than as to what they shall believe or whom they shall worship. Hotu Matua thoroughly realized that the religious faculty of Easter Island lies in the stomach. The Polynesians, like the early Indo-Europeans, show in their language that the abdomen is the realm of thought as well as of emotion. The Easter Islanders put the belief into practical form. To fill the stomach of the living was to them the surest way, if not the only way, to honour the dead and to worship the gods. And the old Polynesian gods were to them non-existent ; they had forgotten or let lapse all knowledge or mention of the occupants of the Polynesian Olympus, Tane, Tangaroa, Rongo, Rangi, Papa, Tu, Maui. The nearest they come to a reminiscence of the great mythology of Polynesia is in a prayer for rain which addresses a god of the sky called H i r o , probably the W h i r o who did such wonders as a voyager in the Society group, and in a legend of a king, T a n g a r o a , who swims from a distant land to the island. The whole religious and mythological atmosphere of Easter Island is on a lower plane than that of any other island in Polynesia. The cosmology is still lower. And yet the cyclopean works of sepulture on it seem to imply an effort to immortalize, if not deify, ancestry, the basis of most elements of Polynesian religion. The names and words of the dialect have often to find derivation in other Polynesian dialects ; the name for the statues (m o a i) has not found any satisfactory etymology ; perhaps the Eastern Polynesian word " *moa* " " sacred " and the common Polynesian root *i* for " ancestry," the basis of " *i v i*," might furnish explanation of their purpose " sacred to ancestors."

CHAPTER XIV

THE MARIONETTES

(1) *The Easter Islanders of to-day are perfectly callous about the* a h u s *and images.* (2) *It is not the cyclopean stones they have used to get advantages from the supernatural or the natural, but a stone shaped by nature to imitate what they want more of.* (3) *In the use of these charm-stones and mascots they are Melanesian; but so are the cultivated Europeans of the twentieth century, who believe in the omnipotence of charms and mascots.* (4) *But they also believed in what was shaped by the hand of man, especially in wooden composites like the lizard-headed human body that guarded the porch and scared trespassers.* (5) *There is no fear of the two small indigenous lizards; nor is there anything in the legends or mythology, as there is in New Zealand, to account for the dread of such fabulous monsters.* (6) *Stone was preferred to wood for images and memorial purposes, and in this Easter Island differs from New Zealand and most of Polynesia, probably because there were no forest trees on the island and plenty of soft breccia; but in the archipelagoes around there must have been great forests to supply the great levers and beams and great double canoes.* (7) *But there is a decided break in the cyclopean stone record when Hotu Matua's expedition arrives.* (8) *When Tuukoihu resumed the Polynesian record of wood-carving he had scant material to deal with, and had to make his statues subhuman instead of, like the stone images, superhuman.* (9) *He had two palaces, one on the south coast and one on the west coast.* (10) *Returning from the latter he had the good luck in the twilight to come across the idea he wanted to express the no-longer-living as the gigantism of the stone images had done, two figures asleep on the road so famished as to show the ribs; he at once carved the first skeleton image that was in wood to memorialize the dead.* (11) *A nightmare of two female* t a t a n i s *scared him into making the little images female as well as male and even both together.* (12) *But the skin-and-bone images brought only frowns to the faces of his subjects, reminding them of nothing but famine and death. He would make them laugh and be cheerful; so he made them dance and gesticulate till the humans laughed to see wood ape flesh.* (13) *The aquiline nose was a laugh at his own feature (his name means " nosy ") and the goatee was the favourite beard of Easter Islanders.* (14) (15) *and* (16) *The only kinship to be found in Polynesia for the dancing images or marionettes is in New Zealand, and amongst its blond forest-haunting aborigines, and in the Hawaiian islands; but the latter are clothed.*

(1) SORCERY PREFERS PEBBLES TO CYCLOPEAN STONES.

One of the singular things about Easter Island sorcery is that it is unconnected with any of the carved stones. After all the boundless labour and striking primitive art spent on the burial platforms and the images it is somewhat surprising to find that no use was made of them to appease the hostile and often destructive forces of Nature, or to get concessions or blessings from the gods or the dead. In Rarotonga and Tahiti and the Marquesas such magnificent burial-places could not help becoming altars or temples. There is to this day a callousness in Easter Islanders about these memorials of the dead, who are supposed to have been ancestors of the living, that is in strange contrast to the tendency to ancestor-worship amongst the Polynesians. An Easter Islander will gleefully haul the skulls and bones out of the vaults of an *ahu* in which

A STONE HUT AT ORONGO DILAPIDATED AS MOST OF THEM NOW ARE

ENTRANCE TO BURIAL VAULT UNDER AN AHU

he has just boasted that his ancestors, even immediate ancestors, have been buried. If I had liked I could have filled a good-sized ship with skulls from Easter Island; but my knowledge of the artificiality of the Polynesian skull repressed the desire. There must be a hiatus in the ancestral line that connects the dead whose huge statues adorned the platforms with the Easter Islanders who begin their history with Hotu Matua.

(2) Neither *maori* nor *iviatua* made any attempt to take advantage of the sepulchral magnificence of their island to work miracles or even to link it up with the supernatural. The imagination of the islanders has never been touched by the wonders and mysteries of their speck of earth as that of scientific and quasi-scientific Europe has been since its discovery. What sorcery resorts to in order to work a point over not only the supernatural but the natural is not these unexplained cyclopean works, or even any stone carved by the hand of man, but any obscure pebble or boulder that the "prentice hand" of nature has tried to mould into imitation of something else. If a rounded stone has taken on even the most distant suggestion of the head or mouth of a fish, then it is hung up in the fishing-canoe and is expected to bring a miraculous draught of fishes. If a boulder looks like a swollen abdomen or *vulva*, then it is recognized as the one thing that, if put on the beach, will draw shoals of flying fish into the surf. If a pebble lengthens out like a banana, it becomes a *m a e a m a i k a* that placed in a banana hole or circle will make the trees bear prodigiously. And when an *a r i k i p a k a* was sent up into the hills to pray for rain in order that the crops might not wither or die, he took up a white pebble to plant so that the earth might be encouraged to produce tubers abundantly.

(3) This is one of the most primitive forms of sorcery, even more primitive than catching an *a k u a k u* in a net and burning it, or getting hold of a wandering soul and jamming it back into the body, beginning at the big toe-nail, like the Hawaiian sorcerer. It is exactly at the same stage of development of the reasoning powers as the use of the *m a n a* stone in the Solomon Islands for increasing the coco-nut crops. In fact, this is the one feature of Easter Island culture that has most kinship with the Melanesian. But the anthropologist of a few thousand years hence who is investigating the curiosities

K

of folklore he will find in the Europe of the twentieth century
will be surprised to see such an array of mascots and talismans
in his museums from an ancient age that left such marvellous
ruins of great edifices. If he still continues to study Melanesia,
he will be certain to find a strong Melanesian affinity, if not
a Melanesian substratum, in the people that trusted these
m a n a objects for the bringing of all that was good.

(4) **THE WOODEN LIZARDS.** Though these natural stone
imitations of other objects formed the largest department of
their armoury for the conquest of the immaterial, they were
not all their sorcery ammunition. They trusted more to the
shaping hand of nature than their modern brethren, the
believers in the cult of the mascot ; yet they were not afraid
to include in their armour or weapons of offence, when they
advanced into the realm of the intangible, objects shaped by
the hand of man. Their doors were protected by a stone
at times artificially, oftener naturally, simulating a human
face or other form under the sill or one of the posts. But by
far the most efficient protection for the house of at least
the less poverty-stricken, was the four wooden lizards
(*m a n u u r u*) that stood in pairs on either side of the porch
of the *h a r e p a e n g a* or stone-foundationed house. They
were about four feet long, a foot longer than the lizard-headed
wooden clubs used in warfare and dancing, and they housed
each an *a k u a k u,* an immaterial being of some sort.
Whether the war-weapon had this indwelling spirit or not it
was intended to terrify by its very appearance. So there was
no such efficient watchdog for a house as those four wooden
lizards ; Easter Islanders, especially women and children,
shivered with terror before them. There are only two small
lizards indigenous to the island, one about the length of the
forefinger (*e h u e h u*) and another twice as long (*u r u u r u -
k a h u*), harmless and unfeared by the natives. What gives
the terrifying power to their wooden brethren is their composite
character ; they have with the lizard head a human body.
It seems to be the combination of different animal elements,
especially if the human is introduced, that expresses the
Easter Island idea of the supernatural.

(5) **COMPOSITE MONSTERS IN POLYNESIA.** And here we
have another intimate affinity with New Zealand. On the
carved bargeboards and lintels of the Maori large houses
and storehouses it is the combination animal form that is

A SANTIAGO COMPOSITE OF LIZARD AND HUMAN FORGUARDING THE PORCH; DESCRIBED
BY DR. AURELIANO OYARZUN, DIRECTOR OF THE SANTIAGO ETHNOLOGICAL MUSEUM, AS
COMING FROM EASTER ISLAND

one of the most striking features. So frequent is the recurrence of the *m a n a i a* in these masterpieces of the wood-sculptor that the word is sometimes used for ornamental carved work ; and so frequently has it lizard elements, especially a lizard head, that it has come to be applied to the lizard, and as a combination form so like is it to the sea-horse that the word is applied to the hippocampus. But behind the Maori awe of lizard combinations there is a far-back mythological basis such as there is not in Easter Island. There is nothing here equivalent to the lizard-gods of New Zealand to justify the dread that the natives had for a stake that had a lizard-head carved on a human body. The Maoris not merely feared the immaterial lizard as the source of internal disorders, as the Easter Islanders feared the *a k u a k u* of people recently dead ; but the *t a n i w h a s*, or combination monsters whom their heroes did deeds of might to subdue, had something of the lizard in them, and they had many gods or demons in lizard form, some masculine like *M o k o n u i*, others feminine like *N g a r a r a - h u a r a u*. The lizards of New Zealand are no more formidable than those of Easter Island, though one of them, the *t u a t a r a*, is a foot or more in length. Their fear of them goes back to the fatherland, Hawaiki, and monstrous lizards are reported by their legends to have followed them to their new land. Yet it is possible that the saurian forms found in some of the rocks of New Zealand may have given shape to their terror of the monstrous and the supernatural. For in a new type of carved lintel recently found, differing entirely from the known Maori styles of wood-carving, the delicate wings held out by the squat central human figure suggest the skeleton of such a monster of the prime laid bare by some rock fissure. But that the idea of lizard monsters goes back to the traditions of the fatherland is evident from the importance that it attains in other Polynesian groups. Samoa and Tonga give a reptilian tail to *H i k u l e o*, the ruling deity of their paradise, B u l o t u, probably the origin of that of the great Fijian god, N d e n g e i. In Mangaian mythology lizards appear. But it is in Hawaii they attain as terrifying forms as in New Zealand, living as they did like the Maori t a n i w h a s, both in the earth and in the water. And there seems an affinity between the fact that Hawaiian chiefesses especially feared them and the special mention of women as fearing the wooden lizards of Easter Island.

(6) **WHY WAS STONE PREFERRED TO WOOD?** What makes
the *m o k o - m i r o* especially significant is that it is of
wood, a medium that the architects of the platforms and
the sculptors of the images do not seem to have considered
as of importance from either an artistic or a religious point
of view. The Maoris of New Zealand, with the great forests
at their command, considered timber as the proper material,
not only for their canoes and houses, but for their carved work
and their sepulchral memorials, though they occasionally
erected forts and even religious memorials of stone. The
Hawaiians and the Tahitians, though they built their open-air
temples (*h e i a u s* and *m a r a e s*) of stone, furnished them
generally with gods of wood. And the Marquesans though
preferring stone, and that cyclopean stone, for their *m a r a e s*
and even for the statues that were to be built into their altars,
carved wooden images to set on them. Perhaps the reason
the megalithic builders and carvers of Easter Island did not
choose wood was the absence of the thick-boled trees ; the
m i r o (sophora) and the *n a u n a u* (bastard sandalwood),
the only two trees that ever grew on it of old, never grew
higher than twenty feet and are at the best but slender-
stemmed. But we hear of Hotu Matua coming to the island
in huge canoes ; native tradition has titanized them into a
mile long, just as B e h r e n s , the historiographer of
Roggewein's discovery turned the natives into giants between
whose legs his marines could walk erect ; and we hear of
T u u k o i h u , Hotu's lieutenant, building a double canoe
on the island. And the great levers (*a k a u e*) fifteen feet
long and proportionately thick and the immense beams of
the aerial ropeway needed to fill the huge holes cut in the rim
of R a n o R a r a k u are evidence that tradition recognizes
timber far greater than could ever have been grown on the
island. Again, perhaps it may have been the comparative
softness of the *b r e c c i a* of Rano Raraku that drew the
carvers away from wood as the medium of their art ; were
it not for the pebbles, large and small, that bind it together
and keep it from mouldering away, it is as easy to cut as
steatite. But, when they had the features of the face and the
long fingers to cut, wood would have been far easier to carve
and far more durable than the material they chose. And it
is manifest that the great levers and beams which must have
come from the archipelagoes around indicate ancient forests

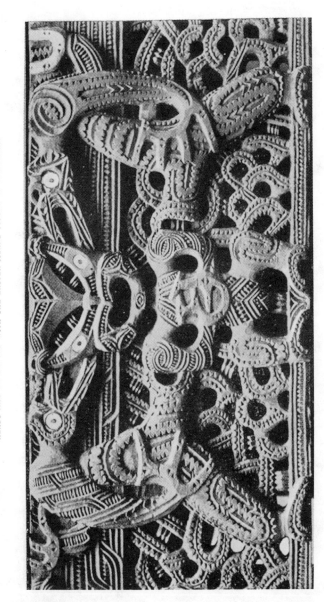

CARVED BOARD FROM THE FRONT OF A FOOD-STORE IN THE AUCKLAND MUSEUM. THE COMPOSITE MONSTERS WITH BIRD-HEADS MAY BE RANGED WITH THE EASTER ISLAND FIGURE OF *Makemake*.

A PART OF THE FRONT OF A MAORI CARVED HOUSE, WITH CARVED COMPOSITE MONSTERS

in them, capable of supplying timbers for huge double canoes. Though there is a tradition that Hotu Matua brought in his craft a stone which he cut into three, there is evident in the clients of the *a h u s* and the images a distinct preference for stone for the purposes of memorial art and a depreciation of wood as being a merely utilitarian medium. This may have arisen from the abundance of great timber in the old forests of the archipelagoes.

(7) **THE THREAD OF CYCLOPEAN CULTURE IS SUDDENLY BROKEN.** There is also evident in the history of the island a clear breach with the past of megalithic culture. All work in the sculptors' workshop suddenly ceases ; the huge images that are being dragged miles over the exceptionally rough surface of the island are as suddenly abandoned far short of the platforms they were intended to adorn ; any later sepulchral memorials are shapeless heaps of loose stones gathered from the surrounding flats or slopes, or roughly shaped so as to rise to a point or to imitate a European boat, the meaning of *p o e p o e* not being canoe, but boat. All the stone carving that is done on the island thereafter is the petroglyphic, such as is found at Orongo or on the boundary stones, or on the fallen images, or the softer blocks of their platforms, or on their still softer hats. The great timbers already brought to the island in the shape of double canoe or titanic lever, or canoe-sledge to haul the statues in so as to preserve their features and surfaces intact were a godsend to the isolated people and enabled *T u u k o i h u* to build a large double canoe on it and to erect high timber super-structures on the cyclopean foundation-stones tooled by the builders of the burial platforms.

(8) **THE GENESIS OF THE RIBBED WOODEN IMAGES.** But it enabled him to do more, to resume the tradition of Poly-nesian wood-carving which the unlimited resources of Easter Island in the way of stone material had broken. He had to use what was to hand till the young *m i r o s*, which they had brought with them from abroad and planted, had grown into trees. But he had not such wealth of material as his predecessors, the stone sculptors, had had to deal with ; he could not, he dared not, make his carvings rival the size of the images on the *a h u s ;* nay he had not timber enough to make anything he carved attain the size of their originals and models. If they were to be in human form then they

must be cut subhuman and not superhuman in size. What they lacked in quantity they must make up in quality; the details must be more realistic and striking than the great statues on the platforms. If he was to get the most out of his material he must make the portrait memorials of the dead more human in the face, whilst bringing out their immaterial nature in some special feature. They had become *a k u a k u s ;* he must ensure their recognition as no longer of this life, just as his predecessors secured it by making their images titanic.

(9) **THE LEGEND OF TUUKOIHU AND HIS PALACES.** That is perhaps the natural genesis of the *moaimiro,* the little wooden images of Easter Island, which are as peculiar for their dwarfness as the Rano Raraku statues are for their gigantism. But tradition was busy ages ago with their origin and has recorded it in a legend. The great ruler, *Tuukoihu,* had two palatial residences, one on each of the two sides of the Easter Island triangle, which his chief, Hotu Matua, had not made his own ; they had landed on the northern side, which possessed the only protected cove in Anakena Bay and the only two shell-sand beaches, Anakena and La Perouse, on the coasts. The second in command naturally took the more precipitous coasts, the west and the south. About the middle of the west coast, behind the great platform of *A h u T e p e u,* he had plenty of cyclopean foundation-stones which the builders of the *a h u* had tooled for the residences of those who came to bury the dead or to celebrate their memory. Here he erected his largest palace, with a splendid round house for his cooking and many lesser houses for his retinue. About the middle of the south-coast, inland from the magnificent platform of Hangahahave, he chose the outcrop of a high volcanic dyke, that had weathered and broken up into its constituent crystals only in its lower part, for his other palace ; he built up the solid wall of the rock with a stone wall so as to support the house placed above it, and set in his huge foundation-stones on the flat ; whilst he set other and lesser stones for subsidiary buildings, the most important of which was to be the house for his earth-oven (*u m u*) and cooks. Tuukoihu must have been himself a *b o n v i v a n t,* however much the people might suffer from famine, he made such a prominent feature of the cook-house in both of his palaces. And the name of his south coast palace has been handed down by tradition as *H a r e k o k a,* the house of the cockroach,

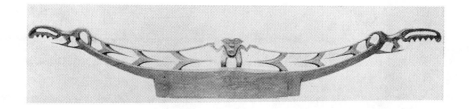

AN ANCIENT LINTEL FOUND RECENTLY IN THE AWANUI SWAMP, NORTH OF AUCKLAND, NOW IN THE
AUCKLAND MUSEUM. THE CARVING IS QUITE UNLIKE THE USUAL MAORI STYLE

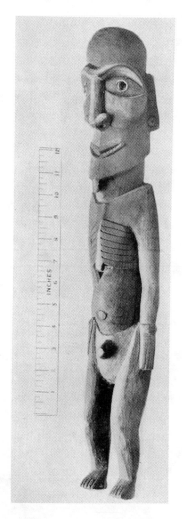

A RECENTLY CARVED *moaimiro* PROCURED
BY THE AUTHOR IN EASTER ISLAND IN 1922

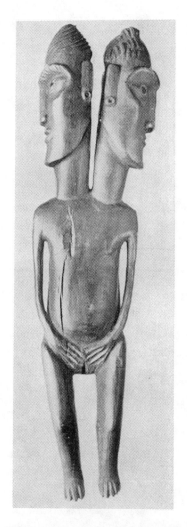

DOUBLE-HEADED FEMALE *moaimiro* BROUGHT
BY THE REV. EVERARD ROE, CHAPLAIN OF THE
CRUISER " FLORA " FROM EASTER ISLAND IN
1906 AND PRESENTED TO THE AUTHOR

though the native words for cockroach are *n g a r a r a* and *p o t u p o t u* .

(10) **THE MAKING OF THE FIRST RIBBED IMAGE.** He had doubtless duties on both coasts as governor. And one evening, as he was returning from the west coast, he came across a sight that made him pause and laugh. There in the middle of the road lay asleep two beings in human form but reduced to skin and bone. He took a good look and began to resume his way when a great shout from a neighbouring hill, P u n a p a u , the hill whence the red hats of the statues had come, startled him for a moment. But with his usual clear intelligence he took in the situation and regained his self-control. The shout was intended to waken the sleeping skeletons, and did awaken them ; for it carried to their ears the warning that a stranger had been inspecting their uncovered ribs. He was alone and saw that he would be at the mercy of these enraged aborigines who had been driven into the mountains by the new-comers and then driven frantic by famine. He saw the skeletons resume their *m a h u t e* mantles and make for him, rage on their faces. He calmly went on as if nothing had happened, and, as there is practically no twilight in Easter Island, darkness fell and concealed any feelings on his face that might betray his guilt. They stopped him and asked, " Did you see our nakedness ? " But like a man of the world and an Easter Islander he sturdily denied the charge and went on. They were not too sure of his word and were afraid that he would make them the laughing-stock of the island. So they followed him to *Hare Koka* and hung about the place for several days and nights. But they never heard him utter a word about the sight he had seen ; they never heard either him or the people he spoke to laugh. At last they came to the conclusion that *M o a h a* , their fellow-clansman, who awakened them with his shout from Punapau, had been having a jest at their expense. They went in to *Tuukoihu* and apologized to him for misjudging him and told him their names, *H i t i r a u* (the native word for the red hats) and *N u k u t e M a n g o* . He accepted their apology and went along with them some distance to make sure that they were finally gone. But so deeply had their skeleton figures impressed him that he resolved to record it in wood. He had now got the very feature that would symbolize the state of the dead ; the ribs with nothing but the skin on them,

and the hipbones jutting out from the sides would easily convey to every one the idea of an *a k u a k u*. He had been searching long for some such symbol to express in the memorial images he was trying to carve out of wood what their titanic size had conveyed in the stone statues on the *a h u s*. So afraid was he lest any detail should fade from his memory that he sat down at once and carved the first *m o a i k a v a k a v a*, or images showing the effects of emaciation that meant death. Of course, in the legend as told the aborigines are spoken of as devils in contrast to the strongly human and well-fed characteristics of one of the two great pioneers of the island.

(11) **TUUKOIHU HAD TO MAKE WOMEN IMAGES TOO.** Unfortunately he had seen only masculine devils, and had accordingly made his skeleton images only masculine. He soon discovered the mistake he had made in ignoring the other sex; and the other sex had more to say in the Easter Island household, and through the household in public life, than in any other Polynesian branch except the Maoris of New Zealand; they did their share in the wars and expected to do their share in peace and after death as *a k u a k u s*. He had done a hard day's work making little images, all of them men, and fell asleep; and as he slept he had a horrible dream; he saw two women *t a t a n i s* come at him with the most violent gesticulations; they announced themselves as P a p a a H i r o and P a p a a K i r a n g i and deafened him with their talk; they pointed to his parts with threatening gesture, and in fear he drew on his *h a m i h u n e*, or perineal band. But he was so terrified that he awoke. And he resolved never to submit to such agony again. So he sat down and did justice to the *a k u a k u s* of women by carving the *m o a i m i r o* female as well as male. Tradition does not tell it in the form of legend; but there must have been a sequel; he must have had another nightmare. For he has handed down to later generations of carvers a third type, a two-headed image; for up till recently, *moai miro* have been made consisting of a figure with two heads and the traditional name is *h a u a*, or double.

(12) **THE DANCING IMAGES.** But he had not reached the true goal of all his artistic efforts. Hitherto he had been working in the interests of religion; he had been endeavouring to lay the ghosts of the dead by making representations of

them that would be as unmistakable as the stone statues on
the *a h u s ;* that would gratify their vanity and get rid of
them as nightmares and perhaps also as malignant workers
of evil on their friends and neighbours ; and so he had helped
to allay the terrors of the living. Perhaps by going further
he would be able to cheer and amuse them as well. He chose
his other and greater palace on the west coast for his new
experiment in carving. They were not now to be the suggestions
of the famines that the people had so often suffered since that
first great period of starvation after the sources of their food
had gone down. They were not now to be representations of
skeletons. The skin-and-bone times were painful memories ;
he would abandon everything that would bring the thought
of them back, and make his wooden images like full-fed men ;
no ribs or thigh-bones would show now. He manufactured
them by the score and made them so that their legs and arms
should take the attitudes that those of the dancers of the
h o k o h o k o assume. Then he arranged them so that they
could be hung on a cord all round the roof of his three hundred
feet long house ; by another cord he could keep them whirling
round, whilst with a third he could control the movements
of their limbs. And when the people crowded round there
they saw the little wooden images dancing the *h o k o h o k o ,*
as they gyrated round the roof of Tuukoihu's house. And
they laughed as they contrasted this with the picture of famine
and the malignance of ghosts that they had seen in his
rib-and-thigh-bone memorial images. He had found the true
secret of the management of his Easter Islanders. Through
all their history they have loved to live for the moment and
forget the hateful things of the past and shut their eyes to
the hateful things that might come. They were beings of a
day, ephemeral as their winged insects ; why should they not
enjoy the sunshine whilst it lasted and shut out the thought
of the night that no amount of care could prevent from
falling ? It was the stone statues that had inspired him with
the thought of the skeleton-images. The grisly figures only
brought frowns upon the faces of his subjects ; it made them
think of times of famine, when it was feasting alone that they
enjoyed ; it made them foresee death with a shudder when
they preferred to welcome it as the last narcotic ; it brought
before their eyes the malignant ghost that haunted them and
persecuted them with sickness and death. His carving magic

had brought smiles to every face, and he had at last willing
and loyal subjects. His House of the Cockroach (Hare Koka),
the factory of the ghost images on the south coast, was forgotten
and his palace on the west was remembered all through
tradition as The House of the moving, dancing images
(*Ko te Hare Hakahaere Moai*).

(13) **THE FEATURES OF HIS RIBBED IMAGES.** The idea
of marionettes seems almost as much beyond the elementary
culture of Easter Island as the great burial platforms and
the gigantic stone images set on them. Carved wooden statues
have their like, not in the other branches of the Polynesians
alone, but all through the Pacific Ocean, from Alaska to
New Guinea, from Japan to Peru. And the special features
of Tuukoihu's ribbed wooden images are as easy to trace and
account for as the totem poles of the north-west coast of
America, or the wooden Buddhas of Japan and China. The
outstanding bones are manifestly the symbol of the emaciation
of periods of starvation such as are not infrequent on small
infertile islands occupied by an improvident people like
Easter Island and the Chatham Islands. The strongly aquiline
nose of all the ribbed images was probably a feature of their
creator ; for *T u u k o i h u* means " The erect one of the
nose." The goatee beard was doubtless one of the distinctions
of his face ; as it was noticed by voyagers as not infrequently
worn by Easter Islanders ; *v e r e* , the native name for beard
means especially the beard on the chin. Even if he had not
put these features into the figures he first carved, his imitators
would be certain to adopt them in carving their figures of the
a k u a k u , just as the sculptors of the stone statues, being
all Longears, gave all the images long ears.

(14) **WHENCE HIS MARIONETTES ?** It is much more difficult
to account for the story of the dancing movement of the
m o a i m i r o . There are the *w a y a n g* figures of leather
in J a v a . But these are meant for shadow-plays depict-
ing the deeds of the great heroes of Indian history. The
nearest to it that we can find in the Pacific is " the working
of the wooden marionettes that were caused to imitate *h a k a*
dances " mentioned by Mr. James Cowan in an article in the
June number, 1921, of the " Journal of the Polynesian Society,"
as taught by a blond aboriginal forest-people to a Maori chief.
It is more than likely that moving images or marionettes were
an early invention of the human race and belonged to many

ONE CORNER OF THE FINE EASTER ISLAND COLLECTION WHICH DR. WALTER KNOCHE, OF SANTIAGO (CHILI), HAS MADE. WOODEN *moaimiro* (30, 31, 32, 35, 36, 37, 38, 39, 40, 44, 45, 46, 48, 49, 50, 52; 33, A FEMALE IMAGE); THESE ARE COPIES OF TUUKOIHU'S MARIONETTES, AS THEY HAVE NO RIBS SHOWING EXCEPT NO. 40; TWO OR THREE OTHERS BESIDES 33 MAY BE FEMALE IMAGES; 44 AND 49 ARE SINGULAR FOR THEIR SQUATTING ATTITUDE AND THEIR HANDS WITH SIX FINGERS SPREAD UPON THEIR BREASTS; 50 SEEMS TO HAVE THE VISOR MENTIONED BY FORSTER; 34 IS AN INSTRUMENT FOR THE DANCES; 54 IS A HAND ALSO PROBABLY HELD IN THE DANCES; 42 IS AN *ua*, OR DANCE CLUB; 41, 47, 51, AND 53 SHOW THE CRUDER ART WHEN DEALING WITH STONE; 55, 57, 58, 62 TO 70 ARE *toki*; 56 IS A HATTED *toki*; 59, 60, 72 AND 73 ARE SPEAR-HEADS (*mataa*).

parts of the world like cat's cradle. The conditions necessary to their appearance and development are some skill in wood-carving and plenty of wood to carve, just as those necessary to the persistence of cat's cradle are skill in making good string and plenty of fibre to make it of. And the latter conditions are much more common than the former. It is only amongst a wood-carving people that marionettes have the chance of surviving. Almost all branches of the Polynesian race carved in wood. But it was only the inhabitants of New Zealand, especially the early inhabitants, that carried skill in wood-carving to a high pitch. It is a singular thing that Easter Island, which is known chiefly for its work in stone carving and tooling, should have in its traditions a maker and worker of marionettes. It is one more of the affinities between this island of Eastern Polynesia and New Zealand. And one might not be far wrong in conjecturing that if Hotu Matua called at New Zealand, T u u k o i h u was one of the forest P a t u p a i a r e h e that he brought with him.

(15) **HAWAIIAN, ASIATIC, AND EUROPEAN PUPPET-SHOWS.** The only marionettes that persisted in Polynesia up to our own day were those of the Hawaiians, the *H u l a K i i*, or dance images, described by the late Dr. Emerson in his "Unwritten Literature of Hawaii." They were operated as late as Kalakaua's reign in the eighties of last century, when that king was attempting to revive the old Hawaiian autocracy and as its basis the old Hawaiian customs. They are, therefore, the only puppets in Polynesia of the working of which we have any detailed knowledge. Like our Punch-and-Judy show they were used as the actors in a drama. "The arms were loosely jointed to the body," and "the performer stood behind a screen," and "imparted to the puppet such movements as were called for by the action of the play, while at the same time he repeated the words of his part; words supposed to be uttered by the marionette." The plays were evidently reproductions of Hawaiian customs and struggles and intrigues; and many of the utterances were in the form of songs sung to the sound of the *i p u*, or calabash drum. The pictures Dr. Emerson gives of three, Maka-ku, the boasting warrior, Nihiaumoe, the voluptuary, and Maile Papaka, the sweetheart of the little victor over the braggart, show them carefully dressed in bark-cloth. And this clearly differentiates them from the puppets of Easter Island and New Zealand;

there is no mention of any clothing in the traditions of these latter. But the three point back to a common origin, in the fatherland, Hawaiki. There probably the Polynesians, before they spread all over the Pacific, indulged in dramatic performances of puppets carved out of wood and having eyes of mother-of-pearl. It was the gestures and actions of the figures themselves that the spectators watched and not their shadows thrown on a screen ; they are thus differentiated from the *wayang* plays of Java, and show a close affinity to the Punch-and-Judy shows of western Europe. So close, indeed, was the resemblance that Dr. Emerson at first suspected the Hawaiian marionettes to be a modern imitation of the European; but he found on further investigation that the suspicion was untenable ; " the words used as an accompaniment to the play " are in many cases long obsolete and " bear convincing evidence in form and matter to a Hawaiian antiquity " ; and one performer says that " it was at Berlin she witnessed for the first time the European counterpart of the *hula Kii*, the Punch-and-Judy show."

(16) There is perhaps another feature that differentiates these Hawaiian puppet-plays from those of Tuukoiho. There is no mention in the tradition of his concealing himself from the observation of the onlookers, whilst in Hawaii the manipulator was hidden as in the Burmese marionette plays and the Punch-and-Judy shows. It seems to affiliate them rather with the still popular marionette shows of Japan, in which the director of the puppet makes no attempt to conceal his manipulation of them ; they go far back in Japanese history and form one of the origins of the popular plays, as is seen in the stiff, mechanical movements of the actors on the stage of the Kabuki theatres. This openness of the manipulation is not a feature of the puppet-plays of the West, which are probably in direct descent from those of Greece and Rome. Whether it belonged to the marionettes that have been found in Egyptian and Etruscan tombs it is impossible to say. The East as a rule preferred to conceal the source of the puppet-movements and in China and India and Further India made the shadow fall on a screen. From India came the preference into Java, though the Javanese puppet plays that deal with more modern times and not with the ancient myths of heroes make no use of the shadows ; the figures are not flat but round and more lifelike, and the performances can take place

MAILE PAKAHA   HAWAIIAN MARIONETTES   NIHI-AU-MOE

From Dr. Emerson's "Unwritten Literature of Hawaii."

by day. Which of these two types, the unconcealed and the screen and shadow, came first it is not easy to decide ; but that, like all dramatic performances, they originated in ceremonial religion is highly probable. Where they have divested themselves of all religious meaning and aim only at entertainment, they have doubtless had a long course of development. Tuukoihu's dancing puppets strongly contrast with his rib-exposing wooden figures, in being purely for the amusement of the people, whilst the latter have a distinctly religious significance ; and the contrast is probably one of development in the submerged empire, the religious figures being the more ancient.

CHAPTER XV

WOOD CULTURE

(1) *The larger Polynesian areas had shelter for defeated peoples and hence have legends of extra-human beings like fairies. In New Zealand these are generally wood-elves, because they dwell in the great forests.* (2) *Easter Island has no wood-elves because it had not and could never have, forests, its only two trees being slender-growers, the bastard sandalwood (the naunau the same as the ngaio of New Zealand) and the miro, the same as the yellow-flowering kowhai of New Zealand.* (3) *They never had big or oceanic canoes after Hotu Matua; their best freightcraft was the mat-raft (pora).* (4) *But the men were proud of their great oceanic past and wore constantly the reimiro in memory of the huge old canoes; the legends show consciousness of far-distant islands, but no one gets thither or thence in canoes.* (5) *The cyclopean foundation-stones of tooled adamant made the flimsy superstructure a mockery; the low belly-crawling door belonged to all Polynesian houses however large.* (6) *The scarcity of timber made them often resort to subterranean houses and cave-like houses of stone.* (7) *They differed from all other Polynesians in having no vessels of wood.* (8) *But the most convincing proof of their scarcity of timber was that they used the Polynesian word for wood,* r a k a u, *in the sense of "wealth"; and legends like "The Tree from the Tomb," reveal that the one thing they valued most was a tree.* (9) *Wood was a necessity of life for house, canoe and weapon; yet it had to go up in smoke; without it in the earth-oven they could not cook.* (10) *So scarce was it that some of their old weapons had to become ceremonial.* (11) *Wood became their sacred material and was devoted to making their talismans and memories of the great past, the mimic oceanic canoe (reimiro), the imitation of the coconut, the tablets of the sacred script.* (12) *Eyraud thought their dancing and singing before the little wooden images was no worship because the only reason for it was that their fathers did it before them.* (13) *The dance and song before the little wooden images were undoubtedly worship as the feasts at the burial platforms were. The great images and the little were both called* m o a i *(sacred to the ancestors).* (14) *Yet they respected both as little as the Tahitians respected their wooden gods or* t i i s, *although hanging the wooden images round their necks when they went to feast before the stone ones.*

(1) **WOOD ELVES IN THE LARGER POLYNESIAN AREAS.** One of the striking things about the larger Polynesian areas like H a w a i i and New Zealand is that they have a considerable folk-lore of faerydom. The M a n a h u n e in the former and the P a t u p a i a r e h e in the latter, fill the same rôle as the brownies and fairies and gnomes in Europe. They live just beyond the outskirts of civilization in the mountains and forests, and venture down into the haunts of men only in the night, when the humans are safe asleep. Sometimes by day they are heard singing or calling from height to height in the far distance or seen dimly moving when a mist veils the mountains. Now and again one of them gets united to a human and there are offspring, or a human blunders up into their recesses and settles. But there is, as a rule, isolation. The mountain-dwellers are fenced about by the impenetrable wall of extra-humanity built by the fears

146

and fancies of those that dwell on either side of it. The coast-dwellers keep in touch with the mundane and commonplace by their internecine wars and their sea-travel and the arrival of new immigrants. In Hawaii these extra-humans are stone-workers, generally cyclopean stoneworkers; in New Zealand, with its great forests, they are forest-dwellers and workers in wood. They are undoubtedly the remnants of defeated peoples who have found shelter in the central recesses of the great islands untrodden by the foot of new-comers and coast-dwellers. From them, doubtless, the later immigrants from the central Pacific into New Zealand learned their skill in wood-craft, and doubtless, too, many forms of art in wood perished with the extinction of the conquered and the failure of the conquerors to recognize their merit.[1] The larger area of New Zealand and its more extensive forests account for the greater variety of these fairy peoples in Maori tradition and legend. But most of them are forest-dwellers and have a facility in the manipulation of trees and timber that seems to the Maori story-tellers superhuman. This is especially the case with the *Hakuturi*, or wood-elves. R a t a , when he is preparing an expedition to rescue the bones of his father from the hands of the sea-hunting fairies, the P o n a t u r i , goes into the forest and cuts down a tree large enough for the keel and body of his canoe. When he returns in the morning the tree is back in its old place. Again and again the incident occurs and he feels baffled. But at last he gets into touch with the elves and in a miraculously short time his canoe is made and ready for launching. A similar legend is told of the forests above K o n a on the north-west coast of H a w a i i .

(2) **NO FOREST TREES ON EASTER ISLAND.** In Easter Island there are no traditions like this. There are extra-human beings; but they become devils and *tatanis*, wizards, and witches, and have no connection with forests or wood-carving or the making of canoes. In fact, there never was a forest on Easter Island and never could have been. It is not merely the lack of humus or the porosity of the island letting the rain that falls go through like a sieve and so preventing the formation of valleys or streams or the violent winds that behead trees venturing beyond the low height of their fellows. It is the absence of all vegetation of the nature of forest trees.

---

[1] See p. 134 for a carving recently found in a New Zealand swamp having no affinity to Maori carving.

The *naunau*, probably the bastard sandalwood, now extinct, the sacred tree of the natives, sacred perhaps because of its perfume, was never large enough to put into the timbers of their houses or canoes. The only tree that they got their wood from to make their tablets and weapons and dancing clubs and little images was the *miro;* this is the *sophora tetraptera* or yellow-flowering *kowhai* of New Zealand, a tree that is never accounted a forest tree; its girth is too slight to supply large timbers and its height rarely reaches more than twenty feet. It is completely different from the *miro* of New Zealand and Tahiti, in the one case the *podocarpus ferruginea*, in the other the *thespesia populnea*. I am more inclined to accept Cook's description " without wood " and Forster's " not a tree above ten feet " than Behren's glowing account of the vegetation, although it is possible that in the half century between the natives with their usual improvidence may have used up the trees of any size in their earth-ovens and otherwise. Quite recently a Chilian missionary planted two or three acres with vines, and, though they had begun to bear, the people finding it too far to go for firewood one winter cut them all down to use in their *umus;* Cook and Forster have proved to be the most accurate of observers; Behrens evidently wrote his monograph from memory when he reached Europe, if we are to judge by his inaccuracies and fantastic exaggerations.

(3) **THE PAUCITY AND SMALLNESS OF THE CANOES.** None of the voyagers but remarked on the smallness and fewness of the canoes on the island. Forster speaks of "their canoe patched up of many pieces "; and La Perouse says of them : " They are composed only of very narrow planks, four or five feet long and would at most carry four or five men. I saw only three on this part of the island and I should not be surprised if in a short time, through the want of wood, there should not be one remaining." There are really three sizes of canoe; one was but a rough low raft without keel or prow or poop; a slightly larger had two sharp ends matted over with rushes; the largest, called *vaka vaero*, was about eighteen feet long and two broad and had, as Forster says, " an outrigger made of three slender poles," and it had projections sloping upwards from bow and stern[1]; it is the canoe that La Perouse gives a picture of and was used for going

[1] See p. 26 for picture.

MANGAREVAN RAFT AS DEPICTED IN DE RIENZI'S "OCEANIE." THIS WAS THE ONLY CRAFT
OF THE GAMBIER GROUP, AND MAY HAVE ORIGINATED THE EASTER ISLAND LOW RAFT

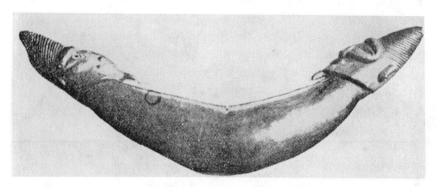

REIMIRO DESCRIBED BY DR. AURELIANO OYARZUN, DIRECTOR OF THE MUSEUM OF ETHNOLOGY
OF SANTIAGO IN CHILI IN "LA REVISTA CHILENA," VOL. 25, 1921

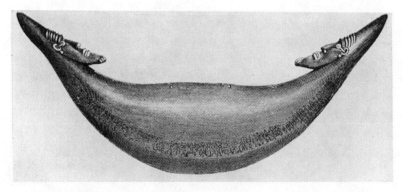

REIMIRO IN THE BRITISH MUSEUM BROUGHT BY THE "TOPAZ" IN 1888 FROM EASTER ISLAND

out to the deeper water to catch the bigger fish, especially *kahi*. The poorness of the timber for canoes is brought out by the word they use for keel; it is the word all the other Polynesians use for " body "; the only part of any thickness in the largest canoe was the keel and hence it was called "*tino*." But perhaps the best proof of the island's poverty of timber was its commonest method of transport along the coast. Those who went to one of the numerous feasts were expected to bring all they had raised in their cultivation and all they had got out of the sea; the usual procedure was to weave a mat of rushes, six or eight feet long, wrap the provisions kind by kind in the folds of this from one end; and when the whole had been folded over and become solid, the ends of the flat roll were made so secure that no water could enter. On this provision raft, or *pora*, the visitor to the feast laid himself, whilst he put one of his arms round it; then with the other limbs left free he swam along the coast. It must have been one of the commonest sights of the island to see the surface of the ocean full of swimmers and their *pora* making for the feast; it was only an odd householder or two who had a canoe to go in. And the swimmer was the better off of the two; for he had not to bail the whole way as well as paddle; the canoe, caulked with dried banana leaves (*kakaka*) or dried grass (*para*) leaked continually; it might have been as easy to go to sea in a sieve.

(4) **MEMORIES OF OCEANIC VOYAGING.** This is a complete contrast to the traditions of Hotu Matua's arrival. His canoes were large, ninety feet long and six feet deep, says one; a mile long, says legend; and were capable of carrying each from a hundred to a hundred and fifty men besides much cargo, several months' provisions and water for the crew and passengers and many trees, tubers and seeds to plant. Whether they were single canoes as in the north of New Zealand or double as in the south it is difficult to decide; for the report that makes them double adds "and balanced by outrigger or small canoe." It is likely they were double, though the stone one of tradition is single; for the only other large canoe mentioned by tradition, a canoe built on the island, was double. They had undoubtedly high prow and stern like the Tahitian and Hawaiian double canoes. For the later deep-sea fishing outrigger had this, and the *reimiro*, the fashionable wooden ornament worn by men at the feasts, if

L

not always hung from the neck, is supposed to be a reminiscence of the ancient big canoe, though it tapers off too much
from the middle to the fore and aft parts for that. That it
was the symbol of a great tradition is evident from its being
the constant ornament of men when they were not asleep
and from its being carved so frequently on the statues, the
a h u s and the red hats. It was the next best thing to having
a caste or profession of canoe-makers like most of the other
Polynesian islands to be able to wear this badge of a great
memory. If it indicates anything nautical, it indicates that
in the great days of old, the days of forested archipelagoes,
there were large single canoes made with swan's-neck bow
and stern. There was manifestly no far-voyaging after *Hotu
Matua's* day; for there was no craft built capable of facing
oceanic storms and billows or carrying provisions for more
than a few days. In some of the legends there is the consciousness of far-distant lands; but the travel to and from
them is never by canoe but by some means of the same order
as the magic carpet or ring of The Thousand and One Nights.
The witches who go to a far land to get a sleeping potion for
their Endymion take a rainbow as their road; the paragon
of beauty, who is carried off on the back of a turtle to a
far-off island and married to a royal magician, escapes home
on the back of a turtle; and the supernatural dyers who
come from a distant land to teach the secret of a fast yellow
dye come on wings; it is only King T a n g a r o a who
swims all the way from his island kingdom. The memory of
the voyages to and from far-away lands had come from the
times before the great catastrophe; but it had to find other
means of travel than canoe if it was to get into the budget
of the Easter Island story-teller.

(5) **THE HOUSES POOR IN THEIR TIMBERS.** Much the same
tale of a great past suddenly snapt and slowly tapering
off into insignificance is told by the cyclopean foundation-
stones.[1] They are heavy enough to bear edifices of the same
order as the burial platforms. The poor little lath-and-straw
imitation of an upturned canoe they usually bore is absolutely
out of proportion. Eyraud (Brother Eugenio), the first
missionary, does mention a superstructure more in keeping
with the foundations: " There are built in the place of the
feast great cabins higher than the ordinary." But they were

---

[1] See p. 8 for a photograph of one.

of flimsy material and, like the *p a i n a* figure, only meant
for the occasion. The ordinary house he compared to "a
mussel half opened, resting on its hinges." But the upturned
canoe that almost all the voyagers compare it to is a more
exact analogy ; and, as some of them were three hundred
feet long, it indicates that the canoes, of which they were a
memory, were some of them single and huge. Whether the
superstructure that originally stood on these great tooled
stones at the time when nobles were being buried in the
platforms was higher than what they afterwards held it is
difficult to say ; it was probably solider and more durable,
as there would be greater timbers to deal with ; and the porch
they had was continued into the impoverished era, as it needed
no great amount of timber and there was but a low entrance
to protect from the weather. The large paved court in front
was continued, as it needed only stone, and there was plenty
of that at hand ; it was the open-air drawing-room for con-
versation and rest like those in front of the great men's club-
houses and at intervals along the roads in Y a p , one of
the most westerly of the Carolines.[1] The low, narrow entrance,
which compelled visitors to get in or out on all fours, if not
on their stomach, belonged to the most palatial houses of old ;
it was not peculiar to Easter Island ; it was characteristic of
all Polynesian houses. It was only in the house of the Maoris
of New Zealand that there was any attempt at a window ;
Cook, in observing how low the door was, adds, " There is a
square hole near the door serving both for window and chimney,
near which is the fire-place." This development was probably
due to the colder climate necessitating fires indoors to sit
by during the winter ; the Polynesian earth-oven had generally
a separate roof over it ; and in some of the better-class Maori
houses there was a louvre in the roof to give exit to the smoke.
In the tropical islands of Polynesia there was not so much
need of a second hole either for the emission of smoke or the
admission of sunlight. But to this day the houses in Japanese
villages have no other escape for the smoke than below the
eaves, in spite of their long and severe winter. The Easter
Island house was pitch-dark, the only relief being a small
wicket by which a person's share of food was handed in
directly to him. La Perouse found two doors in one house,

[1] See p. 132 for a photograph that gives the proportions of the
entrance.

both of them less than two feet high ; but that house was
three hundred feet long and might accommodate more than
two hundred people ; so large was it that " he was almost
certain their houses were common at least to a whole village
or district." But that was probably a guest-house for a feast,
or a general meeting-house of a village like the *wharepuni*
and the carved house of the New Zealand *pa*.

(6) **THE STONEHOUSE RARE AND DIFFERENT IN FORM.**
Cook has no hesitation about the wretchedness of the common
dwelling-places : " Their homes are low, miserable huts con-
structed by setting sticks upright in the ground at six or
eight feet distance, then bending them towards each other
and tying them together at the top, forming thereby a kind
of Gothic arch. The whole is thatched over with leaves of
sugar-cane." And the Easter Islander had no need for most
of the six houses that the Hawaiian noble generally had ; he
had beside the common sleeping house, a special house for
beating bark-cloth ; but he had no need for a separate eating-
house for women, because his women had managed to get
rid of that taboo ; nor did he need a separate house for the
family idols, as he had none ; whilst he went in the opposite
direction of a special house for women at the birth of a child
and welcomed everybody of either sex to witness the event.
Moreover, there were other types of houses in Easter Island
besides the canoe-bottom-shaped. Forster describes another
kind : " Besides the poor huts we observed some heaps of
stones piled up into little hillocks which had one steep perpendicular side, where a hole went underground ; perhaps these
cavities sheltered people." This type of house was the model
and origin of the pyramidal burial platform that was the most
shapely form of *a h u* after the catastrophe. And La Perouse
noticed that " some of their dwellings were subterraneous."[1]
Had they visited Orongo they would have seen that the houses
there, too, were a kind of cave adapted to the special kind of
laminated stone to be found at hand.[2] So it was with the
circular and elliptical houses, ruins of which are to be found
in several parts of the island ; this was the form especially
adapted to the countless stones found everywhere, the *débris*
of the lava outcrops that have weathered into their crystals.

---

[1] See p. 102 for pictures of Orongo stone houses as they were till
recently ; most are now dilapidated as in the above photograph.
[2] See p. 112 for picture of round tower and subterranean house.

STONE FISH RECENTLY FOUND UNDER AN OLD WALL THAT HAD FALLEN; EVIDENTLY A TALISMAN FOR THE INCREASE OF FISH. I HAVE SEEN SIMILAR FISH-LIKE STONES IN THE MARQUESAS

A SHORT CLUB FROM EASTER ISLAND FROM WHICH THE REPLICA OF THE MAORI *patupatu* MENTIONED BY COOK MAY HAVE DEVELOPED

THE *ao* AND THE *rapa*, TWO SACRED CLUBS USED ESPECIALLY IN THE DANCES, EVIDENTLY IN THEIR ORIGIN DOUBLE PADDLES. *Ao* IN EASTER ISLAND DIALECT, MEANS ALSO "A SPOON" AND "A SHOVEL"; IT IS THE SAME AS MAORI *hako*, "A SPOON," AND HAWAIIAN "HAO"; "*rapa*" MEANS "A PADDLE" IN PAUMOTAN

THE *ua*, THE SACRED CLUB USED CHIEFLY IN THE DANCES; IT IS EVIDENTLY FROM *rua* (TWO), BECAUSE ITS HANDLE IS A DOUBLE HEAD. THE WORD IS ANOTHER INSTANCE OF MARQUESAN INFLUENCE; *ua* IS "TWO" IN MARQUESAN, AND IT APPEARS IN EASTER ISLAND *haua*, FOR A DOUBLE-HEADED WOODEN IMAGE—*See also No. 42 in picture facing page 142.*

It was this plentiful stone that dictated the form of the towers for the navel-strings, the towers for watching the approach of the turtles and the shoals of fish and the fort-like fowl houses. The material was ready to hand everywhere.

(7) **NO DOMESTIC UTENSILS OF WOOD.** The Easter Islander preferred timber for his house whenever he could get it; and it shows how limited the supply was that he had so often to resort to his unlimited supply of stones; the stone house, whatever its form, had all the darkness and discomfort of a cave, a name it often bore; the wood and thatch structure admitted some air and sunlight, and had the advantage of being liable to be burned down in the frequent wars and so rid of its accumulated filth and live stock. But the surest sign of the scarcity of timber was the almost complete absence of dishes and domestic utensils of wood. The wooden *kumetes*, or food dishes, and the feather-boxes of Polynesia are a distinctive mark of its culture, quite apart from the finger-bowls, slop-dishes, and spittoons of the Hawaiian group. There was nothing of this in Easter Island; instead there were in use shells (*takatore pane*) and calabashes (*ipu*); for they had no coco-nuts to make vessels of as most of the other Polynesian islanders had. They could not think of any receptacle that was not a gourd, although one paint-grinding mortar of stone has been found in the centre of the island; happily they had two sizes; the large one was used as the tub in which the bark of the *mahute* was soaked, but never, as in Hawaii, as a vehicle for carrying goods hung in a net on the ends of a shoulder pole. The smaller they used as a casket for their feathers, and also as drinking cups. But so scarce were even these that a household had often to carry its fresh water soaked up in grass laid in a banana leaf, and when they wanted to drink or wash squeezed it out. The *miro*, their only timber tree, and hence their one word for timber, was not large enough or hard enough to make dishes out of.

(8) **THE TREE FROM THE TOMB.** If anything was needed to confirm the report of the scarcity of timber it was the use of the word *rakau*. In Polynesian it properly means a branch of a tree or timber. In the dialect of Easter Island it means " wealth," " treasure." And the legends bear this out, and especially one, " The Tree from the Tomb "; it is as follows : An old man had lived all his life in a cave because

he had never been well enough off to get wood for a house. He saw his wife die in it, and as he felt his strength begin to fail he was afraid his son would die in it too, still unsheltered. So he called him and before breath failed him he bade him bury his body in the neighbouring platform of Tongariki. A week after the burial a tree would spring from his bones and with this he would be able to build a house for himself. His neighbours, when he told them the prediction, only mocked him. But, when it sprang and grew into a stately tree, they called a public meeting and resolved that it belonged to them. The youth tried persuasion and protest in vain; so he prayed the *a k u a k u* of his father to transplant it elsewhere. And sure enough the communizers of the tree saw it pass through the air away over the hills and they begged the youth to get it brought back that they might give him a share in it. But he had had enough of their public benevolence, and he followed the floating tree over the hills. He saw the direction it was taking and going to the village that was its goal told the people that it was coming and that he would share its benefits with them. They saw it take root in their midst and for generations they were able to sit in its shade. But, what was best, he cut great branches from it and shared them with his fellow-villagers. And still it grew and grew. And though he cut it down to make a house and a canoe, it continued to spring and grow and be a source of wealth and benevolence to him all his life. His old neighbours near Tongariki were filled with chagrin, not at the thought that they had entertained an angel unawares, but that such a source of treasure should have passed out of their hands.

(9) **THE NECESSITIES OF WOOD.** None but the dwellers in a comparatively timberless islet could have manufactured such a story. We will not be far wrong in calling the period in the history of Easter Island after *Hotu Matua* its age of wood. What had gone before was its age of stone. Now, whatever they valued most they made or imitated in wood. It was their gold, their jewels, their precious stones. Those forested archipelagoes that had once encircled their island had been their G o l c o n d a if only they had known. But like the migrant tree they were gone and nothing could recall them or take their place. They needed it for their houses and canoes and could not get enough of it for these purposes. They must have it for their earth-ovens; cooking must go on

if they were to live ; they grudged seeing the precious material go up in smoke ; but what else could they do ? They could live without houses ; for there were caves and plenty of stone to build artificial caves ! They could live without canoes ; for they could use their mat-raft, and they would get plenty of fish in the shallows where they could wade or swim and plenty of crayfish and eels and snakes by diving. The first foundation of life was the *u m u*, and the *u m u* they must keep steaming whatever else they might do without.

(10) **WAR AND WOOD.** What they did keep their timber for was their war-weapons. They must have a shaft for their *m a t a a;* else their warfare would be toothless. They must have a flat piece at least two feet in length to make their short oval knob-handled clubs. They must have a long thick piece to carve the lizard head and human body on ;[1] with this *m o k o m i r o*, or wooden lizard, they could do wonders on the skulls of their enemies, not to speak of the magic effect on their minds of the monster with the indwelling *a k u a k u*. Even more important was it for one of the joys of the festival, the dance ; how could they join in the *h o k o h o k o* or impress the idea of their prowess in battle on the minds of the row of young women in front of them without a lizard club in each hand ? And when a friend was murdered or slain by an enemy how was an Easter Islander to proclaim vengeance on the slayer unless he had in each hand one of the flat, oval, handled clubs called *t i m o i k a* ?[2] And here we touch upon the use of wooden implements for religious purposes. It was a religious duty of the avenger to lay the corpse on the burial platform, and go on turning it over in order to kindle his wrath and keep it warm. And many of the old weapons of the archipelagoes had been since their emergence set aside for ceremonial and religious purposes. There was the long *u a* which with its double-headed handle and its baton end had been so effective in the making of Makemake's empire ; that had to be reserved for the sacred dances now that Makemake was their great god ; they could not use it in mere secular strife. Then there were two famous weapons of the archipelagoes, the *a o* and the *r a p a*, two clubs that had once been paddles, first used as weapons in sea fights when the ordinary clubs had been lost and then found to be doubly

---

[1] See p. 134 for picture of their humanized lizards.
[2] See p. 34 for picture of this baton.

effective, as the blade at either end might be brought down with crushing result on the skull of an enemy. There is an attempt to differentiate the two ends in both the *a o* and the *rapa*, but the differentiation cannot conceal the original double-bladed paddle, as in the similar Marquesan dancing club (*parahua*). Whence such a paddle could have come is a difficult question; it is to be found only amongst the American Indians and for use in the E s k i m o *k a y a k*. It is only one of many features of Polynesian culture that seem to point to the North Pacific. The paddle of the Easter Islanders must have been ridiculously inefficient in the water compared to these two clubs broad-bladed on either end.

(11) **THE SACREDNESS OF WOOD.** But Makemake was the centre of the new worship, and what he had used in battle must be a club and remain a club however much it might look like a paddle or however useful it might be in propelling their canoes; and it would now be sacrilege to put it to so secular a use. To what more exalted purpose could the precious wood be put than to make these implements which were so essential to the religious dance? Then there were the two great talismans of all good luck, the *r e i m i r o*[1] or " precious thing in wood," constantly hung on the breasts of men, reminding them of the huge craft their ancestors sailed in to distant lands, and the *t a h o n g a,* or " thing of value," worn on the breast by women to remind them of the times when their ancestresses had wealth of coco-nuts to make oil for their hair and body on festal days. No better use could the most valuable material on the island be put to than the making of these mascots that drew their magic from the great past. But best of all the uses of wood for keeping faith alive was to make the tablets on which the *r o n g o - r o n g o* could be etched. Their priests, the *m a o r i s,* knew every prayer and hymn and genealogy that the various combinations of characters were intended to bring to their mind; and they were all brought up from childhood to recite them led by the *maoris*, though they knew not what the characters meant. These were all that remained of the traditions and liturgy of Makemake's realm; they had been saved by Hotu Matua from the wreckage of the culture of the past. And now they had become precious as talismans like the skulls of that great pioneer's successors even when they had

[1] See p. 148 for pictures of the *reimiro*.

lost the life and brains that had dwelt in them. The *Kohaurongorongo* had to be copied on new tablets so that every household might have them. For though they had lost their meaning, they had the magic of a charm; they could bring fertility to their women as the king's skull could bring fertility to their fowls.

(12) **DID THE EASTER ISLANDERS WORSHIP THE MOAI MIRO**? The precious wood was sanctified by being etched with those potent though unintelligible characters. And here the question arises, why so much of the rare material was used every generation in making the little wooden images, the *moai miro?* Were they only for the amusement of the carvers and for use as marionettes? Why did the men wear them round their necks at every festal meeting and at every sacred dance? The first missionary, the courageous Eyraud, was the first to mention them: "In all the hovels are found some little statues of some thirty centimetres in height which represent the figures of men, fish, birds, etc. These ought to be idols. But I have never seen any honour rendered to them. Sometimes I have seen the natives take these statues, set them in the open air and make certain gestures accompanied with one kind of dance and song." He adds that he believed that they did not know what they were doing; "they did merely what they saw their fathers do; all the philosophy they can give of it is that it is the custom of the country." What else is their worship to the majority of worshippers in any religion but doing what they saw their fathers do, or the custom of the country? It proves rather than disproves that the Easter Islanders with their gestures and dance and song were worshipping the little statues. Dance and song are exactly the methods that many primitive peoples employ to worship their gods, even though they may pay little attention to them in ordinary life and even thrash their wooden representatives and mutilate them if they have not got what they prayed for.

(13) All the evidence we have of the religious worship of the Easter Islanders indicates that it consisted of dance and song with the still more important exercise, for a people often harassed by famine, of feasting. Their festivals at the burial platforms have every appearance of being a religious service; for the priests, the *maoris*, get them up and recite and sing the *rongorongo*, the ancient liturgy, and lead the dances

at them. This may be the mere mimicry of the ancestor-worship that is the spirit of much of Polynesian religion ; but it is worship. The white *p a i n a* figure set up at the festival was supposed to represent the dead parent of the man who presided at it ; it was perhaps the nearest they could come to the magnificent representations of the dead in stone the predecessors of Hotu Matua had set up on the great burial platforms, the *m o a i* (probably meaning " sacred to the ancestors "). These little wooden figures were also called *m o a i ;* which implied that they were representations of the dead. The ribbed figures and then the female figures, representing the women *t a t a n i s* of *Tuukoihu's* nightmare, were meant to stand for the dead. The marionettes, an afterthought, were for the amusement of the people and had nothing that could be called sacred or religious about them ; they were open or unconcealed magic, and were made and dealt with as secularities ; it is these that are made to this day to sell to foreigners. My guide described one which his father gave to the Americans of the *Mohican* in 1886 ; it was four feet high, it had exaggerated male parts and its legs were astraddle. The representations of " fish, birds, etc.," which Eyraud mentions may have been a relic of primeval totemism and may have been used, like the charm-stones, for the increase of the animal-food they stand for. They seem to have dropped out of the fancy of Easter Island carvers once the new religion and the new civilization threw the old beliefs into shadow. The little ancestral figures had a better market. A stone fish recently found under an old wall was probably one of those totemistic figures, though my guide insists that it is a lizard.

(14) The others had been a different proposition ; they were meant, like the *p a i n a* figure, to be substitutes for the great stone images of the *a h u s .* As ancestral representations they were sure to receive something of the kind of worship that this primitive people were capable of. And that is exactly what the first missionary describes, dance and song before them in the open air. It was not likely to be very lasting or sincere in a people who had no world of spirits beyond the grave and believed that the ghosts of the dead were nothing if they were not malignant and fortunately soon became nothing. The want of reverence for them that Eyraud observed is at least no worse than that which Moerenhout described thirty years before as shown by the Tahitians to the wooden

representations of their lesser gods: The *t i i s* were the children of Taaroa and Hina and " spirits inferior to the gods, but intermediate between organized and unorganized beings." " These spirits were little respected ; the images were sold or broken when the owners were dissatisfied ; yet they were feared and were used by the sorcerers for their evil ends. Their images were placed at the ends of the *m a r a e s* and guarded the boundaries of sacred places." So the Easter Islanders left the little ancestral figures unhonoured in their houses ; but when they went to their festivals, one of the nearest approaches to religious worship that they made, they hung them round their necks.

CHAPTER XVI

THE ARTS

(1) They had plenty of bone, turtle shell and obsidian, but never thought of using them for inlay work like the Melanesians, except for the eyes of the wooden images ; nor did they follow the New Zealanders in the use of human bone further than to make a fish-hook of it ; wood was the precious material. (2) Their tools were amazingly inefficient, their drill no nearer to the Polynesian cord-drill than the hand-driven terebra shell. (3) They made but limited use of the human bone that cannibalism so plentifully supplied. (4) With their bone needle and wooden thimble they quilted their rough bark-cloth in order to strengthen it. (5) As in other Polynesian islands there was a special house for making bark-cloth ; for to complete a sheet the whole day was needed, one woman pounding and another splashing on water to bring out the mucilaginous sap ; no Polynesian clothing would stand this continuous moisture ; so the cloth-beaters had to be naked. (6) And there was but the narrowest supply of bark ; most had to go without, and use up what they had in fly-whisks in order to assert their claim to their own skin. (7) There was even scantier material for their mats and hats and baskets and girdles, the rushes in the crater-lakes ; there was no pandanus. (8) They made no attempt at design, their dyes being few and scarce. (9) The magnificent featherwork of the rest of Polynesia dwindles down in this islet to hats and royal banners ; (10) for they were limited to the grey and white and black of seabirds ; there were no land birds. (11) For a people that had so little material for clothing and indulged so much in swimming and diving an indelible ornamentation of the skin was an absolute necessity ; they were not Melanesians, and this had to be tattooing and not cicatrization. Had they come from Rapa or the Chatham Islands they would have left the skin unpunctured. (12) They were one of the most highly tattooed branches of the Polynesian race. (13) Their tattooing points rather to New Zealand than to the Marquesas for origin, though its purpose was only to beautify as in Tahiti. (14) But it was connected with religion ; for the maori or priest was the tattooer. (15) A legend of the introduction of the art shows that it was exotic ; (16) it was evidently from New Zealand, and there came with it the art of spoiling it by smearing it over with paint.

(1) THE EASTER ISLAND USE OF BONE, TURTLE SHELL, AND OBSIDIAN. Wood was certainly the most valued material in Easter Island. It was used for most ornaments and charms like greenstone in New Zealand. It was preferred for weapons, for all chiefly and sacred clubs or batons, and for all the new sculpture and carving. We might almost call it the sacred and royal material as stone had been in the era before the catastrophe. Bone and stone and shell were only subsidiary to it as a rule. From the backbone of the shark came the white of the eyes of the little images ; from the obsidian came the dark centre or pupil. It was the only instance of that inlaid work which is so beautiful on the food bowls and canoes of the Solomon Islands, and on the breast ornaments of parts of eastern New Guinea. Not that they had not material for it ; they had at times plenty of turtle shell and there were the cowrie[1] and a small iridescent shell called *r e i* that went

[1] See No. 7 in picture facing p. 188.

to the making of shell necklaces (*r e i   p i p i*) for the women. But it does not seem to have come within the range of their art to inlay. They used the shell of the turtle to make a girdle for women; they cut it into eighteen-inch slats and tied them on cords in triplets, so that it should be flexible and fit to the waist; and with *t i* leaves and water they polished the *h o n u* plates till they shone and reflected objects in them—the closest approach any branch of the Polynesian race made to a mirror except the Hawaiians in their polished rounded black stones set in water, perhaps an imitation of a Japanese metal mirror from some junk driven on to their shores. The same process of polishing might have made as good a mirror from their plentiful obsidian; a look at the slope of *O r i t o* in the morning sunlight might have suggested it; it gleams and shimmers all over it like running water. But they were too much obsessed with the idea of its use for spear heads to look beyond that[1]; they have a special legend of the discovery of its piercing property; before they had shod their spears with pieces of gourd shells; but a boy had his foot cut by the volcanic glass and thereafter they utilized the discovery that it would pierce human flesh better than gourds. It was the same with their use of human bone; they could have had unlimited quantities of it from the vaults of the *a h u s* and from the bodies they so frequently feasted on; but they never thought of making use of it till some fisherman became dissatisfied with the stone hook and got the hint in a nightmare from an *a k u a k u* that a hook made of one piece of human bone or of two pieces tied together would be more efficient.[2] This was doubtless a suggestion that came in with the immigrants from New Zealand, although it is a contrast to the lavish use of human bone made by the Maoris for *h e i t i k i s*, flutes, whistles, and combs, as well as hooks. They used the snout of the swordfish in the same way as they used the tooth of the shark and the chips of obsidian, for piercing the lobes of the ear, for shaving the head, for etching the *rongorongo*, and for tattooing. But they never thought of using these sharp edges and points for cutting hollows in wood for the insertion of pieces of turtle-shell or obsidian.

(2) **THE SMALL STONEWORK OF EASTER ISLAND.** The

---

[1] See Nos. 1, 2, 3, 4, 5 of picture facing p. 22, and also 59, 60, 61, 72, 73 of picture facing p. 142.

[2] See Nos. 3 and 4 in picture facing p. 188.

m a o r i s or priests were really the successors of the sculptors and fell heir to their art of stone carving and tooling. As etchers of the characters on the tablets, they naturally developed the art more in the line of petroglyph than of·statue. And it is marvellous what they have done on the rocks of Orongo with the tools that were their legacy from the past; these were the two stone chisels, the big and long chisel (t o k i p a n e p a n e) and the slenderer and long chisel (t o k i k a i k a i); the adze (t o k i o h i o), and the drill (t o k i m o k o m o k o). The drill was an amazingly inefficient tool for making holes in stones, compared with the usual Polynesian cord-drill with its wooden flywheel and its rotary motion; it was a mere wooden-handled terebra-shell rotated by the rubbing of the hands as in the Australian aboriginal method of making fire; water was used in the hole to make it run better, or, if water was not available, saliva. It is difficult to understand how they bored the inch-deep holes for the wooden posts in the adamantine basalt of the foundation stones; once bored they could be freed of irregularities by the triangular obsidian file with rough side (*h e r e h e r e* or *m a t a r i k i*). It is easier to understand the achievement of the well to which the natives conducted Cook " cut deep into the rock," or of the deep well at V a i h u to which the elder Forster was led by the " h a r e e k e e " or the cisterns, one nine feet in diameter and fourteen feet deep, seen by Thomson on P o i k e plains or the cups he saw in a rock on the promontory beyond to represent the stars. The rocks chosen would be like the stuff of the statues, not of the hardest. It was easy for them to cut the *r e i m i r o*, or complicated geometrical figures on the images, or on the red hats, or the *k o m a r i* and *a o* on the back of T a u r a R e n g a. But to carve the Makemake with such exactness in relief on the rocks at Orongo was more difficult, though not so difficult as on the blocks of the *a h u s* or on the foundation stones; that would probably need the larger hand-drill as well as both the big chisel and the slender. The wide and deep holes on the rim of Rano Raraku would be no difficulty; the filling them with thick beams from an island that had no forest trees would be the difficulty. Whether the deep holes in the rocks which Thomson came across were fish-ponds is disputable, so improvident are Easter Islanders. Lacking coco-nuts for cups and timber large enough for dishes, they might have

CARVING ON ROCKS AT ORONGO

CARVING ON ROCKS AT ORONGO

taken to stone for domestic utensils, as even some Polynesians well supplied with wood have done. But the only stone dish I have heard of is a mortar for grinding paint found recently in Rano Aroi. The singular thing is that where all the other Polynesians have used wood for their cloth-beater, the Easter Islanders have used stone, sometimes a beach-stone untooled, but oftener carefully rounded by the chisel. Stone-charms to increase a crop or a shoal of fish were more in their line. They would go to endless trouble in carving a rough stone, or even a hard beach pebble, into the shape of a human face or a human vulva just to bring good luck.[1] I have a rough basalt tooled into the shape of a fish, recently found under a pile of stones[2] ; my cicerone thinks it a lizard ; whatever animal it simulates, it was meant as a charm.

(3) **THE USES OF BONE.** Why they did not make more use of the bones their cannibalism so freely supplied or of the vertebræ of the large fish they caught, the bonitos, the dolphins, and sharks, is puzzling. We can understand why whale ivory fails to come into the list of their materials as it comes in most Polynesian islands. For they had no canoes to tackle even a sick whale ; and there were only two small beaches for dead whales to be thrown upon. An occasional cetacean vertebra, or even a dead whale has been found amongst the rocks ; but not enough to suggest its constant use in art. Only shark-oil, and never whale-oil, is mentioned amongst their toilet requisites. Thomson speaks of the *t i m o i k a*, of which he gives a picture as made of whale-bone ; he probably means the bone of a whale. It is easy to believe Forster when he says : "The only ornaments which we saw were flat pieces of bone in the shape of a tongue or like a laurel leaf, which both sexes were hanging on their breasts together with some necklaces and ear jewels made of shell." They did use the vertebræ of the shark for bone ornament ; but these ornaments he refers to are the *tahonga* and the *r e i m i r o* and they were usually made of wood ; no specimen in bone has been recorded in recent times as far as I know. But they may have used it in older times ; for another fact that he records is unique ; his father's party "saw the representation of a dancing woman's hand carved in wood."[3] What distinguished the hand of a

---

[1] See Nos. 41, 47, 51, 53, 68 in picture facing p. 142.
[2] See Chap. XV, par. 13, for stone fish in picture facing p. 142.
[3] See No. 54 in picture facing p. 142.

woman dancing from the hand at rest it is not easy to see, unless the artist was able to represent the rapid quiver of the fingers. The bone of the whale, on the rare occasions when it was found, like the vertebræ of the shark, was used to make the plug for the ear-hole ; bone was also used to make the sewing needle and occasionally the netting needle (h i k a). But the sewing needle was not used without the *p a o a*, or thimble, a flat strip of wood about nine inches long with a groove along its whole length ; this was placed under the pieces to be sewn and the needle was, after piercing on one side, guided by the groove across and then thrust through again.

(4) **THE USES OF BARKCLOTH.** We are on less uncertain ground when we come to the material which had to be sewn or netted. It is seldom we hear in Polynesia of bark-cloth being sewn when it is torn ; it is generally mended by wetting and beating another piece over the rent. But in Easter Island it was quite common to sew pieces together, probably because the cloth was extremely coarse and showed the interlacing fibres.[1] Forster speaks of meeting a crowd in crossing the island : " A very few of them had a cloak which reached to the knees and stitched or quilted with thread to make it the more lasting." This cloak was the *n u a* worn only by the well-to-do. The usual habit was to go naked but for the girdle and the perineal band (h a m i h u n e) passed from front to back between the legs, these being made of bark-cloth or rush matwork ; and on the back of some of the images, as, for instance, on the images fallen head down on the *a h u* of Anakena beach, there is a circle above the representation of the girdle that doubtless stands for the loop in tying the band to the waistband, whilst the spiral on each buttock may be an attempt to conventionalize as an ornament the flying ends of the girdle which, in the case of women, at least, was twelve feet long, so that it could be undone and, set below the chin and under the arm-pits, enable them to carry a burden on their back (a k a v e n g a). The women, when not at work, often wore a *m a r o a*, or petticoat, like the Tahitian *p a r e u;* when at work in the fields or in fishing they had only the *h a m i h u n e* on ; but when they were engaged in beating bark-cloth they were always nude, as in all the Polynesian islands ; for water had to be splashed

[1] See p. 98 for photograph of Easter Island barkcloth.

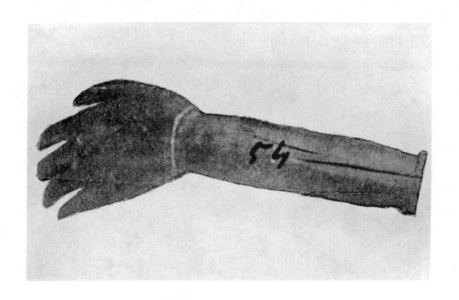

A CARVED HAND USED IN THE DANCES

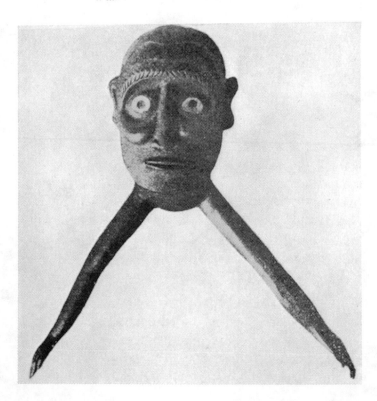

A DANCING BATON IN SHAPE OF A TWO-ARMED HEAD

plentifully on it, and their belt and band, whether cloth or matting, could not stand so much wetting.

(5) **THE MAKING OF BARKCLOTH.** Hence it was that they always had a separate little house for making cloth. Two women were needed for the operation ; and they had to keep at it all day without break, else the piece would be spoiled. One knelt at the beam of wood for beating it on (*t u t u a*, but in Mangareva meaning a beater), and with the round, generally tooled, stone two feet long by one broad (*m a e a t u t u m a h u t e*) kept pounding the pieces of white mucila-ginous inner bark together. The other kept carrying water in a gourd and pouring or sprinkling it on so as to keep all moist and bring out the glutinous quality. For days the rolls of it had been soaked in water in a long calabash (*k a h a*). After it was all welded into the sheet required it was spread out in the sun to dry ; and when thoroughly dry it was ready for dyeing, if it was to be dyed. In Easter Island it was more commonly worn undyed and white as on the *p a i n a* figure and in the masked dances. But the gallants and superior people generally had it dyed yellow with the colouring from the turmeric root. Forster, in describing the dress of the crowd he met, adds : " Most of these cloaks were painted yellow," or, as he puts it before, " orange colour." In Tahiti, and especially in Hawaii, there was a great variety of dyes and even shades of colour ; in the former, ferns and other natural forms were placed on the sheet so as to bring out white ornaments on the coloured ground ; whilst in Hawaii there were special patterns carved on wood to impress varied geometrical combinations in a different colour on the funda-mental colour. Even for the ordinary *t a p a* for the common people grooved beaters were used in order to introduce design into the texture and dye. In Easter Island there was too little material as well as too little dye to allow of much variety.

(6) **THE POOR SUPPLY OF MATERIAL.** In the larger Poly-nesian groups the *t a p a* makers were not confined to the paper mulberry for material. In Hawaii, for example, the *mamake*, which grew in the woods and needed no special cultivation, was almost as important. Then there was the bark of the hibiscus (*h a u*) and for a less fine kind the bark of the small branches of the breadfruit tree. None of these ever grew in Easter Island. The only bark-cloth plant it

M

ever had was the *m a h u t e*, which therefore gives its name instead of the usual Polynesian word *t a p a* to the cloth. It is now to be found only round the lake in the depths of the crater of Rano Kao. But that it was always scarce has most of the voyagers as witness. La Perouse says : " Mulberry trees are very rare, having been destroyed by the droughts. Such as have survived are only three feet high, and these they have been obliged to encompass with walls to secure them from the winds ; it is remarkable that the height of these trees never exceeded that of the walls by which they are sheltered." And Beechey, half a century after, shows that this state of things had continued : " The cloth mulberry tree produces so small a supply that a part of the inhabitants necessarily go naked." " Most wear a girdle of red *tapa*, or of a wild kind of parsley, or of a species of seaweed." There was no room for luxury of clothing here ; there could be no selection for the rich and poor as in Hawaii and Tahiti. What the poor had to cover themselves with in the night was a dry banana leaf or the grass that usually covered the floor (*mauku tai*) or thatched the roof (*mauku uta*) ; they tied this grass (*e r i k u*) in bundles and drew these over them as they drew them over the narrow low entrance to keep out the rain and the cold. And the *m a h u t e* had to serve a variety of purposes. Out of it they made a sunshade for their eyes, there being few or no trees to shelter under. Forster speaks of a modification of this that was braided : " The women wore a great wide cap of very neat matwork which pointed forwards and formed a ridge along the top and two large lobes behind on each side, which we found extremely cooling for the head." It was this combination of head-covering and sun shade that perhaps explains the form of the red hats of the statues with their hollow rim below. Out of the bark-cloth also they manufactured an even more essential thing for the barest comfort on an island that has a small indigenous fly, the arrogant, pertinacious owner of the human skin ; this was the fly whisk (t a v i r i v i r i), which in the tropical islands of Polynesia was the special baton of chiefship and kingship, but here the only chance a man had of establishing his right to his own face by day. They never manufacture a fan ; it was not hot enough.

(7) **THE SCARCITY OF MATERIAL FOR MATWORK.** But it was not comfort the Easter Islanders ever thought of in looking

CHISELS OR ADZES OR HAMMERS FOR CUTTING THE STATUES FOUND BESIDE UNLAUNCHED STATUES ON THE OUTER SLOPE OF RANO RARAKU (1, 2, 3). SMALLER TOKI USED FOR CARVING THE FEATURES OF THE FACES (4). POLISHED ADZE NOW RARELY FOUND ON THE ISLAND (5). STONE FISH AMULET FOUND RECENTLY UNDER A WALL THAT HAD FALLEN (6).

after their skin; as Eyraud says: " The natives have no
interest in protecting themselves from the heat or cold, but
only to decorate themselves with clothing; in the feasts they
load themselves all they can." Because of the scarcity of
bark-cloth they had to resort to other sources of ornamentation. The usual alternative in Polynesia was the mat or
hand-braided textile. But in the tropics there were several
plants that supplied material for this besides the reeds and
rushes which grow wherever there is sufficient fresh water;
but by far the most important was the *p a n d a n u s*, the
leaf of which when soaked and scraped and split supplies the
finest of all threads for braiding; it is a characteristic feature
of every tropical island in the Pacific, whether high or low,
volcanic or coralline; for its seed can stand saturation with
salt water for months without losing its vitality, and it is
therefore a natural and universal immigrant. But it never
reached Easter Island till Messrs. Salmon and Brander introduced it some fifty years ago. Nor is there any plant like the
New Zealand *phormium tenax* to take its place. It is as poor
in material for matting as it is in material for bark-cloth.
The result was that mats were even scarcer than cloth. The
fact that the word for mat, *m o e n g a* (in other dialects
" a thing for sleeping on ") is monopolized by the special meaning of a corpse-wrap or coffin shows how rare it was for use
by the living. It was of course used for its original purpose,
a covering during the night. Eyraud says: " The little mat
that covers them is full of insect life "; and again, " I have
never been able to get over my repugnance when I see them
swallow with the agility of a hen the numerous insect parasites
they collect from the little mat that covers them." It had its
day use; but it would be its night use that would especially
stock it from the grass on the floor. The only source of this
matting was the rushes that grew round the lakes in the
craters. It was this, too, that was the source of the beautifully
braided long girdle that women wore round their waist and used
as a carry-all. It is still a common thing to see women riding
down the slopes of Rano Kao with a bundle of reeds in front
of them. But in the old days, when there was no European
stuff to eke out clothing, there must have been a run on the
reeds, since not merely mantles, sleeping mats and their little
straw hats, but all their baskets, were made of them. Their
lack of wooden dishes and coco-nut cups made these *k e t e s*

the universal receptacle[1]; there was the foot-long *k e t e r a u -
h i r i* for use at meals, the four-foot long and four-foot deep
k e t e t u r u a for carrying and the six-foot long and six-foot
deep *k e t e t u k u n g a* to hold the food from the great
earth-ovens at the feasts.

(8) **MAT MAKING AND DYEING.** They seldom attempted
the geometrical patterns and edgings that usually distinguish
Polynesian matwork; they were satisfied with making some
finer and softer, like the *N i i h a u* mats of the Hawaiian
group, for special occasions like marriages, and with dyeing
them one bright colour, usually yellow. This effort to reach
more artistic work and finer colours is seen in the legend of
The Old Matmaker. She lived alone away up the slope of
Rano Aroi and gained a reputation all over the island for the
beauty and fineness of her products. But she was baffled in
her efforts to get a satisfactory and fast yellow; she tried all
sorts of mixtures of the usual materials and failed. One
evening, as she was seated at her porch thinking over the
problem, she saw two great shadows against the sky; she
thought at first they were *m a k o h e* making their way to
the south coast from Motu Matiro Hiva. But they grew in
size and it was soon plain that they were men on wings. They
landed in front of her and she invited them to rest a while.
They told her that they were dyers in a far-off island and in
dream there appeared to them a woman-dyer baffled with the
problem of a yellow colour and begging them to come to her
island. They had the secret of that dye and they had come
to communicate it to her provided she kept it to herself; she
swore she would keep it. And then they got a stone and shaped
it into a mortar for grinding the stuffs they had brought, and
with twigs from a neighbouring tree they made a sifter. They
showed her how she could get her material from the R a n o
including the red from the *p u a* tuber and the juice from the
sugar-cane. They manipulated it all so that when a mat was
soaked in it, it became a brilliant golden. Her cries of delight
drew some rival matmakers who were out in search of material
for colouring; and seeing the brilliance of the mat and the
three busy with the process, they burst in upon them to learn
the secret. One of the strangers made off on his wings towards
the sea; but the other, in attempting to hide the secret,
was caught and stoned to death. Thus the *r e n g a*, or

[1] For *kete* see Chap. X, par. 14.

AN EASTER ISLAND FEATHER HAT MADE AS MOST COMMONLY IN
ANCIENT TIMES OF THE FEATHERS OF FOWLS; USED IN THE DANCES

THE *Broussenetia papyrifera* (*aute*), THE SOURCE OF THE BEST
BARKCLOTH IN POLYNESIA

yellow dye, came into Easter Island and became the property of all.

(9) **THE FEATHER-WORK OF EASTER ISLAND.** We get an
even more difficult and rarer material of Polynesian personal
ornament when we come to feathers. In Tahiti and even in
New Zealand feather-work was of great importance as a fine
art ; certain feathers were reserved for the heads of chiefs
and kings ; and the feather mat with its checker-work of
colours was the ceremonial mantle of only the noble and
wealthy. But it was in Hawaii that the art reached its greatest
development in decorations for the heads of gods and chiefs
and in caps and mantles and robes that were the work of
generations. Here the art surpassed that of the Pacific coast
of America. In Easter Island it spent itself chiefly on decoration
of the head, the most sacred part of chiefs in Polynesia. The
feather-hat was the first thing that the early voyagers noticed.
Behrens observes how some whom they took for priests round
the images " had the head quite shaven and wore a bonnet
made of black and white feathers like those of the stork " ;
" the most aged had on their heads plumes resembling the
ostrich." Forster, a far more accurate observer, sees the
feathers of the *makohe* and the *kena;* " They protected
their heads from the sun, many of the men with a grass ring
two inches thick, covered with great quantities of the long
black feathers which decorate the neck of the man-of-war
bird. Others had huge bushy caps of brown gulls' feathers " ;
" and still others wore a simple hoop of wood round which a
number of the long white feathers of a gannet hung nodding
and waved in the wind." There was a considerable variety
of feather hats: the *hau kurakura* of the red-tail feathers
of the tropic bird, donned when going into battle, and though
the king never fought he generally wore a feather-hat called
veri just before a battle ; *hau vaero*, a hat for the dances,
made of the tail feathers of the white-tailed *tavake; hau
teketeke*, a hat with a ridge or crest ; *hau tara*, a
hat with rough or bristling feathers ; *hau moroke*, a
hat of Mother Hubbard shape. This last was like the
moroke, a feather decoration in front of the king's house.
Along the road leading to it on either side was a line of poles
covered with alternate belts of white and black feathers,
called *huhu;* and on the porch were two *maros* or cords
of feathers as his ensigns or flags, and two of them just within

the porch. This (*m a r o*) was also the name of a circlet of feathers worn by men in the dance.

(10) The Easter Islanders had only a limited range of colour for their feather-work. They had nothing but sea-birds and fowls, and the feathers of these, except for the red tail feathers of the *t a v a k e*, were all black, grey, or white. The dark wings of the frigate-bird had evidently something sacred in them ; for they were used as the distinctive ornament for the head of the *paina* figure. The women resorted to other methods of ornamentation. Their girdle was especially long and handsome ; when they wore a shorter, it was the *k o t a k e* beautifully braided of human hair. Next to this the most distinctive ornament worn by women, along with the wooden *t a h o n g a*, was the shell necklace, the *r e i   p i p i* of iridescent shell and the *r e p u r e v a*, cowries strung on human hair.[1] Both men and women wore the hair long, so that the human hair used in these girdles or necklaces must have been supplied by both sexes. In Hawaii the *h o l o k u*, the necklace of human hair with the white ivory ornament, was a mark of nobility in women. In Easter Island there was no distinction of class and such a necklace was only a mark of prosperity. Both men and women tied up (*u r u*) the hair in a topknot (*p u k a o*) like the men of old Japan and the men of most Polynesian groups. This will largely account for the height of the red tufa hats placed on the heads of the great images.

(11) **TATTOOING IN POLYNESIA.** But for a people that had only bark-cloth for dress, a material that unless water-proofed with coco-nut oil will go to pieces in rain and in the sea, and that had but little of that, there was only one permanent form of personal decoration and that was tattooing, unless they were Melanesians and preferred cicatrization. With a tropical people, given to much bathing in the sea, swimming and diving, there was an absolute necessity to use but little clothing and to adopt some form of skin-ornamenta-tion that would not wash off. Had the Polynesians been a negroid people or even come slowly through a negroid region and crossed with some of its inhabitants, this would have been secured by means of scars fixed and raised by cutting the flesh and keeping the wounds open. But where they did not adopt tattooing the Polynesians made no indelible marks on the

[1] See No. 7 in picture facing p. 188.

skin at all. This was the case with the Chatham Islanders and the people of Rapa ; and in their case it was probably due to the coldness of the climate not encouraging nudity of body. The Austral Islanders, who are just within the tropics, may owe their untattooed skin to the same cause. But why the Easter Islanders, who are almost as far out of the tropics as Rapa, did not follow the example of that island is not so easy to determine. It may be due to immigration of highly tattooed peoples. The Maoris migrated from the tropics to a cold climate ; but all the effect was to shift the finest tattooing from the body to the face, not to make them abandon it altogether.

(12) **EASTER ISLAND TATTOOING.** The Easter Islanders were one of the most highly tattooed branches of the Polynesian race, only the Marquesans rivalling them and some of the Paumotans. It was the fashion for both men and women to have the whole body and face tattooed, though the length and pain of the process made many women shrink from completing the operation ; they had it only from waist to knee and on the lips and cheeks and forehead. The voyagers were as much struck with the result of this art as of feather-work. Behrens as usual describes it inaccurately as *painting* : " their bodies were *painted* with all kinds of figures of birds and other animals." Forster is more accurate : " They were all prodigiously punctured on every part of the body, the face in particular." The women were also punctured with something like the patches on European court ladies' faces. Beechey is more detailed in his description : " Tattooing is here practised to a greater extent than formerly, especially by females, who have stained their skins in imitation of blue breeches. Besides this, some of them tattoo their foreheads as well as the edges of their ears and the fleshy parts of their lips." " The males tattoo themselves in curved lines upon the upper part of the throat, beginning at the ear and sloping round below the underjaw. The face is sometimes nearly covered with lines similar to those on the throat, or with an uninterrupted colouring except two broad stripes on each side at right angles to each other. Most of their lips were also stained. Some had the body thoroughly stained, but most only a small space. All the lines were drawn with much taste and carried in the direction of the muscles as in New Zealand."

(13) **THE WHENCE OF THE ART.** Considerable elements in

the tattooing seem to point to New Zealand as the source and not the Marquesas or Paumotus, where though the whole body and face are often covered, it is with designs less refined than those of the Maoris or the Easter Islanders. The lines on the face and body are drawn horizontally and roughly. The Maori preferred the curve and the spiral; the Easter Islander had curves about the head and spirals over the lower ribs. The Marquesan, and to some extent the Easter Islander, was fond of figures from life, flowers or birds or fishes or even human busts or faces. The Maori preferred an arabesque, though the Marquesan sometimes adopted in his tattooing the arabesque of his carved clubs, and the Easter Islander occasionally varied his picture by arabesques. The blue breeches of the Easter Island women and sometimes of the men are much the same as the tattooing of Samoa and Tonga, and as that on some of the Maoris as described by Cook. As far as one is able to gather from tradition there was nothing totemic in the tattooing as in one case at least it was in Tonga. It did not, as in Hawaii, denote the noble or the brand of the slave, nor was it used in mourning. It did not indicate the tribe or the deeds of the tattooed or his ancestors as in New Zealand. Its main purpose was to beautify, as in Tahiti. Every woman was proud of it when it covered her whole body and face. Probably it was also meant as a symbol of courage and endurance; for to go through the whole process was ten years of pain, and some succumbed to the suffering. In the case of the *p u h i* tattooed by the *m a o r i* on the cheeks of the virgin and the canoe on the cheeks of the men, it was clearly intended to carry a meaning; whilst the lizards tattooed on the chest and back of the men probably had the same significance as the lizard-headed club they took into battle and the dance. The women had this lizard only painted on the breast for the feast and afterwards washed off.

(14) **THE TATTOOING OF VARIOUS PARTS OF THE BODY.** It was the *m a o r i*, or priest, that did the tattooing; he was the successor of the sculptors and should have been an artist, and yet Easter Island tattooing is rather a collection of varieties than a work of art like the face of a New Zealander. He began with tattooing at Orongo circles on the buttocks and bands on the arms of the young women, the *p o k i m a n u* and, if virgin, the *p u h i* on her cheeks; and equivalent forms on the young man on M o t u n u i, the *p o k i t a k e;*

THE TATTOOING OF A MAORI MARRIED WOMAN

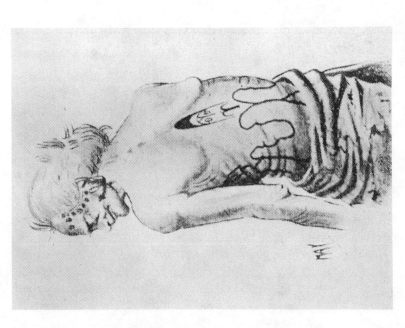

THE TATTOOING OF AN EASTER ISLAND WOMAN WHO SAW THE PERUVIAN RAID IN 1860 (From "Tres Notas sobre La Isla de Pascua," by Dr. Walter Knoche of Santiago, Chili. The Author's photograph of tattooing failed).

the *r a p e* was tattooed on the breech as amongst the Maoris. He was called as tattooer *t a k o n a*, as was also the tattooed, from *k o n a*, the thigh, as he began with that part of the body. *P a r e* was the tattooing on the waist and the calves of the legs; *p a r e p u*, a face tattooed on the abdomen; *p a e p a e*, tattooing on the lower part of the back; *r i m a - k o n a* or *p i r i u k o n a*, that on the hands; *p u r a r i k i*, that on the back; *u m i u m i*, that from the lips to chin on both men and women; *n g u t u t i k a*, that on women's lips; *h u m u*, that on the upper part of the feet, and *m a t a - p e a p e a*, that on the eyelids. The *a o*, or dance club, was tattooed on the back of both men and women.

(15) **A LEGEND OF TATTOOING.** That the art came from abroad seems to be indicated by the legend of *H e r u* and *P a t u*. Two surpassingly beautiful women on *P o i k e* enslaved the husbands in the neighbourhood and were reputed witches. But they had heard of a method the inhabitants of other islands had of making themselves more beautiful and of an old woman at *O r o n g o* who had the secret. They set out and at last stumbled on her house and were invited to rest and eat. But they saw smoke rising from Motunui and found out from their host that it was two men, *H e r u* and *P a t u*, who had recently arrived there. Their curiosity was piqued and they swam across after getting from the old woman the secret and the materials to realize it. They found the men out fishing, but slowly insinuated themselves into friendship that ended in matrimony with them. The two fishermen got tired of their beauty and their airs and set out for a journey on the mainland. When they were gone the women each became the mother of a boy and they called them *H e r u* the younger and *P a t u* the younger. The men did not return; and the boys grew up on the islet, handsome and skilled in fishing and swimming. The mothers were long suspicious of the truth; but at last two wizard friends from another isle showed them in a dream their husbands settled in new homes. They called their boys and told them their history and the secret of making themselves beautiful for ever and the hiding-place of the materials to apply it. Then, calling on their patrons far away, they went to the top of the islet and vanished. The boys, finding themselves alone, tattooed themselves and set out for the mainland to find their fathers in the place their mothers had indicated. From the

rim of R a n o K a o they saw a great crowd on the shore by T o n g a r i k i and made for it. They found going on a competition in surfing and entered it. On their *pora* they swam far beyond the others and came rushing in on a huge billow. When all was over they went to a well of fresh water, and, washing, lay down to rest; and some youths approached with calabashes for water and as each drew his calabash fell to pieces; afraid of the sorcery that could have done this and suspecting the two strangers of it, they fled and told their fathers, who were none else than the older *Heru* and *Patu*. The old men sent them to bring the strangers, and when they were brought, recognized them; they were handsome and the very image of their mothers. So they sent their other children packing and took the two into their households and asked them how they made themselves so beautiful. The youths told their story and taught all the neighbours and ultimately all Easter Islanders how to be beautiful for ever.

(16) **SPOILING BEAUTY BY PAINT.** This sounds as if art were exotic; and the finer lines, the tattooing on the face and especially on the lips, and the use of spirals seem to point to New Zealand as the country from which it came. But the Easter Islanders were not satisfied with this indelible beauty; they must have paint as well. And so they spoiled the work of art by daubing it over. Forster described the result in the women: " they painted their natural clear brown colour of the face with a reddish brown," " over which they laid on the bright orange of the turmeric root or ornamented themselves with elegant streaks of white shell lime." And Beechey, half a century after, described the painting of the men: " Some people had their faces painted black, some red, others black and white, or red and white, like clowns and two demonlike monsters were painted entirely black." The black they got from the tattooing powder, the soot of the *ti* leaf, the red from the tuberous root of the *pua*, and the white from the earth on R a n o K a o called *kiea* or *marikuru*,[1] but later from the white arrowroot of the *pia* plant which was all over the island. The use of this led them, when flour was first given to them, to think it was white paint; and instead of using it for food they rubbed it all over their bodies. That this " painting the lily " was exotic is probable and that

[1] See No. 11 in picture facing p. 188.

it came from New Zealand is not improbable after reading Cook's description of the Maori custom of painting over the tattooing : " The women paint their faces red which, so far from increasing, diminished the very little beauty they have. The men's faces were not in general painted ; but some were rubbed over with red ochre from head to foot, their apparel not excepted." He evidently regretted that they should so overdo the art of beautifying and spoil the " a m o k o " which " resembled filigree work and the foliage on old chased ornaments " and no two alike. It is one of the ironies of anthropology that this " painting the lily " and overlaying beauty with flour has reappeared not amongst primitive peoples but in the most civilized strata of modern Europe.

CHAPTER XVII

THE QUEST OF FOOD

(1) *The Polynesian rat was a vegetarian and a prolific breeder, and escaping the voracity of the Easter Islander perished before its carnivorous brethren and cats from European ships.* (2) *The fowl was probably indigenous in the Pacific ; and all the introductions of domesticated animals went down the improvident gullet of Easter Islanders, pig, dog, goat, sheep, rabbit.* (3) *The fowl escaped the* umu *and the Easter Island appetite by aid of the fortifications called "fowl caves."* (4) *Of tubers the taro needs much moisture, and this is not to be found here.* (5) *The yam is considered insipid though the legend of the monopoly by growers in Hangaroa, and the defeat of the ring by a frigate-bird seems to show that it was once more valued.* (6) *Sweet potato was their staple of food, and is practically the equivalent of food in the language ; but though especially suited to such a dry island, it did not prevent famines ; and their colossal improvidence, probably due to the absence of long-voyaging, neglected the making of* poi, *the universal Polynesian provision against famine.* (7) *The banana is only seasonal, the sugar-cane used chiefly for thatching and the dracaena (ti) chiefly for the tattooing powder from burning its leaves.* (8) *They rely most on the products of the sea, and are the most skilful fishermen and swimmers and divers.* (9) *By diving they get huge crayfish, which sometimes got them, as is seen from the legend of the king and the crayfish, which, till he secured it, disposed of numberless divers ; such fear has this produced that they place an imitation crayfish at their doors to scare off trespassers.* (10) *The eels down in the depths and the seasnakes are caught by a running noose ; but the cuttlefish by hand.* (11) *The women gather the shellfish and limpets, but avoid cannibal cave because the blood of a* tatani *wounded by the sweetheart of a girl, being drunk up by a limpet, wrought vengeance upon her ; trying to get it off the rock it carried her out to sea.* (12) *The dream of a skeleton led to the substitution of the hook of human bone for the old stone hook.* (13) *Elaborate preparations are taken for catching the tunny* (kahi), *and taboo prevents its being exterminated.* (14) *They had many kinds of nets for fish that went in shoals.* (15) *But they trusted more to charmstones than to hooks or nets.*

(1) **THE RAT IN POLYNESIA.** In an island so little capable of cultivation and so far from all other land the fundamental problem was not what to eat but what could be found to eat. There were no animals except the rat and the fowl. The rat was plentiful, though now almost extinct ; but it was a mere mouthful, especially for such a hungry people. It was the same as the edible rat of New Zealand and the other Polynesian areas, not much larger than a mouse, black and long-furred, as a vegetarian, fed on the most barren islands, plump and tasty ; one of the features of the male was the testicles large out of all proportion to the body. It was extremely prolific and made up for its smallness by its numbers, till the cat arrived, and following the cat the two so-called European rats, which did not arrive in the West from Asia till well on in our era, one of them not till the ships of the crusaders brought it. These new-comers were twice as large and ten times as voracious and, unfortunately for the little native,

carnivorous. The two types must have hived off early in Asia, and the little vegetarian got quarantined on the islands of Polynesia and saved for thousands of years, a cave and tree dweller, whilst his congeners swarmed into the hives of men, the thieves of all human foods and the carriers of the worst of human diseases. Had these bold burglars and brigands been the rats that got into the *débris* of the hypothetical Pacific continent there is no question that the Polynesian would not have carried them in their migrations as they carried the little vegetarian. Its breeders and spreaders of Polynesia were a highly sporting race, and when conquest led to monarchies and nobilities in some of the larger groups it became the victim of sport. In Tonga and Hawaii the bow and arrow that had never become war-weapons in Polynesia were used to shoot rats; in the latter group they were gathered together in a pit and shot at by the nobles; in New Zealand it was the sport of old men and boys and again it was the only use of the bow. But in New Zealand as in other Polynesian areas it was encouraged mainly as a food, or rather as a titbit, reserved as a rule for the chiefs. In Easter Island it was so highly valued as a luxury that it became the medium of exchange; no one would refuse a bunch of rats when anyone made an offer for any of his goods.

(2) **THE FOWL AND THE MAMMALS AFTERWARDS INTRO-DUCED.** It is more than likely that, though, like the rat, the fowl was carried by the Polynesians in their migrations, it was also an occupant of the central Pacific Islands when men first reached them. For there is no taboo for women on the flesh of fowls as there is on that of the dog and the pig. It is one of the strangest anomalies in the history of Easter Island that when all the other animals that have been landed on it were eaten out before they could establish themselves the fowl survived. Whether it was down the gullets of the inhabitants that the primeval pig and dog vanished or into the maw of the ocean with the sinking of the archipelagoes it is impossible to say; we know that they existed before the catastrophe; for their Polynesian names survived in the language (*p u a k a* for animal and *k u r i* for cat). Hotu Matua, the universal provider of Easter Island, brought porcine and canine animals with him (*p e p e k u* and *p a i h e n g a*); but tradition tells us that they were both eaten out before they established themselves. Again, La Perouse put a boar and sow on shore,

but with certain misgivings as to the result. " I do not flatter myself that the pigs I present them with will flourish." And tradition again tells us his misgivings were justified ; they were taken up to P o i k e and a great pit dug for them, and they were fed on the best, sweet potatoes and bananas ; the sow had a litter and they were distributed in pairs over the island. There must have been a lover and breeder of animals up on that barren plateau ; but the voracity of his countrymen made the experiment impossible ; they all went the way of their predecessors, leaving like them only a new name for a pig (o r u from their grunt) in the language. But the benevolent French voyager had more hopes of his two other experiments ; " the goats and sheep, which drink little and love salt, will succeed here." The only success they had was to leave their native-manufactured names in the language, a p a i h o r u (manifestly a combination of p a i of Hotu's dog (p a i h e n g a) and the new name for the pig (o r u)), and m a m o i for the sheep, perhaps from its cry. It would have gladdened the heart of La Perouse to see the tens of thousands of sheep now covering the island ; another Frenchman from Tahiti brought the first consignment, but brought with them new grass seed to raise feed for them, and European guardians to save them from the native earth-oven ; then Anglo-Saxons came in early this century with their wider knowledge of sheep and better breeds and, making the natives shepherds, have raised the numbers to tens of thousands and are improving their chief purpose here, wool-bearing. Another experiment was made with goats ; but there are none now on the island. The rabbit was introduced ; and Pierre Loti, on his visit in 1871 with the French warship, the *Flore*, was pestered by the natives wanting to sell him rabbits ; they had generally several hung at their girdle. They have gone the same route as the pigs, dogs, goats, and sheep, leaving only the French-derived name r a p i n o in the language ; that an English-derived word r a p i t i has taken its place shows that a later experiment was tried and again failed ; Australians would add " much to the benefit of mankind " ; have they ever tried the intro- duction of a colony of Easter Islanders into their continental island as a cure for the rabbit pest ? The way in which new introductions vanish was vividly brought to my mind when I was riding amongst the a h u s in the north ; I had been told that the partridge had been introduced recently ; a sudden whir from below a huge statue fallen by the way reminded me of the fact; my guide was ahead; he got off and hauled a young partridge just feathered from the nest underneath the image; what became of it I do not know; but it vanished into his bag. That the cat has not yet been completely exterminated is probably due to the fact that it and its mate came off their ship " on their own " and lost all signs of domestication in the caves amongst the rats. In the other islands of Polynesia its name (*p u h i* and *p o p o k i*, poor pussy) and Tahitian *p i i f a r e* ("stick to the house") indicates that it came off the ship with its human friends. Its appropriation here of the old Polynesian name for the dog (*k u r i*) tells its own story.

(3) **WHAT SAVED FOWLS FROM THE UMU?** Why the fowl should have escaped this improvident voracity of the natives is a problem not easy to solve. Its use for the ceremonial and dancing would not have saved it; for there were still the sea-birds to get decorative feathers from. Its commonest use by the naturally sportive Polynesian for cock-fighting would not have saved it; for though the Easter Islanders used it for this purpose it was only rarely; it was not one of the outstanding events of their festivals; they are not so fond of sport as the Tahitians or Hawaiians, the Tongans or the Maoris. It was for the need of feathers for the kings' ensigns and ceremonial hats, probably the only sign of their kingship. Hotu Matua saw the absolute necessity, if there was to be any distinction between royalty and subject, of conserving the one source of royal decoration. He might have secured his purpose by *taboo*, making the people afraid of eating the flesh of fowls lest they should get some appalling disease. But he had probably used up his stock of diseases in *taboo* for essential foods, fish and birds. At any rate, the measure he took for the conservation of fowls was to make it the fashion to build great houses or caves for them, with walls thick enough for a fortification. In these the chickens were safe from marauding hands at night; by day the owners could keep an eye on them. It would be a task for even the most skilful native to take those great walls to pieces, and the noise made by tumbling the huge stones off them would waken the owners in the neighbouring house. Yet tradition tells of one fowl-thief so expert that he used to send notice to an owner of a chicken-house that he was going to raid it and yet he would get off with the plunder. But that

only one such expert has his story told and that the story is told as a wonder shows that those *a n a m o a* had been successful in their purpose ; young chickens were enabled to avoid the *u m u* of the night-prowler and so to hand on their species throughout the generations.

(4) **TARO AND YAM.** With no animals to manure it and no forests or fruit trees to shed their leaves, it is no wonder that there was little or no humus on the island till the modern age of sheep and cattle. The first party from Tahiti that visited it to see what it could be used for reported that there were great bare patches all over it, without grass or herbage of any kind ; and since that when trees are cut down no vegetation springs up spontaneously on the ground thus freed from the drain on its resources and laid open to the sun and rain ; there is no seed stored up from former vegetation in the soil. Further, there are no streams as the rain filters away through the porous soil and rock till it meets the solid imper- meable basalt that is the base of the island, flowing out as springs between high and low tide. Hence there are no valleys, the work of the erosion of streams, to accumulate good soil on their banks and flats and hollows. There are ponds inside the old craters where the rain, prevented from escaping down- wards by the impermeable plug in the throat of the old volcano, accumulates under a felting of reed-roots ; and where these are not too deep there is a soakage and often a shortlived stream over a breach in the rim as is the case with Rano Aroi in the north centre. Here *t a r o* can be grown with something approaching to the irrigation that is generally employed for its cultivation in most other Polynesian islands. But most of the *t a r o* that they raise is grown in artificial hollows where a weathered volcanic dyke has spread a blanket of its crystals over the ground and so conserved some moisture ; and the stones protect the tubers from desiccation by the sun's rays. Hotu Matua with his Polynesian knowledge and predilections brought about a dozen varieties ; amongst the best of them were *t a r o k o r o m a r u i*, small but excellent eating ; *t a r o n g a a t u*, as good, but large with foliage like a rush ; others were *t a r o t u a n g a m e a*, red and large, *t a r o h o r e h o r e t a p a t e a*, black, two white- fleshed *n g u n g u h a h a t e a*, and *n g e t i* and one of great size, *h a r a h a r a*.

(5) But *t a r o* had too little ground fitted for it, and needed

too much care, and produced too little to be a favourite tuber. *Y a m* was not much better, though, if properly grown, it produced a tuber as large as a man, as some who have seen them this size testify. And it had this advantage over *t a r o* that it would grow without irrigation. But the natives say it is insipid and not worth the growing. But this cannot always have been the opinion, if we are to trust the legend of The Frigate-bird's Theft. A great gardener called R a p u had every variety of Easter Island tubers in his garden at *T e K o h e* on *P o i k e* except yam and he was even said to have produced others by hybridization. But he longed for the plant that he had not got and offered every kind of inducement to its monopolists in H a n g a r o a for a set; but they refused, and in order to prevent him getting one they peeled the skin and top off every tuber they traded off and burned the peelings. But one night R a p u saw a *m a k o h e* hovering over his garden as he worked and he threw it the tastiest bits of his plants as well as the fish he had just caught. It fluttered down and he told it that he was anxious to get a bit of yam. It flew away west and hovered over *H a n g a r o a* till it saw an old man carrying tops of yam to plant. It swooped down and carried off one in its beak to P o i k e. It dropped it on a piece of R a p u ' s garden that had just been turned over with the digging-stick (*o k a*); it fell foliage down; but when the gardener came out in the morning and saw it already shooting, he turned it over and covered it with earth. He watched all day for his avian assistant; and as he saw it winging its way from the cliffs empty-pouched, he held up his choicest fish to it and called it. As it settled down by his fish, Rapu said to it: "My dear Kotemanu Haarongo; you are too clever to be a mere pirate of the air; you should be a gardener; see how your yam is growing." And the bird, on his journeys to and from M a r o t i r i, never failed to visit R a p u, who, when the yam grew into a long tuber, cut it into many pieces and by the help of the *m a k o h e* distributed them all over the island and defeated the selfishness of the monopolists of Hangaroa. But so little are the yam and the taro necessary to the well-being of the Easter Islander that their cultivation is neglected and in a drought they are apt to die out. It is probably an occurrence of this sort that has led to the belief that all the varieties of *t a r o* and *y a m* brought by Hotu Matua died when his successor, Maurata, died in Peru in 1863.

N

(6) **THE SWEET POTATO, AND WHY NO POI?** The real stand-by of the Easter Islander is the sweet potato (*k u m a r a*). He can eat it raw or cooked like the yam, and he can get a huge crop of it with little cultivation. But what makes it his chief food is that it can be grown in the driest of soils; and there are few places on this island but are almost permanently dry. It grows none the worse for an occasional shower; but as soon as moisture accumulates round the tubers they rot. It is exactly the plant for Easter Island; for there is seldom more than forty inches of rain in the year, and the soil seems to be dry a few minutes after the heaviest shower; its drainage is perfect, in fact so perfect that it is imperfect for everything but *kumara*. All the voyagers speak of the abundance and excellence of the sweet potatoes. They had not much variety in cooking them. They sometimes stoneboiled them in the large calabash (*k a h a*); but they were far the best steamed in the earth-oven. They had practically no coco-nut to make flavouring for puddings such as they cooked in the tropical Polynesian islands. This may be one of the reasons why they never made the *p o i* which is the distinctive food of all Polynesia. But the two main reasons were that they were exceptionally improvident and that they never had a canoe after the catastrophe that could go a long voyage, even more than a mile or two from the shore. The two reasons are probably closely related. The necessities of a long voyage cultivate the faculty of foreseeing; without careful provisioning and forethought no voyage, however long it is meant to be, can be long. They had not the breadfruit from which the Tahitian *t i o o* was made for famines and long voyages. But the low coralline islands had not breadfruit, and yet made the fermented paste called sometimes *p o i* and sometimes *m a i;* and even volcanic islands like the Marquesas, which had breadfruit, preferred to make their *p o i* of *t a r o*. And Easter Island had *taro*, which, if the natives had cultivated it carefully, might have been grown in sufficient quantity to make the fermented paste for times of scarcity. And that they had periods of famine we know, not merely from the word for it in their language (*h a k a - m a r u a h i*), but from their traditions; they were often reduced to eating the skins of bananas, the peelings of their tubers, the bark of the banana stem, and the root of the *t a n o a*, or seaside convolvulus, although that inflamed the

eyes and swelled the tissues and sometimes caused death. Their rooted cannibalism originated in hunger. The gorging at their feasts of the whole produce of their land meant often subsequent famine. No Polynesian people was ever so improvident, although the cessation of the taboo, the basis of the chiefly organization and power, has, by removing the compulsion to work, brought out the tendency of the village communism of Polynesia to idleness and lack of forethought in providing for the future. As long as the Polynesians were long-voyagers they knew the evils of improvidence. And doubtless the main reason for Easter Island standing out as the awful example of this vice is that since the catastrophe the natives could not and did not make long voyages. The last Easter Islander to look ahead of the moment was Hotu Matua. The natives had not even the forethought to ask the gods for success in their raising of food ; only when the crops were in danger of dying did they go to the king and get him to send an *a r i k i   p a k a* to pray for rain. In Hawaii and most other Polynesian areas they feared the possibility of their crops failing and on planting they prayed to the gods for success, and on harvesting showed their gratitude by offerings to them. There is no record in tradition of such a custom amongst the Easter Islanders. And this is due not so much to lack of religion as to lack of forethought.

(7) **BANANA, SUGAR-CANE, AND TI.** They might have used the banana as well as *t a r o* for the making of *p o i*. For Hotu Matua had provided the island with about half a dozen varieties of it, some of them different from the varieties to be found in other Polynesian islands, one, for example, triangular in the shape of the fruit that is very sweet and has under the skin flesh puffed out and more like a soufflet than paste. The names of some that he brought were *maika puka-puka, m. korotea, m. hihi, m. pia, and m. pahu* (this kind now extinct). But bananas are a seasonal crop like breadfruit and not to be relied upon for a time of scarcity unless it is fermented or dried. Another seasonal crop was sugar-cane ; but it was never very successful in the island ; it rarely flowered and never ripened, so that it had little or no sugary sap in it. The natives relied more on the root of the dracaena (*t i*) for their confection ; baked in the earth-oven, it had far more sweetness in it than the sugar-cane. But it was more valued by the natives for the tattooing powder from its burnt

leaves, just as sugar-cane was more valued as a thatch for their houses than for its juice.

(8) **NATURAL FISHERMEN.** Next to the sweet potato it was the seatrove that furnished most food for Easter Island. The sea was ever present to every native, and from infancy boys and girls were accustomed to swim ; they were not only not afraid of salt water but delighted in it. And as they grew older they dived without fear to great depths ; they were, perhaps, the most expert swimmers and divers in the Pacific Ocean. For the lack of timber made canoes scarce, small, and leaky. By preference the men and women who went to the festivals took the route by sea, and chose the *p o r a*, or swimming mat-raft, as their conveyance. When a foreign ship arrived it was far easier to swim on this than to launch and paddle a leaky canoe. The voyagers therefore report crowds of swimmers, few canoes. Beechey's boats passed a rock far out in the sea swarming with women who had swum out to it ; it was like an islet of sirens. Many, too, kept swimming after the boats, and when one young and good-looking girl was taken into one of them she did her best to help the the others in the water to get in.

(9) **THE KING AND THE CRAYFISH.** It was little wonder that they were expert fishermen ; and they had to be ; for no island had ever more difficult conditions for successful fishing. Most of it was faced with precipitous crags, against which the billows dashed incessantly ; some of them were inaccessible from above and unapproachable at their base. There were only three small beaches accessible by a canoe and that only at certain seasons. And where they could get down the rocks into the water, the irregular rocky bottom was a danger unless to an expert swimmer and diver. In the caves and crevices of the rocks below they knew where to find crustaceans, some of them of considerable size ; the coasts of Easter Island, like those of Juan Fernandez, abound in gigantic crayfish, which are usually called in Spanish *langosta*, or lobster. They never used the wicker basket or trap so common in the other islands of Polynesia ; and they could not set nets as in Hawaii, because the haunts of the prey were amongst craggy and sharp rocks. It is one of the commonest sights along the coasts to see the naked fishermen disappear below the water and in two or three minutes appear with a huge crayfish in each hand ; when down he sees the long

feelers searching around for food or he tempts them out by tasty baits, and then he seizes them and pulls the animal out. The dangers of this pursuit are crystallized in the legend of The King and the Crayfish. Some parts of the north-west coast are so much frequented by these great crustaceans that many fishermen are seen to dive together into the depths. Once upon a time two of the boldest went down, and only one came up with his catch. He waited, thinking his mate was about to bring up a larger haul. Minutes passed and no head appeared above the surface of the water. Something must have happened, their friends on the shore called to him. Summoning up courage he dived again ; but he came up soon with a look of terror on his face ; it was then he remembered the stories of fishermen having disappeared in this very corner ; and he told the spectators that a gigantic crayfish had darted out of a cave at him and he escaped by the skin of his teeth. The king had heard of the frequent disappearances and called some of the most expert fishermen and divers to the place ; he sent one of the most experienced down in order to make sure that the enormous crayfish was not the product of imagination. He came up and said that it was a reality and that its residence was a cave large enough for two or three men to enter. So the king got the strongest *hauhau* ropes he could find and made a great net of them. He went down with the last diver and fixed it right across the mouth of the cave and came up. After recovering, he went down alone with thirty feet of the rope and bound the feelers of the monster to the meshes of the net through which they were thrust. He came up with the other end in his hand and giving it to the strongest men he could find in the crowd bade them haul. Soon appeared above the water the head of a crayfish of enormous proportions ; it must have been preying on fish and on men for centuries. It was cooked in one of the largest ovens that had ever been made on the island and hundreds of people came to the feast. There were no more disappearances of divers on that side of the island thereafter. The king must have learnt net-capture from Hotu Matua or some other far traveller in Polynesia. That the crayfish had terrors for Easter Islanders is shown by the fact that they used to make one of bark-cloth and paint it red ; this *ura* having an *akuaku* in it was placed at the door to scare off trespassers.

(10) **EELS, SNAKES, AND CUTTLEFISH.** But there was

other game than crayfish for venturous divers down in those
fissured and cavernous depths. There were conger eels, some
of them of great size. But with their slippery bodies it was
impossible to catch them by hand. So the fisherman took
down with him a simple apparatus consisting of two sticks
about eighteen inches long, and on the end of one a running
noose controlled by a string attached to the other and on the
end of the other a bait which hung right in the middle of the
noose[1]; with this the eel was tempted out of his retreat and,
following the dangling bait, he thrust his head through the
loop and the diver drew the string so that it cut deep into the
neck of the fish. He took other eels by the same method
and there were many of them from the two-foot long *koreha
te puni* and *koreha tapitea* to the *koreha haoko*, six-foot long,
and the huge *koreha tokotoko ari*. Sea-snakes (*k o e h o*)
were caught similarly and were eaten as readily as eels. And
they had often to dive sixty or seventy feet to get the eels.
The divers did not fear either conger eels or snakes; nor did
they fear the cuttlefish (*h e k e*), though it was feared all over
the Polynesian islands and even turned into a deity in some.
The wonder is that the people chose the crayfish for a monster
instead of the octopus in their legends. But it seems as if
they had no *h e k e* as large as the octopus in tropical
Polynesia. For they caught them by hand; both men and
women went out to catch them on moonlight nights. There
were two kinds they preferred for eating, the *h e k e p u k a -
p u k a* with tentacles about eighteen inches long and suckers
on the ends of them an inch across, and the *h e k e k o r o t e a*
with tentacles four feet long and suckers only about half an
inch across. This enjoyment of the cuttlefish as a food extends
over the Pacific Ocean up to Japan. In Hawaii the capture
of the cuttle fish was as eagerly pursued as in Easter Island;
but the method of capture is a contrast to the seizure by hand
in vogue here. The Hawaiian fisherman had noticed the fondness of the squid for the cowrie (l e h o); so, long ago he
manufactured a hook that would take advantage of this;
he shaped a stone like the cowrie shell and between the flat
bases of the stone and a cowrie he placed a stick with a hook
of bone on its end before tying them together; he covered
the hook with leaves and lowered it to the haunts of the
cuttlefish. The Easter Island fisherman had a small cowrie

[1] See No. 1 of picture facing p. 188.

and he had the bone-hook; but he adhered to his primitive method of wading or diving and seizing the tentacles. He did not even follow the Samoan and Tongan method of a hook wrapped up in ti leaves (l a k e i) to catch the cuttlefish.

(11) **THE VENGEANCE OF RAERAEHU.** The women, too, engaged in its capture by night, always having one of the little baskets attached to the girdle for *h e k e*, the others being for big crabs (*p i k e a u r i*), little crabs (*n a h e n a h e*), *p a t u k i*, fish about half an inch long and *p a r o k o*, fish about an inch long. They were especially the collectors of shellfish, as is evident in the legend of *H a u t e r e;* she was a beautiful girl who lived at the foot of Rano Kao; and one of the two devils, Raeraehu and Matamatapea, who lived on its slopes, fell in love with her, not as a sweetheart, but as a dainty morsel for his palate; her parents and lover stabbed him when he was following her, and as he dragged himself to his home he stopped to quench his thirst at the spring of fresh water close to Cannibal Cave just below where I write. As he lay drinking his wound burst out in a fresh stream of blood, and a limpet attached to the rock on which he lay drank it up, and Raeraehu swore an oath that he would have vengeance for his wound. Years passed, and Hautere went down to Cannibal Cave with a friend, H e n e r u, to gather shellfish. On a rock by the spring she saw a huge limpet and sent off her mate to get a large stake to knock it off, as her digging stick was not large enough. When Heneru returned both Hautere and the limpet were gone, and as she looked out to sea she saw her friend's *o k a* floating on a great billow. The neighbourhood came to the conclusion that the devil of Rano Kao had had his vengeance through the limpet that drank his blood; and women became shy of the little cove by Cannibal Cave as a source of shellfish.

(12) **HUMAN BONE THE BEST FOR HOOKS.** There is evident in Easter Island fishing customs something of the Polynesian taboo against women as fishers. They took by hand and generally at night, returning to their home in the morning to do domestic duties and then go to sleep. As an illustration of this division of labour in fishing, the same fish, about eighteen inches long, but plump, with blue skin and red mouth, has two different names; when caught by women at night, it is caught by hand and is called *t u a m i n g o;* when caught by men during the day it is caught by hook and is called

r a e m e a . Spearing fish, a common sight still, was naturally
the employment of men, as the spear was their chief weapon
in war. But hooking also belonged to them, for it was the
commonest method of deep-sea fishing. According to the
legend the only hook in old times was the stone hook, beautifully ground or polished of the hardest stone to be found on
the island ; the round one, like an interrogation point, must
have been a task of many months to drill and rub it down
out of a single large stone ; and not much less would be needed
to manufacture the much rarer angular stone hook. (The
Maoris had also the stone hook, as is evident from the use of
m a k a "a stone" for "a hook.") And this long process
must have been a far more serious objection to them than their
barblessness. But legend tells how a royal scion was weary
of attempting to catch fish with the stone hooks and falling
asleep with fatigue dreamed that an ancestor came to him
in the form of a skeleton and invited him into a canoe ; they
went out to sea and the ghost took a piece of his own bone
and made a hook and fished ; and the rapidity with which
he caught fish by this means astonished the sleeper so much
that, when he awoke, it was deeply impressed on his mind.
He went off to the ancestral vault in the *a h u* in the morning
and took a piece of bone ; out of it he manufactured secretly
a hook like the angular stone one he had been accustomed to
use ; by the aid of a cord he made out of two pieces a good
imitation of the older hook and went out to fish ; he caught
well but not as quickly as the skeleton in the dream. Then
he remembered that the ghost had whittled the bone so as to
have a notch below the point and he made a hook of one piece
like that. He was astonished at the shortness and ease of
the task compared with the manufacture of the stone hooks.
His success in fishing amazed everybody. And the fishermen
resolved to get his secret, as he would not tell it. Once he
went out in the twilight to fish ; and, following him on their
mat-rafts, they leaped into his canoe as he was pulling up a
k a h i , and the secret was theirs and the island's. No burial
vault was safe after that. And so Easter Island is again in
contrast to the rest of Polynesia, which hides the bones of
the dead or at least of the aristocratic dead in secret places
lest they should be made into fish-hooks. To this day the
stone hook is occasionally used for the bigger fish. But most
think that it never catches any and that human bone has a

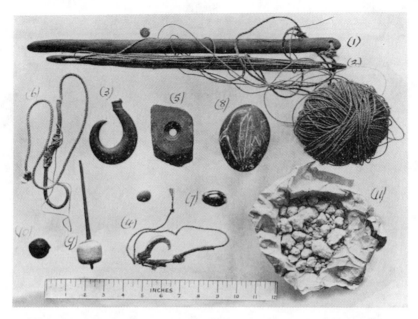

(1) THE APPARATUS FOR CATCHING EELS AND SEA-SNAKES
(2) THE EASTER ISLAND NETTING-NEEDLE, THE SAME AS THROUGH ALL POLYNESIA AND ALL
    EUROPE; THE STRING WAS MADE FROM THE BARK OF THE *hauhau*
(3) AN ANCIENT STONE HOOK
(4) AN ANCIENT HUMAN-BONE HOOK
(5) THE BEGINNINGS OF A STONE HOOK; THE DRILL DID MOST, THE OBSIDIAN RASP DID THE REST
(6) A MODERN EASTER ISLAND HOOK OF BENT BRASS
(7) THE COWRY OF THE ISLAND
(8) A STONE TALISMAN WITH A SHARK PETOGLYPHED ON IT
(9) A WOODEN EASTER ISLAND TEETOTUM
(10) THE SMALL NUT FOUND AT THE BOTTOM OF CLIFFS AND WITH STICK PIERCING USED AS TEETOTUM
(11) *Kiea* USED FOR PAINTING THE BODY WHITE

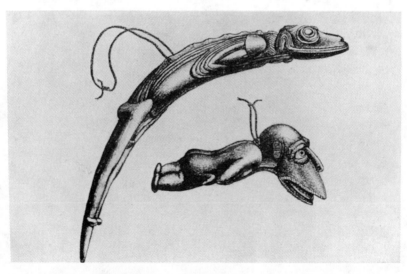

ARTIFICIAL FISH-TALISMANS FROM EASTER ISLAND; IN THE BRITISH MUSEUM

special virtue, quite apart from the barb, that stone can never have. Maui, the hero who pulled up the islands of New Zealand, had the same faith in human bone.

(13) **THE KAHI, OR TUNNY.** The bone hook is preferred for shark and *k a h i*, the deep-sea fish that has always been valued by the islanders. This latter is said by some to have been reserved by the kings for themselves by means of taboo. Whether that was the case or not they were afraid lest it might be overfished and the rite at Orongo was evidently established to prevent that; at any rate, the people were persuaded that deep-sea fish were poisonous till the first egg of the sooty tern was ceremoniously borne along the south coast. The value attached to the *k a h i* is evident when we know the elaborate preparations for its capture. They first had to take a little fish called *a t u r e* as bait; and to procure this a bag of sea-fleas had to be got out of a hole full of seaweed (*r i m u*) that stank to sicken. This bag and the *a t u r e* net were taken out in a canoe and the net was sunk four or five fathoms; then the fleas were let loose and the *a t u r e* rushed in shoals to catch them; the net was drawn up and seldom less than a hundred was the haul. The *a t u r e* were then split and their heads pounded into a pulp. The end of the line was enveloped in the little fish and the hook placed in the middle of the pulp; a stone was fastened on as a sinker and the line run out; the *k a h i*, after swallowing the bait and hook, ran a long distance and the line was made long enough and strong enough to stand the strain.

(14) **NETS AND THE NANUE.** But the fish that went in shoals were netted; and there was a considerable variety of nets, all of them brought from Motu Matiro Hiva (now Sala y Gomez) by Makemake, the great god of the Miru, or royal clan. There was one like a *kete* (basket) but much larger, called *kupenga tuku;* there was a small net for small crayfish and little fish called *kupenga puhi;* and there was *kupenga paroho* for catching the tasty little fish (*paroho*) which was taboo for the kings. But there were also large nets, a long seine net for use by day (*kupenga maito*) and one for use by night (*kupenga viri*). The *kupenga tukutuku* was a round net which one man swam far out to sea with. But it needed four or more men to manipulate the *kupenga tahuri* which was for the bigger fish that went together. The women never made use of the net, though they made the

a t u r e net. It was the older men who made all the nets for the bigger fish, as well as the stone hook, the holes in the stone for which were bored by the hand-drill with the small *terebra.*[1] But some of the best fish for eating were caught by the hook from rocks. The *m a h a k i* is one that is full of oil and supplies much of the oil butter that the natives eat. Fish oil is too valuable to be used for the hair; for that, shark oil (*nako*) was used as a rule. Fish oil was put into a *kumara* or *taro* leaf and taken as a tasty morsel. But one of the most highly appreciated fish for both its flesh and its oil was and is the *n a n u e*, which has a legend all to itself. A baby was left in its *n u a*, or blanket, on the beach whilst the mother gathered shellfish; suddenly she heard its voice away out on the waters and it was singing " Oh, the blanket, oh ! Kapura and Mahina carry me away." She swam out and brought it back, but opening the blanket found it dead. She laid it down and wept. And again it was swept away by a wave. She heard it singing out to sea and as dawn appeared she saw it sink and in its place she observed swimming along the *n a n u e* it had become. It is evidently manufactured out of the resemblance of *nua* and *nanue* and the fact that the fish appears especially at night and on moonlight nights; the names of the witches that carry the body away, *Kapura* and *Mahina,* mean " bright fire," and " moon." And occasionally rude stone weirs are made in Hanganui Bay, the scene of the legend; and this fish is found in great quantities in them at dawn when the tide has receded.

(15) **SORCERY AND FISHING.** But the thing to trust to was neither weir nor net, neither stone hook nor bone hook. Without a *m a n a* stone there was bound to be no great success in fishing. Whenever they went out in a canoe to fish they hung in it a stone that had some resemblance to a fish. There was a special charm-stone for every important fish. And they could never catch flying-fish at all unless they had set up *k o t e - t a k a p a u* now at Mahatua on the east of Poike; it was about two feet high and was shaped naturally like a *v u l v a*. It used to be at *Hangaroa* on the west coast; but *Hotuiti* believed in its magic power over flying-fish and by means of a cunning wizard and his rope was able to haul it over to their part of the island. All this was sorcery; the nearest they came to religion in fishing was when they fished

[1] See No. 5 in picture facing p. 188.

from a canoe; they kept silence all the time lest the
akuakus should come and frighten the fish away. The
Polynesian usual method was to have special tutelary gods
for the craft. In Hawaii, for example, there were temples
and altars with different forms of worship established. Every
fisherman had his own, and had taboos which no other paid
attention to. He had special prayers and incantations for
every kind of fishing. Perhaps the Easter Island charm-stone
was not very different, though some of its methods differed;
for example, when other Polynesians used poisons to stupefy
fish for capture, the Easter Islanders, though in their legends
they knew poisons, never used them in fishing.

CHAPTER XVIII

THE QUEST OF PLEASURE

(1) *A nation's pleasures form one of the best tests of its culture.* (2) *The Polynesia of voyagers was a region of " Messalinas " ; but there were traces of a purer state of society and a hardier environment.* (3) *The imperial and warlike vein in the Polynesians points back to a temperate zone for its origin ; it was never bred in the tropics.* (4) *The climate and the niggardly soil of Easter Island should have bred a hardy race.* (5) *But all observers report in them nothing but futility ;* (6) *whilst the* ahus *and images and the script indicate an imperial race.* (7) *All the voyagers report their lawlessness and licentiousness.* (8) *Their life was as undisciplined and dissolute as in the rest of Polynesia only after the taboo of the chiefs had lost its power ; the thought of death was never to interfere with the pleasure of the moment.* (9) *The whole arrangement of the feasts and the work was exactly fitted to bring up a huge crop of loafers.* (10) *But dancing was next to feasting as a religious exercise, limited only by the want of a torch or the candlenut.* (11) *The dances had little movement of the feet in them ; the top-spinning dance was perhaps the least monotonous ; the* maori's *presence introduced the religious atmosphere.* (12) *The singing was as primitive and monotonous, and they may almost be said to have had no musical instruments.* (13) *Their masks imitating certain animals were probably totemic.* (14) *Their games were as poverty-stricken as the rest of their culture, though containing some of the games that are world-wide.*

(1) **PLEASURE AS A TEST OF CULTURE.** One of the tests of a race or nation is the pleasures it indulges in. Their variety gauges its versatility and inventive capacity. Their purity or grossness indicates the moral phases of its nature. Their comparative importance or unimportance shows the strength of its will. Its command of them or abandonment to them measures how far it will go in the line of self-development. Of course, many, if not all, of these have their roots in climate. Yet some nations that have lived in the same latitude have bent their pleasures and relationships to pleasures in entirely different directions. The Romans and the Greeks both came from the north and from a race of Indo-European speech, and they came south into the same latitude and almost the same zone of climate ; and the history of no two nations could be so violently contrasted, especially in relation to their pleasures. So Japan and the north of China, in all ages the heart and fountain of all things Chinese, are not far separated in latitude and climate ; yet there is almost as great a contrast between the character and history of the two as that between Rome and Greece.

(2) **THE POLYNESIAN FAR PAST ENVIRONMENT.** There are marks upon the history and character of the Polynesians

192

that seem to indicate an earlier environment of a more hardening type than that in which the European voyagers found them. They were losing the adventurous courage that had made them the Vikings of the Pacific. They had no longer the nerve and boldness that had distinguished not merely their gods but their heroes, whether semi-divine or purely human. Their imaginations were no longer stirred to discovery by the suggestion of far-distant islands undiscovered. They had no longer kingdoms to conquer or mould unless they had migrated farther from the equator and reached the temperate zone like the peoples of New Zealand or nearly reached it like the Hawaiians. All but the common people, who had the hardest of lots, were given up to a round of pleasures that were sapping their will-power and any morality they had had. In some of the Polynesian areas there are relics of a greater respect for chastity than they had even the most distant hint of in the society the voyagers found. Tahiti was the New Cytherea, an arena of licentious revel. Scarcely an island that Cook and La Perouse or Bougainville or Beechey visited but found the women " Messalinas " and the men ready to offer their wives and nearest relatives as prostitutes. This is a complete contrast to the institution of the *p u h i*, or virgin, in the chief's family amongst the Maoris, of the *taupou* or virgin hostess in every Samoan village that had a chief, as it is to the rule in Samoa that every noble bride shall be proved to be without stain, and the rule in Easter Island that every young unmarried woman should go up to Orongo and have the *puhi* marked upon her cheek, if she were shown to be a virgin. These are isolated customs and they are manifestly from ancient days. For they persisted into days when every thing had more likeness to the manners and customs of that licentious migratory dramatic brotherhood, the Areoi of Tahiti. They are indications all the more striking that they are isolated in a sea of licentiousness. They are from their surroundings all the more convincing evidence that in a previous stage of Polynesian development there had been a state of society comparatively purer, and an ideal of family morality more in accord with primitive life. It is one of the features of Polynesian culture that place it lower than Melanesian. The seclusion of Melanesian young women before marriage and the separate house for Melanesian young men produce a state of social purity more in consonance with the

ideals of Western Europe than the picture of Polynesian
society presented to us by the early voyagers. Pleasure, and
that often licentious pleasure, seems to be the end and aim
of the life of the *a r i k i* when they are not engaged in
warfare.

(3) **AN IMPERIAL VEIN IN POLYNESIAN CULTURE.** It was
warfare that was the one saving feature in their culture.
For it bred vigour and self-control, courage and boldness in
enterprise, even though it also bred ambition and tyranny
and cruelty. Without this constant feature of Polynesian
life, the race would have wiped itself out by licentiousness
and sterility before the Europeans arrived. Infanticide and
abortion became customs fixed through sheer necessity, the
necessity arising from increasing over-population in the
slowly decreasing areas of the sinking fatherland. They were
continued in the new colonies by the increasing love of
ease and pleasure ; the women would not take the trouble
to bring up their children ; it would interfere too much with
their round of pleasure. Had the men not had constantly
intermittent war to stiffen their wills and tissues, they too
would have succumbed, and the whole race would have rushed
down the steep of G a d a r a . Happily there was an
imperial vein in the thoughts of the leaders of the various
communities. It is this imperial vein that distinguishes the
Polynesians from all the people to the west of them till we
come to the coasts of Asia and clearly indicates a temperate
zone origin. Had they come from the Malay Archipelago or
even from India they would have been saturated with the
tropics and tropical life, the very environment that in the
Pacific was sapping their energies when they were first discovered. No masterful or imperial race ever came out of the
tropics or ever will come out of them. Even in the warmer
parts of the temperate zone the rulers of empire generally
came from the colder north. Whence would the Polynesian
leaders have drawn their vigorous wills or their imperial
impulses in coming from Indonesia into the central Pacific ?
They would have tropical environment and nothing but
tropical environment all the way. They would have come
across no people who thought beyond the village except for
war with the next village. Had they started with the imperial
instinct, such as they showed in every large group of islands
they landed on, it would have filtered away long before they

reached their final destination. The imperial ambitions that produced a Kamehameha and a Pomare in an environment that was marked by licentiousness and decay must have had its origin and heredity in some climate different from that of the tropics.

(4) **EASTER ISLAND FITTED TO PRODUCE A BOLD AND HARDY NATION.** Is there any indication of a similar contrast in the history of the people of Easter Island ? By rights, they should have grown more hardy and self-controlling by having shifted away out of the tropics. The climate is cool and with its oceanic surroundings bracing. Nature is niggard rather than lavish. Half the vegetable products that seemed to the first European sailors who visited tropical Polynesia to make it a paradise are absent from this little island ; and the other half that have been brought here lead most of them a life in death, so hard is the struggle with wind and the evanescence of moisture. The voyagers had no struggle here as they had in the other Polynesian islands to keep their sailors from deserting. There is scarcely an instance of a European marooning himself here ; whilst there are few islands in the tropical Pacific, in Polynesia, or Micronesia, or even Melanesia in which voluntary European exiles do not live. The mammals can scarcely be said to exist in the fauna ; there is but scant bird life and that only sea-bird life ; the fish are scarce and hard to catch. We should have had in such an environment one of the hardiest of races, strong in will-power, full of self-control, vigorous in action, and delighting in the exercise of their energy. There are no extremes in the climate ; it is neither too hot in summer nor too cold in winter; and yet there is every occasion and need for the application of vigour and industry to make Nature support human life. It is exactly the island we should have expected to produce a race of adventurous sailors or a band of bold raiders and conquerors.

(5) **EASTER ISLAND HAS BRED ANYTHING BUT A BOLD AND HARDY NATION.** Yet we find in all the accounts of the voyagers and first missionaries the description of a people lacking in everything that makes a great or even vigorous community. The life is of the meagrest and yet marked by the licentiousness of the more prosperous and luxurious branches of the Polynesian race. It has no order or discipline, least of all self-discipline. Their chief skill is thieving. Their chief living art is tattooing and painting their bodies, their

chief artistic devotion the making of feather hats. So little are the great burial platforms and the titanic images in evidence as a part of their actual life that Eyraud, after his nine months amongst them, never mentions them. So small a factor in their existence was the script that none of the voyagers observed the tablets, and only by accident did Bishop Jaussen of Papeete come to the knowledge of them though Eyraud had said in his letter that there were some of them in every hovel. The *a h u s* were to them only the places where their feasts took place. The tablets were kept vital only by the recitations of the *m a o r i s;* had the festivals not kept them before their minds they would have been of less account in their lives than the fallen and broken statues. As it was they were not on a much higher plane than their charm stones or the sorceries of the *i v i a t u a s*.

(6) **A STARTLING ANOMALY.** But for these two drifts out of a great past that had almost passed into oblivion—the burial platforms with their images and the script—this people would have at once dropped into insignificance even among ethnologists ; there was little to observe in their culture that could not be better observed in all the other islands of Polynesia. To explain the startling anomaly there has to be assumed in the vicinity a people the same yet different, a Polynesian people like the existent islanders, yet with all the imperial ambitions and all the power to realize them that Kamehameha exhibited in the Hawaiian group and Pomare in the Society group. And the tradition of Hotu Matua reveals to us a leader of such a people, with all the imperial ideals and but poor arena to work them out in. He is, without doubt, the last of the race of rulers who moulded an empire out of the archipelagoes seen by Davis, and planned and partially realized an insular and central mausoleum for themselves and their nobles such as no imperial conqueror has ever conceived. It was only men of imperial ideals and great deeds, and men of boundless resources who could have brought such a script into working order and left recorded in it their traditions and liturgy, who could have not merely conceived but carried out to a great extent the idea of a memorial island ringed with magnificent burial-places and avenued with gigantic images of the great dead.

(7) **THEFT, ESPECIALLY OF HATS, THEIR CHIEF SKILL.** The contrast between this result and the description of the people

of the island given by the first observers of them is startling.
If we are to trust the description (and there is everything to
confirm it), we have a people here who are little more advanced
than the youngest children even amongst the most primitive
Polynesians. Their treatment of visitors could only be excused
in children not far out of infancy. None of the voyagers
discovered any of the dignity or *savoir faire* that they noticed
in the other Polynesian areas. Cook speaks with admiration
of the manly reserve and self-control of the chiefs in New
Zealand, in Tonga, in Hawaii, and even in Tahiti, in spite
of the emotionalism of the people of that island. There was
at least some order in those parts ; the common people kept
their impulses under in presence of the *ariki*. He noticed a
tendency to thieving from strangers as one of the weaknesses
of all the groups, probably arising out of the village communism that made every man feel he had a natural right to
a share in what anyone had, but in Easter Island he describes
it as absolutely capricious and uncontrolled. No amount of
generosity seemed to put any sense of shame into the thieves.
La Perouse, who had resolved to suffer all without retaliation,
cannot refrain from condemning their lawlessness and lack
of gratitude or other human feeling ; in being helped down
from one of the *a h u s* his hat is whipped off by the helper ;
and when he comes on board he finds all his crew hatless and
handkerchiefless. No visitor but notices how they pilfer in
the act of receiving gifts. Hats were evidently a special
temptation for them all through, doubtless because they had
been a special symbol of power in the archipelagoes around,
as is evident from the red hats that the memorial images had
placed on their heads. One of their favourite stories has as
its subject the stealing of a fur hat. A great ship arrived off
the coast early last century and a boat put off with three
passengers. One was manifestly a missionary ; for he had a
mantle that reached to his heels and he wore a tall red hat of
fur ; the second had besides a straw hat, trousers, as also had
the third, who had only a sailor's cap on. It was too much
for the islanders to see on the head of a stranger that hat so
like in size and form to the hats of the statues ; hardly had
the missionary landed before it was snatched off his head and
disappeared in the crowd. Bareheaded, the clergyman made
back for the boat, with the usual shower of stones from the
natives ; when he was on board of it he turned and called to

o

the crowd: "I am your father, T e p a n o." It reached
the ship and the ship sailed away. The Mangarevans declare
that the bishop, and not merely his hat, was seized and that
he was cooked and eaten, as a great hole that was the earth-
oven testifies to this day. The hat has vanished; but one
who told me the story saw it when he was young, adding that
he thought the missionary was from Chili or Peru, as there
was a nun on board the ship.

(8) **NO THOUGHT OF DEATH MUST INTERFERE WITH
PLEASURE.** The Easter Islanders had evidently no more
restraint when strangers arrived than a gang of mischievous
boys. There appeared to be no authority to establish or keep
order. Their social state was as unorganized and corrupt as
that of the other Polynesian islands after the abolition of the
taboo had dissolved the authority of the chiefs and left the
common people free and uncontrolled, ready to be idle and indulge in every whim; and this long before the missionaries or any
Europeans had approached. Their life seemed to the voyagers
dissolute beyond anything they had seen in the other islands.
The women freely offered themselves to the sailors. The men
dealt in them like goods to be traded off. And if they could
not get the possessions of the strangers by this traffic, then
they stole them. Their one guide was the desire of the moment,
their one aim to have it satisfied. So they hated to be reminded
that life would end and all its desires and pleasures. Eyraud
in his nine months on the island had the longest opportunity
any observer had for watching their character before Christianity was introduced. His description brings out more
clearly than any their lawlessness and enjoyment of the
moment. One incident he narrates tells how deeply they
resented all reference to the end of life. One day he wanted
to impress his patron and monopolist, T o r o m e t i, with
the heinousness of theft, an act of which he had just committed.
He thought he had a fine theme for his sermon in the recent
death of P a n a the Easter Islander, who had been brought
back from Peru to Tahiti and had returned to his native land
with him. He warned the muscular tyrant that some day
the same fate would overtake him; scarcely had he uttered
the words "e p o h e e," "Thou shalt die," before the listener
was seized with wild terror and anger; he seemed as if struck
with lightning. And for at least a fortnight wherever he went
he heard the cry in tones of fear and condemnation, "The

stranger has said 'Thou shalt die!'" Whether his words had been taken as a threat or a divination, all looked upon him as an offender who had done something heinous in mentioning the obvious fact that life would come to an end.

(9) **THE SEEDBED OF INDOLENCE.** For to them life was one unbroken pursuit of pleasure. After it they would be hateful, malignant *a k u a k u s* for a brief period. To remind them of that end was to thrust a ghastly thing into their web of pleasures. And a poor thin web it was; by far the meagrest in Polynesia. Even their feasts, for which they made such preparation, were almost childish in their methods of entertainment; though they had originated in religion and retained a certain religious atmosphere, their chief pleasure lay in gorging. The opening of the *u m u* was the commencement of all that was divine. For this they had attempted to outrival one another in the number and variety of the foods they brought, chickens, fish, rats, bananas, t i root, sugar-cane, taro, yams, sweet potatoes. He who brought most was most envied and praised. And, though his family might starve for weeks or even months after, he would bring all his crops and all the results of his fishing. It was a delightful arrangement for the idlers and loafers, of whom there were always plenty and to spare in every Easter Island village. Eyraud says bluntly, "They live in indolence." It was the women that, though they did not do the planting, did all the hoeing and harvesting; it was they who collected the main seatrove, the shellfish, the crabs, the cuttlefish, the small fish that came in shoals; it was they who looked after the cooking and all the household work; it was they who made the bark-cloth and the mats, the baskets and all the small nets; it was they who went into the *r a n o s* to gather the material; it was they who carried the fresh water from the springs on the beach to drink or to wash. And the old men, who feared getting knocked on the head, did most of the rest, the making of the larger nets and the hooks and the gathering of the bait; it is more than likely that they did the bulk of the planting. What was left was the net-fishing and deep-sea fishing and the diving. With communism at the basis of society one cannot imagine a finer seed-bed for raising a crop of loafers. The result is embodied in the story of "Hupe's Banquet." Hupe got, by begging or borrowing, a bundle of *kumara* runners; he was a big strapping fellow, but girded at having to carry them home.

When he got them there he planted a few and then went in to have a sleep. A neighbour, a *tatani* with a vein of humour in him, saw the performance and resolved to have a laugh at Hupe's expense. So he planted all the rest of the runners, and when Hupe awoke the job was all done. The same occurred with all the other gifts of his friends. He made no inquiry as to how the miracle had been worked, but attributed it to the discernment of Providence in showering gifts on the deserving. It was the same when the crop grew and the weeds grew better ; he must have his rest however high the weeds grew. And again his deserts were duly rewarded ; the weeds vanished. The tubers grew and grew till at last he thought he would let his friends and neighbours see how virtue was rewarded. He invited them all to a great banquet. But the night before it was to come off, the humorous *tatani* came in the dark and got the tubers all away without disturbing the foliage or the soil. He lay low and watched results. Hupe spread out all the leaves that were to be the table of the banquet and got a huge *u m u* all aglow. Then he went with his *o k a* to dig part of his wonderful crop. He thought somebody had been meddling with the first lot he tried to dig ; so he went on digging ; for the guests were dropping in. There they sat on the ground by the *u m u* and looked at the perspiring *Hupe*. At last they began to realize that there was going to be no banquet, and the would-be host began to realize the dilemma he had got into ; he asked them to excuse him ; he had forgotten some of the viands and had to go over the way to get them. The *tatani* laughed and laughed till his sides almost split as he saw the guests saunter off in twos and threes, a wicked grin on their faces and a threatening fist held up. They had begun to see, what the humorist knew long ago, that Hupe did not intend to return. He had to go somewhere else to trust to Providence. I fancy this tale must have been invented by a woman or an old man ; the numerous Hupes of Easter Island would say, by an old woman.

(10) **DANCING NEXT TO EATING.** But it has to be acknowledged that there was more than feasting in the feasts. It was not the teeth alone that were exercised ; the arms and legs and even the trunk had some exercise. For dancing, next to eating, was the most important of the festal pleasures. Forster says that the Easter Island youth who came on board Cook's ship chatted freely with *Hete hete* the Tahitian ; but

he could talk of nothing but dancing (*heeva*). For those " new Cythereans " were, if anything, fonder of the amusement than the Easter Islanders ; in almost every part of the island scarcely a day passed without a re-union of the young men and young women all nude and glistening with coco-nut oil or sandalwood oil. And when it came to the district to entertain the *A r e o i s* there was lubricity *in excelsis ;* the lowest grades of that brotherhood set no bounds to their obscene dramatic exhibitions, especially when the torchlight braved the ghosts. The best material the Easter Islanders had for night dances or torches for fishing was sugar-cane and banana leaf ; they had no cocoa palms to contribute their fronds and no candle-nut trees to light up the house or dancing ground with their oily flare. They had to go to bed in the dark and the dances had to be postponed when night fell and that was never much later than seven. Moreover, they were far more afraid of the ghosts than the Tahitians were. Hotu Matua's failures with the Polynesian plants perhaps leaned more to virtue than his successes ; the coco-nut palm and the candle-nut, which went into Rapa even farther from the equator, would have enabled the festivals and dancing routs to go on all night as well as all day. There would have been still greater and still more frequent famines.

(11) **DANCING, SPINNING TOPS, AND RELIGION.** None of the Easter Island dances had either the *verve* of the New Zealand *h a k a* , or the lubricity of some of the *hula* dances of Hawaii, or the *u p a u p a* dances of Tahiti. There is no up and down movement of the hips or of the abdomen. They are more like the *s i v a* of Samoa or the *o d o r i* of Japan. They are even more static than most of the Polynesian dances. Perhaps the most mobile is the dancing in file, one woman followed by one man in a long row, on the *k a u n g a* or paved strip in front of the *a h u* . They bob the body down with a bend of the knees as in the old-fashioned curtsey and, as they straighten up, hitch a few inches forward, the fingers all the time rapidly quivering ; all to the singing of the older men and women who squat on either side. In the *hokohoko*, the usual dance at the feasts, a row of young men with a *m o k o* , or lizard-headed weapon, or a wooden head with outstretched arms in both hands, faces a row of young women, who sway their bodies from side to side whilst they sing. At the *k o r o* , a favourite was the spinning dance ; the young men in a row

and young women in a row spun tops as they sang : " *Kanini te makoi nau opata ; kara tuu te makoi miro rakerake ; kanini koi te makoi oone o te Rano e Kane.*" " Spin, spin the coco-nut top from the cliffs ; ill turns the top that is made of wood ; spin, spin the top that is made from the clay of the Rano." This refers to the three common types of top ; the first is made of a reddish-brown flattened round nut about an inch thick and two inches in diameter found in considerable quantities in the crater of Rano Aroi and at the foot of cliffs on the north-west coasts, and said by the natives to be small coco-nuts ; a round pin with sharp fire-hardened point is thrust through the middle of it.[1] The second is whittled out of *toromiro* wood into the form of a teetotum.[2] The third is a sun-baked cone of clay got at the foot of Rano Raraku. There is a fourth consisting of a conical stone of some size, which is kept rapidly whirling by two or more men. These were sometimes spun for divination purposes like the *n i u* or coco-nut of western Polynesia. At Orongo and at Haremoai the dances had perhaps more of a religious character ; wherever the *maori* or priest had much to do with the proceedings it may be assumed that there was meant to be a religious atmosphere ; they sang the *rongorongo* at the *p a i n a* and thus introduced the primeval liturgy as accompaniment of the dances ; in fact, it was the youths and maidens specially trained by them that generally supplied both the music and the dancing. *T a u* was the word used for reciting the tablets ; but *a t a* was a more sacred word with the same sense ; and when it was prefixed to a word as, e.g. *a t a u i* and *a t a k u n i k u n i*, it lifted it above common life into the atmosphere of the old liturgy.

(12) **SINGING AND MUSICAL INSTRUMENTS.** The singing was monotonous, generally consisting in the repetition of a word or phrase. Eyraud describes how at the *p a i n a s* " the people meet in groups, placing themselves in two lines and begin singing. The poetry is very primitive," but varying with the event that has recently struck their fancy, as, e.g. the epidemic of smallpox which had just passed when he was there ; that was the subject of their song then ; " they merely repeat the fact, sometimes only the word that denotes it " over and over again. The favourite songs were : (1) *a t e a t u a*, in which the man who sings is the *a t u a* ; (2) *a t e*

---

[1] See No. 10 in picture facing p. 188.
[2] See No. 9 in picture facing p. 188.

hakakakai, a war song meant to work evil on the enemy; (3) *ate hereu*, a lullaby for the crying (*reu*) child; (4) *ate hei*, sung by men and women in the *hoko-hoko* dance; (5) *ate koro hakaopo*, sung by a row of young men and a row of young women when they were making the white straw hats (*hauteatea*) or dyeing the *nua* (mantle) half white, half red. It was little wonder their singing was so primitive when their musical instruments might almost be said to be non-existent. They had no bamboo; it was one of Hotu Matua's misses; for it is all over Polynesia and it now grows well in the island. But they could have bored sugar-cane or even a piece of *miro* to make an instrument to blow. They had not the noseflute of Polynesia, with its two finger stops; they had plenty of human bone like the Maoris; but they had not even the bone whistle of that people, let alone the bone flute or bone flageolet. The only thing they ever whistled through was a natural hole in the top of a three foot high stone over on the north coast near *Mahatua* platform. Nor had they anything that could be called a drum; they had not the timber to make the old sentry-awakening wooden gong of the Maoris. They had both small gourds and large calabashes and they caught many sharks; they never thought of making the shark-skin-ended drums that are so common throughout the Pacific Ocean. The only approach to a drum they made was to dig a three-foot deep hole in the ground between the rows of dancers and in the bottom of this place a gourd half filled with dried grass; over this they laid a flat laminated stone such as they used to make the roofs of the houses at Orongo. On this they danced with the naked feet and so got some sort of resonance. They struck sticks together in rhythm like the other Polynesians; but they never thought of placing the end of the struck stick in the mouth as a resonator like the Maori *pakura* and the Hawaiian *ukeke*.

(13) **MASKS.** With such primitive music their dancing could be nothing else than primitive, even that with the sacred clubs, the *ao* and the *rapa*, originally, as is clear from the form, double-bladed paddles like the Marquesan dancing clubs. For the dance, whether religious or not, they made up like a modern actor with grease and paint, just as they made up the images. And when they did not conceal their tattooing with this temporary colouring they sometimes put on masks of *mahute*; these imitated the animals they feared or admired

or wished more of ; a favourite one was that of the frigate-bird
(*m a k o h e*), another one was of the seal (*p a k i a*), and a
third was the head of a dog, and that must go back to *Hotu
Matua* and his dog (*p a i h e n g a*). Unlike those of *Melanesia*
they had no connection with secret societies or ghosts ; they
were never monstrous in form or intended to scare. The
p a i n a figure and the reed and *m a h u t e* figures seen by
Gonzalez and by Langlé of the La Perouse expedition approach
nearer to a suggestion of the supernatural than these. These
were used in the ordinary dances and, as most of them imitated
animals, they may possibly have had a totemic origin. For
they were used in praying *a t e a t u a* for animals that
supplied them with food, like fish, crayfish, and rats. The
mask seen by Cook on his first voyage in Ulietea (Raiatea)
has much more analogy to the Tamate masks and Dukduk
masks of Melanesia ; in a dance " the performer put upon
his head a large piece of wickerwork about four feet long of a
cylindrical form, covered with feathers and edged round with
sharks' teeth " ; it was called a *w h o u*, probably the same
as the Easter Island *h a u*, a hat.

(14) **EXERCISES AND GAMES.** One of the striking things
about Easter Island culture is that there are fewer hardening
exercises than in the other Polynesian areas. Like most, they
had tobogganing down the slopes (*h a k a n i n i p e i*) ; for
this they used the stems of the banana tree. So had they
surfing (*n g a r u*) ; but they never used a surfing board ;
they came in on the inrushing billow either without anything
to lean upon (*t i a e v e*) or they used a mat about six foot long
and three feet broad made of rushes (*n g a a t u*) ; this was
called the *p a p a n g a r u*. They had few or none of the
exercises that usually prepared the Polynesian warrior for
battle, like wrestling and boxing, and spear throwing and
parrying. Their chief game of this kind was *t u n a*, an
exercise in throwing stones accurately. They had no games of
chance or guesswork, or imitations of battles, like the Hawaiian
stone chequer-board, or *p u h e n e h e n e*, a woman's guessing
game. They had ball games (*hura huraka*, to play ball) like
the Tahitians. They had not lost the spear—or reed-ricochet
game (*t e t e k a*) that remains in the Tongan *j i k a* and
Samoan *t i ' a*, or the universal water-ricochet game of skip-
ping stones known in Europe as " ducks and drakes." The
nearest approach to a game of gambling, like the Hawaiian

m a i k a or "bowling alley," foretelling what may chance, was their *p u k e*. A ring of stones was set up, as, e.g. in front of *A h u H a n g a t e e* on the south coast, about twenty-five feet in diameter. Round this, inside the stone circle, men ran, whilst spectators outside tried to hit them; he who escaped most was supposed to live longest. Children's games were most of them imitations of those of adults; they surfed and swam and tobogganed, and they made, and still make, kites of *m a h u t e* (*manu hakarere*) with very long tails. They played rounders and prisoners' base and hide-and-seek (*hiko hiko kete*) and other games played by children all over the world. They jumped the rope and threw stones. But seesaw was introduced by the missionaries. One of the universal amusements of the world has been kept up by the generations of children till the present day; it is cat's cradle, or, as it is called in Easter Island, *k a i k a i*, a variation of the *a i* and *w h a i* of other Polynesian Islands. One was made for my benefit; it was "the bird"; two strings were stretched horizontally and parallel; one between the forefingers of the two hands and the other between the roots of the thumbs; the ends of these two were, by looping over the taut parallel sections, made to form a double zigzag which simulated well the body and bent wings of a bird. As it was getting made a song went on, beginning: Kami mea no, to koro hami mea, tara ke tu aere, Kamiri no, to koro tangata tuao iti Ohiro, karave tangi noa mahaki ke makohe, etc. It was evidently the frigate-bird and his deeds that supplied the subject of the song; and further on in the song the bird islands, Motunui, Motuiti, and Raukau are introduced and the scene of the bird-watching, O r o n g o. The form produced on the strings was much like the cicatrice of the frigate-bird raised on the shoulders of the Solomon Islanders. The bird *par excellence* among Easter Islanders was the *m a k o h e*, or frigate-bird, which they could see any day hovering overhead as it made from its nesting-place, S a l a y G o m e z, towards the haunts of the fishing-birds, the *k e n a*, the *t a v a k e*, the *m a n u t a r a*, on the bird islands off Orongo.

There is evident in all this quest of pleasure the same poverty-stricken culture as in their quest of food. So much of what they received from the Polynesian ancestry have they forgotten or ceased to use that the contrast with the memorial stone-culture of the island is sharp and striking.

CHAPTER XIX

WAR

(1) In Melanesia constant warfare has driven society into its constituent atoms, villages. (2) In Micronesia and Polynesia, it has welded society into feudalism with an imperialistic tendency. (3) In Easter Island constant warfare did not prevent confederation or the assembly of all the people at the feasts ; and hence, unlike Melanesia, there is but one language with not even dialectic variations. (4) It was most unlike Melanesia in that it had a king, and most unlike Polynesia in keeping the king out of all relationship to war. (5) As in all other Polynesian communities there grew up the profession of sorcerer that monopolized communication with the supernatural, and left the official priests the merely ceremonial. (6) Their war outfit was of the meagrest. (7) Besides the spear, their chief projectile was stones of which the island is a perpetual ammunition factory ; they had no sling and so became deadly in their aim with the hand. (8) Their fighting net was unique in the Pacific, an adaptation of the net that closed the house entrance at night, and used only for catching an enemy who had taken refuge in a house or cave. Why they did not turn the ahus into fortresses is one of the mysteries of Easter Island if they built them. (9) The battle was but a scrimmage and generally ended in a sociable banquet on the slain, but, if for deeper causes than retaliation for a murder, it went on till the defeated were exterminated or reduced to slavery. (10) War was not always merely to fill the larder ; it was for vendetta as is shown in the legend of " The Mother's Vengeance." (11) It also shows that cannibalism was not confined to times of war. There was no god of war, and the war was often one of extermination. Hence the seeming discrepancies in the numbers estimated by the various voyagers.

(1) WAR IN MELANESIA AND ITS SOCIAL EFFECTS. In the Pacific Ocean life was as a rule organized for war. In Melanesia and Papuasia every village had to be on guard against its neighbours ; it never knew when there would be a raid or an ambush. Some islands like Rubiana in the west of the Solomons spent their whole life in head-hunting expeditions to other islands. The Rubiana warriors almost exterminated the people of Y s a b e l, an island to the east ; the few remaining inhabitants had to build what were practically forts in high trees provided with heaps of stones, their chief ammunition ; there they lived in perpetual terror. This constant fear of war and preparation for war absorbed the energies of the people and moulded their social forms all through the Melanesian area. It was the commonest thing to see the women returning from the garden in the forest laden with its products and the man stalking along near her, spear raised in the right hand, and all his other weapons ready at his belt. So even in these days of greater peace one can see the little canoes go off from W a l a early in the morning to the coast of M a l e k u l a, the woman with her digging-stick and nets

ONE OF THE COMMONEST SCENES IN PAPUA : THE HUSBAND MARCHING BEFORE HIS HEAVILY BURDENED WIFE WITH SPEAR
IN READINESS.—*Photograph by Mr. Money, formerly missionary at Collingwood Bay, North Coast of British New Guinea.*

to hold the produce, the man with his musket over his shoulder. It is this state of affairs that has relieved the man of every duty in the cultivation and the hut and thrown it on to the shoulders of the woman. He is the richest man who has the largest number of wives; the old men monopolize the young women and the young men have to take the old and outworn.

(2) **WAR IN POLYNESIA AND FEUDALISM.** Though war is the main purpose of society in Micronesia and Polynesia, it has become an amalgamator as a rule and not a separator. Individual islands are not torn up into their constituent villages; there is some dominant chief in each whose authority prevents perpetual civil war. Even groups have been made to bow to some conquering will. The result is a complete contrast to the state of all the islands to the west of Tonga except Fiji, which was early Polynesianized and later Tonganized. Society is organized on a feudal basis with rigid division of classes, each bound by strict duty to that above it. The higher chiefs owe warlike service to the dominant chief or king; the lower chiefs serve under a higher, and command the loyalty of the r a n g a t i r a s, or employers and organizers of the common people. Word goes out from the central power that there is to be war; and every warrior with full equipment and commissariat has to appear under his immediate commander, who marches his band into the meeting-place of the army. And in peace tribute follows the same course, the common man being left but a fraction of the produce of his toil, all the rest passing through the various ranks who take their toll and hand on what remains to the king. This tendency to feudalize society for war purposes led to empires in both Micronesia and Polynesia capable of cyclopean stone erections that after the submergence of so many islands around seem to have been miraculously set up.

(3) **EASTER ISLAND WAR ORGANIZATION COMPARED WITH MELANESIAN.** It is one of the mysteries of Easter Island that it is so differently constituted in its society, not only from Polynesia, but from Melanesia. It was organized for war as in both of these areas, but on lines that are neither Polynesian nor Melanesian. It was broken up into constituent villages, or rather districts, all round its coasts; these are often called clans; but they each seem to owe their unity to local proximity rather than to common blood or common descent, real or assumed, with the exception of the M i r u, which was a

real clan keeping its genealogies right back to the comrades
of Hotu Matua and trying to preserve its blood pure from
inter-mixture with the rest of the people by means of a taboo,
the breach of which led to painful consequences in the intestines.
This discrete organization of society has a certain superficial
resemblance to the state of things in the Melanesian area. Each
local unity is internally organized for war and seems to have
been constantly in fear of war or engaged in it, like a Melanesian
village. But in Melanesia each village has its own dialect
different from its neighbour's and as a rule unintelligible to
it. In Easter Island all the peoples spoke the same language;
there were not even separate dialects; there is no record of
even a variation in the pronunciation of a word. What this
means is that, in spite of the perpetual wars, there was as
frequent mutual intercourse. And another feature that distinguishes this war organization from the Melanesian was the
tendency to confederation for war. Those on the north coast
north of Anakena Bay and those on the west coast north of
H a n g a r o a B a y tended to join the *M i r u* in any conflict.
Those on the south coast on the south-eastern and south-
western promontories tended to coalesce with the T u p a -
h o t u about R a n o R a r a k u. The one alliance went
under the name of K o t u u, the other under the name of
H o t u i t i. But this arrangement was by no means rigid.
Tupahotu joined with the Miru and others to rescue Ngaara
the king from its neighbour and usual ally, the Ngaure. There
is nothing in Melanesia like such alliances or confederations.

(4) **THE MIRU KING AND THE POLYNESIAN.** Another
feature that puts Easter Island social organization into sharp
contrast with that of the Melanesian area is the existence of a
kingship. This rather brings it into resemblance to that of
Polynesia. But there are striking differences. The Polynesian
monarch was generally so by right of conquest and remained
so only by right of superior force, although like all his great
chiefs he was supposed to be of divine descent, if not divine.
The *M i r u* king in Easter Island was acknowledged by all
to be king and to have divinity in him. But he was not so
by right of conquest. In fact, the condition on which he was
to be recognized as king was that he must never engage in
battle or take sides in any war. He was one of the most
remarkable instances of the *rois faineants*. He was allowed
to do nothing when alive but ceremonial acts; and when he

died, it was his skull, emptied of brains, of course, that fell heir to his divinity; there was no better recipe for increasing the brood of chickens than a royal skull. There is only one power he had that brings him into kinship with the Polynesian monarchs. They were at the mercy of the omens or the will of the gods when they wanted to go to war, and these were at the mercy of the priests, generally the high priest. It was an absolute essential that they should have some hold over that great functionary. When the position became vacant, they filled it with a relative, as a rule a brother, or, occasionally appropriated it to themselves. The king of Easter Island never declared war or entered into war, and so he had no need to get a lien on the will of the gods. But he had the choice of the priests, or *maoris*, and doubtless took care to select the men who were most friendly to himself. The *maoris* had, at least at first, considerable influence over war decisions and thus indirectly the M i r u king had some relationship to war.

(5) **THE RISE OF SORCERERS TO POWER.** But there grew up an unofficial profession that took the real decision out of the hands of the *maoris;* this was the sorcerers, or *i v i a - t u a s*, who in their sanction and origin had no connection with the king. They owed their sanction and selection to their success in trading upon the superstitions of the people. They were the uncrowned kings or queens of the supernatural world. And it was their vaticinations, their announcement of the will of the gods that always decided the question of peace or war. The *maoris* had to be satisfied with the merely formal and ceremonial. That this was a natural growth, a consequence of the arrogance of the official media of the divine will, is at once evident when we find in all the other monarchies of Polynesia the rise of a similar profession to power. In Tahiti, for example, the sorcerers became so powerful that even the priests entered their ranks. The great chiefs and the kings hung upon their words; the great ladies flattered them and clung to them, and gave them favours like *Rasputin* in Russia before the debacle. As long as the charlatan who proclaimed himself the mouthpiece of the gods still went into trances and announced the divine will, he had at his command some of the noblest of the aristocracy. As long as he wore a piece of *t a p a* on his arm, that was the symbol of his intercourse with the supernatural, he had the ladies of the chiefly ranks in his train as subservient parasites.

There was not all this incense about the sorcerers of Easter Island ; for some of them were women.   But, if their success in curing disease by burning the ghosts was patent and their vaticinations did not too often turn out untrue, their reputation and power were boundless.   It was to their interests to stir up war.   Just as the Tahitian sorcerers found their power increase the more of war there was, so the *i v i a t u a s* saw the chances of their vaticinations being on the average likely to be correct, if the arena for them became wider.   The wide area of superstition in a Polynesian community gave them ample scope in private life.   But when they lived in a monarchy, their ambition was to have power and to control the destinies of their fellows through the king and his counsellors.   Even in Easter Island where the king was but a shadow, they made themselves of great importance by stimulating the leaders of their neighbourhoods to fight with neighbours.   There is little doubt that the profession of *i v i a t u a* was one of the chief factors in keeping Easter Island in a constant ferment of war.

(6) **WEAPONS AND THE PREPARATION FOR BATTLE.** And yet the *maori* kept hold of some of his old relationships to war. Whenever a local unit had resolved to fight another, it called for the *maori* and he went up to Orongo and entering the house in which the statue Taura Renga had been accommodated by burying the lower half of its body in the earth of the floor, (another instance of the idea of the sculptors that the images should be set in the earth), he placed his feather hat (*h a u*) on its head.   And the *maori* of the unit that had become hostile, when he came up to do some ceremonial, saw this and he knew then that war was inevitable.   This seems to show that the *maori* of each clan had a hat that by the arrangement of its feathers indicated which he belonged to ; probably every local unit so arranged its feathers and the colours it used for painting the body and face that its members were recognizable in battle or in ceremony.   It is just possible that each had a distinctive combination of the tattooing forms, as the New Zealanders had upon their faces to indicate their tribe and lineage, though there is no tradition of such a distinction.

Each *maori* warned the warriors of the locality to prepare. There was not much to prepare ; for like all Polynesians they had no shield ; they parried spears with their clubs and spears, and, though this is not given as a definite tradition, they must have had, like all other Polynesians, exercises for their young men in catching or parrying javelins thrown at them. This is what is implied in the tradition that Hotu Matua trained the boys he brought in his canoe and those born afterwards in throwing and parrying imitations of spears ; he put them in two lines facing each other and gave the younger *hekekeohe*, the flower-stalk of a tall flaglike plant, to fight with ; to those somewhat older he gave the *miro* shafts (*kohau*) of warriors. They saw that their rude conical or semi-circular obsidian spear points (*mataa*) were sharp and firmly tied on. They got their clubs, the two-foot long club with broad rounded sharp-edged blade and the long lizard-headed *moko*, to see that there was no flaw in them and that they would give an efficient blow. This last they trusted most, for it had a magical power in its lizard head, the same as belonged to the *manuuru* (lizard heads) that guarded the porch of the house from marauders by the influence of the *akuaku* in them. The obsidian point of the javelin must have been adopted instead of the piece of gourd, or in older times coco-nut shell, sharpened, before 1775 ; for Forster in speaking of their weapons says : " Some had lances or spears made of thin ill-shapen sticks and pointed with sharp triangular pieces of obsidian. One of them had a fighting club made of a thick piece of wood about three feet long, carved at one extremity ; and a few others had short wooden clubs exactly resembling some of the New Zealand *patoo patoos*, which are made of bone." This was the *paoha*. In fact most of their weapons seem to have been modelled on those of the Maoris. An uncommon weapon was a wooden sword called *paoa* which seems to have been like the, as uncommon, whalebone sword of New Zealand called the *hoeroa* or long knife. This would be used by only a few, as also would be the sawlike snout of the swordfish (*heheu*). It is difficult to explain why this never suggested to the warriors the making of weapons with sharks' teeth such as were made in the Gilbert Islands and more rarely in Polynesia ; for example, in Hawaii they made a sword like a saw by means of sharks' teeth, a knife with one or two in it, and a short weapon capable of being hidden in the hand with but one used for getting at the brains or bowels of an enemy. The Easter Islanders had an unlimited supply of sharks'

teeth ; for they were always catching the shark. Their
failure to use them in making weapons is probably due, as
so many of the gaps in their Polynesianism are due, to their
lack of ingenuity and initiative.

(7) **PROJECTILE WEAPONS.** What would occupy most of
their time in preparing for battle was the selection of stones
to throw. There is no lack of such ammunition anywhere
on Easter Island. But only certain forms would be fitted
for efficient and accurate projection to a distance. They
preferred large stones for throwing and through long practice they were most expert in throwing them. And doubtless they brought their hand in by competitive practice.
Beechey observed when they were adopting a hostile attitude
that " some few were throwing large stones at a mark
behind a bank erected near the beach." Their facility and
exactness in hitting a distant mark has been noticed by
several of the voyagers ; and Eyraud thought that their
preference for killing by stoning was due to their objection
to the shedding of blood, as he noticed the horror with
which a woman saw him kill a fowl with a knife ; they
always kill it by wringing the neck and burying the head in
the ground. But this is not in accord with their use of the
m a t a a, and the indulgences in cannibalism. And there
used to be a very large obsidian flake, about two foot by two ;
tied to a large stake it was used to assassinate people when
they were asleep ; a specimen of it was found in a cavern
of *M o t u n u i* some few years ago. This is like the use of
the *a k a u e* or huge lever in the legends for killing *t a t a n i s ;*
and is a contrast to the sixteen-inch dagger used by the
Hawaiians, who hung it at the wrist as the Maoris did the
mere. They had no retrieving weapons like the Maori
k u r u t a i, with its long cord, or any spear-thrower like
the Maori *k o t a h a* or *k o p e r e.* Some recent observers
have spoken of a sling ; but it was not brought in till the
late sixties of last century, and it brought its name (*h u r a*)
with it ; the word appears in Roussel's vocabulary. The
Hawaiians not only used a sling, but prepared their stones
with great care, shaping them like an egg. It was probably
because they had no sling that the Easter Islanders became
so expert in throwing stones. Whenever a stranger appeared
they pelted him with stones and soon pelted him to death.
In the legend of the Fur Hat the missionary and his com-

panions were driven into their boat by stones. When King Tangaroa lands after his long swim to help them, they give him a shower of stones. And any Easter Islander who returned after being away for some years was thought to be a ghost and was greeted with stones.

(8) **THE NET, THE JAVELIN, AND FORTIFICATIONS.** But Easter Island had a contrivance that is unique in Polynesia unless we except the Maoris. It was a net of stout cord or rope like the Papuan net for catching pigs. Thomson, in telling the story of Oroi, says : " One peculiar feature of the tradition is the allusion to the fighting net, which must have been something after the fashion of those used in old Roman times. These nets are represented to have been square and weighted at the corners with stones. A lanyard was fastened to the centre and the net was thrown over an antagonist, who was beaten to death while entangled in its meshes." But if we are to trust the traditions and some of the legends, it was used chiefly, if not only, for catching an enemy who had got into a cave or house ; the net was thrown over the narrow entrance and the prisoner secured in attempting to get out. It was probably suggested by the net that was the only means of closing the entrance to the stone-foundation house, as also was the net employed by the sorcerer to secure the ghost that had been the cause of sickness in a house in order to burn it. They had no bows and arrows and so prove themselves Polynesians, though some of them used the projectile for mere amusement and not for war. The projectile that they preferred was the javelin and that an inefficient one ; they threw with an underhand movement of the little finger. The Polynesians trusted more to hand-to-hand fighting ; and yet few of them had fortifications to fight from. They chose rather the battle in the open, trying to get the advantage of an enemy by position. It was the Maoris that, amongst Pacific Ocean peoples, were conspicuous by their earthwork, moat and palisade fortifications. And that makes all the more striking the only attempt at such a fort in Easter Island. This is the earthwork entrenchment so conspicuous on Anakena Bay, on the top of the conical hill *Maunga Hau Eepe*, or the Hill of the Longears. Tradition attributes it to Hotu Matua. The only other earthwork known on the island is a long mound inland from Akahanga called *miro oone*, or ship of earth, a very modern attempt to express their admira-

P

tion for European ships by imitating them. They still keep up the *miro oone*, but only of timber and canvas. The other Polynesian islands, when they made any protection for the defenceless during war, generally built it of stone, like the Honaunau, or city of refuge, in Hawaii. It would have been the easiest thing in the world to build such strongholds in Easter Island so vast is the material that lies ready to hand. And one of the fundamental mysteries of the island is that a people who could build such marvellous cyclopean stone walls as appear on some of the *ahus* did not proceed to turn them into fortresses when they anticipated the coming of a formidable enemy. Many of them have been built quite close to a spring of fresh water on the beach. And the bending of the wings so as to surround the spring and the approach to the sea, would make an ideal place for spearmen to fight off enemies and for women and children to be protected from the outrages that they generally suffered after defeat. Considering the indignities that they had to bear when conquered, including reduction to practical slavery, it is an amazing thing that if these people on their own erected those great stone burial platforms to honour and protect the bones of their dead, bitter necessity did not drive them to use their old skill in moving vast stones and fitting them together to protect the living and defenceless.

(9) **THE BATTLE AND ITS METHODS.** When all was ready for action, if the king was present, he put on his feather hat called *veri*, though that was all he could do in the combat. To keep his inviolability he must not take any share in the fighting. But the *maori* raised the *rongorongo* tablets or the *ua* or the *ao* or the *rapa* and marched into the fray. This was different from the action of the Tahitian priest in carrying in front of the army the wooden image of the god; the purpose was that the first victim might be offered to it. It was rather as an ensign like the *amo* of the Maori priests in New Zealand, to give a lead to the troops and to put heart into them by making them feel that if the Miru king could not fight with them at least the insignia of his god *Makemake* might be in their midst. It may have been that the conch shell was blown. When Beechey sent on shore Lieutenant Peard with a party, they had to retreat towards their boat; for they " saw a man in cloak and feather head-dress attended by several others armed with clubs coming to the landing-

place; and this hostile appearance was followed by the blowing of a conch shell, which Cook and others think never augurs good." And the tradition is quite clear that they had a conch shell which was blown in war times. It is quite possible that the night before they may have lighted warning-fires or watch-fires on the heights, or the coast. Beechey says: " The natives lighted fires and followed the ship along the coast, their numbers increasing at every step." The fires that Behrens saw at the *a h u s* and conjectured to be altar fires in the worship of the images or of the sun are probably to be explained as watch-fires warning allies and others of the beginning of a battle, though Forster thinks they were for cooking. It is probable too that just before entering into battle they danced the *a t e h a k a k a k a i*, or war dance, as the Maoris of New Zealand danced the *h a k a;* this dance was supposed to injure and weaken the enemy, as well as to put enthusiasm and courage into the ranks. Women attended to the commissariat as well as sometimes joining in the fight; for there was not only an advance guard of young men (*k o p i r a e*), but an advance guard of women (*v i e r a e*). It may be that the *m a o r i s* did fearsome grimacing and uttered the wild war-whoop as the warriors did in New Zealand and the priests in Hawaii. When the battle did occur it was what we would call a riot or a scrimmage; there was neither order nor tactics in it. Every warrior hit where he could and killed as many as he had opportunity to kill. And, when the immediate cause of the war, the assassin of one who had belonged to the attacking clan, was slain, hostilities ceased, and if there were any dead the combatants on both sides settled down to an amicable banquet on them. If the war had not issued from a *h e h e v a*, or a desire for revenge for a murder, but from deeper and less personal causes, then there was fighting *à l'outrance*. The enemy was injured by every means fair or foul; his houses were burned down, his crops destroyed, his women and children slaughtered; it was in fact a war of extermination. But if the enemy acknowledged their defeat, they became *k i o s* of the conquerors; they had to work and slave for them all the rest of their lives. This is given as the reason why so little cultivation was done on the island; the masters would expect all the food-raising to be done by the conquered; the slaves would work as little as possible, caring not if they themselves died. Sometimes the defeated took refuge in a cave or on small islands off the coast, as once on Motu Tautara, north of Hangaroa, and then the victors made the refuge a livestock preserve, taking out at a time as many as were wanted for the earth-oven.

(10) **WAR AND CANNIBALISM.** It has been asserted with considerable probability that one of the chief causes of the continual wars was the need of supplying the larder with fresh meat. One of their legends contains an incident illustrating this. A *Tupahotu* woman with her daughter were travelling over from the south coast to Hangaroa and on the way they were both outraged and killed by one of a hostile clan. A Tupahotu man came across the dead bodies and recognized them. He carried the news through his clan; they rose and marched against the clan of the assassin, but when he had been slain, the battle ceased and the two clans cooked the dead and feasted on them. The reason for this state of affairs is that they never killed in peace for the sake of getting meat. But the legend of The Mother's Vengeance seems to point in the other direction. A canoe-carpenter was absent from his home, near Anakena, building canoes, when a friend called at his house and asked for a meal; his wife said she was all alone (her little boy was away on the beach) and could not accede to his request; he threatened her with death, and, as a last defence, she declared that her child when he grew up would cause his death by a wound on the right thumb. He slew her, cooked part of her and took away the rest to supply his household. When the body was all eaten he remembered the threat of the woman before he killed her and resolved to add the boy to his larder and make the threat impossible. But the ghost of the mother always appeared at the right moment and prevented him fulfilling his purpose. The cannibal assassin in time became so afraid of the ghost that he shut himself up in a cave to prevent the threat being carried out. His friends tried to get him to come out, but he always shouted the name of the youth. They resolved to cure him of his mania by bringing the boy. They had difficulty in getting him; for he was generally out fishing. But at last they secured him and bringing him to the cave they shouted his name and said that they had brought him. The hermit burst out of his cave in a tempest of fury and clutched the youth by the throat in order to kill him; but the boy, in the struggle for life, got the thumb of the strangling right hand

between his teeth and bit it through. The would-be assassin let go and fell and, to save himself from another such attack, the boy lifted a stone and brained the madman as he lay on the ground.

(11) This story seems to indicate that cannibalism was not confined to times of war; it was the regular way of finally disposing of an enemy or even of the wife of a friend. But it seems to have been exceptional; else this would not have been a solitary legend. There can be little doubt that, if a clan ran short of provisions, it was the easiest way for getting the larder filled to stir up a little war; besides it gave vent to old grievances and often succeeded in disposing of a criminal; it was the only way they could get justice, as there was no authority in the island to investigate or punish; the king was king only in formal or ceremonial matters. Nor was there any god of war as there was in so many of the larger Polynesian areas to whom they could appeal and so satisfy the religious consciences of the weaker who longed for vengeance but dare not go to war. None of the clans, not even the Miru, had a war deity; each had only a god for general purposes, though drawn by Hotu Matua's devices into acknowledging the *Miru* deity, *M a k e m a k e*, as supreme. It was in accordance with this that after a battle the warriors went to the *m a o r i* and told the number of men they had slain so that he might record it in the *k o h a u i k a*, or tablet of the victims. When commissariat, glory, and justice were all secured by a successful war and continued to act as incentives to war, it is no wonder that wars were almost continuous. They were not all devastating; but even a single exterminating war, that involved both alliances, would have a noticeable effect on the numbers of the population. The estimates of all the voyagers, ranging from eight hundred to three thousand, are probably all not far from accurate; the seeming discrepancies would be explained by the occurrence of a war of extermination in the interval or the absence of all wars of extermination for a time.

CHAPTER XX

SOCIAL INSTITUTIONS AND CUSTOMS

(1) *There was strong family life with unlimited* patria *potestas, and power to dispose of one's land or personal property ; and yet there was village communism and polygamy as the marriage-tie was no tie.* (2) *None of the clans but the Miru had a r i k i or nobles or chiefs ; but village communism had not destroyed the distinction between rich and poor.* (3) *There was no public life except the festivals ; and family life was the only social cement.* (4) *Parents secluded the boys and girls till fourteen, a contrast to Polynesian licence ; it was the married women who offered themselves or were offered to the voyagers.* (5) *The seclusion of girls is illustrated in the legend of " The Happy Elopement," * (6) *and the seclusion of boys by that of " An Easter Island Endymion."* (7) *The patrilineal dominated with a trace of the matrilineal as in the rest of Polynesia ; so there was endogamy in the Miru, with a trace of exogamy in the freedom of matrimonial choice amongst the other clans.* (8) *The women had almost freed themselves from their Polynesian taboo shackles.* (9) *They were admitted to all religious privileges except that of being* maoris *or priests.* (10) *But they were not eligible to monarchy, though there is one tradition to the contrary. The kingship was too much of a mere priesthood to break away from the Polynesian doctrine of the unholiness of woman.* (11) *In the household, when a baby was born, the father went to bed. If a girl it had a fair chance of being killed according to Polynesian custom ; whether girl or boy it might be given to another household, adoption being an alternative to infanticide, though not to the as common abortion. If it remained in the family it was massaged, especially in the head and nose before the gristle passed into bone.* (12) *There was some idea of eugenism, but the general uncleanness of the caves and houses in which the boys and girls were secluded would obstruct the effect of eugenism, and the inhumanities they saw when they came out would blunt all fine feelings.*

(1) **FAMILY LIFE OR COMMUNISM ?** One of the problems about Easter Island is how far the family was developed and as a pendent how far there was community of goods and community of wives. There is great variance of opinion on these two questions. Behrens, the first observer, says : " It appeared to us that each family had its own hamlet apart from the rest." La Perouse like Eyraud nearly a century after him thought that the huge house in which hundreds slept at night indicated a community of goods. Whilst the free way in which the men offered the women at hand to the sailors led some to believe that there was community of wives. This was probably due to their unconscionable practice of thieving, and to polygamy ; a man could have as many wives as he wished, though most limited their wishes to two or three. Just as in the rest of Polynesia there was no ceremony at marriage, the only essential being a feast given by the bridegroom. Polynesian matrimony had no such connection with religion as is apparent in almost all the other events of

early life. There was more connection with it in Easter Island than in any other Polynesian area. The sons and daughters had to be kept in seclusion by the parents till they were of marriageable age and then they were taken up to Orongo to let the *maori* or priest examine and certify that they were virginal ; and the father could say yea or nay to the request of a young man for the hand of his daughter ; if she was good-looking she must have a good-looking bridegroom. The *patria potestas* was supreme in the disposal of the daughter. This does not look as if there was no family life. Of course, the girl, once disposed of, had the right to say whether she would remain with the man to whom she had been given or go somewhere else to a man of her own choice. The marriage tie was an exceedingly loose knot ; it could be undone as easily as it could be made, a feature in which Easter Island is in perfect agreement with all the rest of Polynesia. The free disposal of women was based on the right to unlimited polygamy and the absolute power of the husband over the wife. With regard to community of goods, there was throughout Polynesia a tendency to village communism, and when a man returned with the result of his labours either from abroad or from his garden, every man in the village thought he had a right to share in it. It is this, among other things, that accounts for the small amount of cultivation there always has been on the island ; a man raised or fished only as much as his household needed. The continual feasts supplied all that was necessary for the idle ; they could wander from feast to feast and have as much as would fill their stomachs for some time ; whilst the industrious felt they were sufficiently rewarded for giving all their produce for the feast by the applause of their fellow-feasters. There is a singular contrast to this in the right of every man to divide up his land on dying amongst his children, and the right to say whether his personal property, his *a o*, *paoa, ua, moai miro, mataa, kotake* (belt of human hair) and *hami* should be put into his *moenga*, or death-wrapping, or left in his house for his children. Moerenhout is much nearer the mark when he thinks that the great houses were meant for the celebration of feasts. Eyraud his first night on the island dropped into one of the great guest-houses during a festival ; if so many regularly slept in one of the great houses near the *a h u s*, what was the need of all the others for so small a population as the island carried ?

(2) **WERE THERE CHIEFS?** Behrens goes so far as to say that " in each house or family the most ancient governed and gave his orders." He could find no sign of a chief or prince ; " they appeared and spoke without distinction." Eyraud thought Torometi, who had been on a whaler as far as San Francisco, " was visibly a chief, though it is difficult to explain in what chiefship consists." He had certainly great ascendancy over his neighbours and afterwards was picked out by Dutrou Bornier, the pioneer of farming on the island, for his right-hand man. There were certainly no chiefs except in the sacred clan of the *M i r u*. That is one of the distinctions of Easter Island from all the other Polynesian areas, which always had chiefs great and little. The clans of Easter Island were led promiscuously. There were no hereditary chiefly families but in the *M i r u;* that clan seems to have absorbed all that distinguished the *a r i k i* in other islands, power, privilege and divine descent. Of course, there were poor and rich in the other clans, as is evident in the *h a r e p a e n g a*, or stone-foundation house, and all its arrangements ; and yet we should have expected the Polynesian village communism to have destroyed this distinction between rich and poor in an island that had no hereditary classification of ranks except the impotent *M i r u*. It was doubtless the well-to-do who formed public opinion in each clan and practically selected the leader in war. But the leadership was never allowed to harden into hereditary aristocracy.

(3) **A STRONG FAMILY LIFE.** If we are to trust the traditions and the legends, there was a powerful family life in the community. No relative dared neglect the duty of vengeance when a man or woman of the family was slain. The nearest must become the mourner and avenger (*t i m o*) and stir the whole clan to fight against the clan of the assassin. In some of the legends this duty of vengeance becomes a hereditary vendetta. The child unborn must take up the cause of his slain father when he grows to manhood. In " The Mother's Vengeance " the boy has to pursue the slayer of his mother till he has killed him. There is a special potency in Easter Island family life, all the stronger that there is no public life in the clans and no sign of the appearance of the *a r i k i*, the nobility of the other Polynesian communities. There would have been no bond of community if the family bond

had not been strong. In the language the phrase for one who is a blood relation is *tangata hare,* a man of the house ; the same as " hind " in English, which originally meant a son or daughter of the *" hive,"* or house. This alone would be enough to disprove Eyraud's conjecture that they all lived together in one big house, with community of goods and without separate family life.

(4) **SEEMING CONTRADICTIONS.** There is one custom that could not have arisen, still less have been put into practice, if there had been no family life. Parents kept their sons as well as their daughters in seclusion up to puberty ; this was called *h u r u* . Neither boy nor girl was to indulge the sexual passion during immaturity or until the *maori* had examined them and declared them virginal. Then, and only then, could they be admitted to training for the choruses at the festivals ; then, and only then, were they supposed to be marriageable. This is a striking contrast to the custom of the rest of Polynesia, where the boys and girls were allowed perfect freedom till they were married ; the only exceptions to this were the institution of the *p u h i* , or virgin daughter of the chief, amongst the Maoris of New Zealand, and that of the *t a u - p o u* , or virgin hostess, in every Samoan village that had a chief, along with the examination of the Samoan chief's daughter *coram populo* before marriage to see that she was virgin. The young Easter Island woman had to be certified as *n i r u* (virgin) and have the symbol of virginity tattooed on her cheeks by the *maori* before she could be presented for marriage or for the school of singing and dancing. This seems absolutely incongruous with the reports of the voyagers on the Easter Island women and their conduct ; they offered themselves freely to the sailors ; they were all " Messalinas." These were doubtless the married women, who after once having been given in marriage were free to make their own selection afterwards ; the husbands, as the temporary proprietors, would be within their rights in trading them off for what they considered more valuable goods ; the young women, that is, the girls under fourteen, as that was the age of marriage, would all be secluded in caves ; it was doubtless this that made the voyagers, like Cook, think that the women were only a third of the number of the men.

(5) **" THE HAPPY ELOPEMENT."** There is no doubt about this being the custom if we are to trust the legends. Two of

them will illustrate. "The Happy Elopement" shows how girls were immured in caves till the marriageable age. The fame of the beauty of a girl who had lived all her life secluded in a cave on the outskirts of *Rano Kao* had stirred the imagination of all the youths in the neighbourhood, and one, *L e p a o*, was so smitten with the report of it that he set out to find her cave; he spent days and nights wandering around the slopes and precipices of the mountain till his friends set him down as mad. His father, Punga, stung by the criticisms, tried again and again to bring him back to common sense and work. Failing in his efforts he resolved to break an oath of secrecy in order to save his son. The parents of the girl, believing in the wisdom of their old friend Punga, had confided to him the secret of her whereabouts. He told his son; and the son rushed incontinently to the cave and found her beauty all it had been reputed to be. He was a handsome youth, and when the two met, it was love at first sight. They ran away to the house of his father; and when the mother came to the cave with the morning meal, she found it deserted. With her husband she searched everywhere to see what had become of their daughter. Failing in their search, they thought of their wise old friend Punga, and resolved to ask his advice. As they came up to the house they were amazed to find the son of the old man and their daughter sitting arm in arm on the porch. They recognized the manly beauty of L e p a o and, as they saw they could not have chosen a better son-in-law, they laughingly accepted the inevitable.

(6) **"AN EASTER ISLAND ENDYMION."** "An Easter Island Endymion" illustrates the seclusion of boys. Old bald-headed Ohovehi saw that his boy Ure was so handsome that, afraid of the consequences when he got out into the world, he kept him in isolation even when he had passed puberty, so that when eighteen years of age he had seen no face but that of his father. But the fame of his beauty had gone over the island and two witches of Poike, Kavaaro and Kavatua, could not resist the temptation to see and perhaps capture so handsome a youth. They waited till his father was well out of the way and then entered his cave, professing the desire to have his criticism of their efforts in matting; his father, in order to keep him absorbed, had taught him to net and mat, the occupations of women and old men; they had brought a piece of their braiding to compare with his. And

as he was busy explaining to one the difference between them and the secret of his art, the other by crooning monotonous songs made him fall asleep. Then the two wrapped him up in his own work and carried him off to their cave high up the *P o i k e* cliffs. They had heard of a narcotic in a far-off land that would keep him so buried in sleep that they would enjoy his beauty for ever. But *Nuahine-pikea-uri*, who lived in a cave below, caught some words of their consultation as to how they could get it, and suspected something of the truth. And when they had set out on their quest by climbing the bridge of a rainbow, she clambered up into their cave and, undoing the bundle of mats, found inside it sound asleep her own grandson. She awakened him and told him what had occurred and the dangers that threatened him. She bade him, when they offered him food, pretend to eat it, but slip it down so that it would fall into her cave ; and she herself would supply him with food in the absence of the witches. They returned with the narcotic and mixed it in his food, day after day ; they were amazed to find that he fell into no deep, abiding sleep. They went off to their white wizard and complained ; he gave them stronger narcotics. But still they returned and said that even these had no effect. So he gave them a potion that would practically kill him and yet render his tissues vital and beautiful as if living. This failed likewise. So they resolved to let him live and be awake at his braiding and netting as long in the day as he liked. But he was homesick away from his father, and pined to return to his old cave ; and as he sat at his work he sang a lamentation, the burden of which repeated the name of his father, Ohovehi, over and over again. Two fishermen used to come daily and fish not far from the cave and every day they heard his lamentation and wondered what it meant. And once they took their catch to a great festival near his old place of residence and his father heard them tell the story of the lamentation and repeat the words. He had found at last what had become of his boy and he made for the cave of his grandmother in the cliffs of Poike. She bade him be cautious as the two witches were cunning. So she arranged to have two great nets made and instructed her grandson what to do when one was let down over the cave of the witches. She took the other to her own cave and had it fixed so that if he fell he would be caught in it. So next day, when his captors were out and he saw the net dangling in front of him, he followed instructions and seizing its meshes clung to it. He was soon free and, with his father, went back to their old residence. On their return, the witches, seeing the bird flown, suspected who had managed the flight and began to take vengeance on Nuahine below; persecuting and chasing her they would soon have killed her, but that she turned herself into a black crab (*pikea uri*) and took shelter deep in a crevice of the rocks; for, like all the people of Poike, she had command of sorcery. Knowing the wiles of her enemies, she was certain that they would transform themselves into creeping things so as to get in to their Endymion again; but she warned him to kill every creeping or crawling creature that came into his cave except a little black crab. He followed instructions again and killed everything that crept or crawled into his retreat; but he spared a little black crab that got in. The result was that his two persecutors were killed and his grandmother came permanently to protect him from sorceries.

(7) **EXOGAMY AND ENDOGAMY.** It is plain that the family was by no means insignificant in its influence. And the ruling principle of it was, as in the rest of Polynesia, patrilineal. If a man married into another clan, his children accepted the gods of his clan as their own and not those of their mother's clan. But there is a relic of an older social system; as in most Polynesian communities all cousins were called brothers or sisters, and the nomenclature of all blood-relationships considered rather the generations than the actual paternity or maternity. Even the marriage relationships were carefully classified. There were two different names for presents made to relations by marriage; a present given directly to them was called *vaaino;* but when a father gave a present to his daughter-in-law and she gave it to her father, mother or brother, it was called *mahia* or *hemahia*. And between the clans and within the clans there was complete matrimonial freedom. They were all exogamists except the *Miru*. It was the tradition, if not the rule, for all *Miru* people to marry within the clan; and for this purpose there was a taboo on exogamic intercourse; the man or woman of another clan who had irregular, or even matrimonial, connections with one of the Miru was supposed to suffer for it; he or she was harassed with intestinal troubles (*tutae-hihi*) and not the *Miru* man or woman; and the ordinary

headache of a man or woman who was not married to a *Miru* was *puoko ngaruru*, the common Polynesian word for a headache; but if he or she was married to a *Miru* a headache was supposed to result that had a special name of its own "*ahe*." A thoroughly sensible Easter Islander who is married to a *Miru* woman has told me that he is quite sure all the colics and headaches he has suffered from were due to this and this alone. There are even relics of a still older exogamy as there are in some other branches of the Polynesian race. One vigorous Easter Islander told me that in order to secure his wife, he had to run after her and catch her. This is still to be found amongst the Maoris of New Zealand; and in Hawaii the custom of making the bridegroom or his relatives throw a *tapa* over the head of the bride seems to be a relic of the same exogamic capture.

(8) **TABOOS AGAINST WOMEN.** All these origins and customs were bound to have a depressing influence on the position of women. And throughout Polynesia this is expressed partly in taboos that exclude women from many foods and privileges. But for some reason these are not so drastic or so extensive in their action in Easter Island. The most prominent taboo on women in Polynesia forbidding them to eat with the men or even touch their food had lapsed. Even in Pitcairn Island, where the blood of the mutineers of the *Bounty* might have been expected to introduce the European attitude to women, it is the Polynesian taboo that still holds; the women cannot sit with the men at meals; they have to wait till the men have finished eating and then sit down to table. Some time or other the Easter Island women had got the taboo abolished. But as to food, a part of it still lingered; they could eat fowl; but they had to ask permission to eat from the father, husband, or brother. What their rights as to the eating of pig or dog were we do not know; for neither, when introduced, established itself on the island. The dog and the seal were reserved for the king, when they appeared. As for the turtle, its visits were so rare that the rights of women to its flesh are not mentioned; but, as the shell was often made into a belt which women wore, it is more than likely that they were allowed to eat its flesh. As for the rats there was evidently no taboo; for they formed one of the delicacies of the festival, and women took their full share in them. In human flesh they were accorded full rights; for, in spite of the sensitiveness

of the people on this point since the introduction of Christianity, there are many of the oldest women in the village
who ate it long ago and one fine old lady herself candidly
acknowledges that she did. And this was probably because
they took their share in the battle that led to the cannibal
banquet. It is safe to say that they did not usually kill in
time of peace in order to eat. And, though they were as much
given to infanticide as the rest of the Polynesians, they never
killed the infant in order to eat it, as the people of Rarotonga,
Raivavai, and Rapa used to do. There was probably a taboo
against women using nets, though not against their making
them ; they never used the net or the hook in fishing.

(9) **WOMEN LESS PROFANE IN EASTER ISLAND.** Nor were
they ever considered too unholy to take part in religious functions. In all the other Polynesian areas the temple was pro-
faned by the footstep of a woman however noble; it was taboo
for women to take any part in a ceremonial that had anything
to do with religion. In Easter Island, the young woman was
connected up with religion on her issue from seclusion ; she
was taken to the *m a o r i*, or priest, and he imprinted indelibly on her cheeks, her buttocks, and her parts, his religious
certificate that she was fit to become a wife and mother in the
community; she became the *p o k i m a n u*, the bird child
under the protection of the great protector of the birds, the
god M a k e m a k e. The *maori* was his priest and, though
he was the god of the Miru to begin with, he had become the
god of the whole people, and though his priests were at first
chosen by the king only from the Miru, they were later chosen
from all the clans. Women then, having upon their persons
the sign of the god of the community, had the right to see,
if not take part in, his ceremonials. Afterwards, when as
a wife a woman was about to bear a child, she went up into
the house where Taura Renga stood half buried in the earth,
and the *maori* in his red and yellow girdle (*taura renga*) painted
a red line and a yellow one round her abdomen. Thus again
the seal of religion was set upon her. And to all the feasts
was she admitted as freely as the men. She could not become
a *m a o r i ;* but she could be trained by the *maori* to sing and
dance as well as the young men ; and under the guidance
of the *maori* she took an active part in every festival by
singing and dancing. And there is little doubt that their feasts
were their substitute for the Polynesian temple services. The

p a i n a was not worship of the gods in our sense of the term ; it was not even a conciliatory feast to the dead although always held at one of the great burial platforms ; it was a conciliatory feast to the living in honour of the dead ; that this was considered religious by the community we may take for granted, inasmuch as a *m a o r i*, or priest, superintended it all. A woman could not be a *maori ;* but, when the unofficial profession of intercourse with the supernatural sprang up, woman asserted her right to be in it and her claim was not rejected. She not infrequently became an *i v i a t u a*, or as the name might be translated by help of cognate Polynesian vocabularies, "a representative of the clan in its dealings with the supernatural"; of course, it was of a clan that was not the Miru ; for the *M i r u* had no *akuaku*, or ghost, and could not have an *i v i a t u a*, as the supernatural element that the *iviatua* dealt with was the *a k u a k u*.

(10) **THE KINGSHIP IN EASTER ISLAND.** That the Polynesian taboo of women had not always existed is evident in the fact that if there was no male heir a woman might become chief or even monarch, and, the singular matrilineal relic in the most monarchic of the groups, Hawaii and Tahiti, that a noble or royal woman handed on her nobility or royalty to her offspring by a commoner whilst the noble or royal man did not, and in the little less monarchic Tonga, where royalty when it landed in a woman had especial potency. There was no trace of this in Easter Island ; the kingship went to the eldest son as soon as he married and had a household of his own. And yet there is a singular fact about the last days of the *Miru* monarchy that seems to indicate its Polynesian affinity. *K a i m a k o i*, the son of Ngaara, resigned his kingship when he had no son of age and his eldest girl had married and become head of a household ; she became queen till his eldest son, *M a u r a t a*, married ; then she resigned and he became king. Her name is not recorded in the list of monarchs, nor is the name of any other queen. It looks as if the occurrence were abnormal. But the list has an artificial air about it, as if it had been manufactured in later times. There was no reason why a woman should not succeed in an island that had removed so many of the Polynesian taboos from women. But the *M i r u* kingship had absorbed all the divinity of the Polynesian theocracies without their power. And, as it monopolized sacredness, and all its functions

consisted of ceremonials and religious functions, it may have fallen heir to the Polynesian idea that woman was profane and incapable of any religious act or ceremony and so excluded her from kingship. An island like Easter Island was exactly fitted for monarchy; for it has no valleys or dividing ridges, such as Rapa and the Marquesas have to an extent that made single government impossible; but it had contingents from Marquesas and also from New Zealand, where the great forests and the mountains still stood in the way of unification. And these contingents may have brought a strong objection to real kingship, whilst the circumstances of the island after the catastrophe rendered concentration of real power an impossibility. The divine side of kingship had therefore to be forced to an extreme in order to give it any weight. Even the commoners of the clan were all *ariki* and had the divinity of chiefliness; they monopolized rain-getting, an important function in an island that has far too little rainfall to satisfy the bibulous character of its soil and rocks. And once divine always divine; the captivity of *Ngaara* did not destroy his divinity; as long as he was prisoner with the *Ngaure* his religious and ceremonial functions went on as usual; all the *maoris* came to him with their tablets; all the reviews and festivals went on for the islanders.

(11) **THE COUVADE, INFANTICIDE, ADOPTION, AND MASSAGE OF THE INFANT.** No Easter Island woman could shake off the Polynesian taboo so far as to assume an office that had absorbed the essence of divinity. She had to be satisfied with the lowlier function of domestic duties added to a good share in the raising of food and in fishing. Her chief function was, of course, the bearing and raising of children; for how could the generations go on without that? But man had to pretend to take his share in the labour; when the infant was born, the father went to bed "so as to make it strong"; the number of days he went to bed depended on his strength or indolence. I have not heard of the *couvade* in any other Polynesian area, and was doubtful about its existence till one of the most intelligent and trustworthy of Easter Island men assured me that he always went to bed for a day or two after a baby was born in the household in order that it might live and be strong. But before this masculine *mana* could be applied it had to be decided whether the baby was to live. For infanticide has been an institution in

all parts of Polynesia, whether from reasons of necessity or reasons of luxury. In Hawaii a child might be killed at birth or one or two or even more years after. In Tahiti if a child lived half an hour it was allowed to live; but both sexes might be sacrificed. In many it was only the female infant that was put out of life, and that was where war was constant and renewal of the bands of warriors was an absolute necessity. In Easter Island dialect there is a special word for it, *t i n g a i - p o k i*, or killing of the child; and the infants chosen to be killed were generally the girls, as war was always going on. There was another question to be decided soon after the baby was born and allowed to live; it was, to whom should they present it? It was the better alternative to infanticide. But if it were a mere alternative to infanticide it was not so to abortion, which was almost as common in Polynesia as infanticide. That infanticide and adoption still exist side by side is one of the anomalies of Polynesia not so easy to explain, especially when we know that abortion was not less common than the former. It looks as if the two customs were the relics of two different environments. Abortion and infanticide belong most commonly to a hard environment though they also appear amongst luxurious livers. They rarely become a fixed habit sanctioned by public opinion unless it is a public necessity; the life of the whole population must be threatened with famine before such a sanction could be given. The habit is rooted in the far past of Polynesia; it is so fixed, as to be almost instinctive; probably it was a necessity of the slow submergence of the fatherland; for it exists in every branch of the race. But adoption, though common, is not so nearly universal; it is the natural product of a prosperous environment; the more prosperous are ready to bring up the children of the less prosperous, and the poor naturally look to it as their means of relief. Finally it becomes the fashion in a community and every family either adopts or presents for adoption and sometimes even both. There are few homes in the village of Hangaroa here but have both children of their own and adopted children. Having decided on both saving the infant and bringing it up, the first thing to do was to massage the baby; the skull had to be given the fashionable Polynesian shape, flat back, sloping brow and domed crown; the nostrils had to be flattened out; the fingers had to be made long and slender; the knees and ankles had to be made

Q

strong and flexible for swift and safe passage over the stony surface of the island. This had all to be done before the gristle hardened into bone. And doubtless mothers varied in the strength of the applied hand ; and the result is much variation in some of the parts and features that were supposed to be changed in babyhood.

(12) **EDUCATION AND INHUMANITIES.** And after the infancy how did they deal with the children ? In the olden days the father secluded his boy and the mother her girl. It was therefore isolated education they had. And that the father had often some eugenic purpose in his mind is evident in the fact that if he had a healthy handsome boy, he would refuse to sanction his marriage to an ugly or deformed or unhealthy young woman ; and when his girl had beauty and health he would never bestow her on any but a strong well-made youth. This should have resulted in a perfect race full of strength and beauty. But there were other features of life that obstructed such a result. Immurement and seclusion often leave the social qualities undeveloped, and seclusion in a narrow space must have greatly interfered with the development of the physique. And we have only to consider the lack of cleanliness in those dark dank caves and houses to see that no amount of eugenism would ever save the race from degeneration. The floor was covered with grass, the haunt of every crawling and creeping thing. The mat-mantle or blanket was full of livestock, as Eyraud testifies. The hair was as full. For, though they had plenty of bone for the purpose, they never made a comb. Their only comb was their fingers (*k a t u*). And the hair was generally long in both sexes. No wonder that the greatest kindness and courtesy was to sit down and "dislouse" (*h a h a r i*) a friend or child ; and no wonder that the first shout of the *t u u r a*, or servant from Motunui, to his employer when he had found the first egg of the season was "Shave your head," and that the bird-man for the year had as his first duty to shave every hair off his head and face, his moustache and beard, his eyebrows and his eyelashes. These might all be harbourers of the unclean and crawling or jumping ; and the unclean could not be pleasing to *Makemake,* the patron of the sea-birds and the fish. The *a o* must be free from impurities when he did the *r o k u n g a*, the dance with the egg in his hand, along the coast in the presence of all the people. After the children

were brought out of their seclusion into the world they must
have witnessed much that blunted all finer feeling and
obstructed all realization of any eugenic ideal. They would
see the rough unfeeling treatment of the sick. In some parts
of Polynesia they buried the sick alive, stifling their cries with
a shred of *t a p a* . If the Easter Island youths and maidens
did not see that, they saw the old people stoned to death
because they were useless. All the effect of their seclusion
from such sights and of the careful choice of mates would be
lost in a few days amidst such inhumanities.

CHAPTER XXI

POLYNESIAN

(1) *All observers have contrasted Melanesian and Polynesian in stature, physique, stoutness of leg, face and hair.* (2) *Easter Islanders are Polynesian with a difference ; they have a slenderness and poor musculature that differentiate them from the race the images represent.* (3) *Their complexion is very varied, often white, their face and body lean.* (4) *Their lips thin and showing resolution like the statues which have the face and expression of a race of conquerors, their chins being as large as the under jaws in most of the burial vaults.* (5) *There is no sign of racial mixture ; the race of the images was better fed ; it had a larger abdomen and muscular arms ; but the head in both shows the effect of massage.* (6) *All agree that their features are Caucasoid ; those of the images are exaggeratedly so ; and there are many traces of a blond race as in the rest of Polynesia.* (7) *They are Polynesian in all their vegetable foods, and especially in those they resort to in famines.* (8) *And they were Polynesian in all their animal foods, though their colossal improvidence ate out the pig and the dog more than once.* (9) *In all their clothing and ornamentation, especially tattooing, they are entirely Polynesian.* (10) *All their arts were Polynesian, though limited by scarcity of material ; but they are differentiated from both Polynesia and Melanesia by almost complete absence of musical instruments.* (11) *In warfare and weapons they are Polynesian as distinct from Melanesian.* (12) *The farther we get into the world of spirit the likeness is less.* (13) *And in the absence of all belief in a life beyond death they are differentiated from both Polynesian and Melanesian ; their priesthood differs from the Polynesian, but still more from the Melanesian, which is non-existent.* (14) *As in Polynesia there is a king—a contrast to Melanesia ; and the king is divine, but he is un-Polynesian in being a mere ceremonialist.*

(1) **POLYNESIAN AND MELANESIAN.** No voyager, from Cook onwards, but has noted the contrast between the inhabitants of the central and eastern Pacific and those to the west of them south of the equator. The former are scattered over an area five thousand miles by three thousand, on islands that are so numerous that the region has been called Polynesia, or the realm of many islands. The latter occupy islands that though exceedingly numerous are comparatively close to one another ; and the region has been named not from the character of the islands, but from the colour of the inhabitants, which is sometimes not far from black, M e l a n e s i a , the island region of the blacks. But there is a much deeper contrast than in the colour of the skin. The features of the latter are generally negroid, often heavily negroid ; those of the former may have a trace of the negroid in them, in the nostrils and often in the lips ; but the former is largely artificially produced soon after birth under the stimulus of some aristocratic ideal of beauty. In the hair there is a still more striking contrast ; the one is curled up and even tufted ; the

FOUR GENERATIONS OF AN EASTER ISLAND FAMILY. THE GREAT-GRANDMOTHER
WAS A MATRON WHEN THE PERUVIAN RAID OCCURRED

A GROUP OF EASTER ISLANDERS TAKEN IN 1922

ANOTHER GROUP OF EASTER ISLANDERS TAKEN IN 1922

other is straight without lankiness and instead of that a tendency to waviness, whilst the colour is often reddish-brown (the Polynesian *k e h u*) and generally in children bronzy until puberty. The stature of the one, though often fairly tall, shows on the average the influence of an aboriginal pigmy or negritto people. That of the other is the tallest in the world, in individuals not seldom rising well above six foot. But perhaps the greatest distinction is in the legs ; the negroids to the west have little or no calf to the leg ; the other race is marked by the stoutness of its legs, surpassing all other races in this respect. But in making this comparison it must not be forgotten that the Polynesian race has saturated all the eastern shores or islands of the various Melanesian groups ; this is due to the dominance of submergence in their region, their oceanic canoes and the prevalence of the trade-winds from the east through the greater part of the year.

(2) **EASTER ISLANDERS AND POLYNESIANS.** How far has this Polynesian physique passed into the Easter Islanders ? To judge from those of to-day there is on the whole less of the negroid than in a large number of Polynesian islands ; for it is rapidly going out of fashion to flatten the nostrils of the infants, and the lips are often thin and the features almost completely European. But it may be said this is due to intermixture with Europeans, although there have been far fewer European settlers than on any other equal area in the Pacific Ocean. The best witnesses are the voyagers and visitors before there was or could have been European infiltration. Behrens is the first to report on their physique : " These islanders are in general lively, well-made, strong, pretty slender, and very swift of foot." Here we have the first hint of a contrast to the Polynesian, in their slenderness ; but this is doubtless due to their scant fare and hard life. In the report of Cook's Third Voyage by Mr. Anderson on the Tahitians it is said : " The muscular appearance so common amongst the Friendly Islanders and which seems a consequence of their being accustomed to much action is lost here, where the superior fertility of their country enabled the inhabitants to lead a more indolent life." Easter Island is even less cultivable and less productive than Tongatabu and its neighbouring coral islets ; but it has less opportunity for developing the musculature, inasmuch as it has none of the ocean canoes of Tonga and none of its reef-protected waters. Hence

the Easter Islanders have none of the stoutness of the Polynesians of the elevated islands and none of the muscularity of
those of the low islands. And the statues represent a race
that had a different environment; the sculptors avoided
cutting their legs in stone; but they made the arms a special
feature, and these are striking for their size; they are not
only long, but broad; they represent arms that have had
their muscles exceptionally developed. Then the hands bent
in at right-angles to them from the wrist seem to be set to
hold an exceptionally large abdomen; and in some of the
statues fallen inland the abdomen is huge. These images
evidently represent a race that was well-fed, like the Polynesians
of the rich volcanic islands.

(3) **THE TESTIMONY OF THE VOYAGERS, THE IMAGES AND
THE BURIAL VAULTS.** Behrens continues: " They are in general
brown like the Spaniards; some were also found pretty black
and others who are quite white." There are others of " a
reddish complexion as if burnt in the sun." This variety
of colour, from white through reddish-brown to black, constantly reported by visitors to the island was undoubtedly
due on the one hand to the seclusion of the young people till
puberty and to the lack of shade on the island once they
entered on the open-air duties of manhood and womanhood.
Cook also notices the " slenderness " of the race, though
" brisk and active " with " good features and not disagreeable
countenances." Forster says the people were " of a middle
stature, but very thin," " they are inferior in stature to the
natives of the Society and Friendly Islands and to those of
New Zealand, there being not a single person amongst them
who could be reckoned tall." Yet " the man who jumped
into the boat " was " about five foot eight." " Their body
was also lean and their face thinner than that of any people
hitherto seen in the South Sea." " Their noses were not very
broad, but rather flat between the eyes; their lips strong ";
" their hair black and curling."

(4) Beechey's officers estimated the average height to be
five foot seven and a half inches, which is not far off the
Polynesian average. He thought them a handsome race,
especially the women, with " fine oval countenances and
regular features " and " smooth high-rounded foreheads ";
" rather small and somewhat sunken dark eye." " The nose
is aquiline and well-proportioned." " The lips when closed

AN EASTER ISLAND MAN AS FIGURED BY HODGES, THE ARTIST OF COOK'S EXPEDITION

form nearly a line, showing very little of the fleshy part and
giving a character of resolution to the countenance." The
last picture of the Easter Islander of 1825 could almost stand
for a description of the lips of the statues. And, though the
prevailing type of nose amongst the statues on Rano Raraku
is slightly concave, if not tip-tilted, in a considerable number
it is straight and even somewhat aquiline. It is their great
and prominent chins that, added to their firm, thin and pouting
lips, give them the look of commanders and conquerors. And
in most of the burial vaults that I tried in the larger platforms
I found a huge underjaw well filled with strong teeth, a feature
of most of the skulls ; these great jaws were often lying apart,
the skulls to which they belonged having mouldered away.
Paymaster Thomson in working through the fine *a h u* of
Akahanga was struck with the " extraordinary size and width "
of the " lower jaws " of the skulls. Nor did all of the skulls,
that looked long when first observed, turn out more than
medium when measured, and most of them showed in the
somewhat flattened back and the sloping brow that the
Polynesian massage at birth had been used on them. And
this artificial ideal is exaggerated in the heads of the images.
The thigh-bones were also long and stout.

(5) Moerenhout was not long after Beechey in his visit to
the island ; and as he was there to try and get divers for his
pearl fishery in the Paumotus he had longer time and more
opportunities for observing the natives. He argues : " If
the islanders are browner than the people of the isles farther
north, it is that their island is less covered with trees and
shrubs. Some of the women are almost as white as those of
the south of Europe " ; " almost all the men are robust and
muscular ; the women for the most part are delicate and
pretty." " There came on board a handsome young native
six foot high, of noble figure and imposing mien. He had the
air of a Hercules." It is he too who declares generally of the
Eastern Polynesians : " In six years' voyaging and constant
observation I have never seen anything of mixed race."
" Never any individual with ' *c h e v e u x   c r e p u s .* ' " " They
are always tall with high brow, open face, lively and large
eyes, nose a little flattened and face oval." And the flattened
nose, he knows, was largely produced, like the flattened back
of the head by " *comprimer et petrir* " at birth, in Tahiti at
least ; " for a flat nose is considered a great beauty amongst

women." And more than thirty years after Eyraud declares of the Easter Islanders : " their colour, though a little coppery, differed little from that in Europe, many being entirely white." And Gana on the *O'Higgins* in the Chilian expedition of 1871 describes the natives as " of medium stature, great eyes, protuberant brow, fine nose, flattened nostrils, hair faded black or yellow, large mouth, regular lips," " fine swimmers, yet of no exceptional muscularity."

(6) **EVIDENCE OF A LIGHT-SKINNED ELEMENT IN POLYNESIA.** There is a general consensus on the European-like features and colour of many of the natives of Easter Island. And the faces of the images confirm this Caucasoid impression ; they are oval, straight-nosed, large-eyed, thin-lipped and short in the upper lip, the features that distinguish or are supposed to distinguish the highest ideal of beauty of the north-west of Europe. There are also many indications of a blond race having penetrated into Polynesia. There is the story, in at least all the larger areas in which there were refuges for a defeated people, of a golden or red-haired race that crossing with some of the conquering immigrants have left the *u r u k e h u*, or light-haired families and children. Moorea, the island opposite Papeete, was of old called " the island of fairy folk with golden hair." In Hawaii they worshipped Cook as their golden-haired god *L o n o* returned to his original home, and the priest led him with high ceremonial and offerings to the great stone truncated pyramid that was the temple of the god. In New Zealand the T u r e h u, a light-haired aboriginal race away up in the mountains of the Urewera country, crossed with the immigrants and so left numbers of *u r u k e h u* in that region. But it is the *P a t u p a i a r e h e* that are especially referred to as the purest of the blond-haired races ; and Mr. James Cowan has shown in the June and September numbers of the *Journal* of the Polynesian Society for 1921 that the wise men of the Ngatimaniapoto tribe have traditions of this fair-skinned people having lived in the fatherland Hawaiki. In the September number he tells how one of the *Patupaiarehe* called Tarapikau still guards their sacred places on Mount Rangitoto, and how any Maori trespassing in them sees their red-haired pigs or their red flax or their red eels in the streams and is carried off to the top of the mountain. Red is their distinctive colour, the term generally applied by Easter Islanders to

Europeans. And *u r u k e h u* is often translated "red-haired." Even the Gilbert Islands in Micronesia on the outskirts of Polynesia have a legendary land of blond people called *M a t a n g*, to which the spirits of their dead go ; and for a year or two before coming out at the great dance (*r u o i a*) the girls are blanched. So the aristocracy of most Polynesian areas blanched their daughters by keeping them out of the sun. And the Easter Islanders kept a blanching house near some of their dancing places ; and one of the aims of the seclusion of both boys and girls was doubtless to make them fair in the skin for the matrimonial choice as in the Gilbert Islands *r u o i a*. And still can one see in the village fair skins as well as dark, and children that have bronzy hair and almost blond complexions. And, as I pass native girls, with the sun shining through their hair, there is a glint of reddish-brown in it ; and in the village there is a family that is completely red-haired.

(7) And thus in physique, in hair and features and complexion Easter Islanders show affinity with Polynesia, are in fact Polynesian. So in their foods and plants and methods of cultivation they are fundamentally Polynesian. The basis of their food is one of the three great Polynesian tubers, the *k u m a r a*, of which Hotu Matua brought many varieties. It is the staple here as it flourishes in dry ground and the island has not anything like tropical rain and loses the effect of its showers almost immediately from the porosity of the soil. They grow the *t a r o* also, but only as a secondary food, though it was the chief tuber in the rest of Eastern Polynesia. The *yam* they rarely grow ; for though it gives a large amount of food, the recommendation that probably makes it the chief tuber in Tonga and Melanesia, they think it insipid. Many varieties of both *t a r o* and *y a m* were brought by the great pioneer ; but most have died out and those that are still grown have been brought from Tahiti. Next to the tubers in importance comes the banana ; *m a i k a* is a very old word in the Easter Island language as in Tahitian ; but it was not to Tahiti that they owed their varieties of the banana, *p a h u*, *p u k a p u k a*, *k i r i t e a*, *h i h i* and *p i a;* these were due to the great originator of all Easter Island culture. Perhaps as important was the *p i a* plant which he too introduced ; from this they got their arrowroot, far superior in flavour to that from the South American *m a n i o c*, though

now driven out by it because it is easier to cultivate and more
prolific of the white flour. It grew wild over all the island
in old times, and so plentiful was the flour that they used it as
a white paint for their faces and bodies. The *t i*, or dracaena,
was another Polynesian plant introduced at the start and
used for the Polynesian purpose of making a sweetmeat of
its root by baking it. The sugar-cane was not so important,
as it never flowered in the island, or developed its sweet sap
sufficiently. Perhaps the surest mark of kinship is the foods
that were used in times of famine. The Easter Islanders
were driven to use the root of the beach convolvulus
(*t a n o a*) though they knew its poisonous effects, and so were
the Hawaiians driven to eat it at times (*k o a l i a i*). The
k a p e or *a l o c a s i a m a c r o r h i z a* was used at such
times in Polynesia ; but it had many poisonous elements
which had to be steamed out by long cooking in the *u m u*.
In Easter Island it was and is regularly grown as an ordinary
food in spite of the long treatment its tuber needed. Most
Polynesians resorted to cooking the roots of certain ferns.
The Maoris and the Easter Islanders used the roots of the
commonest, which grow freely over the stoniest and barrenest
portions of their country. And in the cultivation of their
land the natives of this isolated island were as truly Polynesian
as the largest and most central. They used the digging-stick
(*o k a*) for all the operations. Thus were they fundamentally
Polynesian in all their vegetable foods and cultivation of
them.

(8) **ANIMAL FOOD AND IMPROVIDENT APPETITE.** In all
their animal food it was the same with a difference. Their
fish were difficult to get because of the lack of a coral reef
and beaches and because of the rough rocky bottoms of most
of the coast. So there was less netting and trapping than in
the rest of Polynesia and more diving and catching by hand ;
and the women entered more into the last type, especially at
night. And the scantiness of their vegetable oils made them
keep their fish oils to solidify and eat in leaves, whilst they
used the shark oil, and the oil from fowls for dressing the
hair and painting their bodies. Like all Polynesians they
were fond of eating small fish raw, just as they were caught,
with the salt water upon them. But like the Maoris they did
not use salt water as a sauce for their food, nor did they
manufacture salt like the Hawaiians. It is more than likely

that most of the Polynesians had at one stage in their early history to resort to human flesh as a food, as the eating of it remained in some of their priestly rites, or is mentioned in some of their legends and traditions where the actual habit had disappeared from daily life. Thus in their cannibalism are the Easter Islanders Polynesians; but human flesh was with them merely a food and not a means of enslaving the spirit of the dead or of acquiring his courage or other qualities. In the animals that belonged to the archipelagoes around, the pig and the dog, they were Polynesian with the best. Hotu Matua again introduced them; but the Polynesians who had remained on Easter Island had, probably through a long period of famine, acquired in an inordinate degree an improvidence that is not unknown in the rest of Polynesia. There was no future had any chance against the immediate appetite. So they ate up the Polynesian animals that the great pioneer had again introduced before they established themselves in the island. They did the same by the animals that La Perouse left them, the pig, the goat, and the sheep. They had no more regard for their future in the treatment of the fruit trees he planted, explaining what they were and how useful they would be. The seeds he gave them or sowed they ate up as they did all the cereals that later visitors gave them. The coco-nuts that Hotu Matua planted failed partly because of the climate, but perhaps more from gathering the fruit when young, their procedure with the few coco-nut trees that have been planted from Tahiti. And so it was with the bread-fruit that was brought from that island; and it may be the reason that the pandanus has never taken root or flourished on the island. Only what could persist of itself could withstand this colossal growth of improvidence. This was the case with the small native rat; it was exceptionally prolific; it could live anywhere as it was vegetarian; and it was difficult to catch till the cat came and the carnivorous rats from European ships and cleaned it out. It was the pioneer of all things Polynesian who introduced it, a purely Polynesian species, taken by all the migrations to their new colonies.

(9) **POLYNESIAN IN THEIR CLOTHING AND ORNAMENTATION.** The sources of their clothing and ornament had not to encounter this improvidence of appetite. But the fundamental bark-cloth plant of Polynesia had almost as great enemies to contend with; the porosity of the island disposing

of the often scanty showers the moment they fell left it almost leafless and wilted all summer and autumn ; and the strong winds of winter thrashed what remained of it to rags. Yet in spring it always revived and sent up vigorous shoots again. And the natives took especial care of it ; they built twelve-foot high walls of stone round any fertile patch that would be likely to retain moisture and planted their *m a h u t e* shrubs in the enclosure ; for they must have bark-cloth for their girdle and perineal band ; and they needed it to protect their skin from the scorching sun of summer and to warm them during the nights of winter, whilst the love of ornament which is a ruling passion amongst primitive peoples also came to its aid ; for it could be striped with colours and could go to the making of masks for the dances and *p a i n a* figures. And in this love of ornament they were not behind any Polynesian people ; they had the Polynesian tattooing and over it smeared various colours in the true Polynesian style. They bored the lobe of the ear like all Polynesians, though they did it more than most. They refrained from inserting ornaments in the septum of the nose or in the nostrils in the Melanesian style. Nor did they colour or bleach their hair with lime or fuzz it out into a busby or scrubbing brush ; it had not sufficient curl in it for that. They tied it up in true Polynesian style in a topknot. They cut it when it grew long to use it for girdles and necklaces as most of the Polynesians did. Their whole personal ornamentation was Polynesian, though scantiness of material set un-Polynesian limits to it. There is nothing foreign to Polynesia in either their clothing or ornament.

(10) **POLYNESIAN IN THE MATERIAL ARTS.** In all their other material things they were nothing if they were not Polynesian. It was only the poverty of their island that differentiated them. They had only one tree or bush to provide them with fibre, the *h a u h a u* (Triumfetta semitriloba) ; but they made their cords from it in the Polynesian way, by rolling it on the thigh. And when they came to make nets of it they used the same netting needle (*h i k a*), the same as has been used in Europe as far back as the Swiss lake-dwellings.[1] Like Polynesians they had no loom such as is used in parts of Melanesia, Micronesia, and Papuasia. They wove everything with the fingers ; and deft they were at it, as even Eyraud,

---

[1] See No. 2 in picture facing p. 188.

the severest critic, allows. They had only the rushes from the
r a n o s to work with; yet their straw hats and *k e t e s*
and mats and girdles show true Polynesian skill in braiding,
though they had none of the variety of geometrical patterns
that distinguishes the products of some of the areas. They
had but a limited supply of colour in their feathers, their
sources being only sea-birds and fowls; yet they managed
considerable variety in arranging them on their hats or diadems,
and in the royal ensigns. They had no land birds and could
never attain the variety and richness shown by the feather-
work of Tahiti and Hawaii. Nor had they any pottery, though,
like the volcanic islands of Polynesia, they had the clay to
make it, an absence that completely marks off Polynesia and
all eastern Micronesia from Melanesia and Papuasia. The
absence drove Polynesia into the use of the coco-nut shell and
the gourd and the making of wooden dishes. Easter Island
had not the coco-nut ; but it had both the large gourd and
the small, and used any sea-shells it could find large enough
for dishes. It had no forest trees and so differs from the larger
areas of Polynesia in having no wooden dishes. It was this
too that limited them in their making of houses and canoes.
The timbers of their houses look ridiculous alongside the
cyclopean stone-foundations, into the small holes in which
they were stuck ; but their general shape, like an upturned
canoe, their thatching and their low and narrow entrance at
once show them to be Polynesian. Their canoes could never
be more than small outriggers of short sewn planks ; but in
spite of this they are essentially Polynesian with the high beam
at bow and stern. Their weapons were, like most of the
Polynesian, chiefly of wood and stone, clubs and javelins,
though the abundance of their supply of obsidian differentiates
the stone points of their spears. Their implements were like
the Polynesian, of wood, and stone, and bone, their agricultural
tools being of wood, their cutting and beating tools, their
tokis and chisels and bark beaters being of stone, and their
minuter tools, like the tattooing needle and the sewing needle,
of bone, bird-bone, or fish-bone, only the point of the drill
being of shell. One of the striking differentiations from
Polynesia is in musical instruments ; they had practically
none, though they had plenty of bone to make flutes of and
plenty of gourds and shark-skin to make drums of ; they did
not even make them of wood like New Zealand, as they had

not timber large enough. And this absence of musical instruments (the only one mentioned is the conch shell for war
purposes), differentiates it still more from Melanesia, where a
primitive Jew's harp and simple panpipes are widespread.

(11) They had the same method of warfare and fondness
for it; they had no shield or bow as the peoples away west
had; they relied most on hand-to-hand combat, and only in
a subordinate way on the spear. Gonzalez in 1771 made a
bow and gave it to a native; but he hung it round his neck
as an ornament. Stones were their favourite projectile as so
often in Eastern Polynesia; nor did they advance to the use
of the sling as they did in Hawaii and Melanesia. In their
exercises as a preparation for war they followed Polynesia
in the game of throwing stones and that of parrying projectiles
thrown at them. Their games, too, were wholly Polynesian:
on land tobogganing and kite-flying, spinning the top and
cat's cradle, and on water diving and swimming, canoeing,
and surfing.

(12) **IN LESS MATERIAL THINGS POLYNESIAN WITH A
DIFFERENCE.** It is as we get into the inner or spiritual sphere
that we begin to see more differentiation than similarity;
but their differentiation brings Easter Island no nearer to
Melanesia. They expressed the joy of meeting again, as all
Polynesians do, by weeping; and till the missionaries bade
them give it up their usual method of welcome was the
Polynesian pressing of noses together. For marriage they
had no more ceremony or religious function than the rest of
the Polynesians; and like them they considered the cutting
of the navel-string and naming far more worthy of ceremony
than uniting a pair for life. And, as all over Polynesia,
separation was easy and licence the rule. At death the chief
function all over was ceremonial weeping and unceremonious
and excessive feasting. The dead were placed generally in
open places near the sea where the flesh could rot away; and
all who touched them were defiled and taboo. And when the
skeleton was fit for it they cleaned the bones and placed them
in their last receptacle, in most Polynesia some secret place,
a cave or the fork of a tree, but in Easter Island without any
secrecy in the burial-vault of an *a h u* .

(13) And here we approach to a wide difference between
Easter Island and the rest of Polynesia, as also all Melanesia.
After death there is no world of spirits. The ghost lingers

about the neighbourhood bent on mischief to the living, but
soon vanishes for ever. It is a striking difference, but is to
be expected in a people that retained none of the ancient
Polynesian mythology, and little or nothing of cosmology.
They have legends; but they are little else than tales of
sorcery and the narrow superstitious life that it demands.
It is quite true that the *iviatua* has a strong resemblance
to the Polynesian *tohunga;* they are both the consequence
of too monopolistic and overbearing an official priesthood
and too deep-seated a superstition in the popular mind. But
they differ in their methods; the *iviatua* not only con-
sults the supernatural to find the future like the Polynesian
tohunga; he gets it out of the sick man and burns it.
His confrère in other areas does not discourage the popular
belief that sickness is due to possession by a malignant spirit;
but he does not catch it and destroy it; he prefers to massage
it and beat it out; but he also professes to be able to put it
back again, and the soul it has gone off with. The Easter
Island sorcerer has done his work when he has netted it and
burned it; and unlike the sorcerer of the rest of Polynesia,
he may be a sorceress. The resemblance between the official
forms of religion is perhaps a little less pronounced; there
are no temples in Easter Island and no representatives of the
gods in wood or stone, unless we take the stone images on the
burial platforms and the little wooden images as standing
for the dead and the dead as divine. The *maoris* differ
greatly from the priests of the other Polynesian areas; they
are all in the service of the god of one clan, *Makemake,*
and they mark all the children and women and the men
chosen by chance with his signs and ceremonials; they are
also the official tattooers; they are the managers of all the
festivals and entertainments; they are the story-tellers and
conservators of the script and the old liturgy; they are the
teachers of the etching of the tablets and of singing and
dancing to the young. The existence of a priesthood with
such wide secular functions differentiates Easter Island from
Polynesia, but still more markedly from Melanesia, where there
is no priesthood of any kind.

(14) They were evidently the product of a deliberate desire
to keep the people busy with entertainment and feasting, to
keep them so full-fed and absorbed that there was not likely
to be rebellion or revolution. The institution has the marks

of artificiality upon it, the artificiality produced by one hand and that the hand of a king. And here there is no mistake about the kinship with the larger areas of Polynesia that admitted of unification of government. The monarch is divine and represents the gods, and in his hands is left all the arrangement of divine things. The feasts, the chief form of religion, are carefully manufactured by the king to cover most of the year; the great pioneer knew his people well and their limitless appetite. And yet there seemed to be the same round in Tahiti; Moerenhout says: " Life was one continuous feast." The founder of them must have had something to work upon. The *paina* coming in spring and summer, when food was plentiful, has a strong resemblance to one of those festivals in Tahiti and the Marquesas, which the *Areoi* came out of their retreat to celebrate, either the coming of the sun or his departure. The ceremonies of the fish-and-bird cult were manifestly at once seasonal and religious, and were connected with the taboo for the protection of the supply of deep-sea fish and sea-birds. The *paina* has got the same appearance of deliberate manufacture and yet must have been based on a seasonal ceremony in connection with food. And its wickerwork figure had its analogy in Tahiti; on the first voyage of Cook they saw in *Tiarapu* " one of their *eatuas*, or gods; it was made of wicker-work and resembled the figure of a man; it was nearly seven-foot high." It was probably used in one of those seasonal festivals. On Easter Island the whole of religion was within the scope of the king; but unfortunately nothing else was; and in this the kingship differs wholly from the Polynesian monarchy.

CHAPTER XXII

IMPERFECTLY POLYNESIAN

(1) *In religion and government they were fundamentally Polynesian as contrasted with Melanesian, which was kingless and priestless and almost sorcererless.* (2) *If immigrants from Rapa had settled Easter Island, they would have taken that Polynesian essential the candle-nut, that other Polynesian essential* poi, *and the habit of feeding the men with it because they were* moa *or sacred.* (3) *A contingent came from the Marquesas as is evident in the large hole in the lobe of the ear, in the combination of cyclopean platform and stone statue, and in the frequent omission of* r. (4) *But the clearest indications are for New Zealand as the source of Easter Island immigration, especially in the phonology and vocabulary.* (5) *So in tattooing the two agree to differ from the rest of Polynesia, especially in the development of the spiral and the curve and in the tattooing of the lips and forehead in women.* (6) *In foods they agree to differ from Polynesia, no kava, no poi, and great stress on the* kumara. (7) *What produced most of their differences was the lack of timber in Easter Island, yet their implements and ornaments, when of wood, were much alike ; even the marionettes exist in both almost alone of Polynesia, whilst in some of their customs they stand alone as in showing the buttocks in order to insult, in having no supercision, and in the use of human bone as fish-hook.* (8) *Easter Island disagrees with New Zealand, as with the rest of Polynesia, in having no world of spirits, but agrees with it in the magnificence of the sepulchres and in placing them by the sea.* (9) *Polynesian mythology vanishes or becomes ridiculous in Easter Island.* (10) *The great god Tangaroa is caricatured.* (11) *And the cosmology of Polynesia dwindles into triviality.*

(1) **THE RELIGION AND THE KINSHIP FUNDAMENTALLY POLYNESIAN.** It is easy to see that Easter Islanders and Easter Island culture were fundamentally Polynesian. Even the religion is so, although large elements of Polynesian religion have lapsed, as if by the same catastrophe that broke off the work of the sculptors and the building of the great burial platforms. It is exactly the same with the governmental machinery ; it is theocratic like that of the larger Polynesian areas ; but the absolute power of that exists here only in name and profession ; there is the divinity but not the authority ; out of the Polynesianism has filtered in passing into Easter Island its only practical element, its feudalistic organization. It retained only the shadow of it in the power to make taboos and rites and ceremonies. The king was little more than a high-priest endowed with absolute religious authority and no political or administrative or judiciary authority. But the essence of it was Polynesian. Even the peculiar provision for renewal of youth and vigour in the kingship, the resignation of the king when his eldest son had

married and established a household of his own, has its roots
in Polynesia. Cook noticed "in the Society Islands and
elsewhere the custom of the eldest son succeeding to his father
even at the moment of his birth, that is, as to titles, but not
as to real authority. The father was regent and had all power."
There was no police in Tahiti as in Easter Island but taboo,
and no justice but reprisal. However different the Miru
kingship may be in its being only ceremonial and religious
from the Polynesian feudalistic monarchy, it was evidently
from Polynesia it drew its main features, and not from
Melanesia, which had neither kingship nor priesthood, nay not
much of even the shadow and rival of the priest, the sorcerer.
It is difficult to see how so purely priest-bred a rite as that
of *Orongo* could have been influenced by a race that had
no priest, or how so priestly and liturgic a script as the
rongorongo could have elements in it drawn from a
culture that had never had temple or liturgy. That the
composite figure of *Makemake* as the patron and protector of the sea-birds and the fish was moulded in Motu
Matiro Hiva and came thence to Easter Island is clear from
the traditions.

(2) **WAS THERE A MIGRATION FROM RAPA?** If differences
from the common Polynesian culture are to prove anything
with regard to immigrant influences from other islands they
must be shown to exist in those islands. One of the islands
that is supposed by some to have sent a canoe with immigrants
to Easter Island is Rapa ; though some two thousand miles
to the west, it is by no means unlikely that such an expedition
might come east ; for, like the destination, the starting-place
is well outside the tropic and the zone of the regular trade
winds from the east, and in winter the westerlies, which are
generally far to the south, reach up occasionally into these
latitudes. And the Peruvian slave-raiders in the Pacific as
late as the Franco-Prussian war, after taking men from the
solitary islands as far north as Penrhyn, came south and took
men from both Rapa and Easter Island. Fortunately a
French cruiser came across the slaver and rescued the captives ;
it set down in Easter Island all that belonged to it and then
made for Rapa, where it left the natives of that island and
one man from Penrhyn, whom I saw surrounded by his fifty-one
children and grandchildren in 1917. It was probably from
this raid that the name R a p a n u i arose for Easter Island,

as the Rapa people who saw it would naturally call it big Rapa, both being high volcanic islands, though there is not much resemblance between the deep-valleyed character of the one and the valleyless character of the other. The upper valleys of Rapa are brightened by the silvery, almost white, foliage of the candle-nut tree (*aleurites triloba*), called in Tahiti *t i a i r i*, from the wood of which, soft though it is, the natives used to make their canoes. The island is farther south of the tropic than Easter Island, and if it flourishes in the one it should have flourished in the other; but it has never been grown in Easter Island, and the natives have had to pass their long nights without the light of that universal torch of Polynesia, the sliver of wood strung with its nuts. Its general Polynesian name, the kindler (*tutui*) and the voyagers' name for it, the candle-nut, show what an essential of Polynesian life it was. Had a contingent of emigrants gone to settle Easter Island, they would undoubtedly have taken the candle-nut tree, or seed of it, with them. So would they have taken their devotion to *p o i* (or rather *t i o o*, following the Tahitian) with them; it is one of the sights of Rapa of a morning to watch the women kneading their *taro* paste for hours on the flat stones of the streams. Nor would they have failed to implant in their new home the strange custom of holding the men sacred or taboo (*moa*) and so incapable of feeding themselves; the most singular sight of all is to see the men seated on the ground and the women popping pellets of *taro* paste into their mouths. Their taste for the flesh of babies would also have gone with them and left its traces on the customs of Easter Island. One feature of their culture might have gone with them and yet not have left its mark; they never tattooed and they might have encountered in their new home the admired ornamentation of the skin already deeply seated.

(3) **MARQUESAN INFLUENCE.** The highly developed tattooing of the whole body amongst the Easter Islanders points to the Marquesans as the source, the only Polynesians, except the people of one or two of the Paumotus, probably settled by Marquesans, that cover the body from brow to toe with tattooed figures; they follow the Marquesans in not merely having arabesques of geometrical designs, but human faces and busts and imitations of natural objects. But there is some other inspiration of the tattooing; for it is not in the

strong horizontal lines and zones of the Marquesan and indulges more freely in the spiral. That a contingent of Marquesans did settle on the island is apparent in the exceptionally elongated hole in the lobe of the ear common to the Easter Islanders and the Marquesans alone of Polynesians. And the use of stilts (*tekiteki*) in the religious festivals seems to point to the Marquesan ornamental and ceremonial stilts ; no other Polynesian people has recorded their use in ceremonials, though the Maoris of New Zealand used stilts in dance and play. The great-stone work might have had its inspiration from other Polynesian islands besides the Marquesas, though their combination of cyclopean-tooled blocks and carved-stone human figures stands alone in Polynesia with that of Easter Island. The human figures carved in stone still existent in Raivavai are not near any great stone *m a r a e s* , though there is a small stone-figure on one ; and those described by Moerenhout as guarding a peninsula on which *t a r o* was grown from the incursions of the sea are not mentioned as standing on any great stone platform. In Pitcairn Island the cyclopean *m a r a e* found on the island by the mutineers of the *Bounty* had four stone statues ; but as banians grew near and the banian is generally found shading the great stone temples of the Marquesas, it is likely that the immigrants who built and then deserted that were Marquesans, perhaps the very Longears who went in the canoes of Hotu Matua to Easter Island. And they may have taken to Easter Island the sacred club that must have been originally a double-bladed paddle ; in Marquesan this is *p a r a h u a ;* in Easter Island it is *a o ;* though *p a r a* is used for a short club. In the language there is some evidence of a Marquesan element amongst the natives ; there are some Polynesian words like *k i o r e* (rat) that omit the *r ;* it is in the dialect *k i o e ;* and Marquesan is the only Polynesian language that as a rule omits the *r.*

(4) **THE MAORI LANGUAGE AND THE EASTER ISLAND LANGUAGE.** But the case is much stronger for immigrations from New Zealand if we take language as the test. One singular feature of the phonology of the dialect of Easter Island as pronounced is that it is often impossible to tell whether *r* or *l* is meant ; of course, all Polynesian *r*'s have a little liquidity and all *l*'s a slight trill. But here one hears a native use a clear *l* and on asking him to pronounce again he makes

A MARQUESAN MEGALITHIC ALTAR BUILT OF ALTER-
NATE RUDE STONE STATUES AND HUGE TOOLED
STONES; IT WAS BURIED WITH ITS SURROUNDING
GREAT STONE AVENUES BY THE ROOTAGE OF AN
ANCIENT BANIAN (THE SACRED TREE OF THE MAR-
QUESAS), TILL EARLY IN 1917 WHEN IT WAS DIS-
COVERED AND UNCOVERED. IT IS 2000 FEET ABOVE
THE SEA ON A PLATEAU WITH STEEP APPROACHES.
MY GUIDE, AN INTERESTING MARQUESAN YOUTH,
SITS ON THE LOWER STEP OF THE ALTAR. IT IS IN
THE ISLAND OF HIYAOA

SPIRAL TATTOOED ON ROCK NEAR KAWHIA, IN NORTH-WEST OF NEW ZEALAND

it *r.* The real fact is that both *r* and *l* are used as in the south island of New Zealand, where one finds amongst names of places *Akaroa* and *Waihola.* The same confusion is evident in the use of both *k* and *ng* in words that have the same sense. There is a combination of this in the name of the great *ahu* on the south coast, *A k a h a n g a ;* the bay must have been called *A k a* as in New Zealand *Akaroa* (Long Bay the same as *Hangaroa* in Easter Island) ; there followed as occupants of it people who use *hanga* as the form for " *bay* " and, not understanding " *aka,*" they added " *hanga* " to " *Aka* " and produced a word meaning literally " *Baybay.*" Easter Island language and Maori are two of the four Polynesian tongues that use an initial *ng.* An instance common to both is the word *n g a r a h u ,* which means tattooing powder in both, whilst the corresponding form in the Polynesian dialects (with *k* or *n* instead of *ng*) means soot or charcoal. But there are many words in the two that vary the form or the meaning slightly, as for example : Easter Island *riha,* a louse, Maori *riha,* a nit ; Easter Island *tahonga,* a talisman, Maori *taonga,* a treasure ; Easter Island *ngaatu,* a bulrush, Maori *ngatu,* the last joint of *raupo* (a bulrush) ; Easter Island *panepane,* sharp, Maori *aneane,* sharp. But such words are very numerous in the two languages, without corresponding forms and meanings in other Polynesian dialects.

(5) **MAORI INFLUENCE ON EASTER ISLAND TATTOOING.** It is not merely in phonology and vocabulary that the two agree to differ from the rest of Polynesia. In the arts they have occasionally the same agreement in difference. Their tattooing, though by no means fundamentally similar, has many similarities. As Beechey points out, in Easter Island it follows the musculature as in New Zealand, whilst in other Polynesian areas it has little regard for the trend of the muscles ; in the Marquesas, for example, it is arranged in horizontal zones that cross the face and the body. Compared with the Marquesan, that of Easter Island has refinement of lines ; of course, that of New Zealand surpasses the other in this respect, especially in the use of the spiral ; in Easter Island a spiral was tattooed on each side of the men's bodies, on the lower ribs. The use of the spiral in decoration and carving is a speciality of these two Polynesian areas ; it is again the Maori that has developed it most and in a surpassingly beautiful way in the stern-piece of the canoes ; but

near Kawhia Harbour on the north-west coast of the north island there are rocks, tattooed with spirals, as on the southeast point of Easter Island, beyond Poike, there are rocks spirally tattooed. The same love of the curve in both tattooing and carving is apparent in both areas as in contrast to the other parts of Polynesia. Then the elaborate tattooing of the face belongs to both, although it also belongs to the Marquesas and parts of the Paumotus.[1] But the elaborate tattooing of the women on the lips and the forehead is peculiar to the two, the Marquesan women having only slender lines across the lips, although Easter Island had much more tattooing on the faces of the women than New Zealand. On the cheeks there was set indelibly by the *maori* after he had found the *poki manu*, a virgin, the mark of virginity, the *puhi*. Yet here again there is affinity; for the natives of New Zealand called the daughter of the chief who was reserved as virgin, *puhi*. The only other area of Polynesia that laid stress on the purity of the chief's daughter, or seemed to have any relic of a primeval respect for chastity, was Samoa.

(6) **IN TABOOS, EATING AND DRINKING, THEY DIFFER TOGETHER FROM POLYNESIA.** Like all the rest of Polynesia these two areas marked the entrance on married life by no special ceremonial, either religious or secular. But in these two alone existed a relic of ancient exogamic capture that almost amounted to a matrimonial rite; the bridegroom had, if only in pretence, to capture the bride, who, in her turn, ran away from him. In both areas the bride's parents often stipulated that the man should live in their tribe, though, following the patrilineal system of Polynesia, the children had to belong to the father's clan and creed; but as in most other areas the status of the man was much influenced by that of his mother—a relic of an older system, the matrilineal. In both the women had attained an exceptional position in the social system, perhaps based on a survival of the matrilineal. In Easter Island they had got rid of the taboo against their eating along with the men. In Tahiti none but the women of the foremost grade of the Areois had gained the same freedom. And, as in New Zealand, they had a great part to play in all the feasts and dances along with the men. This was probably due to their taking a large part in the armed conflicts alongside of their husbands. And in war neither

---

[1] See figure of tattooed Easter Island woman, facing p. 172.

people had the shark-skin-headed drum of the rest of Polynesia, though they had plenty of gourds and caught plenty of sharks. And had Easter Island had such forests or forest trees as New Zealand had, it would doubtless have had also the Maori war-gong of timber. As it was it was driven to make a miserable attempt at a resonant instrument by means of a gourd with a stone above it, on which the men danced. One thing they both lacked which the rest of Polynesia had for influencing the nerves and emotions. Neither of them ever made k a v a , that poverty-stricken substitute for an intoxicant like the toddy farther west drawn from the flower-stem of the coco-palm ; the people of the two could have grown the *piper methysticum* in their latitudes, and they had splendid teeth and doubtless plenty of salivary ferment to turn the root of it into the soap-tasted liquor that dulls and stupifies the senses and attacks the locomotor centres. It was not in accordance with Polynesian nature to abandon the making of it after it had experienced its narcotic effects. The Maoris made an intoxicating drink from the flesh of the berries of the t u t u plant, which grew everywhere in New Zealand ; and they had the word t e w e for its intoxication. The Easter Islanders had no word for " drunk " till they got " taero " from Tahiti ; nor had they any intoxicating drink, though they might have made it out of the *ti* root, or even out of their sweet potatoes. They were satisfied with great feasts of that filling and sustaining tuber. Appetite dominated their system and not the love of drink, though they had to indulge in the brackish water that flowed from the springs on their coasts. This was perhaps the reason that, like the natives of New Zealand, they made no salt and did not use salt water as a sauce. And another agreement with the Maoris as in contrast to the rest of Polynesia was the stress they laid on the k u m a r a ; of the three great Polynesian tubers, that was their preference and their standby. And they cultivated it in the same way by planting it in hillocks of stones. Nor did either of these peoples ever lay the stress on the fermented paste of the tubers and other vegetable products that the other Polynesians did. That the traditions of Easter Island make no mention of p o i or p o i -making is probably due to the fact that they had no great ocean-going canoes after *Hotu Matua* and *Tuukoihu ;* they made no long voyages and did not need foods so manipulated that they would last months, if not years. The Maoris continued to build and use large canoes for deep-sea voyaging; but in the later ages they ceased far-travel; and hence perhaps the small stress they laid on *p o i*. But the other Polynesians also abandoned distant voyages after the great migrations and yet paid great attention to the making of foods preserved by fermentation. This was to provide for the seasons when the breadfruit and the tubers and bananas were scarce. It was the extraordinary improvidence of the Easter Islanders that was doubtless the main cause of their failure to preserve foods against the winter season and their not infrequent periods of famine; but it is to be said that the sweet potato is less adapted for *p o i* than *t a r o* or breadfruit or bananas; and that it can be kept through the winter season. But the greatest foe to the preservation of foods and friend to starvation was the gorging at their feasts.

(7) **RESEMBLANCES BETWEEN THE CULTURES OF EASTER ISLAND AND NEW ZEALAND.** What differentiated the two peoples more than anything else was the splendid forests of New Zealand and the absence of all forest trees on Easter Island. They had in common the *sophora tetraptera*, the yellow-flowering *kowhai* of New Zealand, the *miro* of Easter Island. *Miro* stands for timber and for most things of timber in the latter. But it was not a forest tree and could never grow to any girth. It was from this, however, that most of their implements and weapons and decorations were made. As in New Zealand, their chief weapons were spears and clubs of various forms. Cook and other visitors call attention to the identity of the Easter Island short club of wood with the New Zealand *mere* or *patupatu;* though the latter was as frequently made of bone as of wood and, if a symbol of chiefship, of greenstone. The wealth of timber caused wooden weapons and ornaments to be less valued than in Easter Island, which made its talismans and its treasures of wood, like the *reimiro*, the *tahonga*, the dancing clubs, the *ao*, the *rapa*, the *ua*, and the little images. It is in these last, the *moai miro*, we find another affinity to New Zealand culture, though other Polynesian areas had images of wood. These *moai* stood for the dead like the four-fingered wooden statues of the Maori carved house; the prominent ribs, like the four fingers conventionalized from the claws of a bird, indicated that the beings they represented were beyond life. But even

PART OF THE WALLS OF VINAPU PLATFORM, SHOWING THE CAREFUL
TOOLING OF THE GREAT STONES

A SECTION OF VINAPU, SHOWING HOW THE STONES WERE TOOLED TO
PLAN BEFORE BEING SET

the *moai miro,* used as marionettes, had their affinity amongst
one of the light-skinned races of New Zealand, the *Patupaiarehe,*
who taught their use to the Maoris. The lizard-headed club
of Easter Island, though it has no equivalent in the other area,
indicates the same fear of lizards, and especially composite
lizards, as is shown in the *m a n a i a* of New Zealand. They
had in them the supernatural power, the *a k u a k u*, that
in the *m a n u u r u* protected the porch of the house from
trespassers and people of evil intent.[1] But some of the closest
affinities of Easter Island with New Zealand appear with
Hotu Matua ; his canoes, double according to one account,
single according to tradition, had the high stern and bow-
piece of the Maori war canoes. It is the earthwork fortification
on the top of Maunga Hau Epe by Anakena Bay that shows
most clearly the warlike genius of the Maori and of no other
Polynesian peoples. And, if odd customs or absences are to
be taken as indications of racial affinities, the following belong
to the Maoris and the Easter Islanders alone amongst the
Polynesians ; one of the greatest insults was, as amongst the
Ainu of Japan, to show the buttocks (*hakahiti ki te eeve* as it
was put in Easter Island dialect) ; the universal Polynesian
practice of, not circumcision, but supercision was not used
by either people, and, if anyone was born with the prepuce
split, they laughed at him and mocked him ; and the net was
used in warfare by both. It was more than likely that the
substitution of the human-bone hook for the old stone hook
was brought about by the influence of the Maoris who had,
like several other Polynesian peoples, a horror of their bones
being turned into hooks ; the Easter Islanders had no such
horror, and yet used the bones of their ancestors and relatives
to make hooks of. The Maoris hid away in caves and other
secret places the bones of their dead after the *hahunga,* or
exhumation. The Easter Islanders wrapped the corpse in a
mat (*moenga*) like the Maoris and, when the flesh had rotted
away, placed the bones in a vault with no attempt at secrecy.

(8) **MORTUARY CUSTOMS IN POLYNESIA AND EASTER
ISLAND.** The difference may be due to the complete absence
in Easter Island of belief in a world of spirits ; after a man
dies his *a k u a k u* may linger a brief time about his house
and neighbourhood, but it soon vanishes into nothingness.
But if there is one thing spiritual on which all other Polynesians

---

[1] See pictures facing pages 134, 136.

agree it is that, whatever becomes of the spirit of the common man, the spirit of the chief did not die out, but went to some shadowy land where life proceeded as before, with a tendency to more and greater pleasures ; there were always leaping-off places, often in the west, almost as often in the north-west, sometimes in the north, of the island or group, whence the spirit found its way to the land of spirits. Anderson in the report of Cook's Third Voyage says, "They believe the soul to be both immaterial and immortal." All that a ghost of Easter Island had to do after death was to cause sickness in the living ; and in this there is a parallel to be found in the Tahitian belief that most diseases were caused by the spirits of the dead (*oromatuas*). That the spirit takes its departure by the sea is perhaps the reason why most of the temples, which are generally also places of sepulture, are placed near the sea. This was the case in Tahiti ; and in Hawaii, the whole of the north-west coast seems one long line of *heiaus*, or temples. This cannot be the reason why the line of burial platforms in Easter Island is almost continuous round the coast ; for there was no spirit to take flight over the sea and no world of spirits for it to flee to, unless as in so many other things there is a sudden break here, and the archipelagoes believed in a life beyond death. The likeness lies in the magnificence and number of the places of sepulture. Cook on his First Voyage says of Tahiti : "The inhabitants seem in nothing so desirous of excelling each other as in the grandeur and magnificence of their sepulchres." The people who built and were buried in the *ahus* of Easter Island were by no means exceptional amongst the Polynesians for their love of imposing places of sepulture or for placing them by the sea. Where they do differ is in not making them at once temple and sepulchre. And another difference is that they never plant a tree to shade them ; the Marquesas planted the banian, and the Tahitian the casuarina or ironwood (*aito*) ; the Easter Islander had no tree large enough to give shade. He counted a tree that is now extinct, the *naunau*, sacred ; it is commonly called the sandalwood ; but it is more probably the bastard sandalwood, which has the same fragrance when cut and was often exported to China when the true sandalwood was exhausted. For it is a tree of both New Zealand and Hawaii, in both areas called *ngaio*, the possible source of the Easter Island name *naunau*;

ANCIENT GREAT-STONE WORK IN CALLE DE LA PIEDRA GRANDE, CUZCO, PERU

ANCIENT PERUVIAN CYCLOPEAN STONEWORK

and its companion on the island, the *miro*, also belongs
to New Zealand. There are two death customs in the absence
of which Easter Island improves on Polynesia, the strangling
of wives on the death of their husbands, or of slaves on the
death of a king, and the mutilation of parts of the body in
sign of mourning.

(9) **THE SUBLIME OF POLYNESIA REDUCED TO THE
RIDICULOUS IN EASTER ISLAND.** But, once they had to deal
with what comes after death, the Easter Islanders fall far
below the other Polynesians in moulding a spiritual world or
in evolving a mythology. There is nothing but dull blankness
or triviality. All the great names of Polynesian myth have
been forgotten or sunk into commonplace. Rangi, Papa,
Rongo, Maui have dropped into oblivion. Whiro is a name
of might in Eastern Polynesia, a doer of great deeds and a
conqueror of monsters. In Tahitian myth he is of prodigious
stature and goes down into the depths of the ocean with his
dogs to fight giants and " dragons of the prime." He delivers
a virgin from the power of an enchanter guarded by giant
warriors as Perseus rescued Andromeda. And if his enemies
raised storms his appearance on the surface of the ocean was
enough to calm them. He was evidently, like Maui, in his
origin a sun-god. In Easter Island *Hiro* is a rain-god to whom
the *a r i k i* pray during a drought ; and his heroic adventures
in going into the depths monster-hunting have tapered down
into a king of Easter Island diving to the cave of a colossal
crayfish and by means of a net and rope dragging it up to its
death.

(10) And if there is one name in Polynesian mythology that
surpasses all others, it is that of Tangaroa ; he is the great
primeval god who comes before all creation, and he is the god
of oceanic migrations who leads the blond-haired race into
the Pacific. In Easter Island legend he has become a king
who can do some of the deeds of a sorcerer. He lived in a
far-off island ; yet heard of the degeneracy of Te Pito te Henua
and resolved to go there and bring it back to the old ways.
After a prodigious swim he landed by Tongariki, and the
people who gathered to see him as he landed refused to believe
his story that he was a king and declared he was a seal
(*p a k i a*) to have swum so far. They stoned him and then
put him in an oven to cook ; but he came out uncooked and
vital. Their neighbours to whom they offered so strange a

monster cooked him still longer with the same result. And so he was handed round the coast till one clan declared he stank and threw him into the sea. The only sequel is that a giant called Teteko comes with seven-league strides across the sea in search of his brother and is last seen wading off to Motu Matiro Hiva. In the list of kings there is one that has Tangaroa as part of his name. And on the south coast there are two *a h u s* which are called *Tangaroa* and *Hiro*.

(11) It is the same with their cosmology. The contrast with the Polynesian is striking. If we take for example the genealogy of the primeval forces and stages given in the appendix to White's "Ancient History of the Maori" we are struck with the capacity of the Polynesian mind to deal with abstract conceptions. It by no means suffers when compared with the great cosmologies of Asia and Europe. It is the same if we take the first volume of Fornander's "Polynesian Race." Vague as are the abstractions with which any one of those cosmologies begins, they soon gather into personalities, the gods and demi-gods who work out the creation of the world and of man and pioneer the migrations of men throughout the Pacific. Great figures loom out of the mist of abstractions like spectres of the Brocken. And the nearest we come to this on Easter Island is in the god of the Tupahotu, Raraiahopa, probably an incarnation of *Ra*, the sun. He makes the heavens and the stars, and at last the sea and man. *Makemake*, the god of the Miru and ultimately the supreme god of Easter Island, is composite of bird and beast and fish ; and his work in the creation of man is as trivial as his taboos and ceremonials. The descent to this from the sublime but amorphous conceptions of the Polynesian cosmology is tremendous and can only be explained by a sudden rupture of Polynesianism on Easter Island. It certainly makes the burial platforms with their cyclopean masonry and titanic statues seem absolutely inexplicable.

CHAPTER XXIII

THE AMERICAN COAST

(1) *The tooling and fitting of cyclopean blocks are exactly the same in Cuzco and in Easter Island ; both demanded the same skill and the same organization of vast armies of labour.* (2) *On Easter Island there was plenty of stone, but nothing else to make the megalithic art possible ; in the Andes all conditions existed.* (3) *The coastal empires of Peru were more like Easter Island in having little or no timber, and their great mortuary monuments had to be sun-dried brick.* (4) *Tiahuanaco on the south of Lake Titicaca had plenty of stone and plenty of muscle to haul it ; and the result is a gradual improvement of cyclopean-stone cutting and building till the stage was reached at which one huge block was cut to fit exactly into another.* (5) *The Incas took up megalithism at this stage and with their great resources and enslaved peoples they would have covered all the Pacific region of South America with cyclopean masonry, but for the entry of Pizarro.* (6) *There is no trace in the Polynesian physique or foods or arts of immigration from the American coast.* (7) *Banana, coco-nut, and most surely sweet potato, give ground for conjecturing Polynesian immigration into South America.* (8) *Of arts, the tiputa, or cape, with a headhole in it, may have gone to lead to the poncho ; and the method of making kava may have led to chicha ; but if the quipu, or mnemonic knotted cord, went into the empire of the Incas, it did not go from Easter Island, which never had it.* (9) *The Polynesian earth-oven went into the south of Chili, and so did the Polynesian stone adze with its name "toki."* (10) *In the ruins of Grand Chimu, north of Truxillo, double-walled barracks, with a waterway dug from its screened gateway down to the sea indicate oceanic conquerors and rulers and a potteryless cemetery outside the walls indicates these as Polynesians, and in Lambayeque farther north, there is a tradition of oceanic rulers that used greenstone and the umu.* (11) *Easter Island was not the teacher of the great-stone art to the Andes, not merely because of the difficulty of getting to the coast, but because any migration from it must have taken the script to a scriptless people, and had not the quipu to take.* (12) *There were great and constant migrations in and from Polynesia up till the fifteenth century ; and the pyramid is the favourite mortuary or sacred monument in Polynesia and in the Pacific region of South America.* (13) *and* (14) *The busts of Tiahuanaco and of the valley of Huaraz point to Polynesia as their inspiration, and the combination of these and cyclopean monuments point to the Marquesas. The lack of American maize and tobacco, pottery and gold and silver work, and the absence of Mongoloid traits in the Polynesian physique and face, make it impossible that the influence came the other way.*

(1) **THE MAKING OF CYCLOPEAN WALLS.** Since ever the great-stone work of Easter Island and that of Peru have begun to be compared there has been a tendency on the part of those who know both to find a connection between them. The cyclopean work of some of the burial platforms is exactly the same as that of Cuzco and of the adjacent regions on the Andes. The colossal blocks are tooled and cut so as to fit each other. In the A h u V i n a p u and in the fragment of the *a h u* near H a n g a r o a beach the stones are as colossal as in the old Temple of the Sun in Cuzco, they are as carefully tooled, and the irregularities of their sides that have to come together are so cut that the two faces exactly fit into each other. These blocks are too huge to have been shifted frequently to let the mason find out whether they

fitted or not. They must have been cut and tooled to exact measurement or plan. There is no evidence of chipping after they have been laid. Every angle and projection must have been measured with scientific precision before the stones were nearing their finish. The modern mason knows he can fill up irregularities with lime or cement. In these cyclopean walls the only cement is gravitation, and that can be used only once. With nothing but stone tools, and these generally clumsy and rough, the result is marvellous. Of course there must have been unlimited labour completely organized to haul, raise, and place the blocks. Wherever there are mega-lithic monuments there was absolute power controlling tens of thousands of toilers who were practically slaves. But in cyclopean tooled work there is more ; there must be skill in planning what is to issue from a rough block, there must be breadth of architectural thought to mark out the place that each stone when shaped and finished has to take, and there must be also large drafts of that subordinate skill which knows how, with the tools to hand, the shapes in the architect's mind and plans can be cut out of the roughly hewn blocks from the quarry, or the fractured rocks that lie about. There are implied in all these carefully tooled and fitted cyclopean walls limitless power and resources, the capacity for organizing great masses of men, keen architectural capacity and large armies of skilled labour.

(2) **EASTER ISLAND AND THE AMERICAN COAST.** There is no possibility of these conditions having existed on Easter Island, it is so small and so unsuited to any kind of cultivation, either extensive or intensive. It has unlimited stone for cyclopean work, but that is all that it has ever had of the essentials of great-stone erections. It has never had a forest tree upon it till this past half century, and those that now grow on it are shorn low by the winter winds. It is inexplicable how the beams could have been got on it for the levering of the great stone or for making sleds large enough to keep the gigantic statues intact in transit ; it is as inexplicable how the fibre could have been grown to make the huge hawsers for harnessing the muscles of thousands of slaves to the task of hauling these up hill and down dale for miles, when the *hauhau* and the *mahute* have to be nursed with care inside a circle of high stone walls that will temper the winds to the thrashed and shorn foliage. There was difficulty in

PACHACAMAC, ONE OF THE ANCIENT ADOBE CITIES IN RUINS ON THE PERUVIAN COAST. TWENTY-
FIVE MILES SOUTH-WEST OF LIMA, OVER THE DESERT

ANCIENT CULTIVATION TERRACES HIGH UP
THE ANDES IN THE VALLEY OF CUZCO

ONE SMALL SECTION OF WHAT REMAINS OF THE
EXTENSIVE RUINS OF THE ANCIENT MEGALITHIC
CITY OF TIAHUANACO, ON THE SOUTH END OF
LAKE TITICACA IN THE ANDES

getting enough cordage for nets and lines, so harassed was their only fibre plant, the *hauhau*, by the conditions of its growth.

(3) The Pacific coast of South America, on the contrary, has all the conditions that would make for an extensive use of the megalithic art. On the low coast there is little or no stone; and all the ancient cities and all the mortuary monuments are built of sun-dried bricks. Not that the empires, which rose on the art of irrigation from the inner or eastern cordillera, were not capable of kiln-burnt bricks, but that they had no wood to spare for firing; there were, as in Easter Island, no forests, probably no forest trees. And any shrubs that grew were needed for the beautifully decorated earthenware that is now found in every grave; a fine piece of pottery as well as implements of their trade or profession was needed for the passage of the dead to the other world. The sun was their chief ally in making material for their walls and great pyramids· And in their rainless climate he was always ready for business.

(4) **TIAHUANACO.** It was up on the slopes and heights whence they drew their water that unlimited stone for building permanently was to be found. Down on the coast there was never any rain to destroy their erections; but the sun dried them too much and the winds cut into them; and, in spite of the fragments of pottery that were mixed with their a d o b e s to bind them, the walls failed to keep their sharpness of outline and tended to moulder and decay. The impermanence of their cities and great mausoleums bred in them a longing for a material that would make their works outlast the ages. They climbed up into the Andes and began crudely at first on the south end of Lake Titicaca the moving of great stones to form walls and mounds; the great megalithic city of Tiahuanaco was started with all the old advantages of their coastal cities and none of their disadvantages; it fronted on a great inland sea and the citizens might develop traffic on their *balsas*, or buoyant rafts, without the perils of the often tempestuous ocean. They built this city jutting into the lake; though the ruins are now eighteen miles from it and eighty feet above its level. As it grew in wealth and power it could employ tens of thousands of workmen to cut and tool and haul their great blocks. The ruin reveals several stages in the development of its cyclopean architecture from the rude blocks with the hollow in it for an altar of sacrifice

to the great monolithic gateway covered with carvings, series of crowned kings and crowned condors. There was still the disadvantage of absence of forests; they had no timber to use with lavishness; but they could fire their pottery, so essential for the graves, with dried *llama's dung* or *llarete* or *tola*, and they could make their *balsas* of the reeds and rushes that grew so plentifully round the lake. There was no lack of rain or water for their a n d e n e s , or cultivation-terraces, which they built as high as seventeen thousand feet up the slopes of the mountains; and, if needed, irrigation was easy with tens of thousands of slaves to make the channels. And as they extended their horizon to the east down the *montaña* zone they could have tropical products in plenty and great timbers when they required them. They reached a stage in cyclopean wall-building that cut each block to fit its neighbour just at the time that the recession of the lake left their city high and dry, stranded and far from the means of lake-traffic that had made its greatness. The coastal cities had kept up their kinship with it, and as it grew in power looked up to it as patron and protector; and now that its greatness was fading they made it still the goal of their pilgrimages, and they placed its carved monolithic arch and its carvings as sacred symbols, conventionalized and moulded, on their mortuary vases.

(5) **THE CYCLOPEAN WORK OF THE INCAS.** On the decayed grandeur of this most ancient empire rose another tribe on the western shores of the lake; the ruin had become but a memory when the Incas took up the imperial banner and pushed their way up from the lake to Cuzco, "the navel of the earth." Thence marching north and south and then to the coast of the Pacific they moulded an empire ten times as great as the old Tiahuanaco empire. They took up the cyclopean masonry at the climax their predecessor had reached and began to build their palaces and temples on the same magnificent lines. Before them powerful monarchies had built part of the S a c s a h u a m a n , the great fortress that dominates Cuzco; but their walls consisted of immense blocks merely selected and slightly chipped to fit. The Incas started on the lines of the last stage of T i a h u a n a c o masonry and built that marvellous continuation of the cyclopean fort, the wall that faces the R o d a d e r o ; into it are set tooled blocks, some of which must be hundreds of tons

THE CYCLOPEAN FORTRESS OF THE SACSAHUAMAN ON THE HILL ABOVE CUZCO

THE TEMPLE OF VIRACOCHA, DOWN THE VALLEY OF CUZCO; GREAT-STONE WORK
BELOW, ADOBE WORK ABOVE

in weight, cut and dragged up the valley from quarries more than a score of miles distant. A monarchy down the valley, half-way to the lake, was also conquered, that had evidently drawn its ideas from the *a d o b e* cities of the coast; there still stand the lofty walls of what is called the Temple of *Viracocha* to show that T i a h u a n a c o was not the only model and inspiration for the masonry of the valley; the walls are composite, below stone, above sun-dried bricks, not unlike some of the walls of P a c h a c a m a c, the ruin to the south-west of *Lima*. The Incas, as usual, appropriated what was done and made it their own, though they did not continue to imitate this coastal method of building, except on the coast, where they had not the material that was available on the Andes; they built their Temple of the Sun at Pachacamac of *adobes*, but with niches and buttresses such as they sometimes used in their cyclopean work on the lake and in the mountains. Here was an empire exactly fitted for megalithic creations on a great scale, having its subjects in the hollow of one hand, with the command of almost limitless resources, and almost limitless supplies of labour; and there was ready to hand all the artistic inspiration as well as the artists that the little empires, which it had conquered, had developed. Much was done, especially in and around *Cuzco*, and much was evidently planned for the heights beyond and in the new provinces added to the empire. Peru would have been in a few centuries covered with cyclopean masonry. But there came division and civil war; and in the midst of it the white strangers arrived with their horses and their far-killing engines of warfare. Had Pizarro and his few hundred Spaniards not broken the line of development we should have had on the Pacific coast such a display of great-stone monuments as no region of the world can show. As it is those that exist there are as impressive as any from the megalithic era, before the age of iron tools and lime.

(6) **WHY THE CYCLOPEAN ART DID NOT COME FROM AMERICA.** How far can these two areas of cyclopean stone-work have been related to each other? They were evidently not far off from contemporary in at least their later stages. What was the relationship of Te Pito te Henua, " the navel of the earth," to *Cuzco*, " the navel of the world "? We may dismiss at once the idea that the American coast peopled or even influenced Polynesia, a position that has been argued

s

by many writers who have been puzzled by the accepted theory that Polynesia was peopled by migrations against the trade winds. There is no trace of the Mongoloid eye or hair or cheek-bones in any of the natives of the central or eastern Pacific. Nor would any influences from the American coast have failed to bring its products and its arts ; we should have had maize and potatoes and tobacco in Polynesia long before they took command of it. It would have learned the art of pottery ; yet no scrap of earthenware has ever been found in it. It would have some trace of the delicate gold and silver work that distinguished some of the ancient coastal cities. It would have got the loom of Peru and so expanded or extended its own hand-textile work. Without any sign of these products and arts we may accept it as an axiom that it was not Peru that taught the builders and sculptors of Easter Island their art.

(7) **POLYNESIAN PLANTS IN SOUTH AMERICA.** Is there any sign of the influence having gone the other way ? It is not conspicuous ; but there are indications that seem to point in that direction. To take the products first : the banana is generally acknowledged to be a native of south-eastern Asia ; and it got into Polynesia at a very early stage of its history, if it was not also a native of the hypothetical Pacific continent ; the plantain at least was a native of the mountainous parts of Tahiti and it is a congener of the banana, though it grows its fingers erect instead of pendulous. The great number of varieties of banana grown by the Polynesian argues considerable age in its cultivation. On the Peruvian coast, though it is little suited from its shelterlessness and rainlessness to the growth of the banana, plantain leaves have been found in the ancient graves, according to Stevenson's "Twenty Years in South America" (Vol. I, page 414). And the banana can be propagated only by suckers, so that we must assume that it went on to the coast with human migrations. The coco-nut is a somewhat doubtful case. Mr. O. F. Cook, of the Agricultural Department, Washington, has argued in his two monographs on the subject that it is a native of America ; all its congeners are indigenous to America, whilst it has none in the south-east of Asia ; he quotes from various ancient writers, like Cieza de Leon, instances of what seems to have been its growth in the high Andes of Colombia. But it was in the South Seas that it was developed into being

RUINS OF THE INCAS' TEMPLE AT PACHACAMAC. IT IS OF SUN-DRIED BRICKS

THE *tiputa*, OR *poncho*, AS WORN IN THE CAROLINE
ISLANDS, MICRONESIA. THE PEOPLE IN THE ILLUS-
TRATION ARE NATIVES OF THE RUK ARCHIPELAGO.
*The Indian poncho is seen in the picture of the
Tiahuanaco bust worn by an Indian, facing p. 270.*

the universal provider of the Pacific Ocean; it was in the
South Seas that it evolved the large number of varieties the
species has. It would be by no means difficult of propagation;
for its nut floats for months on the waves and yet retains its
germinative power; I have seen it with a vigorous young
palm protruding from it afloat a hundred miles from any land.
It is by no means likely that Easter Island, which has grown
it so spasmodically, gave it to America. Perhaps some fragment of the foundering Pacific continent adjoining the broad
oceanic strait that always separated America from any Pacific
land may have set adrift coco-nuts that struck the rising
American coast. It was doubtless an ancient accident that
carried the coco-nut eastwards or westwards, and Polynesia
was the immediate transmitter. It is the edible tubers, or
rather, one, the sweet potato, that gives the most secure basis
for assuming Polynesian influence on the Pacific coast of
South America. It is the tuber of the Polynesian areas that
have not tropical rainfall; it is the chief vegetable food of
Easter Island, probably that of the archipelagoes around, as
it always was of the Maoris of New Zealand. It was all over
the north of South America when the Spanish mastered it;
and its name in parts of Colombia was *u m a l a*. South-
eastern Polynesia cultivated it more than any of the other
Polynesian tubers and was the most likely area to have
transmitted it to America.

(8) **POLYNESIAN ARTS AND METHODS THAT REACHED
AMERICA.** Of manufactured articles it is not likely that so
primitive a people as the Polynesians contributed much to
peoples that could so excel in textiles and pottery and gold
and silver work. And yet the *t i p u t a*, or mantle with a
hole in it for the head, which belongs to Tahiti and goes as
far west as the Caroline Islands, is practically the same as
the *poncho* of South America. It is not likely that it could
have come off to the Pacific islands without bringing with it
maize and pottery. It may have arisen in both areas independently; but if it spread from one to the other, it must have
come from Polynesia. Then there is the salivary ferment
common to the two. In South America, especially on its
Pacific coast, *c h i c h a* is still made by chewing maize and
spitting it into a dish and afterwards mixing it with water;
in olden times it was *c h e n o p o d i u m*, or pigweed, that was
chewed to make this intoxicating drink. The method is

exactly the same as that used in making Polynesian *k a v a*.
And the only other fermented drink in the Pacific produced
by chewing is the *b o a r* in Formosa, a product of rice, and
therefore much more recent than *k a v a*. Burney, in the
third volume of his " History of the Voyages and Discoveries
in the South Sea or Pacific Ocean " (pages 137–139), quotes
a passage from Hendrick Brouwer's " Voyage to Chili in 1643,"
and argues that the Polynesian *k a v a* was the original of the
Chilian intoxicating drink obtained by chewing and the salivary
ferment resulting. The passage is as follows : " about thirty
canoes went on board the ships with some cattle, and a large
quantity of S c h i t i e , otherwise called *C a w a u*, which
is a liquor in use among the Chilese, and is thus made. They
take a quantity of a root called Inilie, which they roast in
the sands, or they take it unroasted. This root is chewed by
their women and thrown into a great tub or vessel with water
and some other roots are added. They let it stand a day or
two, when it works like our beer ; some of it is white and
some of a red colour and has a taste like our sour whey."
It has been pointed out that in the Andean region *c o c a*
leaves are sometimes chewed with lime to bring out the narcotic effect, just as *a r e c a* nut and pepper leaves are chewed
with lime from the eastern Solomons west to the Malay Archipelago. But the use of lime in the Andes has come about
only since the Spaniards introduced the snail that in its shell
is the source of the lime. There is one more feature of Peruvian
culture that is widespread in Polynesia and Micronesia ; it is
the Inca *q u i p u* , or system of knotted cords for remembering
facts and especially numbers. It is not so elaborate in the
Pacific Ocean except in the Hawaiian monarchies where the
tax-gatherers had cords with knots to record the amount
each taxpayer had to contribute of each article. Other
systems were in vogue in Polynesia like the short mnemonic
sticks used in Tahiti in going over long prayers and incantations,
or the notches in the Maori *whakapapa*, or genealogical stick,
somewhat the same system as the tally-stick in Europe, and
the aboriginal message stick of Australia ; but none had such
wide use as the mnemonic system of knotted cords which
in Maori was called *t a u p o n a p o n a*. If this system went
from Polynesia into Peru it did not go from Easter Island or
the archipelagoes of which it formed " the navel " ; it had
not the *q u i p u* and did not need it ; for it had the

TOMB OF THE TUITONGAS AGAIN BURIED IN FOREST GROWTH

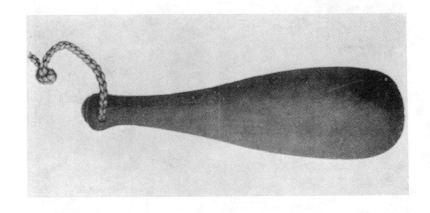

A *mere* FOUND IN A GRAVE OF ECUADOR EARLY
LAST CENTURY

From Rivero and Tschudi's "Peruvian Antiquities."

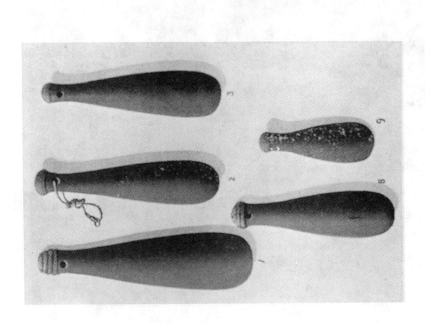

MAORI STONE *meres*, WAR CLUBS WITH CUTTING EDGES

From Hamilton's "History of Maori Art."

rongorongo, or mnemonic script. It is distinctly against the possibility of the great-stone art having gone straight from the region of this little island on to the Pacific coast of America that the most advanced empire of that coast, the Inca empire, did not attain a form of writing and never got beyond the knotted cord.[1]

(9) **THE UMU AND THE TOKI OF POLYNESIA REACHED AMERICA.** There are two more features of Polynesian culture that got on to the Pacific coast of South America. One is the *u m u*, or earth oven; it is one of the most distinctive marks of the culture of Polynesians and went with them wherever they went. It was probably bred in the frozen soil of the wintry north, and belonging to the natives of the north-west coast of America, as it does, it is one of the cues that seem to indicate affinity between them and the Polynesians. It has gone on to the southern coasts of Chili; the *c u r a n t o* of the Araucanians is nothing but the *u m u* of the Pacific islands. A fire is lit in a hole in the earth, with a number of round volcanic stones in the middle of the fuel; when they are red-hot some of them are hauled out and at the same time all the embers of the fuel. Leaves are laid on the stones at the bottom and then a layer of meat in leaves; on another layer of leaves some of the red-hot stones retrieved are laid and a second kind of food is laid down on them, wrapped in leaves. When the hole is filled, leaves and old matting cover it over and the whole is closed with a layer of earth. After a few hours the oven is opened and the food is found perfectly cooked without having lost any of its juices or flavour. Some have abandoned this for European methods, much to their own detriment. Another Polynesian method that got at least into the island of Chiloe is the use of the stone axe or adze used throughout the Pacific; it has retained the Poly-nesian form and the Polynesian name *"t o k i,"* though in spelling it is Hispanised into *"t o q u i."* The canoe of the *C h i l o t e s* has also a strong resemblance to that of Polynesia; whilst they never made or used pottery till Europeans taught them. And the indomitable warlike spirit of the Araucanians has a strong likeness to that of the Maoris of New Zealand; they were never subdued either by the Incas or by the Spanish.

(10) **POLYNESIANS LANDED ON THE COAST OF PERU.**

[1] See Chap. X, par. 3, for Peruvian quipu.

Is there any evidence of Polynesians having landed on the Pacific coast of South America farther north ? If they landed on Chiloe and the southern coast of Chili, it would be the easiest thing for them to sail north ; the wind blows from the south along the Pacific coast all the year round, and the Humboldt current would always be in favour of such a voyage, whilst the attraction of warmer latitudes would naturally draw voyagers who had come originally from the tropics. And in the great adobe ruins of the city of Grand Chimu, stretching fifteen miles along the coast to the north of Truxillo, there are three double-walled enclosures covering each more than a hundred acres ; one of these, that nearest to the coast, has its walls still in good order ; and inside it are the foundations of many large edifices in front of hundreds of small cubicles which were entered only from the roof like the adobe houses of Pachacamac. These could not have been the work-rooms of artisans as Wiener suggests ; there was no entrance for light except the hole in the roof. Taken with the strong high double-walls and screened gateway they are probably the barracks of soldiers, and these the soldiers of conquering intruders who had to guard against the contingency of a rising in this great city and kept these double-walled barracks as a retreat in the last resort. But from the gateway there stretches down right into the surf about a mile off a deep broad cutting that has evidently filled up partially in the centuries. At a short distance from its head stretches a weir of some height with a space cut out in the middle enough to let an oceanic craft in to the dock or shelter within. This was evidently for keeled or deep-sailing canoes and not for the *balsas*, or buoyant rafts, which could be easily hauled up out of the surf on to the beach. The alien conquerors within the enclosures were evidently from over the ocean and wished to have a ready way of escape out to their oceanic highway in case of need. And what definitely indicated them as Polynesians is that outside the northern wall there was a cemetery, and it had been ransacked in the manner of all Peruvian graves, first for precious metals, but afterwards for the decorative earthenware found in every sepulchre. In the heaps of *débris* from this search there was not one scrap of pottery to be seen or found—a most remarkable exception to all the rifled graves that I had seen on the coast of Peru. The only people who could have filled such a cemetery was the Polynesians ; for

INSIDE THE GREAT-STONE TEMPLE OF TEVAITOA IN
RAIATEA, AN ENCLOSURE OF GREAT CORAL BLOCKS UN-
TOOLED ; THE SIZE OF SOME OF THEM MAY BE SEEN
BY THAT AGAINST WHICH THE NATIVE PASTOR LEANS

A *marae* OF TAHITI AS REPRESENTED IN " THE VOYAGE OF THE DUFF," 1799

they alone of Pacific Ocean peoples never made pottery, whilst they were, in ancient times at least, the most adventurous voyagers and the boldest warriors of all time. As a pendent to this may be set a tradition of Lambayeque, an ancient capital town farther north; across the sea came a band of naked warriors who worshipped a god of green stone and dug holes in the vicinity; they ruled for a time and then disappeared. Along with these affinities may be placed the stone cutting club found early last century in a grave in Ecuador; as figured in Rivero and Tschudi's "Peruvian Antiquities" it is the *mere* of the Maoris.

(11) **FROM WHAT PART OF POLYNESIA DID THESE COME?** Up to the fourteenth or fifteenth century there was constant movement among the Polynesians; they set out in large canoes for long voyages over the Pacific. Their aim was probably to find new lands for their folks to settle on, now that so much land in the central Pacific had gone down. Most of them went west, north-west, or south-west before the trade winds; but some of them went south into the regions of snow and ice. Some who had settled in New Zealand were touched with the *wanderlust*, or were driven out by stronger and more warlike new-comers. They would not go far south till they got into the zone of the westerlies, which blow steadily in the same direction all the year round. Once in front of these, they could not avoid getting on to the south coast of Chili, and being borne north by the constant southerly winds. The undefended cities of the coast of Peru, busy with irrigation and the making of pottery and gold and silver ware, would be their natural prey. The influence of Polynesia on the Pacific coast of America was neither impossible nor improbable.

The question is whether they had any influence on the great-stone art. We may rule out Easter Island as the medium of this influence, although there is so strong a resemblance between the work of the two areas. For it would not be easy or natural for voyagers from so far north to reach the American coast; to make sure of reaching it they would have to get far to the south into the latitude of the constant westerlies. And as an actual fact the area of Easter Island had developed a script and in no part of pre-Columbian South America had writing been developed. The great empire of the Incas adhered to the *q u i p u* for all the purposes that writing was intended

to cover ; whilst in Polynesia it was the Easter Island area
that did not use the knotted cords or other mnemonic system.
The influence of the Polynesian art of great-stone work must
have come from some other source and taken some other
direction.

(12) The development of the art in western Polynesia is
almost confined to Tonga, although there are traces of it in
Samoa, in the fallen Stonehenge on the heights behind Apia,
and in the great stepped and truncated pyramids near
Falealili on the south coast of Upolu, and a few slight traces
in New Zealand. We have to look to eastern Polynesia or
its borders for the source. South of the equator are the
Marquesas, Tahiti, Rarotonga, the Austral Islands and Pitcairn
Island that show great-stone work. Rarotonga has *maraes*
that are built of huge cut blocks ; so have the Society Islands ;
those of Tahiti have all gone the way of the road-maker and
-mender. The two great *maraes* of Raiatea are still intact
with their immense untooled blocks torn from the reef or the
hill-side. But none of these are formed of great stones carefully
cut to fit each other's irregularities as in some of the greater
a h u s of Easter Island and in the best work of Andean Peru.
The pyramids of Moche near Truxillo, the larger pyramid of
the sun and the smaller one of the moon, were undoubtedly
built as the sepulchres of kings, and are thus a complete analogy
to the tombs of the *T u i t o n g a s* near Mua in Tongatabu,
though the former are of adobe, the only material available,
and the latter are of great blocks of coral from the adjacent
reef ; they might have had their source and inspiration in the
great pyramids of the Tahitian *maraes*. In the Austral Islands
the chief great-stone work was statues. In Raivavai they are
full-length figures with pedestals deep-sunk in the earth
beneath their feet. There is no sign of the *m a r a e* to
which they may have belonged. Their faces are human, but
grotesquely human, quite unlike the great stone images of
Easter Island, which are only busts and have faces that are
regular in feature and have human individuality upon them.
They have more likeness to the great stone busts that have
been taken from the ruins of *Tiahuanaco* and set up on each
side of the gateway that leads to the church. It is sometimes
stated that ancient South American art, especially in stone,
tends to avoid the human face and figure. But that is by no
means true of *Tiahuanaco ;* a great statue lies headless,

CARVED FIGURE ON BACK OF CYCLOPEAN SEAT LEADING TO THE GREAT
marae NEAR ATUONA IN HÏYAOA, MARQUESAS

ONE OF THE STATUES OF RAIVAVAI IN THE AUSTRAL ISLANDS,
SOUTH OF TAHITI. HALF OF THEM IS BURIED IN THE EARTH

abandoned on its way to La Paz. And crowned human heads appear carved on the monolithic arch along with crowned condors. The last effort of the stone-carver in this centre was human busts carved on the top of tall monoliths of sandstone standing erect in the earth like the busts at Rano Raraku ; but over their surface is traced a fine arabesque of conventionalized human faces not unlike the minute carving on the handles of Mangaian ceremonial axes.

(13) But we have to go to the Marquesas and Pitcairn Island for the combination of great-stone work of the carefully fitted type and the carving of the human figure. On the backs of some of the cyclopean stone seats leading up to the Marquesan *maraes* human figures are roughly carved in relief, and composing the altar of a great *marae*, two thousand feet above the sea and discovered only a few years ago hidden by the roots of a great banian, were alternate carved human figures and plain tooled stones.[1] The stone figures have disappeared from the ancient *marae* on Pitcairn Island, but the banian tree seems to indicate Marquesan origin.

(14) Whether it was from the Marquesas or not that the influence of Polynesian great-stone work was directed towards the South American coast, the likeness of the cyclopean structures of the two areas is sufficiently apparent. Every feature of Polynesian great-stone work is repeated in the great-stone work of the Andes ; and the impetus did not come from America, if we are to judge by the absence of all American products and arts in the Pacific ; it must be the other way, as we find purely Polynesian products and methods on the coast of America and evidences that Polynesian warriors swooped down upon the wealthy cities that were approachable by sea. The most probable history is that since ever the fatherland, Hawaiki, began to be too narrow for its population, expeditions went off in search of new lands ; most went west ; but some must have made for the east by getting south into the latitude of the westerlies. And these may have taken the taste for cyclopean stonework and the art of it ; and from the coast their influence went up with the people of the coastal empires to the high valleys and plateaus of the Andes. They certainly took with them the art of carving the human figure and especially the human bust in stone ; these appear not

[1] See picture facing p. 248.

merely in Tiahuanaco but in the stone images of the Valley of Huaraz in central Peru. But it is in the great ruin to the south of Lake Titicaca that their influence especially appears ; for they naturally, as voyagers, clung to the shores of an inland sea when they left the coast.

ONE OF THE TWO GREAT-STONE BUSTS HAULED FROM THE RUINS
TWO MILES OFF AND SET UP AT THE GATEPOSTS OF THE CHURCH
IN THE MODERN VILLAGE

ONE OF THE FULL-LENGTH STATUES OF TIAHUANACO

CHAPTER XXIV

THE LANGUAGE

(1) Phonology is the most constant phase of a language, and only change of mothers can break its constancy, the moulders of the speech organs in the first seven years of life ; and Polynesian has the most primitive phonology of all languages. (2) There is no tract on the earth but Polynesia that could have kept its people and language isolated for thousands of years ; hence uniqueness of race and speech, primeval in range of sounds and extensive in vocabulary. (3) Grammar is no test of the stage of development of a language or its affinity, as it is ever changing through contact with others ; Polynesian is a starting-point with a plural of the personal pronoun inflected by an affix meaning " three," and implying that all beyond two were uncountable. (4) If this had been a relic of more extensive inflexion reduced by abrasion, other relics would have been found embedded. The only changes arose in the consonants when the dialects faced each other ; for a stricter law than Grimm's controls their changes. (5) Easter Island dialect does not come under this law ; it is capricious in its choice of dialects to follow ; for it has been influenced by many. (6) It had immigrants from Mangareva, Tahiti and the Paumotus. (7) and (8) Marquesan influences the vocabulary somewhat ; but Maori far the most ; very many words are peculiar to Maori and Easter Island dialect ; others explain each other. (9) It is the meagrest vocabulary in Polynesia, and lacks some of the universal words that are essential to Polynesian thought and life. (10) It is impossible to learn the language from existing vocabularies ; they are more Tahitian than Easter Island. I had at last to accept the imperfect English of my Easter Island guide in preference to his Spanish or his native tongue. (11) The pidgin-English of one group is not an accurate guide to that of another. (12) English words have taken far deeper root than French or Spanish. (13) Tahitian almost extirpated the language of Easter Island as it had extirpated those of Rapa and the Austral Islands. (14) No existing vocabulary is a good guide to the language ; it leaves out great numbers of native words, and manufactures or introduces words for things and ideas alien to native life and thought. No language in the Pacific has ever been so mutilated by vocabulary-makers.

(1) THE LANGUAGE POLYNESIAN. The language of Easter Island undoubtedly belongs to the Polynesian, as Cook and those voyagers who knew some of the other Polynesian islands clearly saw. And Polynesian stands by itself as the most primitive in phonology,—the most constant and distinctive phase of a language. It has only twelve to fourteen sounds, when all those to the west of it, from Fiji to the coast of India, have from twenty to forty sounds. This is the mark of a starting-point and not of a goal. It is also the mark of exceptionally long isolation from other languages, or, rather, speakers of other languages. As soon as peoples cross with each other, the phonology begins to change, not for the reason that grammar and vocabularies change, as soon as intercourse begins. These are subject to change right through the life of an individual and a nation. The phonology can change only when the mothers change ; for it is the first seven years of life that mould the organs of speech and hearing and the

271

moulding is in the hands of the mothers or nurses. Change of latitude may make certain sounds more difficult or easy; but without change of mothers too, there is no fundamental change in the range and type of sounds. And, along with the limited gamut that makes Polynesian so primitive goes a phonological law that is as primitive and can be preserved only by comparative seclusion. It is the law of isolation of consonants; no two consonants can be pronounced together; no consonant can be uttered without a vowel following it; in other words, every word and syllable must end in a vowel. But this is not confined to Polynesian; it is the law of the Japanese language away to the north-west, and of the *Quechua* away to the south-east, although these two have far more than the primitive range of sounds. So it is to a large extent a law of most of the languages throughout Melanesia. There is some limitation of it in all those languages, because they are spoken by peoples that have mixed and crossed with other peoples.

(2) **LONG ISOLATION HAS PRODUCED UNIQUE PEOPLE AND LANGUAGE.** Why has Polynesia retained it in all its fullness, whilst retaining its primitive simplicity in range of sounds? It is because it has had perfect quarantine for thousands of years. There is no region in the world but the central Pacific that could afford such a condition. On land there is no such thing as quarantine of race or speech; no mountains or rivers could ever prevent the races on either side of them losing their purity; mutual needs establish traffic; mutual ambitions and hatred lead to wars; conquest modifies both conqueror and conquered; whatever leads to intercourse changes both who intermingle. And the islands and archipelagoes that lie off the coasts of continents cannot exclude traffic or settlement and dare not prevent migration, whilst eager to encourage sea-ventures to the adjoining coast. There is only one region on the face of the earth that hitherto before the era of far-voyaging began has been able to remain quarantined, and that is the central and eastern Pacific. The islands there have through all time been cut off from America by a broad and deep sea; and on the other side the trade winds have barred all but accidental entrance into it since the Micronesian stepping-stones from the coast of Asia have been largely submerged, whilst those through Melanesia have been rising and probably adding to their number. It

is the ideal, the only, region in the world that could keep its isolation through thousands of years, though from it migration might be going on all the time before the trade winds. The result is a perfectly unique race, the tallest and most powerfully built in the world, without pottery, or cereals, or metals, and yet the greatest oceanic navigators before the compass. The result is a perfectly unique language, the simplest, most primitive in phonology, and yet with vocabularies greater than all but the great literary languages.

(3) **POLYNESIAN GRAMMAR.** Grammar is on an entirely different footing from phonology and vocabulary. Its absence or simplicity is no proof of either the primitive culture of the language or of its being advanced. Some of the most uncultured languages are the most complicated in grammar ; some of the most advanced and literary, like English, have got rid of all their formal grammar and have nothing but a grammar of position and particles. Polynesian has the minimum of formal grammar. The only remains of inflexion are as in English in the personal pronouns ; they have a singular, dual and plural, the dual being differentiated by the addition of *ua*, a mutilated form of *rua, two*, to the singular and the plural by the addition of *tou*, a mutilated form of *toru*, three, thus revealing the fact that when these inflexions were created the people who created them did not count beyond *two*, everything beyond being *three* or all. One other inflexion belongs to the personal pronoun, but only to the first person plural ; when a speaker means to include those he is speaking to in " we," he uses the inclusive form, when he excludes them he uses the exclusive form. This formality of grammar belongs to Quechua on the Pacific coast of America and to the languages to the west of Polynesia as far as the Malay Archipelago. There are two other formalities that belong to the Melanesian languages and to some extent to the Malay, but do not exist in Polynesian ; one is the use of the personal pronominal affix at the end of nouns pointing out in each case the possessor of the object indicated by the noun ; the other is the classification of things counted, " round," " flat," " long," for example, by means of special words. The use of *a* and its various modifications at the end of a verb to signify the passive in Polynesian has scarcely passed out of the affix stage into the inflexional.

(4) **PHONOLOGY CONSTANT ; VOCABULARY CHANGES.** This minimum of formal grammar is not due to abrasion through

contact with other languages as it is in the case of English ; else we should have had the relics of other inflexions obscurely embedded in the language, like, for example, "hight," meaning "is called" in English. These remains of inflexions show their origins too plainly to be other than the beginning of the process of turning particles into inflexions ; they are the marks of primitiveness, like the limited phonology. They show that the language has not had to encounter other forms of grammar either by intrusion of peoples who spoke them or by traffic. They reveal the same long quarantine as the phonology reveals. Had great expeditions gone west and returned or gone east and returned, this simplicity could not have remained its striking feature. There were doubtless marauding expeditions returned from the west ; but if they had been of any size, or had settled in the west before returning like the Tongan expeditions to Fiji, they would have brought back pottery and the bow and the shield. And then the vocabulary at least, if not the grammar, would have been influenced to some extent ; the phonology would have re-mained the same, like the household arts, unless enough wives had been brought back to swamp the influence of the Poly-nesian wives completely. But the language retained its pristine purity, though hiving off into dialects that had the phonological peculiarities distinguishing them from each other in the fatherland confirmed and strengthened by the far separation of the different colonies that took them abroad ; yet they retained the bond of contrast that was formed when facing each other and that remained a strict law governing the relationships of the consonants. Each colony dropped out a proportion of its vocabulary retained by others, chiefly through the custom of tabooing words that entered into the names of kings and chiefs.

(5) **EASTER ISLAND PHONOLOGY UNDER NO LAW.** The dialect of Easter Island is out of the range of this strict law. Its phonology is confused. Its consonants follow sometimes one island or group of islands, sometimes another. Like Rarotongan it is constantly omitting the *h*, even that which stands for the *wh* of Maori and the *f* of Samoa ; and it as readily inserts *h* where other dialects have it not. One instance will serve : the Maori word "to escort" is *arahi ;* the Paumotan is *arai ;* the Marquesan is *aahi ;* the Easter Island is *harai*. Sometimes it turns the *h* into *v*, as in *kakava*, " a

shirt," corresponding to Maori *kaha*, "a garment," perhaps mediated by *wh* like *vitiviti*, "a shrimp," corresponding to Paumotan *kovitiviti*, "a shrimp," and Maori *kowhitiwhiti moana*, "a shrimp," from *whiti*, "to spring." At times it compensated for the loss of *h* by the duplication of the vowel, as *aaki*, "to reveal," corresponding to Maori *whaki* and Marquesan *faki* and *haki*. The use of *ng*, *r*, and *k* is similarly confused, e.g. it has *ongapo* for "last night" where all the others have quite regularly *n;* Tahitian *inapo*, Samoan *anapo*, Maori *napo;* again where Maori has *ngako*, Tongan *ngako*, and Samoan *nga'o* it has *nako;* and its *kakaro*, "to dance," corresponds to Maori *ngarahu*, "a war-dance"; where Maori has *whanga*, "bay," it has *aka* and *hanga*. It uses both *r* and *l* and more freely than the south island of New Zealand; and it omits both, though not so much as the Marquesan, or Tongan, which follows Marquesan very frequently in the same words; one or two instances will serve. Polynesian *ero* means "stench," Easter Island *eo* means "fragrance"; Maori for "echo" is *wawaro*, and for this Easter Island has *vavovavo;* *v* or *w* is parasitic between two vowels in both; whilst *h* often stands for *w* or *v* in the other dialects, e.g. *hahohaho*, "outside," corresponds to *waho*, and other Polynesian dialects *vaho*. As in Maori *n* often takes the place of *r*, as in *pini* and *piri*, "close," in *peringi*, "to fall in drops," and *ninini*, "to flow." It has even begun to develop the tendency to use *k* for *t*, which began in Hawaii early last century and is now making way in Samoa, e.g. Easter Island *inaki*, "a share of food at a feast," is the same as Maori *inati*. And the interchange of *p* and *v* are not uncommon, e.g. Easter Island *parei*, "gum from old eyes," corresponds to Maori *ware*, "viscous fluid," whilst in Easter Island "*reperepe*" and "*eëve*" both mean "buttocks." The vowels are not quite so variable; but they vary more than in other Polynesian dialects.

(6) This variability arises from the people that colonized Easter Island, or rather the archipelagoes that used to surround it, having come from various Polynesian groups. Of the groups near at hand it agrees oftenest with Mangarevan and next to that with Paumotan. Its agreement with Tahitian seems to be the greatest; but, if we exclude the words that have come into it after the Peruvian raid, we shall find Tahitian is less predominant in its cognates than these two.

Amongst the more distant areas there are a fair number of words that are to be found only in Samoan, Tongan, and Easter Island dialects. But the influence of these two must have been unimportant ; for they have no effect upon the phonology ; no *s* appears from Samoan, and no *b* or *ts* from Tongan.

(7) **EASTER ISLAND DIALECT AND MAORI.** The two dialects of distant areas that most influence this are Marquesan and Maori. A large number of the Easter Island words that are found in the three dialects nearest to the island are also to be found in Marquesan, not infrequently with a preference for its form. The influence especially appears in the frequent omission of *r*. But by far the most influential of the distant dialects is Maori. There are many words that in either their form or their sense are peculiar to these two dialects ; a short list of some of these is given at the end. Two prefixes are the only formal elements that appear in them and in them alone ; one is *hoko*—used before numerals to make them distributive ; another is *mate* meaning " desire " or " love " and derived from *ate,* " the heart " ; *matevai* means in both " thirst," or " desire for water " ; in Maori *mate* and *matenui* mean " deeply in love " and so does *manava mate* in Easter Island, whilst *ateate* in the latter means " dear." The two languages are fonder of the causative prefix *haka* or *whaka* in its various mutilated forms than any other Polynesian tongue. Some compounds with this prefix are peculiar to them, *hakapura* and Maori *kapura,* " flame " ; *kapuru* and Maori *whakapuru,* " to thatch a house " ; *hakarau* and Maori *whakarau,* " to take captive " ; *hakarere* and *whakarere,* " to forsake " ; *kahorihori* and *whakahorihori,* " to contradict " ; *hakarongo* and *whakarongo,* " to listen " ; *hakarehu,* " to surprise," and Maori *whakarehu,* " to feint with a weapon " ; *hakarite,* " regular," and Maori *whakarite,* " to put in order " ; *hakari,* " aspect," and Maori *whakaari,* " to expose to view." There are some isolated words in one that find their derivation and explanation in the other ; Easter Island *nua,* " a garment," is evidently connected with Maori *whenua,* " placenta " ; *varua,* " ghost," is mutilated Maori *wairua,* which means " double existence " or " spirit " ; *hihoi,* " to divine," is explained by Maori *iho,* " the chief *tohunga* in a canoe " ; *nawe,* " a strap under the chin for securing the hat," is explained by Maori *whakananawe,* " to fasten " ; *piko,* " to hide people," explains Maori *whakapiko,* " murder of guests " ;

inanga, "lungs and heart," is explained by Maori *nga*, "to breathe"; *nanai*, "spider," explains "*ngai*" in Maori puNGAI*werewere*, "a spider"; *vere*, "goatee," is explained by Maori *were*, "to hang," and *werewere*, "wattles of a bird"; *hoangaa*, "nest," is a form of the Polynesian *kohanga* that is explained by Maori *owhanga*; *hokohoko*, "to dandle, to fondle," explains Maori *hoko*, "lover"; *ina*, "not," explains Maori *nanape*, "not."

(8) **MAORI AND EASTER ISLAND WORDS INTEREXPLANATORY.** Some Maori words go into Easter Island with the things they signify, or indicate a similarity in the objects. *Hue* and Maori *upokohue* mean "blackfish"; *kahi* in both indicates a large deep-sea fish. Maori *nanu* and *nanua* indicate an edible sea-fish, like the Easter Island *nanua*, a name which a legend tries to explain from its resemblance to *nua*, "a wrapper," or "garment"; *kaha*, the larger of the calabashes, is the same as Maori *taha*; *pepe* means "a moth" in both; *punua*, "chicken," is the Maori *punua*, "the young of birds and other animals," applied to their only domesticated animal; *kuia*, "the booby," is doubtless the same as Maori *kuia*, "the petrel," and *tavake*, "the tropic bird," is the same in both. The peculiar Easter Island form *toa* for "sugar-cane" is explained by the Maori *toa*, "to throw up a stalk." *Toromiro* exists only in Easter Island dialect and Maori, though it is applied to different trees, a pine (*podocarpus ferrugineus*) in the latter and an acacia-like tree (*sophora tetraptera*) in the former, and although the latter also belongs to New Zealand; its native name there is *kohai*, doubtless the source of the Easter Island synonym for *miro*, "timber," *kohau*. One word that is common to the two would in itself show that both came from tropical Polynesia; it is the Easter Island *hoe*, "a knife," cognate with *oe*, "a sword," and the Maori *hoeroa*, "a wooden or bone sword"; they are from Polynesian *kohe*, "bamboo knife" and "bamboo"; the speakers of both languages left the bamboo behind in the tropical lands they came from. *Kainga*, "fibre from the sugar-cane," has been assumed to be from the Spanish word for "cane"; but it is old and has its derivation in Maori *kaka*, "fibres"; whilst the Easter Island *kakaka*, "grass for caulking canoes," is cognate. So *vave* has been taken as the English word "*wave*," which it means; but *ua* exists in Easter Island, meaning "a wave," cognate with Maori *huamo*, "to be raised in waves,"

T

along with another word *e* or *ve* meaning the same. So Marquesan and Easter Island *vove*, " a widow or widower," has been assumed to be a modification of French *veuf;* but *vo* is another form of *hoa*, " mate," and *ve* is from *vete*, " to untie." *Poporo* in both Maori and Easter Island means both " black " and a species of solanum ; but the species are entirely different, though their berries are used for the same purpose of mixing with a black paint ; in New Zealand it is a bush solanum with a scarlet berry as large as a plum ; in Easter Island it has a small black berry like that of the deadly nightshade, though the foliage is more like the sow-thistle. The distinctive surfing-board of Easter Island, *pora*, " the mat raft," exists in Maori in the two separate senses of " a mat " and " a sea-going canoe," and this brings out the contrast between the two areas with regard to timber for sea use. The much mutilated Easter Island *eeriki*, " floor-covering," has to be explained by Maori *whariki* for " what is stretched out over a thing," " mat " or " carpet." The appropriation of *moenga*, " a sleeping mat," in Easter Island for " a winding sheet " for the dead, throws light on the scarcity of mats and materials for mat-work in the island. And *ahu*, which originally means " a heap," has come in Maori to signify " a sacred mound," before it was appropriated to the great burial platforms of Easter Island. And this is confirmed by the peculiar use of *rumaki* in both dialects and in them alone in the sense of " to bury," the word in each being probably influenced by their use of the Polynesian *rua*, " a hole," in the sense of " grave." And it is not alone the probable derivation of *moai*, " an image," from *moa*, " sacred," and *ivi*, " tribe " or " ancestor," that reveals the people of the *ahus* as ancestor-worshippers. Maori and Easter Island dialects together illuminate the much discussed Polynesian word *atua*, " a god." In Easter Island the form is also *etua*, and *etu* means " a tribe " ; in Maori *whatua* is an ancestor. The identification of divinity with ancestry is easy and natural in a people like the Polynesians, who worshipped ancestors and deified their chiefs even in life.

(9) **THE MEAGREST OF VOCABULARIES.** But, as in all its culture, cosmology and mythology, Easter Island shows great *lacunæ*, so does it in its vocabulary. Some of the most important words of Polynesian are absent here. It is difficult to explain why the word for the ocean, " *moana*," is not to

A GREAT-STONE BUST FIXED IN THE GROUND IN FRONT OF THE FINE BURIAL PLATFORM OF VINAPU, THE ONLY IMAGE NOW STANDING ERECT IN EASTER ISLAND AWAY FROM THE SCULPTORS' WORKSHOP ON RANO RARAKU. IT IS OF THE USUAL BRECCIA, AND HAS EVIDENTLY WORN GREATLY UNDER THE RAINS AND WINDS SINCE THE "MOHICAN" PARTY TOOK A PICTURE OF IT IN 1888, ONE OF THE BEST TESTS OF THE AGE OF THE STATUES

JUAN TEPANO, MY EASTER ISLAND "GUIDE, PHILOSOPHER, AND FRIEND"

be found here ; instead of it there has been manufactured the word *vaikava*, which literally means "salt water"; the compound was open to this application, as the people never used salt water for a sauce, as the tropical Polynesians did. But it reveals that also, unlike all the other Polynesians, they did not look upon the ocean as the great element for voyaging on, but as the narrow rim of the land. A more important *lacuna* is the word *mana*, which in Polynesian covered all that occult power which resides, not only in the supernatural and the ancestors, but in great living men and their deeds and their weapons and instruments. It was probably because there was no sense of this *aura* of the great and indeed no great individuality to embody it or ray it forth that the word dropped out of their Polynesian vocabulary. And that it did not take on the elementary and barbaric mutilation of its sense it assumed in Melanesia leaves not much ground for Melanesian influence ; though the people had great faith in charm-stones, they never applied it to these. The vocabulary is indeed poverty-stricken ; after the Tahitian and Mangarevan words imported in recent times have been rejected there remain but a few hundred words, the meagrest vocabulary in Polynesia. The missionaries were at their wits' end to know how to express the abstract ideas that belong to all religions or the emotions and thoughts they wished to awaken ; and so were the secular visitors, the traders and stock-owners, puzzled how to express the commonest notions of even barbaric culture, so much of Polynesian culture was awanting with its words.

(10) **POLYNESIAN TRANSFORMATION OF EUROPEAN WORDS.** And this is what has made the Easter Island vocabularies so unreliable. I trusted to the compilation published by the Carnegie Institute and studied it and analysed it comparatively for many months before I came to Easter Island ; it not only embodies the mistakes of all the vocabularies it has incorporated, but manufactures new ones by theorizing and professing to correct them ; it combines the maximum of scientific pretentiousness with the minimum of science. When I started going over the vocabulary as given in it with Juan Tepano, the best educated and the most intelligent of the natives, I felt that I had been completely misled by it and had wasted my time. Every third word was not Easter Island at all but Tahitian or Mangarevan ; and a

large number of words current in the dialect were either not given or given in a form or with a meaning that made them unrecognizable. I abandoned the attempt to express myself in the language and took to Spanish, which is now used by the natives, though with an extremely limited vocabulary and an extremely puzzling pronunciation. Tepano insisted on answering in English, though his English words were less recognizable than his Spanish, and I had often to ask him to give me the native equivalent in order to understand his English. The reason why he so persisted in his broken English I afterwards discovered to be the six months' residence in the little community of the crew of the wrecked *Eldorado*. The name of Mr. Edmunds, the manager of the sheep station, he turned first into *eremano*, which I constantly mistook for the Spanish *hermano* and thought referred to his brother; and it got further entangled with the Spanish word for German " Aleman," which he often introduced as against " Inggaris " in his favourite parallel for the Easter Island wars; he next transformed it into *eremoro* and finally into *eremo*. I often referred to the monograph of Paymaster Thomson describing the visit of the American ship *Mohican* to the island : Tepano's father had been one of the native guides and he was fond of referring to it; but his pronunciation of " American " the word he used in regard to it was so like that of " milk," " merike," that I had often to hesitate and ask a question. " A notty man " for " another man "; " palaike " for " flag," " pipera " for " people," " peluk " for " break," " sai " and " set " for " die " and " death " greatly puzzled me at first. He eked out his scanty vocabulary and frequent pauses with stock phrases like " bimeby " and " me speakey you," which might mean past, present or future. But ultimately I got so accustomed to his favourite mispronunciations, and his vocabulary so improved that I understood his English better than his Spanish or native expressions.

(11) The difficulty of the Polynesian in pronouncing European words is obvious when we remember that he had no *b* or *d* or *th* or *g* or *gh* or *s* and that he had to insert a vowel between two consonants, whenever they came together. The result is that a European finds the transformations almost beyond recognition. Nor are the transformations always the same in the different areas ; one chooses one substitute for a difficult sound and another another. A comparison of some of those

that the Maori makes with those that the Easter Islander makes will bring out how little the pidgin-English of one island helps one with that in the next visited. For "missionary" Maori has *mihinare* against *mitinare* here ; for "priest" the one has *piriti*, the other *piripitero*, the latter evidently imitating *presbyterio ;* in the one *hopi* is "soap," in the other *tope*; in the one "letter" is *reta*, in the other *retera ;* "peach" is in one *petiti*, in the other *peti* ; "altar" in one *aata*, in the other *aretare*; "melon" in one is *merengi*, in the other *melone* ; "horse" in one is *hoiho*, in the other *hoi* ; "bishop" is in one *pihopa*, in the other *epikopo*. In Maori the word "biscuits" was turned into *pikiti ;* but in Easter Island the natives saw biscuits taken out of a tin and they threw them away, as they did the seeds and spongy matter of a gourd and called them *karukaruhue*, "the matter inside a gourd." When they got flour they called it, like the Tahitians, *haraoa*, and used it in the way they had used the native arrowroot, as white paint for their faces ; the Maoris called it *paraoa*, but knew better what to do with it. When Easter Islanders first got tobacco, they boiled it and got very sick with the soup, and accepted its name from the Tahitians, who called it *avaava*, doubtless because they saw the sailors chew it and spit as they did when they turned the pepper root into a narcotic liquor ; afterwards, when they got it in the shape of a cigarette, they called it *potu* (short), and when in the form of a cigar, *moke* (English smoke).

(12) **ENGLISH WORDS MORE OFTEN EMBEDDED THAN FRENCH OR SPANISH.** It is strange that though French missionaries and French explorers and French officials had the island to themselves for more than a generation French has left so much less impression on the vocabulary than English ; French words that have got into the language do not seem to have the same vitality as those left by the whalers and shipwrecked mariners. *Rapiti* drove out the original French word for the short-careered rabbit, *rapino ; hoi* for "horse" drove out the French *kevare* (cheval) ; *peni* for the English word "paint" (Maori *peita*) drove out the French *penetuli* (peinture) ; *nieve*, "snow" (French niege), *ani*, "lamb" (French agneau), *toro*, "cattle" (French taureau), and *motare*, "clock" (French montre), are quite dead, probably, indeed, never had any life. It is the Latin words brought in by the French missionaries in the liturgy that have persisted,

though in a very unvital way : *meta* (mass), *miterio* (mystery), *karatia* (grace), *purukatorio* (purgatory), *takarameta* (sacrament), *taperenakero* (tabernacle), *vicario* (vicar), *vinea* (vine), *uva* (grape), *virihine* (virgin), *tatani* (Satan). Only one Spanish word has taken root as yet, though the island has belonged to Chili for forty years ; it is the word for Sunday, *tominika* (Maori *hapati*). The amazing thing is that it is English words that have taken deepest root: *aka*, "anchor" (Maori *haika*); *chot*, "church" (Maori *hahi*); *manua*, "ship" (for man-o'-war); *moni*, "money"; *koropare*, "crowbar"; *puka*, "book"; *purumu*, "broom"; *poti*, "boat"; *nira*, "needle"; *pakete*, "bucket"; *pipi*, "pea"; *paura*, "gunpowder"; *ti*, "tea"; *uira*, "wheel," "helm" ; *tokini*, "stocking," and even a hybrid compound from that, *tokini rima*, "glove." It is evident that it is not merely words connected with the sea and ships; they are well distributed over all phases of life. And often instead of adopting the name of the animal or thing brought in they have a name of their own ; when an American whaler brought the flea from the Peruvian coast a century ago, they adopted the unappropriated Polynesian word for crayfish, *koura*, partly because of some likeness between the crayfish and the flea, and partly because the crayfish was already called *ura* (the red) ; but the main reason was the same as that which drove the Hawaiians to call the new comer "the jumping louse" (*ukulele*), the difficulty of pronouncing the name, which has been turned by the Maori into the unrecognizable *puruhi*. So when the nanny-goat was left by La Perouse, they did not, like the Maoris, call it *nane nane*, but took the first syllable of Hotu's dog, *paihenga*, and adding that to the name of the pig formed from its grunt (*oru*) got the brand-new name *apaihoru*. The dragonfly was introduced some few years ago and they dubbed it *veke*, probably from its tentacles and wings all sticking out like eyelashes (*vekeveke*). But wherever they could get a word in Tahitian for a European thing they never hesitated to adopt it ; perhaps the best instance is the word for "trousers," which the men rapidly accepted as the proper covering for the legs ; where the Maoris attempted the English word and made it *tarautete* the Tahitians noticed how closely these garments clung to the supports of the body and called them *piripou* ("stick-to-the-pillars ").

(13) TAHITIAN ALMOST EXTIRPATED THE NATIVE LANGUAGE.
It was Tahitian that almost extirpated the language of Easter

Island, as it extirpated those of Rapa and the Austral Islands. It was the cultured language of south-eastern Polynesia and had a Polynesian word for everything new as well as everything old. It had begun to be Europeanized by Wallis, and Cook, and Bougainville in the latter part of the eighteenth century and to be influenced by British missionaries before the century closed. It had to alter its official language like Easter Island; about the middle of the nineteenth century it changed from English to French. It was after that that it began to handle Easter Island and made the natives learn French. But it was Tahitian that really penetrated into the heart of its language, because the missionaries, though French, came from Tahiti with a Tahitian liturgy. Even Eyraud, though he came from Chili, seems, during his nine months' sojourn in the island, to have thought in Tahitian; in telling the story of the effect of his warning Torometi that death would overtake him as it overtook their friend Pana, he makes the natives talk Tahitian, " *e pohe e* " (" he must die "). And this was in 1864, before any Tahitian had settled on the island. Not till two years after did the missionaries make way amongst the natives or Dutrou Bornier settle. And the Peruvian raid, with the devastation of the smallpox, that the few returned captives had brought back with them, had reduced the numbers from about three thousand to about a thousand, making the task of conversion possible. And the mission looked to Bishop Jaussen in Papeete as its head and brought the catechism and liturgy in Tahitian and preached in Tahitian. It was inevitable that the native tongue should die out. Some of the preachers insisted that the people should talk in Tahitian and one of them fined them for every breach of this order. And the new converts were loyal and obedient; they carried out all the counsels given them as if they were orders, wherever these did not conflict with the interests of their stomachs and their ancient ingrained habits; they would go as far even as giving up these provided they were only superficial, like the pressing of noses for a welcome.

(14) **DEFECTS OF EXISTING VOCABULARIES.** What saved the remnants of the language from complete annihilation was the departure of the missionaries with three hundred of their converts for Mangareva. Already several hundred had gone to Tahiti to work on the sugar plantations, the act that caused the breach between the clerical and secular authorities. There

were not a hundred left on the island, and these were all concentrated in the village of *Hangaroa*. They were left to themselves and, though the Church dealt with them only through Tahitian, they had the whole week and all their secular affairs for the practice of their native tongue. Roussel had collected a vocabulary of the language before he left, as a guide to French priests and giving them only the equivalents of French words. The result is that it is strained and artificial. He tries to translate into the language ideas and names of things that never entered into the head of a native and never could; the native words are thus beclouded and confused with meanings that they never bore nor could ever bear. It is not merely words for things that were introduced by Europeans like bowsprit, helm, capstan, royal sail, coffin, cannon, musket, saddle, sheepfold, bedstead, sofa, ink, and words for things that never existed on the island, like dove, landcrab, monkey, mouse, negro, palace, brig, bridle, drawers, cage, calico, cascade, caldron, candlestick, key, padlock, coach, farm, harpoon, haricot, plough, bayonet, bronze, tin, iron, tinplate, gold, goblet, diamond, clock, jersey, tinderbox, match, barrel, apartment, lion, cart. He tries to give expression to abstract ideas and things that could by no possibility be thought of by primitive minds; words are given for formula, hypostasis, idolater, lecture, frontispiece, gallows, arbiter, commissioner, angel. It is perfectly absurd when we know the meagre primeval life the people of the island led, a full stage lower in development than all other Polynesian peoples. It is still more absurd when we consider the small vocabulary the people at their best had in use; it consists of the possible minimum that a Polynesian could get on with. And in thus puffing out this slender list of words to look like a cultivated European language the dictionary has left out a considerable proportion of the simple old words. And to make matters worse Mangarevan words are introduced to eke out the meagreness of the vocabulary; one instance will suffice: the Mangarevan *tongi*, " to praise or bless," is used to form, by means of the passive termination, a participle for " blessed," " *tongihia*." To make confusion worse confounded, the language of communication with the natives has been changed from French to Spanish, and, where foreign-trained clerics come in, they are from Chili and know little of Tahitian or the native dialect. What chance has the language had of remaining pure ?

APPENDIX TO CHAPTER XXIV

Short selection of the words that are cognate or similar in Maori and Easter Island languages alone of Polynesian dialects : many of them to illustrate the slight changes in sound and meaning in the two, as e.g. Easter Island K for Maori T.

Maori	*Easter Island Dialect*
ama, posts supporting the barge-board	*tama*, centre post bearing the ridge-pole
aneane, sharp	*ariari=panepane*, sharp
anuanu, offensive	*hanohano*, detestable
areare, free from obstructions	*varevare*, without rocks
atawhai, liberal	*atakai*, generous
ataata, shadow	*ataatapo*, shadows of evening
atamai, to behave contemptuously	*tamaki*, to show off
atanga, beautiful	*atanga*, beautiful
arahi, to lead off as captive, to escort	*harai*, to escort
atuapiko, rainbow	*atuapiko*, rainbow
amatiatia, outrigger canoe	*amatiatia*, outrigger
ahua, to form, make	*raua*, to form
aitua, of ill omen	*aitua*, blackness before storm
amene, to desire	*hamene*, to desire
hapaki, to catch or kill lice	*hapaki*, to crack lice
hangareka, to jest	*hakareka*, to jest
hapopo, an enemy's corpse intended to be eaten	*hapopo*, a corpse from battle to be eaten
hara, excess	*kahara* (a superlative of number)
hau, feather	*hau*, feather hat
hau, to overhang, project	*hau*, the earthwork on conical hill at Anakena Bay
hou, feather	*rou*, feather
hianga, vicious	*hianga*, bad
hihiri, laborious	*hihiri*, difficult to reach
whakaiho, to cut the hair	*hakaiho*, to use the *mataa* on the hair
iki, to devastate	*ikiiki*, to lay waste
ingoingo, spotted	*ingoingo*, dirty
io, muscle	*hiohio*, muscle
iorangi, the emblem of an *atua* carried by a priest in the van of a war-party	*iorangi*, the *ua* or *ao* carried into battle by the *maori*
irirangi, having a supernatural sound	*irirangi*, voices of ghosts or of people at a distance=*tururangi*
kahukahu, membrane enveloping a child when born	*kahukahu*, placenta

kairiri, to find fault with — *kairiri*, to be angry

kaitangata, cannibal — *kaitangata*, cannibal

kanapu, bright — *naponapo*, bright

kari, to dig=*keri* — *are*, to dig=*keri*

karipi, to cut — *karipi*, to cut up and distribute

kapura, flame — *hakapura*, flame

karaparapa, flashing — *karapa*, sunlight in the eyes

kau, ancestor — *kaua*, ancestor

kaui, to lace — *kauiui*, to mend

kaunoni, to writhe — *kaunoninoni*, to writhe

kaupapa, floor — *kaupapa*, canoe floor

kauwaka, human medium of an *atua* — *kauvaka*, sorcerer or priest

kawatawata, yearning — *kavatavata*, desire to speak

kawekawe, strands of a girdle — *kave*, strand of a *taura*

kawei, shoot of a gourd — *kavei*, stem of a fruit

kawhaki, to carry off — *kahoki*, to carry off

kawiri, to twist — *kaviri*, to envelop

kawiu, to be shrunk — *hakaviuviu*, to squat

kehu, brown — *ehuehu*, brown

kerikeri, to rush along — *kekeri*, a squall

kokekoke, lame — *kokekoke*, lame

koromaki, to suppress feelings — *koromaki*, to pine away

mahimahi, to copulate — *mahimahi*, to copulate

makauri, black — *makauri*, black

manana, to wag, wave about — *manana,* to skip

manatu, homesick — *manau*, to remember home

manawaru, fidgety — *manavaru*, afraid

mamanga, to claw — *mangamanga*, to take in the hand

maoa, cooked — *kamaoa*, to open an earth-oven

whakamarumaru, to shelter — *hakamaru*, to shade

mata, flint, obsidian, spear-head — *mataa*, flint, obsidian, spear-head

matapopore, watchful over — *matapupura*, fixed gaze

mataka, red — *mataka*, red

matakite, seer — *matakite*, one who discovers a thief

matatoa, fearless — *matatoa*, conqueror

mau, food products — *mau*, food

mohu, silent — *mou,* silent

manu, a kite to fly — *manu hakarere*, to fly a kite

naenae, failing of breath — *naenae*, asthma

nehu, to bury — *haka-nehu*, to cover up so as to conceal

newha, to doze — *nenehu*, sleepy

ngeru, smooth, soft, sleek — *neru*, a man with long nails who does not work

paenga, site of buildings — *paenga*, foundation

pahao, to catch in a net — *hahao*, to put into a *kete*

pai, handsome — *paina*, handsome

paka, quarrel

pake, a cape of undressed flax

pakipaki, an ornamental border to a cloak

panepane, head

parahirahi, flax sandal

pari, flowing of tide

patiki, a flounder

pohepohe, mad

rakei, to ornament

rangatahi, to move quickly

rangi, seat of affection (obsolete)

rape, tattooing on the breech

rarau, to grasp

rei, cherished possession

rekareka, tickling

renga, yellow

repa, flax cloak

pairua, nausea

ta, to deviate

taharangi, horizon

tahua, courtyard

taingo, mottled

taka, to collect into heaps

tataku, to recite

tao, to weigh down

tareke, small edged tool

tauaki, to expose

taumarere, to fall, to drop

tawharu, to clothe

teki, to drift

tia, a slave, servant

toi, to move quickly

whakatoke, to attack by stealth

toko, to begin to move

tonga, chilled, frozen

tongaku, to fester

topa, to cook

whakatopa, to swoop as a hawk on its prey

tipuaki, crown of head

tua, the future

tuaki, old

---

pakanga, quarrel

pakeke, a rough cloak

pakipaki, black or red pigment dyeing the border of a *nua*

puoko panepane, head

marahirahi, a sandal

pari, rise and fall of waves

katiki, a flounder

pohi, mad

rakei, to adorn

rangatahi, to move quickly

rangi, to love

rape, tattooing on the breech

hakararau, to seize

reimiro, treasured wooden breast ornament

akarekareka, tickling under the arm

henga henga, red

nua hakarepa, mantle for the shoulders

rua, nausea

ta, to throw out of order

taharangi, horizon=*rangi taha*

tahua, paving in front of *ahu*

taingo, covered with sores

hakatakataka, to gather the bones together for deposition in the burial vault

katataku, to count, to read

tao, to carry

reke, knife

tauaki, to hang out clothes

taumare, to drop

haharu, to draw the clothes over

teki, to traverse

kia, a domestic

toi, to hand along

toke, to dupe

toomai, to bring

tonga, winter

ngatu, to suppurate

topa, a feast

katopa, to come down from a seat

tupuraki, where the hair parts

motua, by and by

tuai, old

tuku, to receive, entertain

turehu, to doze

turihaka, bow-legged

tuwhenua, mainland

wairua, spirit

wakawaka, ridge and furrow

weta, excrement

wharo, to abuse

wharo, stretched out at length

whatitiri, a fungus

whenguwhengu, to snuffle

tuura, a servant

rehu, to sleep

turihaka, bow-legged

tuhenua, a rock standing alone

varua, spirit

vakavaka, garden bed

veta, excrement that comes little by little

tarotaro, to chide

haro, to stretch out the hand or other member

hatutiri, mushroom

henguhengu, to murmur

CHAPTER XXV

THE FUTURE OF POLYNESIA AND EASTER ISLAND

(1) The first voyagers found in Polynesia a unique people going to decay, and in Easter Island the same decay, and added to it poor fare, the result of improvidence and indolence. (2) There are in Polynesia both decadence and decay ; the people die out, decaying physically and morally ; but their annals record a great past of voyagings and imperial designs, great cosmologies and mythologies. In Easter Island the decay is patent ; but the decadence is startling, and can only be explained by catastrophe. (3) The decay has been hastened by all that Europe has introduced. (4) Worst of all, the taboo, the basis of the social system, was dissolved ; and there was no more stimulus to work ; the old village communism bred indolence and improvidence. Easter Island had reached this stage a century before the rest of Polynesia. Submergence was at the bottom of its decay, as it was at the bottom of the old Polynesian decadence. (5) Indolence brought infertility, and all over Polynesia the population went down rapidly in numbers. (6) A prediction that was a dirge was falsified by its maker ; Maori decay was arrested by division of the communally held lands. (7) A change from temperate zone to tropics was not the cause of decay, else abortion and infanticide would not have rooted in the race. (8) Polynesia was peopled before the concentration of people in cities on the continent ; and Polynesians are now the victims of the epidemics that were bred by this. But it is venereal diseases that do most havoc ; the old ideal of chastity had vanished and " the new Cythera " became the hotbed of sexual diseases. (9) Malaria has not reached Polynesia, and hookworm has not got east of Samoa ; but leprosy is rife in eastern Polynesia ; an older form of it died out. (10) There were few indigenous diseases. (11) What most reduced the population was slave-raiding. (12) But the decline has been arrested largely by crossing with Europeans and other Polynesians. (13) For they are Caucasoid ; and whatever small part they may play in the great battle of the standards in the Pacific, it will be on the side of the occident.

(1) **A UNIQUE PEOPLE WITH UNIQUE DECADENCE.** When the European voyagers broke into the solitude of the central and eastern Pacific, what struck them most was the similarity of physique, race, culture, and language that prevailed over the vast oceanic area the little islands dusted. There was no such racial and linguistic uniqueness to be found on the face of the earth except perhaps in the Arctic regions of America, one of the last refuges of defeated peoples. Here over this watery expanse they found one of the handsomest and most stalwart races of mankind, separated often by thousands of miles of ocean yet the same. Their foods, their plants, their methods of life differed only where latitude and climate impressed modifications on them. And in the more tropical sections of them there seemed to be the same symptoms of decay, excess of luxury, especially in eating, and a tendency to licentiousness. Wherever they went there was the same over-indulgence in food and drink and venery. Everywhere the women offered themselves freely or were offered to sailors

who had not seen women for long periods. It was all " the new Cytherea," the region where Venus ruled supreme. The experience was new and delightful to European mariners and many wished to settle down in this utopia of Aphrodite. It was with the greatest difficulty the captains could bring away their crews ; and it was doubtless largely at the bottom of the mutiny of the *Bounty*. Easter Island was visited much later than the great areas of Polynesia ; but the same pheno- mena appeared, with this singular difference, that none of the sailors settled or wished to settle on the islet, probably owing to the narrowness of its life and the scantiness of its resources. There was the same over-indulgence in feasting and the same licence in sexual life ; but the life was hard between the feasts ; for there was not much to come and go on in the shape of foods ; there was the indolence of the lotus isles ; but there was also the result of indolence, poor fare and little of it. Men had to eat to live ; but they did not quite realize that they had to live to eat, that energy and work were the first essentials for getting food. And the magnificent *ahus* and fallen titans were but lenten fare for empty stomachs.

(2) **DECADENCE DIFFERENT FROM DECAY.** Moerenhout, who was familiar with eastern Polynesia nearly a hundred years ago, was quite convinced that the race was decadent, and decadent from a great past when land was not so far scattered in these regions. No one who visits the various groups of Polynesia but must have observed the marks of decay, though for much of it that exists now European customs and vices are responsible. But when he thinks of their great achievements in navigation and their great monarchies in the far past as well as in modern times, and realizes their magnificent mythology and the depth of abstract thought indicated by their cosmology it is difficult to resist the idea that the decadence did not begin when Europeans appeared on the scene. And a visit to Easter Island does not remove the idea. Here we see the most extraordinary memorial architecture that the world has seen, and a people indolent, unenterprising, unforeseeing, incapable of any architecture but a thatched hovel, and of any memorial of the dead but gorging at a funeral. And, if we examine minutely their annals and their culture, they reveal the same antithesis to great ideas and great enterprises. Decadence is scarcely the word for this

combination of the sublime and the infantile on the same island. Rupture with the past, catastrophe, is printed plainly on everything that exists, dead or living, upon this oceanic atom. But there are also quite manifest everywhere symptoms of decay such as are apparent in the rest of Polynesia; these are quite separate from the piquant contrast with a great though primitive past. These still go on; that can only be explained by the narrowing of the arena on which the greatness displayed itself. And we have not to search far in the central and eastern Pacific for a true cause. Submergence has been in process through all time and has by no means ceased in our era. It has been and is dominant in this area of the ocean in contrast to the area to the west, especially the south-west, where elevation has manifestly been going on in our geological era at least and is still dominant. The mythology everywhere in Polynesia bears record to the submergence in early human times. And we have within the past century the disappearance of Tuanaki with all its people, and within the past two centuries the disappearance of Davis' Land. How chagrining it is to know that if only Davis had yielded to the desires of Lieutenant Wafer and his crew and visited that long archipelago which stretched away to the north-west over the horizon, we should have had some inkling of the culture and power of the people who used Easter Island as a mausoleum for their conspicuous dead! And it is similar submergences in the central Pacific that will account for the great voyagings of the Polynesians over the ocean and their sudden cessation.

(3) **WHAT EUROPEANS BROUGHT.** But it will not account for the decay that is still going on. Of course, this would not have been so patent or so rapid had Europeans not come on the scene and Polynesia been left to work out its own destiny. These islands have little to thank the intruders for. They brought them European clothing, so little suited to the region and climate, and so sure a breeder of disease as much by its use as by its misuse. They brought them European foods, which happily have not driven out the simpler and more sustaining tubers and fish; and they brought them European methods of cooking foods so radically inferior to their own earth oven. They brought them European religions which, as far as we can see, are still only a veneer over the old and to some extent breeders of pretence and hypocrisy. They

brought them European civilization, another pretentious veneer. But worst of all they brought them European vices and diseases, which, added to their own, have tended to turn their decay into a galloping consumption.

(4) **THE TABOO AND PRIMEVAL COMMUNISM.** Perhaps the most disastrous of all the effects of Europeanism was the dissolution of the power of the kings and chiefs. This was based on what seems to us the most irrational and absurd of all the features of their culture, the *taboo*, which was carried by the rulers and the priests to an extent that made it often ridiculous. But it was the only form of police that existed in the area, and its dissolution meant the dissolution of the social system. To many political creeds of to-day this may seem no evil; but then they hold that all that is established or old had better be dynamited into its constituent atoms so that new theories may have a chance. Yet it was one of the greatest misfortunes for Polynesia that the foundation of its social system melted away before the new creeds; for it left the people without impulse or stimulus to work, even in order to keep life in. Under the old system every one had to work, all the harder that the lion's share of the produce went to the nobles and priests. The fear of the results of a taboo broken kept them constantly at their trades. None of their occupations but were of the health-giving type; they had nothing of the deteriorating tendency of European industrial concentrations; all were open-air and in constant touch with the elements. The result was that they retained their hardy racial vitality and suffered little from disease. It was the nobles that suffered from luxury and over-indulgence, with one corrective in the constant wars. They lost their authority when the people ceased to believe in the taboo and its divine sanctions. There was then no compulsion or stimulus to work and the people were thrown back on their old village communism as the only social system; that is to say, what a man had or produced was not necessarily his; it was as much his neighbour's or any wanderer's who was passing by. This was undoubtedly a substitute for a poor law; but it was also a direct encouragement to the indolent to continue doing nothing for their own sustenance, and a direct discouragement to the industrious to raise more than what would satisfy their immediate and pressing needs. This is at the bottom of the improvidence that is apparent everywhere in Polynesia. What

is the good of providing for the future if what you provide
is every moment in process of being taken from you by one
who is too indolent or too vagabond to provide for himself ?
Let every moment provide for itself. Industry, thrift, and
forethought are useless if they make you no better off, no
better provided against the accidents and emergencies of life.
In Easter Island this sound reasoning began to have its full
effect as soon as the archipelagoes went down with the
organizers and the masters. Hotu Matua's attempt at
establishing a little brief authority by his impotent ceremonial
kingship and his poor little taboos had no effect in stemming
the tide of improvidence that had begun to flow over the
island. The result was that Easter Island was steeped in
Polynesian improvidence before the Europeans came ; there
was no taboo system, except the Orongo ceremonial, to
dissolve and no authority to destroy. It reached the state
of colossal improvidence a century before the rest of Polynesia
had ceased to work or to employ forethought.

(5) **ABANDONMENT OF WORK AND INFERTILITY.** The
removal of the taboo and the dissolution of the authority of
the chiefs had a still more far-reaching permanent effect; it
made the rapid decay of the Polynesian race inevitable. Work
was abandoned by not only the indolent but the industrious,
the only thing that keeps the vitality in full torrent. A
function unused is soon a function in decay ; and that which
keeps all the organs and tissues functioning, regular work,
if abandoned, means the decay of all, including that which
hands on the capacities of one generation to those that follow
and keeps the race alive. Infertility is the doom of indolence.
The race that will not work dies out. And this is the curse
that came upon all the Polynesians as soon as the new creeds
destroyed the taboo and the compulsion to work based on it,
and made them rely on their primeval village communism
for a living. There was not one branch of the race but suffered
rapid diminution during the nineteenth century, especially
as the only other stimulus to use the organs and the talents,
war, came to be abolished also. The Maoris of New Zealand
went down from a quarter of a million to less than forty
thousand. If we take Captain Porter's calculation of the
numbers in Nukuhiva alone of the Marquesas, based on the
nineteen thousand warriors engaged in the struggle between
valley and valley we may set down the population of the

U

group safely at more than a quarter of a million. That was not much more than a hundred years ago; now there are little more than two thousand in all the islands, and they are dying off rapidly.

(6) **THE DECAY OF THE MAORIS ARRESTED.** But in New Zealand the descent has been arrested. It is not much more than thirty years ago that a young Maori student at Canterbury University College, A. T. Ngata, won a prize in the Dialectic Society by an essay on his own race; it was a dirge; he predicted in eloquent language its complete evanishment; it got into the papers and the London *Spectator* had two articles on it. But within half a dozen years after, he had formed a young Maori Reform party; and in his own district, the north-east of the north island, they got the villages to divide up their lands; the communally-held estates, hitherto neglected and covered with weeds, became the property of individuals. There is now no more prosperous or progressive district and no more energetic community in New Zealand; the villages and farms again swarm with children, and some of the villages are lighted with electricity. And the effect is not confined to the Maoris of that district; each census for the last twenty-five years the native race is found to have made an advance in numbers; it is now getting beyond the fifty thousand. The prophet has prevented the fulfilment of his own prediction. The lament is turned into a hymn of jubilation.

(7) **DID THE TROPICS CAUSE DECLINE OF THE POPULA-TION?** Is it possible to stop the decay of the race in other parts of Polynesia by the same means? Some branches have already gone too far down the steep to recover. Others have just stopped the decline without making any advance. There are, of course, more factors in the decline than the social, though that is the chief cause of infertility. The climate has something to do with it. The Maori has returned to the temperate zone to which his primeval forefathers probably belonged; and the sharp winters may have helped him to gain strength of will again and self-control, though it did not prevent his rapid descent during the nineteenth century. The long residence in the tropics was an important factor in that Polynesian decay which was noticeable when the Europeans first arrived in the islands. The extreme heat, added to the constant moisture in the air, softens the tissues and disin-

tegrates the will. It confirms the improvidence and the resulting indolence which the social system breeds. But it had
not produced the infertility which is sometimes set down to it;
else that custom of abortion and infanticide would never have
come to be so deeply rooted in the race as to meet with no
condemnation from public opinion when a more prosperous
environment was found. Had the race become less fertile
through residence in the tropics, no such practice could ever
have arisen, or, if it had, it would have been censured by
public opinion. That it belongs to all branches of the race,
even to the remnant of those who inhabit this little island,
furnishes but one conclusion : it is that it arose in the fatherland before they separated ; for otherwise it would not have
existed amongst those who lived in the rich volcanic islands ;
nor would it have been able to persist in the face of its direct
opposite, adoption. Here in the little village of Hangaroa
with its three hundred inhabitants, all that now remain of
Easter Islanders, the two practices still exist side by side.
And there are few families that are now bringing up alongside
of their own several children adopted from others.

(8) **DISEASES FROM EUROPE.** There is another factor in
Polynesian decay : it is the new diseases introduced by
European ships. One of the proofs of the early quarantine
of Polynesia was the absence of all epidemic diseases such as
have been bred by vast masses of humanity being concentrated
in cities and towns ; so when smallpox or influenza or measles
or consumption got into a group it swept out a large proportion
of the population ; for it found absolutely virgin soil. This
indicates that the central and eastern Pacific was colonized
before the growth of city life on the coasts of Asia and that
means at least five or six thousand years ago. It seems as if
there had been a form of lung disease in Polynesia before the
introduction of the European type ; for long before Europe
had discovered it to be infectious the Polynesians isolated
cases of it ; Tahiti and Easter Island at least did so. But it
was evidently only mild and not epidemic in its results ; it
by no means rendered the patient immune to its European
form, which swept through groups like wildfire. A whaler,
last century, put on shore on Tahuata, one of the smaller
islands of the Marquesas, one of its crew dying of consumption ;
the infection spread from valley to valley, isolated though
they were. It then passed into the other islands, and as one

walks through any of the villages or up any of the valleys
one hears the ominous chest cough that means death ultimately. In the little community of this island there is
undoubtedly much lung disease, and there is no hygiene and
no attempt to prevent the sputum lying about or flying in
the dust with the wind. But it is syphilis left by visitors from
the ships that prepares the seed-bed for tuberculosis and
similar diseases and lays up woe for future generations, if not
annihilation of the people. Venereal diseases are widespread
throughout Polynesia and Micronesia, especially in the islands
and ports formerly frequented by whalers. And where both
are unchecked there is little doubt that the race will die out.
It is doubtless the unceremonied marriage, which practically
comes to no marriage, along with the existence of polygamy,
that has made Polynesia a " new Cytherea " and consequently
the hotbed of venereal diseases. There are the relics of an
ancient state of affairs that was quite different; the former
seclusion of the young girls in Easter Island till puberty, and
the value placed upon virginity in the *taupou*, or virgin hostess,
of a chief's household in Samoa and the existence of the *puhi*
in a Maori chief's family are indications that at one time the
Polynesians laid great stress on chastity. The foundering of
this ideal is part of the decadence observed in the region
before Europeans had much effect on it.

(9) **HOOKWORM AND LEPROSY.** But the isolation of islands
often saves them from epidemics. Easter Island is one of
the most difficult to reach; and it is one of the few islands
in the Pacific that escaped the havoc wrought by the pneu-
monic influenza at the close of 1918. So all Polynesia has
as yet escaped the malaria that is so devastating in New
Guinea and Melanesia, although the taro fields and swamps
are its natural breeding-ground and the mosquito has
found its way everywhere. One of the worse parasitic
diseases that have got into the Pacific is the hookworm; but
it has reached no farther east in Polynesia than Samoa. But
eastern Polynesia has got from the coasts of Asia a worse,
though less rapidly spreading, disease than hookworm: it is
leprosy. The Chinese brought it into Tahiti in the latter half
of the nineteenth century; and thence it has gone into the
Marquesas and is second only to tuberculosis in its ravages
amongst the people of that group. Some of the Easter Islanders
who went to Tahiti to work on the sugar plantations got into

contact with the leper colony there and brought it back when they returned. The result is that it has taken a foothold. There is a leper colony a mile or two north of Hangaroa, and the other day my guide, who is the constable, was called away to take a leper from the village to the settlement, a man in the prime of life, but with his feet all eaten into by the disease. There are still lepers living with relations in the village who have been ill for years and yet have not communicated the disease to those with them. It is to be hoped that the company which runs stock on the island will be successful in its efforts to procure *chaulmoogra* oil, which has cured so many in the Hawaiian islands. There was evidently a mild form of the disease in former times in eastern Polynesia; Moerenhout mentions it as existing in Tahiti and Mangareva in the twenties of last century. And the Easter Islanders have long had a compound word for it, *kiriekaeka*, signifying the milder form which appears in little punctures like mosquito bites; they add *makimaki* for the erosive form. As it is, there are fewer lepers now than there have been for some years. What was called by the Easter Islanders *hereke* or *kiritona* was probably the milder form of it, though from the description it may have been the *yaws* (framboesia) so common in the western Pacific; *kawhanga more* was an erosive and incurable form. Both have died out.

(10) **INDIGENOUS DISEASES.** In the olden days there were not many ailments to cure; the worst were those that came from gorging at the feasts. Indigestion and liver complaints were the real *akuakus* that got into so many people after a death; for there was a great *umu* after the funeral; and the *iviatua* had a fairly easy job by means of the usual steam bath and massage in netting the intrusive demon and burning it. But the same faith in evil spirits and in the sorcerers who have command of them acted the other way too; when an enemy threatened a man and by help of the *iviatua* worked up through black magic the *akuakus* against him, sheer terror often produced the effect required and killed the victim. The results of wars and accidents were as a rule easily disposed of; for as cannibals they knew the place of every bone and organ and could, without much difficulty, mend what was broken or wounded, or extract any intrusive body. They had extremely few serious ailments apart from those caused by belief in *akuakus* and sorcery; for

they lived an open-air life except during the night or rain-
storms, when they crowded into their stuffy, insect-swarming
hovels; and during times of peace when they could not get
dead bodies, and times of storm or taboo, when they could not
get fish, they were vegetarians and ought to have had, but
for their infrequent famines, the large abdomens and plenteous
fat of the tuber-eating Polynesians. Most of their troubles
were cutaneous, pimples, ulcers, and abscesses. One of the
commonest troubles amongst children was called *pia*, from
its resemblance to the flour of the arrowroot; it came out all
white over the skin; and the cure was a plentiful use of hot
water. But there was one terrible disease somewhat like
elephantiasis that, as far as I can make out, never reached the
island; it was called *hopi* by the Tahitians and swelled and
distorted the limbs and features till the victim was a grotesque
caricature of a man; happily he suffered little and was released
by death in five or six years; the different name shows that
it was recognized as different from elephantiasis (*fefe*).

(11) **LABOUR RAIDS AND RAIDERS.** It is diseases from the
old world that have worked greatest havoc. But even worse
than the epidemics the ships introduced (it is said by intelligent
Easter Islanders that there was some widespread, though not
always fatal, sickness after the visit of every ship) was the
havoc worked by the raids for slaves. The Peruvian raid
of 1863 was not the first nor was it the last; early in the
nineteenth century the New England sealer, the *Nancy*, needing extra hands to kill the seal on Juan Fernandez and its
sister island, bound twelve men and twelve women and sailed
away with them from Easter Island; three days out the bonds
were removed and the men jumped into the sea whilst the
women were prevented by the sailors from following them;
the crew put out the boats and tried to rescue the swimmers;
but they would rather die than be taken again; they dived
and avoided the efforts of the salvaging party; their fate
need not be told. It was little wonder that for a generation
after European voyagers were stoned when they landed. It
took the heart out of this homesick people and left them the
prey to disease. The Peruvian slave-raid was a much more
deliberate expedition; one who saw it declares there were
more than twenty ships in Hangaroa Bay; probably imagination has doubled the number. The officers came on shore
with music and with presents in their hands, not excluding

intoxicating drinks. The people drew towards them; but to make sure that all the fish were in the net the crews had gone to all the other coasts and their cordon drew in, chasing all the natives before them till they thought they had the whole population on the Hangaroa beach. Then began the roping of the victims: men, women, and children bound hand and foot were thrown into the boats and taken on board; there were already a thousand from the Marquesas and other islands to the north. The Mangarevans, who had by this time the missionaries amongst them and suspected the designs of the ship that came to their islands, went on board in great numbers, professing to be eager to recruit; they seized the ship and binding the officers and crews took it to Tahiti. The Easter Islanders had forgotten the *Nancy* outrage and had not the missionaries amongst them. Had there not been numerous caves on their island to hide in, it would have been left a solitude. It is not surprising that when Bornier proposed to send to Tahiti three hundred of the natives remaining after this raid and its sequel, the smallpox, which, brought from Peru by the few rescued from slavery, decimated the Marquesas as well as this islet, the missionaries violently protested, fearing the result. But the exploiter was a man of strong will and character and, with his experience as an officer in the Crimean war and some guns that were saved from the wreck of an American vessel, he began his warfare. He set the guns on a height that commanded Hangaroa and, in order to intimidate the clericals and their converts, he sent a shot occasionally into the village. He had a powerful lieutenant in Torometi, the patron and tyrant of Eyraud; when he found any couple who had been married by the priests disagreeing, he brought them up to Mataveri and Bornier, putting a frying pan on his head and a *kimono* over his clothes, mock-ceremonially dismarried them; his aide went even further and any of the young women who had taken the veil and had by no means suppressed their old love of sexual freedom were devirginated by himself or his myrmidons. There could be only one end to this warfare. Bornier sent off his three hundred to the sugar plantations on Tahiti and, at the bidding of Bishop Jaussen, the missionaries went off with three hundred of their converts to settle in Mangareva.

(12) **THE MARK TAPLEYS OF THE PACIFIC.** Was ever an island more shamefully abused by civilization? What people,

however brave and stalwart, would not have had the vitality wrenched out of them by such inhuman treatment ? But the little community, whatever their failings, had the bright side of the improvident as well as the dark. They were cheerful even under these atrocious wrongs. Anderson, in his report on the Polynesians in Cook's Third Voyage, says of them : " Neither does care ever seem to wrinkle their brow ; on the contrary even the approach of death does not appear to alter their usual vivacity." No description could better fit the Easter Islanders of to-day as of all time. La Perouse, in spite of their ungrateful treatment of him, getting stoned after all his gifts, indeed in the act of giving them more, remarks on their insouciance : " They swam off to us a league off shore and came on board with a laughing, careless air." It is difficult not to forget or forgive the innumerable weaknesses of these Mark Tapleys of the Pacific. From every catastrophe and disaster and famine they come up smiling. The worst of it was that now their numbers had gone down to the minimum they had to pair the girls off two years earlier than in their past ; the young women had to begin to be mothers at twelve ; and this has done more to take the stamina out of the community than even their feast-bred famines. The women are old when they should be in their prime ; and the babies die off too easily. Yet the hundred left after all the disasters and emigrations of the sixties have been slowly creeping up in numbers ; they are now three hundred. They are not handicapped in the way so many other races have been in the battle of life by the possession of any intoxicating drink or narcotic ; and yet they are as listless and buried in the pleasure of the moment as if they had such means of momentary oblivion ; the relics of their ancient communism secure that. If we are to trust the evidence of all the voyagers, there have been violent fluctuations in their numbers before they were influenced by Europeans and European evils ; one places them at several thousand, another a generation after at seven hundred, and a few years after that another counts them by the thousand. Droughts and famines and wars would be enough to explain these up and downs. Whether their present three hundred will creep up again into the thousands is a question of hybridization. European blood has put some energy into the race, if we are to judge by some of the half-castes that went to Mangareva and by those of the present generation who have Bornier's blood in them. Shipwrecks are the chief contributors of European blood; and there is manifestly a considerable amount of it in the little community. All over Polynesia this hybridism is apparent; and the natives cross well with Europeans, as well as with the natives of other Polynesian islands. In Tahiti and Mangareva the Easter Island immigrants have remained and formed good hybrids; but this has not arrested decline of population in these areas; there are too many diseases and vices for any such permanent arrest.

(13) **THE PLACE OF POLYNESIANS IN THE FUTURE PACIFIC.** The decay that goes on in most areas is not likely to be stopped permanently unless hybridization puts vigour into the race and their primeval communism is wiped out. It is only a more rapid phase of a phenomenon that has existed in the central and eastern Pacific as far back as submergence has been the dominating factor in the archipelagoes, in other words, since the earliest human occupation of them. That this process of subsidence will cease is not to be expected, though there is not much land now in this region above the waters, and the process will continue to be secular. Migration before the trade winds, which has been going on for untold ages, will probably still go on, even though there are few to migrate, and the settlement of Europeans and their industries and interests have somewhat arrested it. It will be but an insignificant part the Polynesians will play in the great Pacific conflict that is bound to come within the next century or two for the settlement of the standards of life. For tens of thousands of years East and West have been brought up apart, and their ethical, social, and economical standards have taken their own independent lines to some extent. For the first time in the history of the world they are coming face to face in the Pacific Ocean, and if the standards cannot hybridize, or at least come closer to each other, then it will have to be decided some time or other in the future which is to rule the destinies of mankind, the Oriental or the Occidental. And, though the Polynesians have much primeval affinity with the culture of Japan and China, they have practically no Mongoloid elements in their physique and nature. They are altogether Caucasoid, and now they have been inoculated with European culture and creeds there is little doubt as to which side they will gravitate towards in the great battle of the standards.

INDEX

Printed in Great Britain at
The Mayflower Press, Plymouth. William Brendon & Son, Ltd.

NEW BOOKS

ANCIENT TONGA
THE LOST CITY OF MU'A
David Hatcher Childress

Lost Cities series author Childress begins his new Lost Cities of the Pacific series with this book on Ancient Tonga. Childress takes us to the south sea islands of Tonga, Rarotongo. Samoa and Fiji to investigate the megalithic ruins on these beautiful islands. With a vast wealth of old drawings, photos and maps, the great empire of the Polynesians, is revealed in this attractive book. In this new paperback series, with color photo inserts, Childress takes us into the fascinating world of Tonga and the ancient seafarers that Pacific. Chapters in this book include the Lost City of Mu'A and its many megalithic pyramids, the Ha'amonga Trilithon and ancient Polynesian astronomy, Samoa and the search for the lost land of Havaiiki, Fiji and its wars with Tonga, Rarotonga's megalithic road, Polynesian cosmology, and a chapter on the predicted reemergence of the ancient land of Mu. May publication.

218 pages, 6x9 paperback. Heavily illustrated with old drawings, photos and maps. Includes a color photo section. Bibliography & Index. $15.95.   code: TONG May Publication.

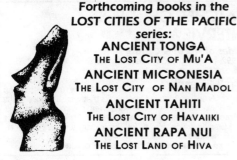

Forthcoming books in the
LOST CITIES OF THE PACIFIC
series:
ANCIENT TONGA
THE LOST CITY OF MU'A
ANCIENT MICRONESIA
THE LOST CITY OF NAN MADOL
ANCIENT TAHITI
THE LOST CITY OF HAVAIIKI
ANCIENT RAPA NUI
THE LOST LAND OF HIVA

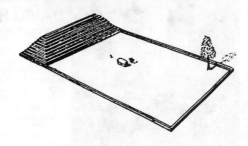

THE LOST CITIES

LOST CITIES OF ATLANTIS, ANCIENT EUROPE & THE MEDITERRANEAN
David Hatcher Childress

Atlantis! The legendary lost continent comes under the close scrutiny of maverick archaeologist David Hatcher Childress. This sixth book in the internationally popular Lost Cities series takes us on quest for the lost continent of Atlantis. Childress takes the reader in search of sunken cities in the Mediterranean; across the Atlas Mountains in search of Atlantean ruins; to remote islands in search of megalithic ruins; living legengds and secret societies. From Ireland to Turkey, Morocco to Eastern Europe, or remote islands of the Mediterranean and Atlantic Childress takes the reader on an astonishing quest for mankind's past. Ancient technology, cataclysms, megalithic construction, lost civilizations and devastating wars of the past are all explored in this astonishing book. Childress challenges the skeptics and proves that great civilizations not only existed in the past, but the modern world and its problems are reflections of the ancient world of Atlantis.

524 pages, 6x9 paperback. Illustrated with 100s of maps, photos and diagrams. Bibliography & Index. $16.95. code: MED

LOST CITIES OF ANCIENT LEMURIA & THE PACIFIC
David Hatcher Childress

Was there once a continent in the Pacific? Called Lemuria or Pacifica by geologists, and Mu or Pan by the mystics, there is now ample mythological, geological and archaeological evidence to "prove" that an advanced, and ancient civilization once lived in the central Pacific. Maverick archaeologist and explorer David Hatcher Childress combs the Indian Ocean, Australia and the Pacific in search of the astonishing truth about mankind's past. Contains photos of the underwater city on Pohnpei, explanations on how the statues were levitated around Easter Island in a clock-wise vortex movement; disappearing islands; Egyptians in Australia; and more.

379 pages, 6x9, paperback. Photos, maps, and illustrations with Footnotes & Bibliography $14.95. code LEM

DAVID HATCHER CHILDRESS RADIO INTERVIEW

On the Lost Cities of North & Central America
In December of 1992, popular Lost Cities Series author, David Hatcher Childress, was interviewed live for six hours on the Laura Lee Radio Show, broadcast out of Seattle, Washington. The subject of the interview was David's book, Lost Cities of North and Central America, with special emphasis on the Smithsonian Institution's cover-up of American history. Other topics that were included in the interview, which also included live call-in questions, were pyramids around the world, the Rama Empire of India and Vimanas, Atlantis and Lemuria, UFOs, an Egyptian City in the Grand Canyon, and more! This audio interview comes on three high-quality 90 minute cassette tapes in boxes.

270 Minutes on 3 audio cassettes, $12.95 code: DHCR

THE LOST CITIES SERIES

LOST CITIES OF NORTH & CENTRAL AMERICA
David Hatcher Childress

From the jungles of Central America to the deserts of the southwest... down the back roads from coast to coast, maverick archaeologist and adventurer David Hatcher Childress takes the reader deep into unknown America. In this incredible book: search for lost Mayan cities and books of gold; discover an ancient canal system in Arizona; climb gigantic pyramids in the Midwest; explore megalithic monuments in New England; and join the astonishing quest for the lost cities throughout North America. From the war-torn jungles of Guatemala, Nicaragua and Honduras to the deserts, mountains and fields of Mexico, Canada, and the U.S.A., Childress takes the reader in search of sunken ruins; Viking forts; strange tunnel systems,; living dinosaurs; early Chinese explorers; and fantastic gold treasure. Packed with both early and current maps, photos and illustrations. An incredible life on the road in search of the ancient mysteries of the past!
590 pages, 6 x9, paperback. Photos, maps, and illustrations with Footnotes & Bibliography $14.95. code NCA

LOST CITIES & ANCIENT MYSTERIES OF AFRICA & ARABIA
David Hatcher Childress

Across ancient deserts, dusty plains and steaming jungles, maverick archaeologist David Childress continues his world-wide quest for lost cities and ancient mysteries. Join him as he discovers forbidden cities in the Empty Quarter of Arabia, "Atlantean" ruins in Egypt and the Kalahari desert; a mysterious, ancient empire in the Sahara; and more. This is an extraordinary life on the road: across war-torn countries Childress searches for King Solomon's Mines, living dinosaurs, the Ark of the Covenant and the solutions to the fantastic mysteries of the past.
423 pages, 6 x9, paperback. Photos, maps, and illustrations with Footnotes & Bibliography $14.95. code AFA

LOST CITIES & ANCIENT MYSTERIES OF SOUTH AMERICA
David Hatcher Childress

Rogue adventurer and maverick archaeologist, David Hatcher Childress, takes the reader on unforget-table journeys deep into deadly jungles, windswept mountains and scorching deserts in search of lost civilizations and ancient mysteries. Travel with David and explore stone cities high in mountain forests and fantastic tales of Inca treasure, living dinosaurs, and a mysterious tunnel system. Whether he is hopping freight trains, searching for secret cities, or just dealing with the daily problems, of food, money, and romance, the author keeps the reader spellbound. Includes both early and current maps, photos and illustrations, and plenty of advice for the explorer planning his or her own journey of discovery.
381 pages, 6x9, paperback. Photos, maps, and illustrations with Footnotes & Bibliography $14.95. code SAM

LOST CITIES OF CHINA, CENTRAL INDIA & ASIA
David Hatcher Childress

The real life "Indiana Jones," maverick archaeologist David Childress takes the reader on an incredible adventure across some of the world's oldest and most remote countries in search of lost cities and ancient mysteries. Discover ancient cities in the Gobi Desert; hear fantastic tales of lost continents, vanished civilizations and secret societies bent on ruling the world. Visit forgotten monasteries in forbidding snow-capped mountains with strange tunnels to mysterious subterranean cities! A unique combination of far-out exploration and practical travel advice; it will astound and delight the experienced traveler or the armchair voyager.
429 pages, 6 x 9, paperback. Photos, maps, and illustrations with Footnotes & Bibliography $14.95. code CHI

THE ATLANTIS REPRINT SERIES

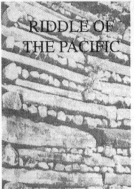

ATLANTIS REPRINT SERIES
RIDDLE OF THE PACIFIC
by John Macmillan Brown

Oxford scholar Brown's classic work on lost civilizations of the Pacific is now back in print! John Macmillan Brown was a New Zealand-Oxford historian and New Zealand's premier scientist when he wrote about the origins of the Maori and after many years of travel though out the Pacific wrote Riddle of the Pacific in 1924. This book, along with The History of Atlantis (1926) are the beginning of our Atlantis reprint series. Don't miss Brown's classic study of Easter Island, ancient scripts, megalithic roads and cities, more. Brown was an early believer in a lost continent in the Pacific. Sixteen chapters in all. 460 pages, 6x9 paperback. Illustrated with maps, photos and diagrams. $16.95. code: ROP

ATLANTIS REPRINT SERIES
THE HISTORY OF ATLANTIS
by Lewis Spence

Lewis Spence's classic book on Atlantis is now back in print! Lewis Spence was a Scottish historian (1874-1955) who is best known for his volumes on world mythology and his five Atlantis books. The History of Atlantis (1926) is considered his best. Spence does his scholarly best in chapters on the Sources of Atlantean History, the Geography of Atlantis, the Races of Atlantis, the Kings of Atlantis, the Religion of Atlantis, the Colonies of Atlantis, more. Sixteen chapters in all.
240 pages, 6x9 paperback. Illustrated with maps, photos and diagrams. $16.95. code: HOA

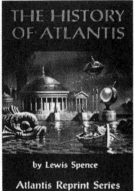

ATLANTIS IN SPAIN
A Study of the Ancient Sun Kingdoms of Spain
E.M. Whishaw

First published by Rider & Co. of London in 1928, this classic book is a study of the megaliths of Spain, ancient writing, cyclopean walls, Sun Worshipping Empires, hydraulic engineering, and sunken cities is now back in print after sixty years. An extremely rare book until this reprint, learn about the Biblical Tartessus; an Atlantean city at Niebla; the Temple of Hercules and the Sun Temple of Seville; Libyans and the Copper Age; more. Profusely illustrated with photos, maps and illustrations.
284 pages, 6 x9, paperback. Epilog with tables of ancient scripts. $15.95. code: AIS •November Publication

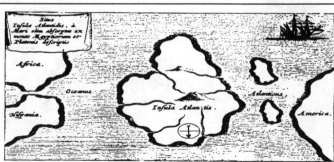

Coming Next in the ATLANTIS REPRINT SERIES
The Shadow of Atlantis by Col. A. Braghine (1940)
Secret Cities of Old South America by Wilkins (1952)

THE MU SERIES

THE LOST CONTINENT OF MU
By Col. James Churchward
Churchward's classic books on Mu are now back in print. First Published in the 1930s Churchward made a sensation by writting of a lost civilization in the Pacific that his teachers in India told him was called Mu. Churchward brings together a wealth of evidence from all over the world of ancient traditions of megaltihic building. His first two books The Lost Continent of Mu and The Children of Mu (Both 1931) contain his own archaeological journeys around the world. His later books, The Sacred Symbols of Mu (1933), Cosmic Forces of Mu (1934) and Cosmic Forces of Mu, Vol. II (1935), examine the origins of civilization, writing and symbolism, plus they explore the amazing science used by the ancients.
335 pages 6x9 tradepaper Illustrated with maps, drawings & photos $15.95. code: LCM

THE CHILDREN OF MU
By Col. James Churchward
267 pages, 6x9 tradepaper, Illustrated with maps, drawings & photos. $15.95. code: COM

THE SACRED SYMBOLS OF MU
By Col. James Churchward
296 pages, 6x9 tradepaper, Illustrated with maps, drawings & photos. $15.95. code: SSM

THE COSMIC FORCES OF MU
Book Two
By Col. James Churchward
269 pages, 6x9 tradepaper. Illustrated with maps, drawings & photos. $15.95. code: CFM2

THE COSMIC FORCES OF MU
Book One
By Col. James Churchward
246 pages, 6x9 tradepaper, Illustrated with maps, drawings & photos, $15.95. code: CFM1

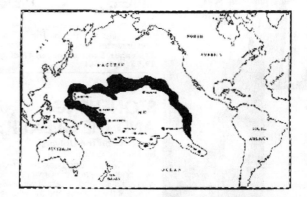

NATIVE AMERICAN STUDIES

TZOLKIN
Visionary Perspectives and Calendar Studies
John Major Jenkins

TZOLKIN is a visionary journey into the heart of an ancient oracle. Jenkins, in both academic and mystical viewpoints, explore the sacred Calendar of Mezoamerica is than a calendar, but an ancient cosmology that includes a mytho-evolutionary system which describes the spiritual and physical unfolding of the Earth. At the heart of this sophisticated philosophy is the Sacred Tree—the Axis Mundi. Prepare for a journey... prepare to to enter the mysterious borderland between night and day!
346 pages. 6x9 tradepaper. Profusely illustrated. $13.95. code: TZO

AMERICAN DISCOVERY
The Real Story
Gunnar Thompson.

Thompson's second book is a state-of-the-art overview of ancient voyages to America, beginning with the Native Americans and continuing through Amerigo Vespucci. The book features Old World art in America, ancient maps of America, chapters on native tribes; Phoenicians; Norse; Celts, Britons, Irish & Welsh; Greeks, Jews & Romans; Japanese; Hindus; Indonesians; Sumerians; Chinese; Black Africans; Scots, Basques, & Portuguese; Polynesians; Egyptians & Arabs. Archaeologist Thompson explores the reasons why Old World voyagers sailed to America and their impact on native culture. Diffusion of plants, diseases, languages, symbols, races, religion, metals, and civilization are examined.100s of illustrations and photos.
400 pages, 6x9 tradepaper, Profusely illustrated, bibliography & index. $17.95. code: AMD

ANIMATED EARTH
Metaphysics & the Whistling Pots of Peru
by Daniel K. Statnekov

An unusual adventure story in which Statnekov is sent on a shamanic quest to Peru to discover the cosmic secret to the whistling vessels that are to be found there. An archaeological adventure of the spirit that illuminates a unusual subject. Something of interest here perhaps for students of harmonics, sound and vibration.
227 pages, 6x9 paperback. 8 Page Color Insert. Other illustrations & photos. Index. $9.95. code: ANE

THE LOST PYRAMIDS OF ROCK LAKE
Frank Collins

40 miles west of Milwaukee lies the pyramid complex of Aztalan and the sunken ruins of Rock Lake. For years rumors of a lost city in the lake have circulated and finally in 1989 a side-scan sonar mapping of the lake was done. This book recounts that expedition and gives the reader background information on the mysteries of Wisconsin. See also ATLANTIS IN WISCONSIN.
212 pages, 6x9 paperback. Illustrated. Footnotes & Bibliography. $10.95. code: TLP

NATIVE AMERICAN MYTHS & MYSTERIES
Vincent H. Gaddis

Veteran Fortean researcher Gaddis's classic book on strange Native American myths and legends. The tribal shamanic knowledge links Native Americans today to this spiritual past, many thousands of years old. Divination and healing ceremonies, the Shaking Tent mystery, Navaho feather magic and other traditions all portend a great knowledge lost to the European colonizers. This book, written by one of the finest researchers of our age, will astound, fascinate and enlighten you to an ancient world hidden in the American landscape.
184 pages, 6x9 paperback. $12.95. code: NAM

THE MYSTERY CAVE OF MANY FACES
A History of Burrow's Cave
Russell Burrows & Fred Ridholm.

This hardback book tells the incredible story of how Russell Burrows discovered a cave of thousands of fantastic artifacts in April of 1982. The cave's walled up entrance in a remote valley of southern Illinois kept one of the most astonishing archaeological discoveries hidden for approximately 2000 years. This discovery, and photos of the artifacts, have created a sensation in the archaeology field, and some well-known scholars, such as Barry Fell, have declared much of the collection to be a fake. Others, such as Joseph Mahan, maintain that the thousands of ancient Hindu, Egyptian, Sumerian and other artifacts, are genuine, and that the cave is but one of a number of such caches. This book chronicles the exciting discovery of the cave, the trials and dangers of getting the story to the public, and a brief description of some of the many artifacts found inside, including statues, coins, engraved tablets, various texts and more. Well illustrated with photos and drawings of the artifacts from the cave.
254 pages, 6x9 hardback, Profusely illustrated, bibliography & index. $24.95. code: TMC

NATIVE AMERICAN

Primitive Man in Michigan

INDIANS AND MICHIGAN PRE-HISTORY

Prehistoric Indian cliff painting

PRIMITIVE MAN IN MICHIGAN
Indians and Michigan Prehistory   **NEW!**
by W. B. Hinsdale
A reprint of a fascinating and well illustrated volume on the huge earthworks, mounds, tools, artifacts, rock carvings and more. Despite its title, this book shows us what a sophisticated civlization once occupied the Great Lakes region. Important chapters on the massive earthworks, ancient pyramids, garden plots, trepanned skulls, more.
229pages, 6x9 paperback, Illustrated. $12.95 code:PRMM

THE DIFFUSION ISSUE
Edited by Donald Cyr
A large format book on the controversial issue of ancient seafarers and the theory of ancient contacts (diffusion) of culture, science and civilization around the world. This book includes articles on Pre-Columbian transoceanic contacts, Chinese ancient world mapagesing, Megalithic man in America, and new world plants in the old world.
122 pages, 9x10 tradepaper, illustrated with photographs & diagrams. $9.95. code: TDI

THE ECCLECTIC EPIGRAPHER
Edited by Donald Cyr
Ogam writing around the world; megaliths and ancient inscriptions, Professor Barry Fell on Epigraphy, more.
160 pages, 10 x12 tradepaper, Illustrated with index, References & Bibliography $9.95 code: ECE

EXPLORING ROCK ART
Edited by Donald Cyr with Barry Fell
A fascinating look at the bizarre and controversial rock art, including the Illinois Thunderbird monster called the Piasa (believed by many to have been a gigantic flying lizard!), Colorado Ogam inscriptions, megaliths, pyramids and rock art in Scandinavia and more are all profiled in this large format book.
128 pages, 8x10 tradepaper, 100 photos, illustrations and maps. $9.95 code: ERA

CELTIC SECRETS
Edited by Donald Cyr
Includes an an analysis of Celtic invasions into Ireland, Scotland and America other Celtic lands of antiquity. Ogam writings, the mysterious "Black Scots", ancient megalith building and more are to be found in this large format book.
117 pages, 9x11 tradepaper, 100's of illustrations, diagrams, photographs. $9.95 code: CTS

THE COLORADO OGAM ALBUM
Photographs of Ancient Inscriptions
Donald Cyr
A large format book from Stonehenge Viewpoint with page after page of ancient inscriptions found at some of the river terminus sites in Colorado. Plenty of interesting ogam writing and other rock inscriptions, plus interesting chapters on the Olmecs and Ogam; the Chinese connection; 23 chapters in all.
128 pages, 10x12 tradepaper. Illustrated with photos, charts & drawings. Index. $12.95. code: COA

303 Main Street
P.O. Box 74
Kempton, Illinois 60946
USA
Tel.: 815-253-6390 ♦ Fax: 815-253-6300
Email: adventures_unlimited@mcimail.com

ORDERING INSTRUCTIONS

➤ Remit by USD$ Check or Money Order
➤ Credit Cards: Visa, MasterCard, Discovery, & American Express Accepted
➤ Call ♦ Fax ♦ Email Any Time

SHIPPING CHARGES

United States

➤ Postal Book Rate { $2.00 First Item / 50¢ Each Additional Item
➤ Priority Mail { $3.50 First Item / $1.50 Each Additional Item
➤ UPS { $3.50 First Item / $1.00 Each Additional Item
NOTE: UPS Delivery Available to Mainland USA Only

Canada

➤ Postal Book Rate { $3.00 First Item / $1.00 Each Additional Item
➤ Postal Air Mail { $4.00 First Item / $2.00 Each Additional Item
➤ Personal Checks or Bank Drafts MUST BE USD$ and Drawn on a US Bank
➤ Canadian Postal Money Orders OK
➤ Payment MUST BE USD$

All Other Countries

➤ Surface Delivery { $5.00 First Item / $2.00 Each Additional Item
➤ Postal Air Mail { $10.00 First Item / $8.00 Each Additional Item
➤ Payment MUST BE USD$
➤ Personal Checks MUST BE USD$ and Drawn on a US Bank
➤ Add $5.00 for Air Mail Subscription to Future *Adventures Unlimited* Catalogs

SPECIAL NOTES

➤ RETAILERS: Standard Discounts Available
➤ BACKORDERS: We Backorder all Out-of-Stock Items Unless Otherwise Requested
➤ PRO FORMA INVOICES: Available on Request
➤ VIDEOS: NTSC Mode Only
PAL & SECAM Mode Videos Are Not Available

Thank you for your order
We appreciate your business

Please check: ☑
☐ This is my first order ☐ I have ordered before ☐ This is a new address

Name				
Address				
City				
State/Province		Postal Code		
Country				
Phone day		Evening		
Fax				

Item Code	Item Description	Price	Qty	Total
CAT	Adventures Unlimited Catalog	N/C		N/C

Please check: ☑
☐ Postal-Surface
☐ Postal-Air Mail (Priority in USA)
☐ UPS (Mainland USA only)

Please Use Item Codes!

Subtotal ➤	
Less Discount-10% for 3 or more items ➤	
Balance ➤	
Illinois Residents 7% Sales Tax ➤	
Previous Credit ➤	
Shipping ➤	
Total (check/MO in USD$ only) ➤	

☐ Visa/MasterCard/Discover/Amex

#_____ Exp. _____

Comments & Suggestions

Share Our Catalog with a Friend

10% Discount When You Order 3 or More Items!